An Introduction to the

Sociology of

Education

SECOND EDITION

An Introduction to the

Study of Education

SECOND EDITION

Edited by David Matheson

David Fulton Publishers

David Fulton Publishers Ltd
The Chiswick Centre, 414 Chiswick High Road, London W4 5TF

www.fultonpublishers.co.uk

First published in Great Britain in 1999 by David Fulton Publishers
Second Edition 2004

10 9 8 7 6 5 4 3 2 1

Note: The right of the author to be identified as the author of this work has been
asserted by him in accordance with the Copyright, Designs and Patents Act 1988.

David Fulton Publishers is a division of Granada Learning Limited,
part of ITV plc.

British Library Cataloguing in Publication Data
A catalogue record for this book is available from the British Library.

ISBN 1 84312 134 4

Typeset by RefineCatch Limited, Bungay, Suffolk
Printed and bound in Great Britain

Contents

Contents

Dedicated to the memory of
Norman Matheson [1926–2000]
My father

Lily Matheson [1927–2003]
My mother

Nigel Grant [1932–2003]
International Scot and friend

Is e an Tighearna mo bhuachaille;
cha bhi mi ann an dìth

Contributors

Estelle Brisard   Research Fellow, School of Education, University of Paisley

Anthony Coles   Lecturer, Faculty of Education, University of Central England, Birmingham

Trevor Corner   Professor of Lifelong Learning, School of Lifelong Learning and Education, Middlesex University

Gareth Evans   Teacher, Barton Peveril College, Hampshire

Nigel Grant   Late Emeritus Professor of Education, University of Glasgow

Richard Hatcher   Director of Research, Faculty of Education, University of Central England, Birmingham

Mary Kellett   Lecturer, Faculty of Education and Language Studies, Open University

Graham Martin   Associate Dean, School of Education, University College Chester

Jane Martin   Lecturer, School of Education, London Metropolitan University

Catherine Matheson   Researcher, Department of Continuing Education, City University, London

David Matheson   MA Course Director, Faculty of Education, University of Central England, Birmingham

Ian Menter   Professor of Education, University of Paisley

Graham Mitchell   Lecturer, Division of Psychology, University College Northampton

John Nisbet   Professorial Honorary Research Fellow, Departments of Education & Sociology, University of Aberdeen

John Stanley   Research Fellow, Instituto Superior da Maia, Portugal

J. Eric Wilkinson   Professor and Vice Dean, Faculty of Education, University of Glasgow

1

What is education?

David Matheson

Education is what survives when what has been learnt has been forgotten.

(B. F. Skinner)

Introduction

THERE ARE SOME NOTIONS which most of us *think* we know what they are and assume that others share the same or similar ideas. These can include ideas such as fairness, equality and justice. They are terms that are easy to use and to feel that we understand what we mean by them but notoriously difficult to explain to others, other than by appealing to common sense and asserting that 'everyone' knows what justice, fairness, equality and so on actually are.

Among these slippery concepts is the concept of education. Education is what Winch and Gingell (1999) term an 'essentially contested concept'. It is one that has a vast range of definitions, none of which is totally satisfactory. For example, we have the common equation between education and school. In this case, what about higher education? Where does further education fit in? And, for that matter, where do we place things we teach ourselves? We can discuss education that includes all of these arenas for learning or we can exclude at least some of them. We may even do as Abbs (1979) does and claim that 'education and school can refer, and often do refer, to antithetical activities' (p. 90). Or we can go even further and align ourselves with Illich (1986) and assert that not only is school the antithesis of education but its main function is to provide custodial day care for young people.

This chapter has as its function to consider what education might be. I intend to do this by considering a well-known attempt at defining education. I will then consider some of the things that education can be for and, lastly, I will consider what it might mean to be educated before briefly considering Education Studies itself.

Defining education

The literature is replete with attempts at defining education and so, at most, I will succeed here in merely scratching the surface. Firstly, there is what we might term the 'elastic' sense of education. This is one, in a manner akin to the manner in which Lewis Carroll's Humpty Dumpty ascribes any meaning he wants to a word, where education means precisely what the speaker, though within limits unknown to Humpty, wants it to mean. This approach capitalises on the kudos attached to the term 'education' and seeks to ascribe to it whatever the speaker wants to give it. The result is a very loose approach wherein terms like 'education' and 'learning' are used interchangeably and the whole notion of education gets diluted to vanishing point. Despite this, as Lawson (1975) says, to call an activity or process 'educational' is typically to vest it with considerable status.

It is a commonplace that humans are learning machines. As Malcolm Tight puts it, 'Learning, like breathing, is something everyone does all of the time' (Tight 1996: 21). A first step then in trying to get a definition of education that is worth the bother is to exclude some activities. Unfortunately this is exactly where the problems start. As soon as we exclude activities from the list of what constitutes education we have to exercise a value judgement and we have to find a good reason for doing so. Nonetheless, at least by going about it this way, if we do decide that education equals school – an all too common assumption – then we have hopefully begun with a definition of education into which school fits, rather than beginning with school and making our definition of education fit into it.

The synonymous use of 'school' and 'education' is, however, hardly surprising when we consider that most of us will have experienced in schools what is arguably the most important part of our formal education. After all, it is there that we tend to have learnt to read, we have developed our skills in social interaction, we have encountered authority that does not derive from a parent and we have been required to conform to sets of rules, some of which might have been explained, some of which may not. School leaves its mark on us and on our personal conception of education but this risks rendering us at least myopic to other possibilities.

One of the most popular approaches to the definition of education, at least in Anglophone countries, is that proposed by Richard Peters. Peters' (1966) contention is that 'education implies that something worthwhile is being or has been intentionally transmitted in a morally acceptable manner' (p. 25). He manages to encompass two significant components: there is not only the end product, there are also means adopted to achieve it.

Peters' definition suggests several areas for exploration:

1   Intentionality and the 'something'

2   The notion of transmission

3   The criteria for ascertaining whether the something is worthwhile

4   The basis upon which moral acceptability is to be judged.

Intentionality and the 'something'

For Peters, education cannot come about by accident. In this he concurs with Hamm's (1989) claim that 'learning is an activity that one engages in with purpose and intention to come up to a certain standard' (p. 91). This implies, inter alia, that those things that we learn incidentally cannot count. Equally it implies that the person fulfilling the function of teacher has some clear notion of what is to be transmitted to the learners.[1] This may take the form of some specific material to be learnt or it may take the form of attitudes to be acquired and opinions to be formed. A question to be asked concerns whether we can ever separate what is being transmitted from the manner in which the transmission occurs. In other words, can the message stand alone from the medium that carries it? Or is the case, as Marshall McLuhan (1967) claimed, that the medium *is* the message?[2]

For Peters, the 'something' refers to knowledge and understanding (and this can reasonably be extended to include skills and attitudes).[3] This in turn leads to several other questions, not least of which is to consider exactly what we mean by knowledge. Knowledge consists of several components. Most notably these consist in their turn of: knowing *how* to do things (procedural knowledge) and knowing *that* (propositional knowledge) certain things exist or are true or have happened and so on. There is also the rather thorny question of how we know that

---

[1] It also implies some sort of examination to see if the learner has come up to the 'standard'. Examination may of course be self-examination, rather than some sort of test imposed or conducted by a third party.

[2] A master of aphorisms and puns, Mcluhan deliberately entitled his book on this subject *The Medium Is the Massage*.

[3] Indeed, if one follows Bloom's (1969) *Taxonomy of Educational Objectives*, then one has to include at least some skills since the hierarchy of cognitive objectives is as follows and the last three listed are clearly skills to be acquired:
- knowledge
- comprehension
- application
- analysis
- synthesis
- evaluation.

Similarly, following Bloom's affective objectives will mean including attitudes in our 'something'.

we know something and just what knowledge is, but this is perhaps beyond the scope of this book.[4]

Understanding is important for Peters since this takes us beyond simply knowing and into the realms where we become better equipped to grasp underlying principles, are able to explain why things are the way they are or why they happen the way they do, and so on. The role of knowledge and understanding in defining education becomes even more crucial when one considers Peters' view on what it means to be educated (see Barrow and Woods 1995: Chapter 1). For Peters, becoming educated is an asymptotic process: we can move towards it but we can never fully attain it. For Peters (1970), 'this understanding should not be too narrowly specialised' (p. 4). Just how narrow is too narrow is open to speculation but this is a point best dealt with later as we consider what it means to be educated.

Transmission

Transmission creates in the mind an image of something passing from one place to another. However, we have to take care to understand just what Peters means by the term. In an age dominated by broadcast media, there is a tendency to equate 'broadcast' with 'transmission'; in other words, one may transmit but we never know who will receive or indeed exactly what they will receive. If Peters equates 'transmission' with 'broadcast' then he clearly is referring to teaching rather than to learning. On the other hand, if by transmission he actually means what we might nowadays term 'successful transmission' (i.e. when the message sent is equal to the message received) then he refers to both teaching *and* learning. Indeed the etymology of 'transmission' would clearly indicate the latter. We need only look at the manner in which 'transmission' was employed in the days before our present media age (in terms, for example, of a vehicle's transmission – which transfers power from the engine to the wheels – which certainly brooks no ambiguity as to the 'message' sent being the same as the 'message' received) to see the justification for this claim. Nonetheless we do live in a media age; transmission has adopted a range of meanings; and so, perhaps Peters' definition might be better altered to use the term 'successful transmission'.

In any case the need for transmission in Peters' definition of education brings with it the idea that, firstly, one cannot educate oneself by means of discovery, although one can by means of educational materials such as books since in this latter case it is the ideas of the writer of the book that are being transmitted via the book. Secondly, there is an implication of a deficiency model of education whereby

---

[4] For discussion of the nature of knowledge, the reader is referred to the *Blackwell Companion to Epistemology* (Dancy and Sosa 1999). For a counter-argument to the commonly held belief that knowledge is justified, true belief, see the Gettier Problem which tackles the inconsistency in the JTB approach with humour and panache. See http://en2.wikipedia.org/wiki/Gettier_problem.

the teacher has 'something' that the learner does not and hence the teacher's task is, at least in part, to remedy deficiencies on the part of the learner.[5] This is a view of education that stands at odds with Freire (1972) and Rogers and Freiberg (1993) who see personal growth *from within* as a central tenet of education and for whom 'transmission' of any 'something' is in effect anathema. For each of these writers, an educator may facilitate learning but nothing more.

Worthwhile and useless knowledge

There are various criteria we might use to mark out *educationally* worthwhile or valuable knowledge from that which is worthless. We might do this in terms of need but in doing so one must take care not to confuse *needs* with *wants*. What I want is not necessarily what I need and vice versa. Again, it is a matter of perspective and relative importance. With this in mind, needs can be defined in terms of societal needs or individual needs. The question arises as to whether the needs of society are necessarily compatible with the needs of the individual. The answer one gives is very much contingent on one's view of the social goal of education and whether one views society as composed of individuals or whether one sees individuals subsumed into society.

There is also the cultural aspect to knowledge to consider. Whether we seek cultural replication, maintenance or renovation or even replacement will play a major role in one's definition of educationally worthwhile knowledge. Our view, not only of the society we have now, but also of the society we want to have, is critical both in determining educationally worthwhile knowledge and in determining what counts as knowledge at all. This is exemplified, in all too many parts of the world, by the way in which some minority (and sometimes even majority[6]) languages have been proscribed in schools. This happened, for example, to Welsh, Scottish Gaelic, Scots, Swiss and French patois, Breton, Catalan to name but a few cases in

---

[5] Being unable to educate oneself by means of discovery stands at odds with Donald Schön's (1984) work on the Reflective Practitioner which has been extremely influential in the United Kingdom in terms of how not only teachers but also medical practitioners, engineers, architects and various other professionals are trained. Schön discusses, among other things, the development of the expert touch, that tacit knowledge that allows us to make adjustments to our practice on the hoof. It is a type of knowing that we see in every skilled craftsperson who knows by apparent intuition just what to do in a given situation. It is a skill that, like any skill, is learnt but it is essentially one that, although a teacher may help one on one's way, one essentially teaches oneself.

[6] 'Majority' is a very relative term. In the UK, English speakers are in the majority but they are very much in the minority in Europe, however we want to define 'Europe', for this too is a relative term: do we mean the *European Union*? If so, then what about Switzerland and Norway? If Europe is that part of the world west of the Urals which sits on the European Continental Shelf (a traditional definition of Europe) then what about Iceland? The Icelanders *consider* themselves European and yet their country is a volcanic island in the middle of the Atlantic and very definitely *not* on the European Continental Shelf. Similarly, 'minority' is relative. Both terms can also be considered in terms of power.

Europe. These languages were effectively designated as educationally (and often politically) unacceptable knowledge in often vicious bids to extirpate them.

Moral acceptability

Peters contends that education must be conducted in a morally acceptable manner. If there were consensus as to what constitutes morality then this exigency would present few, if any, problems. Unfortunately in our present society we see what are termed 'moral values' being challenged on a regular basis. No longer is the teacher seen, if ever s/he were, as an absolute authority on moral matters and this is the case across the whole range of teaching and learning. Our society increasingly sees itself as multicultural (as indeed it has been since the dawn of recorded history – see Grant 1997) and, as such, recognises that there can exist a multiplicity of value systems within one society. This poses the major problem of defining 'morally acceptable'. There are, however, some points of agreement within our society that certain 'educational' methods are simply unacceptable. At the extreme this precludes inflicting physical pain as a means of encouraging learning. Yet it was only in 1985 that corporal punishment was finally outlawed in state schools in the UK. While in theory in its latter years this punishment was reserved for recalcitrant miscreants, in practice it could be used, and was used, as an 'aid' to learning whereby, for example, a pupil might be hit for not spelling a word correctly.[7] Moral torture in the form of denigration, however officially decried, still continues as a not uncommon means of pupil regulation. This can range from sarcasm to denigration of speech patterns and the learners' cultural roots.

The literature, however, tends to highlight *indoctrination* as an immoral means of encouraging learning. Indoctrination is defined as the intentional implantation of unshakeable beliefs regardless of appeals to evidence (Barrow and Woods 1995). Indoctrination is seen as running counter to the very idea of education as it 'necessarily involves lack of respect for an individual's rationality [and hence] is morally unacceptable' (Barrow and Woods 1995: 80). These same writers illustrate their opposition to indoctrination by means of an imaginary Catholic school where all the teachers endeavour to have the pupils wholeheartedly and unequivocally share their belief in Catholicism. The fact that Barrow and Woods demonstrate some remarkable ignorance about Catholicism[8] is beside the point. Their focus is on major areas of belief, on whole-life beliefs, on what one might term '*macro*-beliefs'. What about the lesser ones, the *meso*-beliefs and the *micro*-beliefs? How did we learn that science is objective? That experts are to be trusted? That reading

---

[7] This was the standard practice in the primary school I attended in the 1960s.
[8] This they do, among other things, by insisting that Catholics believe that the Pope is infallible (p. 70). The reality is that the Pope is held under the doctrine of infallibility to be able to make infallible statements under certain circumstances and only on matters of doctrine.

is a necessary prerequisite for any modern society? It does not demand much imagination to determine a welter of beliefs which we usually hold unshakeably and which have been intentionally transmitted to us. There is also the question of the level at which intentionality occurs. While a teacher may not intend to indoctrinate his/her learners, it is quite conceivable and indeed likely that the socio-political system within which that teacher operates demands that certain values and beliefs be transmitted (this is a theme returned to in the next chapter). If we are not only indoctrinated but also conditioned then perhaps the very thoughts we are capable of thinking are restrained and constrained.[9]

In Chapter 4 in this volume, Trevor Corner and Nigel Grant remind us that we are generally better at identifying when others are indoctrinating. When it happens in our own education system we are more liable to call it 'moral education' or 'citizenship'. The question of moral (un)acceptability remains unanswered.

Perhaps a better question to ask is whether one can avoid *all* indoctrination in an educational process. Can one always present a learner with rationales as to why things are as we say they are? Will one always have learners who are capable of understanding such rationales? How does one rationalise to a three-year-old that to stick one's finger in the fire is not a good idea? By explaining the basic theories of thermodynamics and the interaction between skin and hot surfaces? By slightly scorching the child's finger? By telling the child that it will hurt and hoping that one's authority as an adult/parent will be enough to have the child always believe that sticking a finger in the fire is not a good idea? Simply presenting notions as truth is much simpler than explaining them and may be much preferable to demonstrating possible consequences of an action one wishes the learner to avoid. Explanation demands a level of understanding which may simply not exist in the learner. However, even rationalising everything might be construed as 'indoctrination', in that one is presenting the learner and encouraging in him/her a pattern of behaviour and hence beliefs as to its acceptability. One's force of argument may give one such an advantage over the learner that the latter simply succumbs to the belief being proposed. As a teacher one may feel that the learner has agreed with the reasonableness of the belief and has agreed to share it. As a learner one might just feel ground down.

In passing, it can be worth reminding ourselves that 'acquiring a belief is like catching a cold' (Heil 1999: 47). No matter how I might contrive to 'catch' whatever metaphorical virus transmits a belief, no matter how I might believe myself willing to acquire the said belief, it is only when conditions are just right that I will acquire it. However, repetition and reinforcement that the proposed belief is true will help enormously in engendering these conditions. This point is illustrated by

---

[9] See Matheson and Matheson (2000) for a discussion of discourse and the limitations that language can set on our thinking.

the way in which media stories can achieve a life of their own, regardless of how true they are and frequently in the face of powerful evidence to the contrary (Miller *et al.* 1998; Moore 2002).

It seems that the teacher is in a cleft stick if s/he decides to avoid *all* indoctrination. Giving no teaching implies to budding learners either that learning has a low value or that they themselves have. If we offer teaching, we are offering a complete package of beliefs that go with it and implying, if not insisting upon, its acceptability and desirability and hence 'indoctrinating' (Sutherland 1994).

On the other hand, perhaps there is a major argument in favour of critical thinking. Indeed if one's position is that indoctrination *in all its forms and regardless of the intent* is immoral (i.e. if one accepts that Peters' definition of what constitutes education is valid at least in this respect) then the encouragement of critical thinking is essential. Expressed at its least subtle we have Postman and Weingartner's (1976) notion of 'crap-detection' whereby the 'crap detector … is not completely captivated by the arbitrary abstractions of the community in which he [*sic*] happened to grow up' (p. 18). In other words, the crap detector is able to look past the symbolism and theatricals of his/her society and adopt a critical perspective. This is a notion that is most often associated with Paulo Freire and his idea of conscientisation. In dealing with Freire a word of caution is needed: Freire wrote in Portuguese and used the term *consciencização* which, since the Portuguese words for conscience and consciousness are the same, could be translated into English as either *conscience-raising* or *consciousness-raising*, so there is an element of ambiguity about the concept. However, Freire, a gifted linguist, was probably aware of this and hence the double meaning is more than likely deliberate.

Conscientisation is a means of empowerment where the learner decides what is to be learnt and does so in terms of what is meaningful to his/her own existence. The goal of this education is to make the learner more critically aware of the area under discussion, and hence more critically aware of him/herself and his/her environment. The political implications of such an educational goal and its associated pedagogy are immense. In this view of education, there is no received wisdom and everything is open to question. Nonetheless, the quandary outlined above remains, whereby offering teaching in any shape or form, or not at all, constitutes indoctrination but perhaps the development of the critical faculty is the most moral of options in that it encourages the learner to question even the basic premise upon which the learning experience is based (Akkari and Perez 2000).

What is education for?

What education is for is clearly dependent on how we choose to define education and how we determine the relationship between education and the society in which it operates. For the purposes of this section where we look at some of the social goals of education, we shall concentrate on the formal domain. Formal education is above all associated with school, further education and higher education. It tends to aim, at least at some levels, at a qualification and is often associated in the public mind with younger people. Non-formal education requires no entrance qualifications (such as schools certificates or degrees but it may require a certain level of knowledge and/or expertise in the domain in question), may result in no exit qualifications and is more usually associated with adults. The boundaries between formal and non-formal education were never very strict and are becoming even more blurred as time goes on.

Since time immemorial, formal education has been used with a social goal in mind. Every society seeks to replicate itself and finds ways of transmitting what it considers worthwhile to its young and sometimes its not-so-young citizens. In Ancient Greece, for example, the Spartans used a formal school system to instil into their young men the ideas of absolute obedience to their military commanders, extreme courage and resistance to pain as well as what were, for the time, some of the most advanced notions of military strategy. The young women were trained in domestic arts and motherhood. By the same token, it was not uncommon for commentators to complain, as did Seneca during the Roman Empire, that 'we are training children for school, not for life.' From this it becomes clear that it has been held for a very long time that school *ought* to have a social function and that this social function has not always been clear and well-defined.

Since the Reformation, at least, the idea that formal education can be used to reproduce society, mould society or create a new society has been widely discussed and written about in the West. The Reformers sought to create a society based around the *reading* of the Bible which distinguished them from their Roman Catholic predecessors who emphasised the *interpretation* of the Bible given by the Old Church. The social upheaval of the Reformation was accompanied by attempts to literally create a new society based on a literate population. To this end, John Knox *et al.* (1560), in their *First Book of Discipline*, proposed the creation of schools in every centre of population whose aims would be not only to teach basic skills such as reading and writing but also to act as a means whereby the more able boys and girls would learn sufficiently to allow entry to higher education. In this way, the intelligentsia would be kept in contact with the rest of the population and the upper echelons of society would be revitalised by new blood.

This idea of using education for social engineering has echoes in Robert Owen (1835) who states in his *New View of Society* that:

> Any general character, from the best to the worst, from the most ignorant to the most enlightened, may be given to any community, even to the world at large, by the

application of proper means; which means are to a great extent at the command and under the control of those who have influence in the affairs of men.

(Owen [1835] 1965: 85)

It is important to underline here that *character* refers not to individuals but to the communities that they form. The essential point, however, is that for Owen education had the power to shape collections of individuals into communities and to determine the nature of those communities. In other words, education has a major socialising function. This theme is taken up by Durkheim for whom 'education consists of the methodical socialisation of the young generation' (Durkheim 1956: 71). Durkheim also sees education as a means for social reproduction:

Education, far from having as its unique or principal object the individual and his interests, is above all the means by which society perpetually recreates the conditions of its existence.

(Durkheim 1956: 123)

Part of the recreation of itself is the need for economic sustenance if not growth. However, until recently there seemed to be a certain coyness about openly espousing the view that 'the economic aims of education are as legitimate as any other' (Winch 2002: 101). Yet, if education – whether a lifelong activity or as Winch (2002) puts it 'broadly but not exclusively concerned with preparation for life' (p. 101) – does not have economic aims, then why is so much money spent on it? In point of fact, it is fairly easy to establish that the economic aims of education, *especially* when viewed as a preparation for life or as a means of coping with changes in one's economic circumstances, are paramount.

Formal education serves many functions besides those outlined above. It contains examinations and assessments of various kinds which serve to decide, in part at least, the choice of next destinations the learner can move on to. Depending on one's perspective, these can be seen as an opportunity for social mobility or as a means for further entrenching social divides and further ossifying the existing social structure. Formal education may liberate or enslave, expand horizons or confirm feelings of personal failure. But let us note that formal education is seen as a right but seldom as a privilege despite general consensus that it is essential in order for a person to learn how to function within our society.

What does it mean to become educated?

Becoming educated carries with it a number of notions such as the acquisition of *depth* whereby a person understands (increasingly) the underlying principles within an 'area of knowledge'. The educated person will acquire *breadth* in the sense that s/he will develop a cognitive perspective *within* an area of knowledge and *between* areas of knowledge. This implies the creation of linkages across the area of knowledge and into areas which may adjoin or not. This serves not only to distinguish knowledge from information but also to encourage the adoption of differing perspectives on the same domain (an almost essential prerequisite to creative problem-solving). Indeed for Peters (1970), 'being educated is incompatible with being narrowly specialised' (p. 4).

An area of knowledge, by definition, is not an amorphous mass but has certain rules which bind it together. In this view of education, the educated person has to abide by these rules when acquiring knowledge, when handling knowledge and when using knowledge. To take one example, when learning another language, one accepts that the grammar and syntax of that language are rules to be obeyed (as best one can) if one wishes to actually communicate in that language. Failure to obey the rules will make communication difficult, if not altogether impossible. Against this has to be set the notion that fundamental creativity often comes about when the accepted rules in an area of knowledge are bent or ignored and a new, revised set has to be put in place.

We are used in our culture to measure 'being educated' against, for example, level of qualification or extent of acquaintance with some domain or other. In this way, the capacity to expound upon and employ the literary canon, or some other set of knowledge, may be the scale against which one's being educated is measured. Barrow (1999) draws this together with the development of criticality mentioned above and states that 'it is to have a developed mind, which means a mind that has developed understanding such that it can discriminate between logically different kinds of questions and exercise judgment, critically and creatively, in respect of important matters' (p. 139). Such discrimination and judgement inevitably need to be based upon a significant amount of knowledge. Just how much is significant and about what sort of knowledge we are talking is, of course, open to debate and will vary according to circumstances. My being educated in horticulture may be of little use when faced with a burst pipe in my living room.

All this implies that, while we may wax about general education, the sheer scope of knowledge and skills that are there to be acquired, at least in theory, is such that we must forcibly remain uneducated in at least some, if not many, domains. However, Barrow's argument, in company with many others, implies very strongly that education is the antithesis of indoctrination, although, as suggested above, education must perforce contain elements of indoctrination, if only to convince some learners of its own worth.

Education suffers from a variety of definitional problems, not least of which is the frequently false equation between education and studying (compounded by a similarly false equation between learning and studying). Studying implies some sort of examination, if only of oneself. Learning does not. Whether education does is dependent on how one chooses to define it. However, we might do well to distinguish between *education* and *being educated*. If *education* runs into such problems through its simultaneously being a process and a product then why not dispense with the one and concentrate on the other? In this way, discussion of what it means *to be educated* can potentially be more fruitful since the term implies not a process, with all the pitfalls and traps that await even the more astute such as Richard Peters, but rather a product. In this way, it is immaterial how we have acquired the components of being educated; what counts is that we have indeed acquired them.

With this idea in mind, it is worthwhile taking a moment to consider those things that, in your opinion, every person should know and those things that every person should be able to do. Should we value some knowledge and skills over others? If so, which ones? And, as importantly, why should this knowledge and these skills be more important than others? By asking questions such as this, we can begin to establish a canon of basic knowledge – which might be quite sophisticated – as well as establishing a hierarchy of knowledge. Critical in this venture, though, is establishing the rationale for such a set of affairs. In the end we may arrive at the same conclusion as Maskell (1999) who argues that those whom we might term 'educated' are all too often themselves in want of an education, suffering as they do from limited horizons and narrow ranges of knowledge.

We might even arrive at the notion of the *educated public* which, as Wain (1994) tells us, can take a variety of forms but which in all of them seems to imply some sort of community of persons endowed not just with knowledge and understanding across a wide range of spheres but, critically, with a capacity to communicate effectively with each other.

What is the study of education?

Education is unlike most other academic disciplines in that there is no agreement as to what it actually is. In consequence the study of education is somewhat diverse. It begins inevitably from the concept of education held by those directing the study – whether through their role as course managers, as researchers or as funders of research projects.

From the student's point of view?

If one succumbs to the notion that education equals school, then one's view of what constitutes knowledge of education worthy of study (for who really wants to study useless knowledge?) will be somewhat different from knowledge considered worthwhile by one who believes that education is a lifelong process. Unfortunately, there is a widespread tendency to do just that, despite the fact that it closes one's mind to the educational experiences that occur in the longer part of one's life. The excuse given, as Gutmann (cited in Wain 1994) reminds us, is that 'an exhaustive study of the other potential educational agencies in society would be exhausting if not impossible' (p. 155). This is doubtless true but one could just pick and choose as has occurred in the present text and try at least to be representative of what is available.

At least one attempt has been made to establish what students of Education Studies might study and this was undertaken for the Quality Assurance Agency for Higher Education. The result is the *Benchmark Statements for Education Studies* (QAA 2000) which seek to state what a student completing a single Honours programme in the subject will be capable of. Joint and Combined Honours students would be expected to show capability in a relevant selection of the areas.

The benchmark statements represent a compromise between those who argue that Education Studies is a discipline in its own right[10] and those who see it as an offshoot of teacher training. Equally the statements have to accommodate those who emphasise one methodological approach, be this sociological, historical, psychological, philosophical, some combination of these or some other approach entirely.

> Education Studies is concerned with understanding how people develop and learn throughout their lives. It facilitates a study of the nature of knowledge, and a critical engagement with a variety of perspectives, and ways of knowing and understanding, drawn from a range of appropriate disciplines. There is diversity in Education Studies courses at undergraduate level but all involve the intellectually rigorous study of educational processes, systems and approaches, and the cultural, societal, political and historical contexts within which they are embedded.
>
> (QAA 2000: 4)

What is perhaps most remarkable is that, other than the definition given above, the statements never explicitly state what topics need be studied. This should come as no surprise: if there can be no consensus on what constitutes education, there can surely be none on what constitutes Education Studies.

Despite this, Education Studies is perhaps unique among academic disciplines in that all students can bring directly to bear their own experiences and their own process of education. Since we have all found ourselves in situations that involve teaching and learning (and in studying Education Studies we are continuing to do so), then we all have experience that is relevant. In this respect, perhaps the only other domain that comes close in terms of universalised experience is medicine since we have all been sick at least once in our lives.

---

[10] I once heard Education Studies being described as parasitic and proud of it.

From the researcher's point of view?

The various chapters of this book, including this one, together with their references lists, give some indication of the wide diversity of subjects studied by researchers in Education Studies. Fundamentally, one can say that if a topic involves teaching or learning in any shape or form whatsoever, whether in a classroom or in the school of life or wherever, then it is fair game to be researched. Not that one would necessarily get funding, of course.

Like research in any academic discipline, research in Education Studies goes through trends as John Nisbet shows us in the last chapter in this volume. Topics come and topics go. Currently, for example, we see much ink being spilt on the apparent underachievement of boys. In a few years this may have vanished from the agenda. Likewise for notions of teaching and learning. We have seen a growth in recent years of work looking at issues arising out of our multicultural and multi-ethnic society. We have even seen research being conducted on educational research (Ofsted 2000).

Conclusion

In essence, this chapter has been about ideas regarding education and its purpose, as well as briefly considering Education Studies. Ideas when formalised into practice naturally have material impacts and some of these are picked up in later chapters. A negative perspective on such an impact is given by Common (1951) who presents us with perhaps the most cynical view of formal education as social control:

> We learn reading and boredom, writing and boredom, arithmetic and boredom, and so on according to the curriculum, till in the end it is quite certain you can put us in the most boring job there is and we'll endure it.

(Common quoted in Meighan 1986: 75)

Suggested further reading

There is a vast literature concerning the topics we have discussed in this chapter. However, a few texts stand out as especially suitable for the debutant. On the philosophical side there are Barrow and Woods (1995) and Walker and Soltis (1992) who introduce the reader to a wide variety of concepts in the philosophy of education without getting lost in jargon. Freire (1972) is a clear and lucid account of the ideas behind conscientisation while Akkari and Perez (2000) offer a critique of Freire and his ideas. Maskell (1999) presents a strong argument in favour of revising what it is to be educated and advocates an emphasis on great literature. Worth reading, given our increasingly technological society, is Snow's (1959) *Two Cultures* where he decries the breakdown in communication between the sciences and the humanities which extends to almost deliberate ignorance of things scientific by those 'into' literature and vice versa.

Sociologically two texts stand out. Meighan and Siraj-Blatchford (1998) adopt a themed approach while Blackledge and Hunt (1993) is arranged according to major theories and theorists and takes the reader from Durkheim through various Marxisms to the micro-interpretive approach.

References

Abbs, P. (1979) *Reclamations*. London: Heinemann.

Akkari, A. and Perez, S. (2000) 'Education and Empowerment', in C. Matheson and D. Matheson (eds) *Educational Issues in the Learning Age*. London: Continuum.

Barrow, R. (1999) 'The higher nonsense: some persistent errors in educational thinking', *Journal of Curriculum Studies*, 31 (2), 131–42.

Barrow, R. and Woods, R. (1995) *An Introduction to the Philosophy of Education*. London: Routledge.

Blackledge, D. and Hunt, B. (1993) *Sociological Interpretations of Education*. London: Routledge.

Bloom, B. S. (1969) *Taxonomy of Educational Objectives: The Classification of Educational Goals*. London: Longman.

Dancy, J. and Sosa, E. (eds) (1999) *A Companion to Epistemology*. Oxford and Cambridge MA: Blackwell.

Durkheim, E. (1956) *Education and Sociology*. New York: The Free Press.

Freire, P. (1972) *The Pedagogy of the Oppressed*. Harmondsworth: Penguin.

Grant, N. (1997) 'Intercultural education in the United Kingdom', in D. Woodrow *et al. Intercultural Education: Theories, Policies and Practice*. Aldershot: Ashgate.

Hamm, C. (1989) *Philosophical issues in education: an introduction*. London: Falmer.

Heil, J. (1999) 'Belief', in J. Dancy and E. Sosa (eds) *A Companion to Epistemology*. Oxford: Blackwell.

Illich, I. (1986) *Deschooling Society*. Harmondsworth: Pelican.

Knox, J., Douglas, J., Row, J., Spottiswoode, J., Willock, J. and Winram, J. (1560) *A First Book of Discipline*. np: Edinburgh.

Lawson, K. H. (1975) *Philosophical Concepts and Values in Adult Education*. Nottingham: University of Nottingham.

Maskell, D. (1999) 'What has Jane Austen to teach Tony Blunkett?' *Journal of Philosophy of Education*, 33 (2), 157–74.

Matheson, C. and Matheson, D. (2000) 'Educational Spaces and Discourses', in C. Matheson and D. Matheson (eds) *Educational Issues in the Learning Age*. London: Continuum.

McLuhan, M. (1967) *The Medium Is the Massage*. New York: Bantam Books.

Meighan, R. (1986) *A Sociology of Educating* (Second edition). London: Cassell.

Meighan, R. and Siraj-Blatchford, I. (1998) *A Sociology of Educating* (Third edition). London: Cassell.

Miller, D., Kitzinger, J. and Williams, K. (1998) *The Circuit of Mass Communication: Media Strategies, Representation and Audience Reception in the AIDS Crisis*. Thousand Oaks CA: SAGE.

Moore, M. (2002) *Bowling for Columbine*. Dog Eat Dog Films Production.

Ofsted (2000) *Educational Research: A Critique*. London: Ofsted.

Owen, R. [1835](1965) *A New View of Society and Report to the County of Lanark* (Gatrell, V. A. C. (ed.)). Harmondsworth: Pelican.

Peters, R. S. (1966) *Ethics and Education*. London: Allen and Unwin.

Peters, R. S. (1970) 'Education and the Educated Man', *Journal of Philosophy of Education*, 4, 5–20.

Postman, N. and Weingartner, C. (1976) *Teaching as a Subversive Activity*. Harmondsworth: Pelican.

Quality Assurance Agency for Higher Education (2000) *Education Studies*. Available at http://www.qaa.ac.uk/crntwork/benchmark/education.pdf.

Rogers, C. and Freiberg, H. J. (1993) *Freedom to Learn* (Third edition). New York: Merrill.

Schön, D. (1984) *The Reflective Practitioner: How Professionals Think in Action*. New York: Basic Books.

Snow, C. P. (1959) *The Two Cultures*. Cambridge: Cambridge University Press.

Sutherland, M. (1994) *Theory of Education*. Harlow: Longman.

Tight, M. (1996) *Key Concepts in Adult Education and Training*. London: Routledge.

Wain, K. (1994) 'Competing Conceptions of the Educated Public', *Journal of Philosophy of Education*, 28 (2), 149–59.

Walker, D. F. and Soltis, J. F. (1992) *Curriculum and Aims*. New York: Teachers' College Press.

Winch, C. (2002) 'The Economic Aims of Education', *Journal of Philosophy of Education*, 36 (1), 101–17.

Winch, C. and Gingell, J. (1999) *Key Concepts in the Philosophy of Education*. London: Routledge.

2

Ideology in education in the United Kingdom

Catherine Matheson

> To '*idéologues*' one must attribute all the misfortunes which have befallen France.
> Do you know what fills me most with wonder? The powerlessness of force to establish anything ... In the end the sword is always conquered by the mind.
>
> (Napoleon Bonaparte)

Introduction

EVERY CONCEPT IN EDUCATION has varying and various interpretations but perhaps none more so than ideology. As this chapter will show, it is used in a variety of senses and to a variety of ends. To do this, we begin with a discussion of the concept of ideology and show how it has had multiple meanings from the time it was first coined. We then move on to discuss ideology in education and show some of the types of ideology that are used in understanding education, before illustrating some of these types.

The concept of ideology

Ideology is a 'highly ambiguous concept' (Meighan and Siraj-Blatchford 1998: 179), a 'most equivocal and elusive concept' (Larrain 1979: 13) which has many meanings and usages and can be conceived either negatively and critically as a 'false consciousness' or positively as a 'world-view'. The former has a restricted meaning and tends to be used in a pejorative manner to describe a set of undesirable and even distorted beliefs, while the latter has a looser meaning and is used by philosophers and social scientists in neutral and analytical ways. Ideology can also be viewed as a subjective psychological phenomenon emphasising the role of individuals and groups or as a more objective social phenomenon 'impregnating the basic structure of society' (Larrain 1979: 14). Ideology can also be seen either, restrictively, as part of or, more loosely, as equal to the whole of the cultural sphere or ideological superstructure of society.

The word 'ideology' originated with that group of *savants* or intellectuals in the French Revolution who were entrusted by the Convention of 1795 with the founding and management of a new centre of revolutionary thought. These people were located within the newly established *Institut de France* which was committed to the ideas of the French Enlightenment and thus the practical realisation of freedom of thought and expression (Lichtheim 1967).

In its original sense, the word 'ideology' was first used in 1796 by the French philosopher Destutt de Tracy, a member of the *Institut de France* and one of the directors of the highly influential French literary review *Mercure de France*. It was, in the words of one of the *Mercure*'s regular contributors, Joseph-Jérôme Le François de Lalande, nothing more than a name for the 'science of ideas, their rules and their origins' (Lalande in Rey and Rey-Debove 1990: 957). Deriving ideas from sensations Destutt de Tracy undertook to study the 'natural history of ideas' in his *Eléments d'idéologie* (1801–15). He wanted to unmask the historicity of ideas by tracing their origins and setting aside metaphysical and religious prejudices but also wanted this unmasking to reveal a true and universal knowledge of human nature (Hall 1978). Ideology was presented as a science and set in opposition to prejudice and false beliefs because scientific progress was possible only if these could be avoided.

From the start, however, ideology was to have pejorative connotations, one reason being because de Tracy and those who practised it, the ideologues or *'idéologistes'*, were concerned with two logically incompatible concepts of 'ideology': the relation between history and thought and the promotion of 'true' ideas which would be true regardless of the historical context. Following Helvétius, who believed that education could do everything, the ideologues shared his enthusiasm for education (Larrain 1979). After the years of revolution they wanted to educate the French people and above all the young people so that a just and happy society could be established. De Tracy wanted his book to be a study programme for youngsters and explicitly acknowledged that a motive for writing it was the new law (1801) introducing public education.

The other reason for the pejorative connotation of ideology was Napoleon who was the first to use ideology in a truly negative sense. Initially he shared the objectives and goals of the *Institut de France* and even became an honorary member in 1797 (Lichtheim 1967). The *Institut* then facilitated Bonaparte's accession to power, which he achieved in 1799, by helping him win the support of the educated middle class (Hall 1978). However, he abandoned the ideologues in 1803 when he signed his Concordat with the Church and deliberately set out to destroy the core of the *Institut*, the liberal and republican ideas of which greatly influenced the educational establishment. From then on the *'idéologistes'* were ridiculed as utopian visionaries under the name of *'idéologues'* (Dancy and Sosa 1993: 191). After the defeat in Russia in 1812, Napoleon turned on them forcefully and attributed all of France's misfortune to the unrealistic, doctrinaire and ignorant of political practice ideologists or *'idéologues'* as he disparagingly called them (Lichtheim 1967). (It is worth noting that the English language has reversed the pejorative and non-pejorative use of the term.) Nonetheless after Napoleon's demise, the Comte de Tracy who became a well-known personality in France and outside France held an influential salon where writers and scientists met.

It is from this pejorative use of ideology as an undesirable or misguided set of ideas that many modern uses of the word have grown. Continuing this tendency, Marx and Engels used ideology pejoratively to mean a false belief or illusion. In *The German Ideology*, written in 1845–7 but only published in 1927, Marx and Engels, although not clearly defining the concept, use ideology to deride the proposition of the belief in the power of ideas to determine reality. For Marx (and Marxists) ideology was thus often seen as an attempted justification of a distorted set of ideas which consciously and/or unconsciously concealed contradictions in the interests of the dominant class or of a group and served to maintain disproportionate allocation of economic and political power to the ruling class or dominant groups (Marx and Engels [1845–7] 1970). Elsewhere Marx uses the term less pejoratively and gives a sociological interpretation of ideology (Marx [1859] in Meighan and Siraj-Blatchford 1998) where ideology can be defined as a broad interlocked set of ideas and beliefs about the world held by a group of people operating at various levels in society and in various contexts and which is demonstrated in their behaviour. This adds to the ambiguity of the concept of ideology not only because of the competing definitions but also because the set of beliefs operates with several layers of meaning (Meighan and Siraj-Blatchford 1998).

After a period of disuse, the word was revived with the publication in 1927 of Marx and Engels' previously unpublished *The German Ideology* which reinforced the Marxist and central sociological tradition view of ideology as 'distortion of reality' (Bullock *et al.* 1988). The classical Marxist position claims that ideological misconceptions cannot be dispelled by confronting those under their spell with the 'truth' since ideologies contain standards of evidence and argumentation that prevent the recognition of reality as it is (Dancy and Sosa 1993). For Gramsci, and other Marxists, however, ideology is explained in terms of its social role. It is neither true nor false but 'the "cement" which holds together the *structure* [in which economic class struggle takes place] and the realm of the complex superstructures' (Hall 1978: 53). In other words, ideologies are those beliefs that are generated by a particular mode of production or economic structure. For Althusser ideologies are non-scientific beliefs related more closely to social practice than theoretical enquiry (Summer 1979). Lack of space precludes discussion of scientific beliefs as the only true beliefs and hence being free from ideological constraints. More recently, the concept of ideology has seen a renewed (implicit rather than explicit) interest, particularly in feminism, cultural studies and post-modernism in general, for the 'unmasking relations of power and domination implicit in culturally dominant forms of theoretical and social discourse' (Dancy and Sosa 1993: 193).

For my purposes I shall consider ideology in its broad sense of a set of beliefs as opposed to the narrow sense of a set of undesirable or misguided beliefs. Within contemporary sociology one distinguishes between 'particular' ideologies concerning specific groups and 'total' ideologies concerning a total commitment to a way of life. Every ideology is composed of three ingredients: an invariable mythological structure, an alternating set of philosophical beliefs and a historically determined chosen group of people (Feuer 1975). Where ideologies exist in competition there are several outcomes: domination, incorporation and legitimation. In the first instance, we have cultural domination or hegemony. In the second, we have radical ideas incorporated into the traditional ideology. In the last instance, an ideology may achieve acceptance of its beliefs by direct repression or by more indirect means of institutional control such as those of the media, education, religion, law or economy (Meighan and Siraj-Blatchford 1998).

Ideology, knowledge and the curriculum

A curriculum as a package of ideas, together with the manner in which it is delivered (its pedagogy), certainly fits the bill as an ideology. Curriculum heritage is the product of a philosophical tradition which can be traced through historical and contemporary curriculum practice, and in which we find the European triad of humanism (Plato, Erasmus and Locke), rationalism (Plato and Descartes) and naturalism (Rousseau). The first two elements of the triad underline respectively the importance of the human character and especially the feelings and the importance of reason but with both understanding is sought by submission of the individual to an external body of knowledge, while the third seeks understanding in the private, concrete and the natural (McLean 1995). As in much in ideology, the triad's elements are not mutually exclusive.

It is these first two approaches that have dominated curriculum development across Europe and, as a consequence of European influence, across much of the world. In France there is the rational encyclopaedic educational ideology with state prescription of national occupational needs (McLean 1995). In this collectivist tradition upper secondary schooling is subordinated to economic and social planning while general and vocational education are linked in content and control (collectivism). In the pluralist tradition we move towards individualist and humanist approach such as exists in the UK and Germany with a clear separation between general education and vocational training, but in Germany the curriculum is more infiltrated with rational encyclopaedic ideology than in the UK. We also have generalism (as in France and Germany) versus specialism or, some say, elitism in England and to a lesser extent in Scotland (McLean 1995). Naturalism, however, as we shall shortly see, is very present and has been highly influential, especially in primary schools.

Educational ideologies

An educational ideology is any package of educational ideas held by a group of people about formal arrangements for education, typically expressed by contrasting two patterns of opposed assumptions such as teacher-centred and child-centred methods (the Plowden Report, DES 1967) or traditional and progressive methods (Bennett 1976). Going beyond dichotomies, Davies (1969) and Cosin (1972) outline four ideologies of education: conservative or elitist which maintains cultural hegemony; revisionist or technocratic which is concerned with vocational relevance; romantic, individualist or psychological which focuses on individual development and derives from the work of Pestalozzi, Froebel, Herbart, Montessori and Piaget; and democratic socialist, liberal tradition or egalitarian which seeks equality of opportunity and the progressive elimination of elitist values (Meighan and Siraj-Blatchford 1998). These categories are not hermetic, nor are they entirely mutually exclusive; they overlap and indeed an educational ideology might belong to several categories simultaneously. Assuming one accepts these categories as valid at all, the category(ies) to which a particular ideology might be assigned is often a matter of perspective.

Any ideology can be compared with others on the basis of a series of theories functioning as part of an aspect of knowledge, learning, teaching resources, organisation, assessments and aims. The concept of ideology can be used as an analytical tool to compare various patterns of education. Ideologies operate at different conceptual levels and, if categorised into levels of operations, can be compared along the lines of whole education systems, competing ideologies within a national system, ideologies within formal education and ideologies of classroom practice. Ideologies are usually linked with, for example, ideologies of classroom practice being linked to other parts of the educational and political network. The levels at which ideologies operate can be seen nationally in terms of Education Acts; regionally in terms of local education authorities; locally at the levels of educational establishments, rival groups within educational establishment, classroom, teacher/learner interaction and rival groups within classroom (Meighan and Siraj-Blatchford 1998).

One could also distinguish between ideologies of legitimation or implementation, the former concerning goals, values and ends and the latter the means. It can be a worthwhile exercise to consider the ideologies outlined below in this light.

Educational ideologies and politics

By definition education is a political activity in the broad sense, although this does not necessarily mean that it is a party political activity. Politics has to do with power and the distribution of power. Education has to do with knowledge (whether in terms of knowing that or knowing how). If knowledge is power, then education is political. If Gramsci's theory of hegemony is accurate, then politics is an educational activity and education is a political activity. All educators have an ideology whether formally articulated or not or whether they are aware of having an ideology. To subscribe to a particular view of the aims of education is to subscribe to an educational ideology. Debate about the nature and purpose of education is therefore 'bound to be not only ideological but, in the broad sense, political as well' (Winch and Gingell 1999: 111).

Often people think that it would seem that there is a correlation between political views and educational views. The correlation is usually that left-wing political views and support for child-centred or progressive education go hand in hand. This may have been more true at particular times, but it need not necessarily be so. Three examples illustrate the fact that political and educational ideologies cannot necessarily be subsumed into each other, although they certainly overlap.

The first example concerns two Labour personalities who had different educational ideologies. In his Ruskin speech of 1976 (see Chapter 3) the Labour Prime Minister James Callaghan acknowledged his indebtedness to R. H. Tawney who had been one of the originators of the Labour Party programme on education many years previously. Ironically, Callaghan and Tawney had very different views on most educational issues. Tawney defended liberal values, teacher autonomy and social democratic meritocracy. Callaghan in his speech advocated greater state control, teacher accountability and parentocracy, that is, more power to parents and less to the teachers. Callaghan aimed at increasing state control over education and over the curriculum whereas Tawney had fought to remove central Government hold on the curriculum. He feared that Government might abuse its power over the curriculum to serve the interests of industry or political ideologies instead of serving the interest of the pupils who were best served by the professional judgement of the teachers. Callaghan questioned the power of the teachers over the curriculum and thought that teachers should be more accountable to parents and to industry (Brooks 1991).

The second example is that of a Marxist who had nothing but contempt for progressive educational ideologies. Antonio Gramsci, who thought that education had the power to affect political consciousness, advocated conservative schooling for radical politics (Entwistle 1979) and there could be no time for what he considered to be the playful experimentation approach of progressive educational methods. Instead as much as possible of literacy, numeracy, history, politics and economics and science had to be learnt as quickly as possible. In order to be in a position to counteract the dominant hegemony one had to learn what the dominant hegemony learnt through education and much more. Learning had to be done in a concentrated systematic and disciplined intellectual way. Incidentally, the lack of time for playful experimentation and the opening up of the imagination was one of the major reasons behind the erstwhile Soviet Union abandoning in 1931 the very progressive and child-centred Dalton plan which had been introduced from the USA shortly after the Russian Revolution. The Soviet Union needed to industrialise rapidly and discovery methods with self-directed learning were simply not delivering the expertise quickly enough (Grant 1979).

A third example is a form of selective secondary schooling for all, which was introduced by a Labour Government after the Second World War and yet is currently associated with right of centre politics. The Conservative Party has over the last 15 years much criticised comprehensive education which was widely introduced from the end of the 1960s onwards replacing state-funded selective schooling in many areas but not all. However, the Conservative Government did not stop the spread of comprehensive schools but accelerated it. In 1967, the Conservative Party Leader, Edward Heath, could state that 'it has never been a Conservative principle that in order to achieve [selection or grouping by ability] children have to be segregated in different institutions' (Heath in Finn *et al.* 1978: 176).

Political ideas and ideologies evolve and their expression in educational circumstances evolves too. Indeed the apparently same educational ideology can be adopted simultaneously or consecutively by different political ideologies. This is the case not only with selective and comprehensive schools but also with standards and achievement (see Chapters 11 and 12) or equality of opportunity (see Chapters 6, 7, 8 and 9) and more recently the application of market principles to education and the idea of 'privatisation' not only not rejected by Labour but taken even further (see Chapters 13 and 14).

Some examples of educational ideologies

An elitist ideology: the public school ethos

'There is perhaps no better illustration of an elitist educational ideology than that which is held to underpin the education of the ruling class in a country' (Matheson and Limond 1999: 20). This kind of ideology is important not only for the way in which it might be held to form the ideas and behaviour of the ruling class but also for the influence it has on the education of the non-ruling class (Matheson and Limond 1999).

Everyone knows something of the public school ethos or public school spirit. The largely autobiographical novel *Tom Brown's School Days* – whether faithful portrayal or 'romantic fiction and expurgated fact' (Chandos 1984: 45) – has helped reinforce the mystique of the public school ethos as the 'pragmatic, almost unsupervised, trial-and-error, sink-or-swim test for survival in a self-governing community of male juveniles' (Chandos 1984: 38).

Its principal values are those of character over intellect and the importance of physicality. School is a place to train character. It is what came to distinguish the English public school from all other Western approaches to education or educational institutions. It is what 'impresses and amazes foreigners' (Gathorne-Hardy 1977: 75). In France, Germany or even Scotland schools not only drew from a wider social spectrum, but were also academic institutions; character being left to the family (Vaizey 1977). Examples of the public school ethos can be found in *Tom Brown's School Days*. The first example is from the point of view of Tom's father:

> Shall I tell him to mind his work, and say he's sent to school to make himself a good scholar? Well, but he isn't in school for that – at any rate, not for that mainly. I don't care a straw for Greek particles, or the digamma, no more does his mother. What is he sent to school for? … If only he'll turn out a brave, helpful, truth-telling Englishman, and a gentleman, and a Christian, that's all I want.
>
> (Hughes [1857] 1963: 71–2)

The second example demonstrates that Tom himself seems to have fully internalised the importance of physicality and that character mattered more than intellectual achievement, which constitute the fundamental values of the public school ethos:

> I want to be A1 at cricket and football, and all the other games, and to make my hands keep my head against any fellow, lout or gentleman … I want to carry away just as much Latin and Greek as will take me through Oxford respectably.
>
> (Hughes [1857] 1963: 262)

The public schools pre-date the emergence of the British Empire. The most distinguished date to the High Medieval period. The public school ethos is therefore a package of ideas, values and associated practices that have grown up over time. However, it was in the imperial period that their role, nature and ethos became most clearly defined (Matheson and Limond 1999). The main aim of the education of those who attended public schools was to develop a certain sort of character. This would be one in which self-control and 'stiff upper lip' would be of the greater importance as it gave clear imperial advantage. It was well suited to the needs of the army but equally suited to other forms and aspects of imperial service from missionary work to exploration and administration (Matheson and Limond 1999).

Henry Newbolt's poem 'Vitai Lampada' from *Poems: Old and New* (1912) linked together Empire and Public School.

> The sand of the desert is sodden –
> Red with the wreck of a square that broke;
> The river of death has brimmed his banks,
> …But the voice of the schoolboy rallies the ranks:
> 'Play up! Play up! and play the game.'

The Empire is no longer but the public school ethos endures, be it in modified form. *Tom Brown's School Days* gave rise to the public school novel and the public school memoirs. The magic derives from the myth and the myth derives from literature. The public school ethos survives not just because the public school mystique has a firm hold on popular imagination but especially because the public schools continue to educate the ruling class (Matheson and Limond 1999).

The Clarendon Commission (1864), an investigation of the nine leading public schools, found that:

> The average school boy was almost ignorant of geography and of the history of his own country, unacquainted with any modern language but his own and hardly competent to write English correctly, to do a simple sum; a total stranger to the laws which govern the physical world.
>
> (Quoted in Martin 1979: 60)

Nonetheless the public schools were praised for 'their public spirit, their vigour and manliness of character' as well as 'their love of healthy sport and exercise' and above all the fact that 'they have had perhaps the largest share in moulding the character of an English gentleman' (quoted in Martin 1979: 65).

Today the public school ethos endures, not only in about the tenth or so of English schools that are independent schools, both day and boarding schools, and are thus not financed by the state, but it also permeates to some extent the whole of the English education system. More particularly the public school ethos endures in what is allegedly 'education's best kept secret' (Hackett 2001: 10), that there remain in England about 36 state boarding schools where one can get what amounts to a public school place for between a third or half of what it would cost to send one's child(ren) to an independent school. The Government pays for the teaching and parents for food and accommodation for a mere £4,500 to £6,000. Such schools are praised and prized for their discipline, importance given to team sports and excellent exam results (Hackett 2001). Such importance given to academic achievement is a more recent development within the ideology of the public school ethos.

Some romantic or psychological ideologies

The romantic or psychological ideology, derived from the naturalism of Rousseau, was central to the establishment of progressive schools and has had considerable influence on some forms of curriculum revision and on the primary schools. Working within this ideology was perhaps the greatest influence upon the modern primary school curriculum: John Dewey, who argued against the subservience of the child to a curriculum devised for him/her by adults with its logical division of subject matters and little notice taken of the child's interest. For him, 'the child is the starting point, the centre, the end. His[/her] development, his[/her] growth, is the ideal' (Dewey 1906: 21 in Curtis 1965: 162). This centrality of the child to the schooling process can perhaps be said to have reached its peak in the United Kingdom and especially in England with the Plowden Report (DES 1967).

In its own terms, Plowdenism emphasises such things as, 'Learning ... [but] not [by] ... direct teaching ... [and] working harmoniously according to an unfolding rather than a preconceived plan' (Maclure 1973: 313). Plowden's was the pedagogy of learning by doing and following one's interests or enthusiasms (Matheson and Limond 1999). It was influenced by developmental psychology such as that of Piaget, Dewey and Montessori. A long time before Plowden it had been officially approved as an educational ideology in England. The Report of the Hadow Consultative Committee on *The Primary School* (1931) backed the idea that 'the curriculum is to be thought of in terms of activity and experience, rather than of knowledge to be acquired and facts to be stored' (p. 75). The aim of education was to open up the imagination. The cramming of factual or propositional knowledge (knowing that) was condemned, but experience and activity or procedural knowledge (knowing how) were advocated instead. Schooling would be based on scientific ideas of how the child grows and changes. The purpose was to meet the needs of those processes because anything else would be counterproductive in practice if not also morally wrong (Matheson and Limond 1999). Just as the Reports of the Consultative Committee on *The Primary School* (1931) and on *Infant and Nursery Schools* (1933) were full of metaphors about growth and nurture and psychological needs, so was the Plowden Report which stressed that education should foster flexibility and adaptability to an economically changing world. Such an ideology saw the aims of education as psychological harmony and intellectualism as detrimental to that psychological harmony. The importance of getting on with others and understanding them as well as of psychological balance was stressed:

> They will need as always to be able to live with their fellows, appreciating and respecting their differences, understanding and sympathizing with their feelings. ... They will need to be well-balanced, with neither the emotions nor the intellect giving ground to each other.
>
> (DES 1967, sections 494–6)

In the 1960s there was an increasing commitment to child-centred education as local authorities moved away from the 11+ examinations and the number of comprehensive schools increased (Brooks 1991). The Plowden Report deplored that some teachers 'still used books of English exercises and of mechanical computation' (DES 1967 quoted in Brooks 1991: 92). The Black Papers regarded Plowdenism as a libertarian charter and Callaghan's Ruskin speech denounced progressivism. The Prime Minister seemed to have accepted much of the Black Papers propaganda about declining standards, but the ideology promulgated in Plowden was far from being what was actually happening in English schools (Brooks 1991).

Although often half-heartedly implemented, Plowdenism can nevertheless be seen as the British, or more specifically English, culmination of the romantic or individualist/psychological tradition (Matheson and Limond 1999). So Plowden had arguably a non-negligible influence in British primary classrooms until the advent in England and Wales of the National Curriculum with its emphasis on cognitive performance. To its critics it is misguided and even a libertarian charter that promulgates the pursuit of 'relevance' to oneself as the essential criterion of intellectual worth. To its supporters it is 'a truth which has never been fully tested in practice because it has often been misunderstood or overlaid only very thinly as a veneer on existing practices and principles' (Matheson and Limond 1999: 22).

In all, Plowdenism bears a striking resemblance to Montessorism, the theories of Maria Montessori articulated in *The Montessori Method* (1912) and *The Advanced Montessori Method* (1917). The former deals with mentally or socially handicapped children and the latter applies the deriving principles to normal children. In other words, Maria Montessori advocates a psychological method implying that 'the educative process is adapted to the stage of mental development of the child, and to his/her interests and is not wholly subordinated to the necessities of a curriculum or to the teacher's scheme of work' (Rusk 1954: 262). Like that of Plowdenism, Montessori's own child-centred progressive pedagogy with emphasis on freedom and auto-education is associated with the names of Rousseau, Pestalozzi, Froebel, Herbart, Dewey and Piaget. Such a pedagogy aims to replace traditional pedagogy, whereby the teacher maintains discipline and immobility and engages in loud and continual discourse, 'by didactic material which contains within itself the control of errors' and thus 'makes auto-education possible to each child' (Montessori 1912: 371). She later added that 'to make the process one of self-education, it is not enough that the stimulus should call forth activity, it must also direct it' (Montessori 1917: 71).

Montessori's emphasis on interest as a driving force for the learner finds a modern echo in Malcolm Knowles' (1998) idea of andragogy (although, unlike Montessori, Knowles thought primarily of adult learners). Interest as a motivator has, however, a much longer heritage and was defined as 'the doctrine of interest' by Herbart who derived the idea from Rousseau but expanded upon it (Herbart 1816 in Rusk 1954: 210).

Herbart asserts that 'that which is too simple must be avoided' and 'instruction must be comprehensible and yet difficult rather than easy, otherwise it causes *ennui* [boredom]' (Herbart 1901 quoted in Rusk 1954: 225). Herbart further asserts that 'the principle of interest braces [pupils] up to endure all manner of drudgery and hard work', the idea being 'of making drudgery tolerable by giving it a meaning' (Adams quoted in Rusk 1954: 225). The doctrine of interest, however, is to be found in Plato's *Republic*, Rousseau's *Emile* and Pestalozzi's correspondence. Herbart also advocated the principle of recapitulation or spiral curriculum which is a doctrine common to many educators from Plato to Montessori and Dewey. For Herbart, there is no education without instruction and conversely no instruction that does not educate (Rusk 1954). Paradoxically, for an educational ideologist in the romantic tradition, Herbart ascribes to the teacher a centrality which is largely absent from those whose ideas derived from his (Dewey 1923).

A revisionist ideologist: Herbert Spencer

Herbert Spencer challenged the traditional curriculum and 'liberal education' by classifying the subjects, with scientific subjects being seen as most important because the knowledge that enables one to earn a living should come first in the curriculum and literary subjects should occupy the lowest place on the scale (Curtis 1965). Spencer further asserted that 'education of whatever kind, has for its proximate end to prepare a child for the business of life – to produce a citizen who, while he [she] is well conducted, is also able to make his [her] way in the world' (Spencer 1911 in Curtis 1965: 154).

Spencer presents several facets of the doctrine of relevancy (i.e. relevant to the economy and relevant to the learner's future quality of life). The importance of this former facet in educational and economic debate should not be understated. Other than its returning to the forefront of debates with a great frequency (e.g. in Callaghan's 1976 Ruskin College speech), the doctrine begs a great number of questions. How might it be determined *how* a learner is going to earn his/her living? How can we know what economic needs there will be in the future? To what extent does formal education not already instil *pre*-vocational skills? Spencer wrote at a time of economic stability when the future appeared largely to be a direct continuation of the past. Our future now appears much more uncertain but is this reason sufficient to discard Spencer's ideas? Even relevancy to the economy is relative, as is discussed at length by White (1997). There are also questions that arise out of the second facet: the business of life also appears to be in mutation but are there underlying skills and values which the learner need acquire in order to be successful (by some measure or other) in the ways of the world? We no longer have the consensual moral frameworks that we arguably had at times in the past.

Therefore what skills or values need the learner acquire? And who is to decide these? In sum, to apply the doctrine of relevance, be it to the economy's future (or actual) needs or to the learner's future (or actual) needs, we are obliged to decide who is to decide these needs, on what basis (i.e. on what criteria) and to what end(s). Fundamentally, we need to decide what education is for.

Liberal or egalitarian ideology

The democratic intellect

The philosophical underpinning of the Scottish education system appears to stand in opposition to the English education system. Both ideologies associated with the dominant values of each system are linked to the history of education in each country. For Scots of the nineteenth century education had become a badge of national identity, instead of being associated with the privileged ruling class. Education was 'a potent symbol of Scottishness and one of the ways in which a sense of nationhood was preserved without in any way threatening the basic structure of the union with England' (Devine 1999: 389). This 'national' education system had been established by John Knox and his fellow reformers in the *Book of Discipline* in the sixteenth century. Its ideology remained a guiding principle for Scottish education. It was not only meritocratic but according to some even egalitarian, resting on a ladder of opportunity going from parish schools to burgh schools and then universities, although burgh schools could be by-passed and it was possible for a boy who had talent to go from the parish school to university after he had been given some post-elementary education by the parish schoolmaster in mathematics and Latin (Stephens 1998: 1).

Although not an autobiographical novel as was *Tom Brown's School Days*, Ian Maclaren's novel *Beside the Bonnie Briar Bush* exemplifies and reinforces an educational tradition and hence its ideology. The teacher who 'could detect a scholar in the egg, and prophesised Latinity from a boy who was only fit to be a cowherd' (Maclaren 1940: 8) is the leader of the local community. His function is to spot likely talent for intellectual endeavour and then persuade the family to live frugally to save up and the better-off members of the community to give their help to put together the money for the university fees.

The term 'democratic intellectualism' was coined in 1919 by Walter Elliot, then Conservative Secretary of State for Scotland, and is associated with the works of George Elder Davie (Matheson and Limond 1999). The term is used to characterise Scotland's post-Reformation and Enlightenment history (Davie 1961: 75) in terms of thoughtful citizenship, reasoned participation and thriving intellectual debate derived from the fact that until the middle of the nineteenth century Scottish universities nurtured and promoted a set of highly distinctive academic values (Matheson and Limond 1999). The main mechanism of this nurturing and promotion was their concentration on teaching philosophy in a system that only went into decline when forced to change from the 1840s and 1850s (Bell and Grant 1977).

Davie was a lecturer in philosophy at Edinburgh University. He argued that the true nature of Scotland's educational tradition was democratic intellectualism and deplored the way this true nature had been eroded by closer contact with England (Davie 1993). He argued that Scotland's educational ideology fitted broadly within a European tradition of generalist curriculum and philosophy-centred higher education. This was contrasted to the insular and eccentric English narrowness of curriculum and specialised 'Honours' courses. Not only was there a wider access to universities in Scotland but also a wider and more balanced curriculum with the study of philosophy firmly at its centre (Bell 2000). To understand this point fully it is necessary to think of philosophy not as academic subject but as a way of encouraging students to inquire into issues and ideas, morals and metaphysics. In English universities (and at the start of the nineteenth century England had only two, while Scotland, with a tenth of the population, had four) the emphasis was on teaching a precise grasp of Latin and Greek grammar through studying Greek and Latin authors (Matheson and Limond 1999). In Scotland by contrast the emphasis was more on understanding what these authors had said rather than how they expressed themselves. (It was thus far more acceptable in Scottish universities to read classical authors in translation.) The ideas expressed in their words were of greater importance than the words themselves, thus the Scottish interest was philosophical rather than literary (Matheson and Limond 1999). The common sense of the subject was put before questions of detail. An understanding of ancient civilisation was preferable to textual study (Davie 1961). Asking and answering philosophical questions was always of prime importance as was enlightenment over erudition, hence more morals and metaphysics than literature and language (Beveridge and Craig 1989). There was specific teaching of philosophy as a compulsory subject in its own right, but the weaving of philosophical concerns into all other subjects was of far greater significance (Matheson and Limond 1999).

Social democracy

In the period 1944 to 1970 educational policy was based upon the ideology of 'social democracy' constructed by three social groups who formed a coalition: the Labour Party (although supported in much of this by the Conservative Party), educationalists working in sociology and economics, and the teaching profession. The key features of the ideology of social democracy were: a commitment to educational progress through state policy, and a concern with access and equality of opportunity. Reform was via the state (the state being seen as neutral) and was for the benefit of all sections of society, especially the underprivileged. A focus of attention in social democracy was working-class underachievement and wastage of ability and, as a consequence, the idea of non-selective comprehensive schools slowly emerged. Teachers, for their part, pursued professional status and demanded autonomy and control of the curriculum. The notion was promoted, and accepted, that teachers knew best what was best for their pupils.

A clarion call of social democracy was equality of opportunity in education, a notion fraught with conceptual difficulties. In a simple form, equality of opportunity can be seen as open and fair competition for economic rewards and social privileges. The problems arise when one tries to determine what is open and fair. The way in which this meaning shifted in the UK is demonstrated by the move by socialists from supporting selective secondary schools in the 1940s and 1950s to calling for a total end to selection for secondary school from the 1960s onwards. Both the generalisation of selective secondary school and the abolition of selective secondary school were justified on the grounds of equality of opportunity. However, coupled with equality of opportunity was also equality *per se* (Finn *et al.* 1978). Arguably, equality of opportunity equalises the chances people have to become unequal. It is therefore incompatible with any notion of equality as reducing privilege, except perhaps privilege of birth. Equality of opportunity does, however, give rise to the notion of the meritocracy whereby everyone has, in theory, the same chances to go as far as their talents will take them. As this inevitably leads to the creation or at least the sustenance of an elite, it is perhaps best described as an elitist ideology hiding away in an apparently egalitarian one. This only goes to show the lack of mutual exclusivity of the four categories of educational ideology mentioned above.

In the 1970s the ideology of social democracy was finally challenged largely because of its failure to promote economic growth and growing concerns about falling standards and indiscipline in schools. James Callaghan's 1976 speech in Ruskin College, Oxford, effectively sounded the death knell for social democracy in education. Callaghan called for more control of teachers and more accountability from schools. Education, he claimed, should be seen as a means for training young people for work. The effect was the official beginning of the process that led into the National Curriculum in England and Wales with its concomitant national testing, Ofsted and the full trappings of direct state control over school (Chitty 1993).

The best of all worlds or neither one thing nor another

The Third Way

In 1998 Anthony Giddens came up with a new political ideology, the Third Way. (He borrowed much of his ideas from the New Democrats in the United States who a few years before New Labour wanted to be seen to have moved away from the left and towards the right to attract votes.) Giddens' book provoked a storm of interest and controversy (Giddens 1998). He wrote a response to his critics two years later (Giddens 2000).

The Third Way is an attempt to find a path between the New Right and the Old Left as there is a need to move away from the sterile debate between left and right, or between those who favour either the state or the free market doing everything. It was brought about by the realities of the modern world, that is, the dissolution of the welfare consensus, the rapid technological changes of the Information Age, globalisation and the discrediting of Marxism. It aims to combine social solidarity with a dynamic economy, to stress equality of opportunity, not of outcome, and to concentrate on the creation of wealth and not its redistribution (Giddens 1998). What does this really mean in theory and in practice? Its critics say it is an empty concept without any real content, an intellectual cover for those whose principles are sufficiently flexible to accommodate any type of wealth creation and a betrayal of left-wing ideals.

In terms of education, this new ideology is based on the idea that there is no viable alternative to the market economy. So the Third Way is really social democracy because social justice and equality of opportunity are encouraged but instead of the state paying the full cost of this, market principles are necessary to lessen state ownership, state funding and state intervention, and to encourage private initiatives to play their part in the educational process. The Third Way wants to encourage the less talented to succeed as the exclusion of the less able is feared as much as the withdrawal of the most able. This has to be prevented by improving education to such an extent with the help of market forces that someone with money will choose not to pay for their child(ren)'s education. The critics have ridiculed this idea by underlining that this would mean that the state must take so much in tax from everyone so it can afford to offer a state education that would attract those who previously chose to send their child(ren) to independent schools and who now would therefore become a burden to the taxpayer by no longer doing this.

Conclusion

This has only been a brief look at the role of ideology in education and, of necessity, it has been an eclectic look. There is a multitude of other educational ideologies that might equally merit inclusion, but space does not permit this. I have not specifically discussed the ideological precepts that underpin the National Curriculum although some of these are dealt with in other chapters. I have omitted the ideology of the market which has set schools and universities in competition with each other in a bid to attract students and other sources of funding.

I have not considered the ideology of 'privatisation'. Other chapters in this volume take up again the theme of ideology in education under different guises. There are educational ideologies based on gender, 'race', social class, age, culture, the nature of learning itself, to name but a few which are touched upon.

It is, however, worth remembering that few, if any, ideologies actually bear the name openly. Rather we have various collections of notions, ideas and beliefs which may apply better to one level of education than to another (and this can mean, for example, applying better to a macro-perspective than to a micro-perspective or applying better to one level than to another) by which not only is behaviour influenced or even determined, but the very ways in which we think about phenomena may themselves be set. In this light, it can be worth wondering why comprehensive *secondary* school can rouse so much passion but comprehensive *primary* school never has. Is this through a rational choice on our part or is it through our internalising of an ideological precept which precludes the stimulation of heated debates over the possibility of non-comprehensive primary school?

Ideologies are not static. They evolve and they may expire, as did Scottish Democratic Intellectualism, although arguably until the re-establishment of the Scottish Parliament in 1999, this ideology had a few remaining vestiges in the form of the Scottish Ordinary degree which, unlike its English counterpart, is not (usually) a failed Honours degree but a general, as opposed to a specialised, degree. One of the first concerns of the Scottish Parliament was to set out to abolish university fees as this was seen to go against a tradition and ideology articulated within a country that was not only proud of having a wider social intake in higher education than England, but wanted to be seen to promote the accessibility of higher education better than England. The more important role of the teacher within Democratic Intellectualism can also be seen in the fact that the Scottish Parliament decided to substantially increase teachers' salaries.

In terms of the public school ethos, the discourse of excellence and achievement or rather of 'league tables' and 'exam results' is more marketable and resonates better than that of character. The importance of character formation gave way to psychological well-being which was the cornerstone of progressive education. Recently there has been a revival of character education in Britain. The White Paper *Schools: achieving success* (DES 2001) talked of 'education with character' and linked this with the promotion of citizenship education.

Whether any of these, or the other ideologies mentioned, were ever true (or valid as the case may be) is another issue but one we shall not pursue. Truth/validity depends on perspective. What is important in all these ideologies is not their truth or validity but rather the impact they have had and in some cases continue to have.

Suggested further reading

A good further introduction to educational ideologies is to be found in Meighan and Siraj-Blatchford (1998). Blackledge and Hunt (1985) detail and critique various sociological perspectives and the ideologies within which they function. For more on the 'public school ethos' see Gathorne-Hardy (1977) and Walford (1986). For gender balance Walford (1993) and Avery (1991) should be read. For more on the 'democratic intellect' consult McCrone (1992) who gives a good understanding of the background for this ideology while Davie (1961) is essential for a good understanding of his ideas and Lockhart Walker (1994) is also extremely useful. For an examination of the present Government's educational ideologies in its first four years in office, see Paterson (2003).

References

Avery, G. (1991) *The Best Type of Girl*. London: Andre Deutsch.

Bell, R. (2000) 'Scottish Universities', *Comparative Education*, 36 (2), 163–75.

Bell, R. and Grant, N. (1977) *Patterns of Education in the British Isles*. London: Unwin Education Books.

Bennett, S. N. (1976) *Teaching Styles and Pupils' Progress*. London: Open Books.

Beveridge, C. and Craig, R. (1989) *The Eclipse of Scottish Culture*. Edinburgh: Polygon.

Blackledge, D. and Hunt, B. (1985) *Sociological Interpretations of Education*. London: Routledge.

Brooks, R. (1991) *Contemporary Debates in Education: a historical perspective*. London and New York: Longman.

Bullock, A., Stallybrass, O. and Trombley, S. (eds) (1988) *The Fontana Dictionary of Modern Thought*. London: Fontana Press.

Chandos, J. (1984) *Boys Together: English Public Schools 1800–1864*. Newhaven and London: University Press.

Chitty, C. (1993) *The Education System Transformed*. London: Baseline Books.

Clarendon Commission (1864) *On the Principal Public Schools*. London: HMSO.

Cosin, B. (1972) *Ideology*. Milton Keynes: Open University Press.

Curtis, S. J. (1965) *Introduction to the Philosophy of Education*. Foxton: University Tutorial Press.

Dancy, J. and Sosa, E. (eds) (1993) *A Companion to Epistemology*. Oxford and Cambridge MA: Blackwell.

Davie, G. E. (1961) *The Democratic Intellect: Scotland and Her Universities in the Nineteenth Century*. Edinburgh: Edinburgh University Press.

Davie, G. E. (1993) 'The Importance of the Ordinary MA', *Edinburgh Review*, 90, 61–9.

Davies, I. (1969) 'Education and social science', *New Society*, 8 May.

Department for Education and Skills (2001) *Schools: achieving success*. London: The Stationery Office.

Department of Education and Science (DES) (1967) *Children and their Primary Schools (The Plowden Report)*. London: HMSO.

Devine, T. (1999) *The Scottish Nation 1700–2000*. London: Penguin.

Dewey, J. (1906) *The School and the Child*. Glasgow: Blackie.

Dewey, J. (1923) *Democracy and Education*. New York: Macmillan.

Entwistle, H. (1979) *Conservative Schooling for Radical Politics*. London: Routledge.

Feuer, L. S. (1975) *Ideology and the Ideologists*. Oxford: Basil Blackwell.

Finn, D., Grant, N. and Johnson, R. (1978) 'Social democracy, education and the crisis', in Centre for Contemporary Cultural Studies, *On Ideology*. London: Hutchinson.

Gathorne-Hardy, J. (1977) *The Public School Phenomenon 597–1977*. London: Hodder and Stoughton.

Giddens, A. (1998) *The Third Way: The Renewal of Social Democracy*. Cambridge: Polity Press.

Giddens, A. (2000) *The Third Way and its Critics*. Cambridge: Polity Press.

Grant, N. (1979) *Soviet Education*. Harmondsworth: Penguin.

Hackett, G. (2001) 'Boarders on a Budget', *The Sunday Times*, 23 September, 10–11.

Hall, S. (1978) 'The Hinterland of Science: Ideology and the "Sociology of Knowledge" ', in Centre for Contemporary Cultural Studies, *On Ideology*. London: Hutchinson.

Hughes, T. [1857] (1963) *Tom Brown's School Days*. London and Glasgow: Collins.

Infant and Nursery Schools (1933) Report of the Board of Education Consultative Committee under the Chairmanship of Sir William Hadow. London: Board of Education.

Knowles, M. (1998) *The Adult Learner*. Houston, TX: Gulf Publishing.

Larrain, J. (1979) *The Concept of Ideology*. London: Hutchinson University Library.

Lichtheim, J. (1967) *The Concept of Ideology and Other Essays*. New York: Vintage.

Lockhart Walker, A. (1994) *The Revival of the Democratic Intellect*. Edinburgh: Polygon.

Maclaren, I. [1894] (1940) *Beside the Bonnie Briar Bush*. New York: Dodd, Mead and Co.

Maclure, J. S. (1973) *Educational Documents England and Wales 1816 to the Present Day*. London: Methuen.

Martin, C. (1979) *A Short History of English Schools 1750–1965*. Hove: Wayland.

Marx, K. and Engels, F. [1845–7] (1970) *The German Ideology*. London: Lawrence & Wishart.

Matheson, C. and Limond, D. (1999) 'Ideology in Education in the UK', in D. Matheson and I. Grosvenor (eds) *An Introduction to the Study of Education* (First edition). London: David Fulton Publishers.

McCrone, D. (1992) *Understanding Scotland: the sociology of a stateless nation*. London: Routledge.

McLean, M. (1995) *Education Traditions Compared*. London: David Fulton Publishers.

Meighan, R. and Siraj-Blatchford, I. (1998) *A Sociology of Educating* (Third edition). London: Cassell.

Montessori, M. (1912) *The Montessori Method*. London: Heinemann.

Montessori, M. (1917) *The Advanced Montessori Method*. London: Heinemann.

Newbolt, H. (1912) *Poems: Old and New*. London: John Murray.

Paterson, L. (2003) 'The Three Educational Ideologies of the British Labour Party, 1997–2001', *Oxford Review of Education*, 29 (2), 165–85.

The Primary School (1931) Report of the Hadow Consultative Committee. London: Her Majesty's Stationery Office.

Rey, A. and Rey-Debove, J. (1990) *Le Petit Robert*. Paris: Dictionnaires Le Robert.

Rusk, R. R. (1954) *The Doctrines of the Great Educators*. London: Macmillan.

Stephens, W. B. (1998) *Education in Britain 1750–1914*. London: Macmillan.

Summer, C. (1979) *Reading Ideologies*. London: Academic Press.

Vaizey, L. (1977) 'Facts, Theories and Emotions', in G. Macdonald-Fraser (ed.) *The World of the Public School*. London: Weidenfeld and Nicholson.

Walford, G. (1986) *Life in Public Schools*. London: Methuen.

Walford, G. (ed.) (1993) *The Private Schooling of Girls: Past and present*. London: Woburn Press.

White, J. (1997) *Education and the End of Work*. London: Cassell.

Winch, C. and Gingell, J. (1999) *Key Concepts in the Philosophy of Education*. London and New York: Routledge.

3

A brief history of state intervention in British schooling

Graham Martin

Study the past if you would divine the future.
(Confucius 551–479 BC)

A beginning

England and Wales

BEFORE 1870 ELEMENTARY SCHOOLS provision was funded by charitable donation. The donations were worked in isolation of one another and elementary schooling was largely free of any regulatory legislation[1]. The majority of these charity or voluntary schools had the aim of turning the children of the poor into good Christians who would thereby make a disciplined and productive contribution to society. Even with such high ideals and with some continuing fear that revolution might spread from the Continent, there was extensive scepticism over the desirability of educating the poor (Ball 1983: 11). Some influential people saw little purpose in or good coming from educating these children for fear of causing them to be discontented with their allotted lowly place in life. Others in positions of power took quite the opposite view that it was necessary to provide some basic education to improve public order and control not least through the 'lower orders' gaining some spiritual and moral uplift.

Two societies were prominent in establishing charity schools but it should be remembered that their involvement was to support and advise individual schools

---

[1] See Stephens (1998) for a detailed account of eighteenth-century developments in England, Wales and Scotland.

and not to establish any kind of network or organised system of schooling. The Church of England (Anglican) was served by the splendidly named National Society for the Education of the Poor in the Principles of the Established Church (known as the National Society) created in 1811 and affiliated to the Society for the Promotion of Christian Knowledge (SPCK) which had been in existence since 1699. The educational aspirations of the nonconformist churches were served by the British and Foreign School Society (known as the British Society) established in 1808 as the Royal Lancastrian Society.

The aim of these societies was to bring religious observance and morality to the masses and so began the strong connection between church and schooling. The evangelical imperative to deliver education to the largest possible numbers for the least possible cost concentrated on the curriculum of the 3Rs (Reading, wRiting and aRithmetic) and fashioned methods of delivery confined to rote learning and drill enforced by rigid discipline and frequent harsh punishment. Its effects are most vividly conveyed by a description of 1809 which stated that 'a single master could conduct a school of 1,000 children; that one book would serve for the whole school; and that 500 boys [sic] could spell and write the same word at the same moment' (Gordon and Lawton 1978: 130).

Despite financial difficulties and the lack of suitable teachers (not a situation suffered by Sunday schools where the day meant that educated people were not only available but would dutifully give their services), these charity schools began to be seen as making a valuable contribution. In 1833 the Government awarded its first grant for education allotting the sum of £20,000 (in the region of £1.3m in 2004 terms) between the two religious societies to match charitable donations for the purpose of building schools. This was the first time that the state had involved itself in the provision of elementary education but it was accompanied by the clear assertion that there was no intention to move towards a state-run system of schooling. The Lord Chancellor, Lord Brougham, reported in 1834 to the Parliamentary Committee on the State of Education that with regards to the promoting of general education he thought 'legislative interference is in many respects to be altogether avoided or very cautiously employed because it may produce mischievous effects'[2] and that 'it is wholly inapplicable to the present condition of the country, and the actual state of education' (Maclure 1973: 39). His reservations applied to both the funding of schools, where he perceptively anticipated state funding would cause the withdrawal of charitable donations leaving the Government with the full cost, and legislation requiring compulsory attendance.

---

[2] Many commentators would observe that politicised educational changes in the 1980s and 1990s would prove just what a perceptive prediction this was.

Nevertheless, the provision of funding was, almost inevitably, followed in 1839 by the requirement that schools submit to Government inspection and thereby official influence (Stephens 1998). The involvement of the Government with its largely secular intentions created a tension with the church groups which has characterised almost two centuries of educational development in all parts of Britain. Increasingly, Government funding came with an ever more specific stipulation (known as a Code) on what would be taught in elementary schools. This culminated in 1862 with the Revised Code for England and Wales. Through this directive funding was unequivocally linked to the results of inspections, a process known as *payment by results*. This did much to standardise the experience of the children in the elementary schools as it required that careful attention be paid to the basics of education (the 3Rs) in order to obtain the grant. Any excesses in the time spent away from these basics, e.g. on religious instruction, were ironed out and pupils' attendance began to be a matter of concern.

Despite the financial difficulties and the reservations of the country's governors, there was massive growth in the provision of schooling throughout the first half of the nineteenth century due to the charitable support of the established church and the nonconformists. This was worthy in intent but it was patchy and poorly resourced. It was becoming increasingly clear that 'as an educational provision for a rapidly increasing population growing up in a society whose traditional structure had been shattered by economic change, they were clearly inadequate' (Ball 1983: 14).

The degree of civil unrest and lawlessness predicted by some had not really materialised[3] although some large conurbations created to provide a readily available labour force for the rapidly expanding manufacturing industries were already showing signs of social decay. Often these were the areas least well served by schools due to the poor economic plight of the inhabitants and their consequent inability to contribute to the upkeep of a school and the absence of rich benefactors living in such deprived areas. Some notable philanthropic employers provided elementary education for the children of their employees and on a half-time basis for their child labour, but generally the provision of schooling in these areas was poor.

Although the increase in the number of charitable elementary schools levelled off as the century moved through its second half,[4] the interest of the established church and the nonconformists in the education of the children of the poor had been well established. By the mid-nineteenth century there were as many among the dissenters as were in the Anglican congregation but by 1860 schools in England

---

[3] Nonetheless, 'ragged' or 'industrial' schools were created in the 1830s with the specific intention of providing the 3Rs and industrial training for those defined as 'potentially delinquent'.

[4] This was particularly true in the case of the nonconformist British Society as they increasingly looked to extend their flock through charitable activities in the Commonwealth.

supported by the National Society accounted for three-quarters of the school population with some 10 per cent supported by the British Society (Stephens 1998). The moral and social benefits of a populace with at least a basic level of education was beginning to be more widely appreciated and the economic imperative was growing. Conditions were now such that a more planned system of elementary education was seen by some decision makers, but by no means all, as a necessity and that the state would have to take a lead role.

Scotland

In Scotland a similar function as that of the National Society and the British Society was served by the Church of Scotland. Here there had been a form of elementary education from the mid-sixteenth century and there was already a rudimentary form of inter-school organisation which pre-dates what was available in other parts of Britain. Not only were educational ethos and Presbyterian religious faith strongly connected, but the schooling system had been effectively established by John Knox and his fellow reformers in the *First Book of Discipline* in 1560. From the end of the seventeenth century a small amount of local taxes had been used to help the establishment and funding of elementary schools. This meant that the Church of Scotland and from the middle of the nineteenth century the Free Church were running schools with more state backing than in England. A consequence of this was that for Scots in the nineteenth century education was more than a basic instruction and/or scholarship, 'it had become a badge of identity, a potent symbol of Scottishness and one of the way in which a sense of nationhood was preserved without in any way threatening the basic structure of the union with England' (Devine 1999: 389).

The foundations of a structure

England and Wales

By the second half of the nineteenth century the distribution of schools in England and Wales was largely a reflection of the relative activity of the various religious groups and the presence in specific localities of wealthy benefactors, rather than the result of demographic need. This resulted in the poorest urban areas and the sparsely populated rural regions being served least well. It was estimated by William Forster, Vice-President of the Board of Trade and in charge of the Education Department, that although three-quarters of a million children between the ages of six and 12 were receiving some education, at least 1.5 million children were not. To solve this problem the Elementary Education Act of 1870 (known as the Forster Act) aimed to 'fill in the gaps' by creating elementary schools in these neglected areas. The importance of this initiative to Gladstone's Liberal

Government was emphasised by Forster who completed his speech introducing the Bill to Parliament by saying that for Britain to hold her place 'among the nations of the world we must make up the smallness of our numbers by increasing the intellectual force of the individual' (Maclure 1973: 105).

The new schools created by the 1870 Act were controlled by an elected School Board independent of existing structures and were funded by local rates. Through the enactment of a local by-law the Boards could make attendance at school compulsory for enrolled children between the ages of five and 13 and by 1873 some 40 per cent of the population were subjected to such compulsion (Stephens 1998). This expectation increased and by 1880 all pupils up to the age of ten years old were required to attend school. This legislation was also significant in controlling the amount of religious instruction taught in the elementary school curriculum and it established the right of parents in all public elementary schools, including those run by the churches, to withdraw children from religious instruction on grounds of conscience. Further, schools established from this point forward and funded by the local rates would not be permitted to teach any religious observance (e.g. catechism) that was distinctive to a particular denomination.

The 1870 Act was the first step towards establishing a state system of education but its critics saw it as being much more concerned with quantity than quality. The elementary education it made more widely available was seen by some contemporary observers as of very little benefit.[5] There was also considerable reluctance on the part of influential politicians, including Forster, towards the full involvement of the state in the control of education. This was in sharp contrast to the centralised systems already established on the continent of Europe (notably Prussia and France) and is an ideological stance that persists among the New Right to this day (Chitty 1996). Similar legislation was enacted for Scotland in 1872 and this resulted in the majority of elementary schools being transferred to school boards (largely to alleviate the financial difficulties of the church) to the point that by 1891 only 10 per cent of elementary schools were still in the control of a religious charity, notably the Catholic Church (Stephens 1998), thus bringing in a more co-ordinated strategy for schooling some years ahead of the situation in England and Wales.

Although the 1870 Act made elementary education more widely available, it was still subject to fees. By 1890 there was strong pressure, led by the trades unions and Gladstonian Liberals, for elementary education to be free of charge. To resist this desire was seen by the Tory Government as a sure way of losing the recently given working-class vote so in 1891 a Free Education Act was passed (Simon 1965). The progress of this Bill was not without opposition as the Anglicans, and some supporters of the voluntary schools, saw this as reducing

5 Silver (1983) draws on contemporary accounts to explore the opposition to aspects of education we now take for granted, e.g. state control, compulsory attendance, equal access for all, etc.

their revenue thereby making them more dependent on the Government and they were concerned that it would lead to a greater secularisation of schooling.

An Act of Parliament in 1899 created the Board of Education with the remit to oversee everything related to education in England and Wales which it did, in part, by the issuing of regulations or codes. The Elementary Code of 1900 provided voluntary schools (those established by religious charities) with a block grant to replace the previous subject-based system of *payment by results*.[6] This Code specified, for the first time, the particular subjects that an elementary school was normally expected to teach. These were English, arithmetic, geography, history, singing and physical training together with drawing for boys and needle-work for girls. If circumstances made it possible then provision could be made to teach science, French and algebra.

Scotland

If the 1870 Elementary Education Act was a compromise, the comparable 1872 Elementary Education Act (Scotland) was more a continuation of the more interventionist Scottish approach. From 1872 onwards, elementary schools were no longer operated by the Protestant Churches. All elementary schools in Scotland, except those belonging to the Catholic and Episcopalian Churches, became the responsibility of about 900 School Boards created by the 1872 Act. The Act made attendance compulsory for children aged five to 13. Boards had the responsibility of enforcing compulsory attendance and parents had the duty of making sure that their children were educated (Scotland 1969; Stephens 1998). The Act unfortunately required that 'all religious education given in public schools was according to the reformed faith' (Devine 2000: 101). A direct consequence of this was that the Catholic Church and the Episcopalian Church kept their schools out of the public system, and at great sacrifice to themselves because of the considerable expense, continued to run their own network of schools.

Local co-ordination and control

England and Wales

The Education Act of 1902 (Balfour Act) abolished School Boards[7] and created local education authorities (LEAs) in England and Wales. County and county borough

---

[6] In 1900 it was still schools established by the religious charities that educated the majority of children but the best School Boards were beginning to show what could be achieved with greater resources and legal powers (Ball 1983).

[7] Scottish Act of 1918 abolished Boards in Scotland and responsibility was placed with larger bodies which could have a strategic perspective.

councils were given responsibility for elementary and post-elementary schools while the larger non-county borough councils and urban districts had an oversight of elementary schools only (under Part III of the Act). It also permitted, but did not require, LEAs (but not Part III authorities) to create secondary schools if they so desired. Secondary schools were not at this time conceived of as a staged phase of education to which pupils naturally progressed on completion of elementary education; they were few in number and the age range of their pupils overlapped with the senior section of the elementary school. Elementary schools provided education that was seen as complete in itself and most children would spend their entire school career in the elementary school with only the exceptional few being able to transfer and gain the benefits of secondary education. The creation of secondary schools became a popular aspiration which could be funded from the rates so the number of children attending secondary schools increased threefold between 1902 and 1939 (Sharp and Dunford 1990). A succession of regulatory codes served to widen further the curriculum gap between the elementary and the secondary school, the latter becoming increasingly modelled on the academic curriculum of the public school. A 1913 memorandum from the Board of Education (Circular 826) indicated that the secondary school had the two main functions of providing a general education for those who would go on to the professions or university as well as catering for those who would complete their formal education at 16 years old.[8] Reconciling the needs of these two groups, particularly with respect to the need to prepare the second group for the world of work, was identified as a particular challenge for the secondary school and the Board indicated that it would permit some vocational courses in the final year of schooling.

Throughout the first quarter of the twentieth century there was a tension between those who wanted to retain a strong separation between the parallel systems of elementary and secondary education and those who wished for a system that provided primary and secondary education for all.[9] The Education Act of 1918 (Fisher Act) required that older pupils (11 years and above) in elementary schools should be accommodated in separate schools or classes and raised the school leaving age to 14. The Hadow Report of 1927 furthered this desire for a distinct secondary phase of schooling and suggested that the separation should be at age 11 and that all children should be allocated to secondary grammar or secondary modern schools according to the results of examination. The modern school would have the more practical curriculum of the two and pupils could leave at a younger age although the committee wished to have the minimum school leaving age raised to 15 years old.[10]

[8] Children attending elementary school would normally leave at age 14.
[9] 'A secondary education for all' was an election slogan of the first ever Labour Government that took office in December 1923.
[10] Raising the school leaving age to 15 years old was not actually achieved until 1947 and it was 1972 before the school leaving age was raised to 16.

The notion that at secondary level different types of children should receive different types of education gained credence throughout this period. In 1938, by which time more than half of elementary school pupils over the age of 11 years were being taught in separate accommodation (Sharp and Dunford 1990), the Spens Report recommended that there should be three kinds of secondary education: the grammar and modern as previously suggested and a technical school. It suggested that pupil transfer should be possible between the schools and that all three should be accorded parity of esteem.[11] These views were reinforced five years later in the Norwood Report (1943) which had a strong formative effect on what was arguably the most significant piece of education legislation of the twentieth century with regards to creating a truly national system of education or, as it was often described, a national system locally administered.

Scotland

After 1902 a board system was still favoured in Scotland. So the change into a more centralised education system did not happen until 1918 (Limond 2002). School Boards in Scotland were parochially constituted and wholly elected and so for good or ill exercised some independence from local government. These *ad hoc* bodies survived until the Education (Scotland) Act of 1918 which replaced them with larger education authorities which were themselves separately elected for some further ten years. This Act also gave the Catholics and the Episcopalians the reassurances they needed to bring the few remaining church-funded schools into the public system. These *ad hoc* authorities operated from 1918 to 1929 and were replaced by county and city councils in 1929 (Matheson 2003).

The phased and segregated provision

England and Wales

The 1944 Education Act created a Ministry of Education and thereby gave much more power and influence over educational matters to the Government. The LEAs had specific duties but it was the Minister who had the ultimate responsibility to ensure that these were carried out. The beneficial result of this was 'more unity and standardisation in the national education service, and perhaps even a small reduction in the grosser disparities in educational opportunities between different parts of the country' (Sharp and Dunford 1990: 18).

---

[11] The view that all types of secondary school should be seen as of equal worth (parity of esteem) was often expressed from this point on. The view held by the majority of the population that this patently was not the case has fuelled much heated debate in the pre- and post-comprehensive period.

This Act required that education in maintained schools in England and Wales should be free to everyone of school age, that the concept of elementary education be discarded[12] and that LEAs reorganise into 'a continuous process conducted in three successive stages' (Part II.7) namely primary, secondary and further education with the responsibility of contributing towards the 'spiritual, moral, mental and physical development of the community' (Maclure 1973: 224). Children of school age were to be housed in separate schools with transfer between the two at age 11. It was to be the duty of the parents of children of school age to ensure that they were educated according to their 'age, ability and aptitude' (Section 36). However, the Act is not at all clear as to what this actually meant;[13] for example, it had replaced elementary schools with primary schools without any real guidance on how they were different. The way that secondary education should be structured is not specified in the Act but this legislation is widely credited with ushering in the 'tripartite system' of secondary modern, secondary technical and secondary grammar schools as recommended in the earlier reports. The new Ministry promptly issued the pamphlet *The Nation's Schools* in which it set out the very clear intention that secondary schools should be organised on the tripartite principle (Hyndman 1978). Similarly the 1945 Scottish legislation ushered in a bipartite system of senior secondary and junior secondary schools.

In return for financial support, voluntary schools could give up some of their autonomy and become 'Aided' schools, which retained much of their denominational character, or they could surrender the larger proportion of their self-governance and become 'Controlled' schools. The day should begin in all schools with a corporate act of worship[14] and every school established by an LEA would teach religious instruction according to a syllabus agreed by local representatives of denominational groups. The Act stated the general principle that parents have the right to expect their children to be educated according to their wishes (Part IV.76) and confirmed the right of parents to withdraw children from these activities on grounds of conscience (Part II.25).

The Education Act of 1944 was a hugely significant piece of legislation in establishing much greater coherence of provision and a system of education more centrally controlled by the state. In itself it contained little that was innovative as it can be seen from the above how heavily it drew on the wisdom of the preceding years. Its immense impact is, as much as anything else, due to it being the product of the immediate post-war period when the desire was not just to replace what had been destroyed but to reconstruct for a better future. At the core of the Act is a

---

[12] As were the old Part III authorities whose remit extended only as far as elementary schools.

[13] Gordon and Lawton (1978) observe that the word 'curriculum' is not used in the 1944 Act and the only subject considered is religious education/instruction (p. 32).

[14] The only exception was where the physical accommodation of the school made this impossible (Part II.25).

desire to achieve a compromise between all interested parties and one notable way of achieving this was to say very little about what actually went on inside the schools – the curriculum. The decades that followed can be characterised by the craving of successive governments to specify the purpose of education and to delve ever deeper into the details of the day-to-day experience of children and their teachers.

In 1963 the Ministry of Education published an influential report called *Half Our Future* (the Newsom Report) which specifically focused on the school experience of children of average and below average ability and between the ages of 13 and 16.[15] In it the view was expressed that the secondary curriculum should make clear acknowledgement of the world of work and it tried to set out a curriculum that stood somewhere between the rigidity of a 3Rs strategy and the seemingly laissez-faire approach of progressive education. The report draws on an impressive array of data which indicated, *inter alia*, that this group of pupils received less than their fair share of resources from their LEAs and that there was wide difference in reading test scores between schools and between areas, although they did identify a general rise in attainment particularly over the past 25 years. Some two-fifths of secondary modern schools were identified as having serious deficiencies. The Newsom Report added to the growing voice of opinion that although genetically endowed ability undoubtedly exists it was, however, significantly affected by the social and physical environment and so selection at 11 could be leading to a considerable waste of individual talent and national potential.

Differences between Scotland and England

The 1945 Education Act (Scotland) was broadly similar to the 1944 Education Act. These Acts made secondary education accessible to all. The English Act created the tripartite system (grammar, secondary modern and technical schools) while the Scottish Act introduced a bipartite system in Scotland (junior secondary and senior secondary schools, sometimes labelled grammar schools). These remained dominant until the 1960s. The British education systems that had emerged in the first half of the twentieth century had embodied the view that transfer of children from primary to secondary schools was best made at 11 (12 in Scotland) years old and that tests at that age would establish intellectual qualities that were fairly well fixed. Much of this was due to ideas emanating from the new field of educational psychology and particularly the work on intelligence by the English psychologist Cyril Burt. The development of IQ (Intelligence Quotient) tests which claimed to measure a generalised intellectual ability led to the 11+ examination (the Qualifier in Scotland) which selected children for the secondary school to

---

[15] This report was something of a counterbalance to the Crowther Report (1959) that had concentrated on the more able in the school population.

which they were best suited.[16] The secondary grammar (or senior secondary) school would cater for the most able children by providing an 'academic' curriculum suited for those who might progress to university and a career in the professions; secondary technical schools would cater for those with moderate ability through a curriculum focused on their practical aptitude and a future career as skilled workers; while the secondary modern schools took those children who did not fit into either of these categories and would earn their way through unskilled occupations. In Scotland the junior secondary would take all those who failed to gain entry to senior secondary.

Comprehensivisation

Although some LEAs quickly became ardent proponents of the tripartite system,[17] many others were seeing the benefits of one single secondary school serving a community – the comprehensive school. In rural areas this was often a matter of simple expediency. For example in 1949 Anglesey established its first comprehensive school so that there were enough pupils to fill the building (also to create the potential to generate a viable sixth form) and so that children would not have to travel large distances to gain the education to which they had been allotted. In other areas school planning was based on more educational and socio-cultural reasoning. By the 1950s doubt was being cast on the reliability of the 11+ selection methodology and, perhaps more importantly, on the fundamental view that children could be so neatly categorised (Hyndman 1978). Additionally, sociologists and politicians were beginning to see separate schools as unrepresentative of the society they served and as being in themselves socially divisive. Parents were increasingly concerned that the promised 'parity of esteem' was just not there in reality or perception. For these reasons some London boroughs were quick to follow the example of Anglesey. Secondary education became increasingly politicised as the Conservative Governments hardened their support for grammar schools and the Labour Party adopted as policy what had been their principle for some time before, namely the abolition of selection at 11. By 1963 the combination of these factors meant that most LEAs were developing schemes for at least partial comprehensivisation and this was encouraged by the Education Act of 1964. This

---

[16] Sir Cyril Burt has been seen as the founder of educational psychology in England and his work had an immense formative effect on the structure of the British educational systems. However, re-examination of his findings has raised a considerable degree of scepticism as to the reliability, validity and even honesty of significant amounts of the data. This is taken by some reviewers to indicate that at least part of his findings were fabricated (Palmer 2001).

[17] The reality in most LEAs was a bipartite system of secondary schooling as the secondary technical schools proved to be more expensive to establish than either of the others.

enabled greater freedom regarding the age of transfer to secondary education and made it possible to create 'middle schools' catering for the needs of the 8–13 age range (Sharp and Dunford 1990).

Within months of the election of a Labour Government in 1964, the Secretary of State for Education and Science issued an 'invitation' to LEAs (Circular 10/65: DES 1965) to reorganise their secondary provision on comprehensive principles in order to eliminate selection at 11. The circular offered six possible patterns of provision and expected plans to be submitted within 12 months. However, it was 1977 before all but one (Tameside) of the LEAs had presented schemes.[18] Nevertheless, by 1979 well over 90 per cent of children in England were being educated in comprehensive schools (Barber 1996).

In Scotland, 95 per cent of children are educated in the state sector and of these nearly 100 per cent of children are educated in comprehensive schools, a tiny number being educated in specialist schools where selection is on the basis of artistic talent, not academic achievement or potential. As early as 1947 the Scottish Advisory Council on Education had recommended a comprehensive system with a common curriculum core and a common examination. This had been ignored by the Scottish Education Department, but it was only a matter of time before this more egalitarian approach would be adopted. By 1965 already one-fifth of Scottish secondary schools were comprehensive (Bryce and Humes 1999: 39).

From the 1950s through to the early 1970s schools had enjoyed considerable freedom to decide for themselves (with very few checks) what they would teach and how they would teach it. It had become the practice of the Government of the day to issue guidance and advice through 'pamphlets' and 'circulars' rather than directives through legislation. Similarly LEAs would provide advice but often had little evidence on what was actually going on inside schools and classrooms. There was a particular sense of emancipation in the primary schools that had been freed from having to prepare pupils for selection at 11 as they were increasingly adopting a methodology that had been gaining prominence since the 1920s (Simon 1994). This 'progressive' approach to teaching and learning was generally taken to be synonymous with *child-centred* or *discovery learning* and emphasised the importance of the child's experience within a stimulating environment. Barber (1996) has observed that 'This was the time when primary classrooms shifted from the serried ranks of uniformed children learning their tables into the informal, cheerful, buzzing places they tended to be in the 1980s' (Barber 1996: 41).

The importance of nurturing environments and stimulating experience was further highlighted in the Report from the committee chaired by Lady Plowden and entitled *Children and Their Primary Schools* (1967). This inquiry was the first to look

---

[18] A more subtle response was employed by some LEAs who employed the tactic of submitting a scheme that would take up to 15 years to effect. Ample time for at least one change of government.

into primary education since the Hadow Reports of 1931 and 1933[19] and it was tasked to look at all aspects of primary education as well as transfer to secondary school. It recommended positive measures to redress the effects of social deprivation and a shift in the age of transfer to secondary education by the restructuring of the primary phase into first schools for five to eight-year-olds and middle schools for eight to 12-year-olds. The tone of this report is boldly progressive (child-centred) with much concern expressed on imposing rigid subject divisions on the learning of young children (Part 5). It drew on the educationalist's arguments against selective schooling from age 11[20] to make a strong case against the practice of streaming (selection by attainment within year groups) in primary schools, placed great stress on the importance of the relationship between schools and parents, and wished to encourage the steady expansion of nursery education. Schools in Wales were given a similar consideration by a committee chaired by Professor Gittens (1967) who had been a member of the Plowden inquiry. Their strongest recommendations were for the benefits of increased bilingual education and the interesting notion that the quality of religious assembly and instruction would be improved if freed from legislative necessity.

The major debates of this period, then, were to do with the particulars of the learning experience gained in primary schools and progression to and the organisation of secondary schools. But it should be noted at this point that the comprehensivisation of the secondary sector was not simply a debate about structural issues. It encompassed views on what children should be taught in secondary schools, the ways they should learn, the learning groups they should experience, and the relationships between teacher and pupil and between teachers and parents. This debate was further energised in 1976 by the then Prime Minister James Callaghan in a speech at Ruskin College, Oxford. His central point was that schools were failing pupils, parents and the country because not all were providing the standard of education they should have been and they were not sufficiently locked into the economic needs of the nation. He saw the goal of education as being 'to equip children to the best of their ability for a lively, constructive place in society and also to fit them to do a job of work. Not one or the other, but both' (Callaghan 1976: 202). This prompted the so-called Great Debate on education, the agenda of which was largely dominated by industrialists (e.g. the Confederation of British Industry) and caused many teachers to feel that they were being marginalised. It

[19] Sir William Hadow led inquiries into *The Primary School* (1931) and *Infant and Nursery Schools* (1933).

[20] As stated earlier in this chapter, the confidence in the 11+ was beginning to erode. In particular the Plowden Report cited doubts on the accuracy of the selection process, the contrasting provision resulting from this judgement and the effects of segregation by achievement (Chapter 20). (See Maclure 1973: 319–23.)

gave them a glimpse of how the balance of control over the curriculum would change in the forthcoming years. Callaghan's speech was clearly an attack on what had been described elsewhere as the 'secret garden' of education.[21] He emphasised that when matters of education are being considered:

> Parents, teachers, learned and professional bodies, representatives of higher education and both sides of industry, together with the Government, all have an important part to play in formulating and expressing the purpose of education and the standards that we need.
>
> (Callaghan 1976: 201)

The Ruskin Speech and the public debate that followed was not a *'back to basics'* campaign like the one advocated by the John Major Government in the 1990s, but a clear statement that standards must improve and that work in schools must be better matched to a modern technological society (Riley 1998). Callaghan was careful not to subscribe to the reactionary voices (e.g. Black Papers) or become enmeshed in the details of a curriculum debate but he did state his belief in a 'basic curriculum with universal standards' (Callaghan 1976: 202) and 'the strong case for the so-called core curriculum of basic knowledge' (Callaghan 1976: 203). This significant event in the evolution of British education (Phillips 2001) was commemorated at Ruskin College 20 years on by a speech from Tony Blair, the newly elected Labour Prime Minister. In this rather more detailed presentation of the new Government's policy, he too emphasised the need to raise standards for all and especially in the core skills of literacy and numeracy. He saw their task as 'a change of culture – from a commitment to the excellence of the few, to support for the talents of the many' (Blair 1996). There are further echoes of Callaghan in the often quoted phrase 'education is the best economic policy there is' used by Blair in many campaigning speeches.

The commodification of education

Callaghan was not the only moderniser. Similar themes were developed by the succeeding Conservative Government but from a quite different ideological perspective: that of the New Right (Chitty 1996). They held the view that progressive views of education had gained too much prominence (in primary and secondary education) and education should be seen as a discipline for life where children were introduced to knowledge in a controlled and structured manner, and they advocated a return to core values – back to basics. The White Paper *Better Schools*

---

[21] It had been argued from the 1960s that education and particularly matters to do with the curriculum was a 'secret garden' that could be entered only by those who had the key. Access was seen by some to be by the use of obscure technical language and reference to spurious research.

(DES 1985) is a good example of this as it set out the two aims of the Government as being to raise standards everywhere and to reduce expenditure. The extent to which they were intending to become involved in the detail of schooling was evident in the view that broad agreement on the objectives and content of the curriculum was a necessary step towards the raising of standards.

The debate on what the curriculum should contain continued throughout the 1970s and early 1980s with the clear implication that there should be a 'core' or 'entitlement' curriculum where only the essential irreducible features would be prescribed by the Government. This was, however, insufficiently robust for the Conservative Government of Margaret Thatcher. Their intention was to sweep away the powers of the LEAs and the influence of educational pressure groups (e.g. the National Union of Teachers) and replace them with strong central direction but local accountability. Chitty observes that:

> Thatcherism, and its revised version for the 1990s, can be seen as an uneasy attempt to link the principles of the free-market economy with an atavistic emphasis on the family, traditional moral values and the strong state. It involved rolling back the frontiers of the state in some areas, while pursuing policies of repression and coercion in others.
>
> (Chitty 1996: 260)

This ideological belief was embedded in the view that standards in education (and in other social institutions, e.g. the National Health Service) would be driven up by the introduction of a market economy and this led to the commodification of education. The viewpoint was notably articulated by the MP Sir Keith Joseph (later Secretary of State for Education) from about the same time as James Callaghan's Ruskin College speech. It too is concerned with improving the economy but this time by evoking traditional values. Its central idea is that market forces will drive up standards without state intervention. The education marketplace would be self-regulating as consumer choice would lead to provider competition and therefore self-improvement. For individual enterprise to flourish the consumers (largely seen as the parents) must be provided with the information needed to make informed choices. Lawton argues that as a direct consequence of this the 1988 Education Reform Act (ERA) is ideologically facing in two directions as the National Curriculum it created was 'centralizing in the control it exerted, but was also a market device – providing data for parental choice' (Lawton 1994: 92). This is supported by Barber who suggests that 'The basic premise behind the [1987 Thatcher] government's programme ... was that market forces would solve problems in the public sector just as they solved them in the private sector' (Barber 1996: 36). At the 1988 North of England Conference the then Secretary of State for Education, Kenneth Baker, defined the new Education Act as being 'about enhancing the life chances of young people. It is about the devolution of authority and responsibility. It is about competition, choice and freedom ... It is about quality and standards … It is not about enhancing central control' (Batho 1989: 88). Despite this last assertion, when the legislation came along to implement these ideas it gave over 400 additional powers to the Secretary of State for Education.

Moves to diminish the powers of the LEAs and to promote the ideology of the marketplace are evident throughout the 1980s. The 1980 Education Act gave teachers and parents a right to be represented on school governing bodies and required LEAs to justify their decisions and create an appeals mechanism where parents had exercised their preference of school for their child but been turned down (Sharp and Dunford 1990). Parents with limited financial means and who wished their children to be educated at independent schools were given the right under this legislation to make application to the Assisted Places Scheme for fee remission and have this administered directly from the Department of Education and Science.

The 1986 Education (No. 2) Act reduced the influence of the LEA on school governing bodies by giving parents parity of representation and so created a much stronger connection between the school and the community it served. Other sections were concerned with how the school should function and a miscellaneous section dealt with issues that had received recent public attention such as the abolition of corporal punishment, the appraisal of teachers' performance and freedom of speech within the confines of a school. These examples serve to show how schools have become increasingly more accountable to parents and the general public and how the view that market forces would drive up standards was being operationalised. In reality what had been created was a quasi-market (Power 2002), as much control and therefore distortion was introduced to the market by Government measures such as the creation of new and preferentially treated schools and the Assisted Places Scheme. A review of research on the marketisation of education in three countries led Power (2002) to suggest that what is needed is to 'ask how we can use the positive aspects of choice and autonomy to facilitate development of new forms of community empowerment rather than exacerbating social differentiation' (Power 2002: 62).

A National Curriculum enshrined in law

The 1988 Education Reform Act (ERA) turned out to be prescribing much more than a basic entitlement curriculum as every school had to teach to all pupils between the ages of five and 16 the *core subjects* of English, maths and science together with the *foundation subjects* of history, geography, PE, art, modern foreign language (for pupils 11 and over), technology and music. All schools must teach RE and there were 'themes', e.g. personal, social and health education (PSHE), which ran across the subject strands. Welsh was made compulsory for schools in the Principality. With the exception of RE, the Act contained very little detail on the curriculum as it was an enabling device for the Secretary of State to be empowered to create legally binding Orders clarifying the expectations in each subject. These details were worked out by subject groups who worked more or less in isolation and in an apparently random sequence. Unsurprisingly the National Curriculum that subsequently began to take shape[22] was somewhat over-inflated and lacking in cohesion. Commentators have suggested that it 'has suffered from the lack of an overriding philosophy or vision, being based on the assumption that the best way forward was to impose on a school a specified set of subjects, based on the grammar school tradition' (Docking 2000: 81–2). Docking goes on to state how detailed attainment targets, programmes of study and assessment arrangements were expected for each subject even though a rationale for the choice of these particular subjects was never made clear. Others are even less complimentary, seeing this curriculum as a reinstatement of the 1903 grammar school curriculum (Brighouse 1999).

The National Curriculum was and remains much more than some value-neutral statement of what all children should enjoy as their educational entitlement. It holds together because of the glue that is the market ideology of the Thatcher Government. The evidence is all around and not least in the current Department for Education and Skills web site which proclaims that in the view of the Government (a New Labour Government, that is), the National Curriculum has four main purposes: to establish an entitlement, to establish standards, to promote continuity and coherence, and to promote public understanding.

According to the politicians the attainment targets, programmes of study and externally moderated tests that were to be introduced at seven, 11, 14 and 16 would enable comparisons to be made pupil with pupil, class with class, school with school and LEA with LEA. Educationalists were far less convinced that the data from such straightforward tests could have such universal application. The resulting 'league tables' were as notable for what they ignored (e.g. the social circumstances of the school's catchment area, the ethos of the school, school/home links, the history of funding, the profile of the teachers, etc.) as for what they included. The role of parents in the management of schools was increased further through changes to the rules on electing school governors and schools were given greater control of their own budgets through a process known as local management of schools (LMS). The result of LMS was to give school governing bodies massively enhanced control over the day-to-day arrangements of the school and to

---

[22] The early curriculum proposals for many subjects created enormous controversy and heated debate between those who had opposing views on the essence and methodology of the discipline field. The battlegrounds for English and history were probably some of the bloodiest.

impose a corresponding reduction in the power of the LEA. This was the market-place at its sharpest as the money that LEAs had to devolve to schools was according to a formula based on that school's ability to attract pupils.

Furthermore, schools were enabled by the ERA to opt out of LEA control entirely and become Grant Maintained Schools (GM schools) receiving their funding directly from the Government. As an inducement, schools that chose to follow this course invariably enjoyed an enhanced income when compared to other schools in the locality. Despite this incentive the desire to break the ties with the LEA was not as strong as the Government had wished and anticipated (Barber 1996). A similar 'opt-out' opportunity was created for Scottish schools by the Self-Governing Schools etc. (Scotland) Act 1989 but had almost no impact as is evident from the legislation to repeal this option which only applied to one school.[23]

A new type of school was created by the Act which was to be known as a City Technology College (CTC). These were to be sponsored by private donation and were free from the influence of the LEA.[24] They were to have innovative work practices for both teachers and pupils and would generate examples of best practice. Despite being once described by Margaret Thatcher as the flagship of Conservative education policy, they have never attained the numbers or innovative prominence to make them major players in the marketplace. Nevertheless, as Gregory observes, 'The Education Reform Act builds upon the changes already in place and gives the final and fullest expression to the government ambition of putting into place a version of a market-driven national education service' (Gregory 2002: 93).

The determination that educational provision had to improve was further reinforced in the 1992 White Paper *Choice and Diversity* (DFE 1992). The improvement was deemed necessary largely due to the perceived failings of the comprehensive system of secondary schooling. What was seen to be necessary was a greater concern for individual needs and local circumstances, both of which could be better served by diversity in the secondary sector. There was no overt intention to reintroduce selection at 11 but to create specialist schools built on the ideas of the existing CTCs that would cater for particular talent. Specific mention is made of technology schools and, where business sponsorship was acquired, these would be known as technology colleges. Later developments enabled the appearance of schools with specialisms such as languages (1995); sports and arts (1997); and business and enterprise, engineering, science, and mathematics and computing (2002); and schools may apply to develop a specialism in music or humanities from October 2003.

[23] The 'opt-out' clause was abolished by the Standards in Scotland's Schools etc. Act 2000, a clause which applied only to St Mary's Episcopal Primary School, Dunblane.
[24] In most respects the 'technology' can be defined as information and communications technology (ICT) and these schools were to be characterised by an enterprise culture.

In order for parents to exercise their choice, thereby driving up standards, and for schools to be held accountable for their performance, the public were to be provided with regular school inspection reports compiled by the Office for Standards in Education (Ofsted) which was brought into being by the 1992 Education (Schools) Act to replace the infrequent inspection of schools by Her Majesty's Inspectorate of School. Ofsted was to recruit and train its own inspectors and each inspection team had to include a 'lay inspector' who was to have no previous professional involvement with education. The Act brought in parallel provision for Wales while Scotland was not included and so continued with a process that involves external scrutiny from HMI together with school self-review (Dunford 1999). The introduction and development of this inspection regime has generated, in England at least, much passionate debate and has been portrayed as yet another example of the reduction of the teacher's professionalism and the involvement of Government in the day-to-day matters of the school (Millet, Dillon and Adey 2001).

The Education Act 1993, the longest education legislation of the twentieth century, affirms and extends the regulatory powers of the Secretary of State with particular mention of improving standards, encouraging diversity and increasing opportunities for choice. A notable example of these new powers was for the Secretary of State to intervene directly where Ofsted judged a school to be underperforming. The process by which schools attained grant maintained status was simplified and new ways to establish GM schools were introduced. Also these schools were to be funded by either the Funding Agency for Schools (in England) or the Schools Funding Council for Wales. Where more than 75 per cent of the schools in an area chose to 'opt out', these bodies would replace the LEA.

The pace of legislation was building and would not slack. Lawton (1994) reflects on the flood of education legislation between 1979 and 1994 and suggests that it can be summarised as six ideological concepts:

1   A desire for more selection;

2   A wish to return to *traditional* curricula and teaching methods;

3   A desire to reduce the influence of *experts and educational theory* by encouraging common-sense traditional practices (where market choice prevails, experts are unnecessary);

4   An appeal to parental *choice* as a means of encouraging market forces;

5   A wish to reduce educational *expenditure* (a very high priority from 1979 onwards);

6   A process of increased *centralisation* which had the additional purpose of reducing the power and autonomy of LEAs (Lawton 1994: 95) (emphasis is mine).

All of these have been exemplified already and, with the possible exception of 1 and 3, their presence will be evident up to the present day despite the electorate's rejection of the politics that spawned them.

More central driving and some signs of rationality

The three stages of education identified in the 1944 Act are restated in the Education Act 1996 together with a statement on compulsory school age and the duty of parents to ensure their children are educated. Most importantly the Act gave legal status to the views of parents by specifying that those involved in the provision of education were, within reasonable considerations, to 'have regard to the general principle that pupils are to be educated in accordance with the wishes of their parents'. The Education (Scotland) Act 1996 created the Scottish Qualifications Authority, merging the Scottish Examinations Board (for academic qualifications at school level) with the Scottish Vocational Education Council (for vocational qualifications at all levels), and specified its general, accreditation, quality, advisory and incidental functions.

As stated earlier, the substance of the National Curriculum was put together in something of a chaotic manner with disparate subject groups working to tight deadlines. It quickly became evident to educational professionals that its bureaucracy needed simplifying, its intentions needed clarifying and the whole thing needed reducing in scale in order to make it manageable. The task of doing this was given to Sir Ron Dearing who argued in his final report (*The National Curriculum and its Assessment*, Dearing 1994) that its excessive prescription should be removed and the professionalism of teachers restored within a clear framework of accountability. In Barber's view:

> The perspective of the serious, practically minded teacher who had to put it into practice was applied to it at last. Suddenly it all began to make sense. More importantly, Dearing reasserted the importance of professional discretion. He had listened carefully to representatives of teacher unions saying to him that the reason the National Curriculum had driven teachers out of the zone of indifference was that it had undermined their professionalism. He took this seriously.
>
> (Barber 1996: 64)

In 1995 a more streamlined National Curriculum was introduced which gave teachers more flexibility but retained the same number of subjects. Sir Ron was called on again in 1996 to report on the confusing array of external examinations available to the 14 to 19-year-olds (Dearing 1996).

The 1990s had seen an avalanche of regulations and legislation on education culminating in 1997 with heavily market-driven legislation from the outgoing (not that they knew it at the time) Government, parts of which would be repealed in the same year by their successors. The Education Act 1997 extended the assisted places scheme to include fee-paying primary schools and it was made permissible for schools to create admission arrangements that included a home–school partnership agreement to be signed by the parents. Primary schools were to adopt a 'baseline assessment scheme' that would inform the teacher's planning and provide a starting point for the measurement of future educational achievements. For secondary schools, governing bodies were required to set school performance targets relating to the achievement of pupils in public examinations and pupils must be provided with a programme of careers education. Policies designed to promote high standards of behaviour were to be put in place and disciplinary detention outside school hours was made lawful even where there was no parental consent. There were changes to the rules governing the exclusion of pupils from school and the appeals procedure. The powers of Ofsted were extended to include the inspection of LEAs[25] and the Qualifications and Curriculum Authority and the Qualifications, Curriculum and Assessment Authority for Wales were created to replace both the National Council for Vocational Qualifications and the School Curriculum and Assessment Authority.

Before very much progress was made on these measures, the Conservative administration found themselves out of office for the first time in 18 years. The first contribution of the Labour Government was the very brief Education (Schools) Act 1997 which was enacted within months of the election. It abolished the provision of funds to assist with the fees of pupils attending private schools (Assisted Places Scheme) in England and phased out the scheme in Scotland. Soon afterwards they published their first White Paper titled *Excellence in Schools* (DfEE 1997) in which, much to the surprise of many and albeit given a new spin, New Labour endorsed the Conservative idea of specialist schools. The party that had long championed the cause of comprehensive schooling on grounds of equality was now adopting the stance that 'standards matter more than structures' and the post-comprehensive era had begun (Chitty and Dunford 1999). Education was to be put at the heart of Government and this would benefit the many and not just the few. The Government would work in partnership to raise standards, underperformance would not be tolerated and intervention would be in reverse proportion to success (Docking 2000). The new Education Secretary also announced a further review of the National Curriculum and the Conservative Government's idea of introducing into the daily activities of primary schools a dedicated hour for literacy and one for numeracy.

The White Paper led to the School Standards and Framework Act 1998 which was the first major piece of education legislation enacted by the new Government

---

[25] Ofsted's powers were further extended by the Teaching and Higher Education Act 1998 to include the inspection of initial teacher training.

and boldly stated that the raising of standards was every school's main priority. LEAs were required to produce an Education Development Plan for the approval of the Secretary of State and he was given further powers to intervene where standards were not acceptable. The structure of the school system was altered yet again by redesignating maintained schools (including grant maintained schools) as community, voluntary (aided and controlled) as foundation schools, with specialist schools being allowed to select 10 per cent of their entrants according to their ability in the favoured field. A clear sign of the relaxation of the strictures of the National Curriculum was that secondary schools were allowed to make arrangements so that some of their pupils could receive part of their education in FE college. LEAs were tasked with limiting the size of infant classes, setting up Early Years Development Partnerships and provision was made for the creation of Education Action Zones (EAZs). An EAZ was to bring together schools and other interested partners with the purpose of collectively raising the quality of their provision in socially disadvantaged areas.

It was clear from the White Paper and this legislation that there would be no about-turn in education policy despite the electoral change. The desire for a more equal and meritocratic society is evident but there was no wholesale dumping of Conservative policy. Perhaps the most surprising part of this, given earlier Labour Party rhetoric, has been the continuation of the diversity of provision in the secondary stage (Whitty 2002; Phillips and Furlong 2001). What had become the traditional left-of-centre arguments in support of the comprehensive school had been replaced by a call for specialist schools. By September 2003 some 38 per cent of secondary schools were designated 'specialist' schools. The controversial nature of the policy was given added zest when an unfortunate slip by the Prime Minister's official spokesman declared that 'The day of the bog-standard comprehensive school is over' (O'Leary and Owen 2001), which saddled the Government with the apparent view that the majority of comprehensives were 'bog standard' – an interpretation vigorously denied. However, Labour politicians soon turned this around to the view that no longer was the 'one size fits all' view of secondary schooling acceptable. It is evident that similar thinking is being applied to primary schools as they are encouraged to develop a 'distinctive character' by 'developing strengths in sport or music or special needs or working very closely with the local community' (DfES 2003a).

The revisions to the National Curriculum announced in 2000 included for the first time a clear set of goals. The three core subjects of English, maths and science remained but the eight foundation subjects were increased to ten by the addition of information and communication technology (ICT) and citizenship. Of these ten only ICT, PE, citizenship and RE are compulsory at Key Stage 4.

The Standards in Scotland's Schools etc. Act 2000 aimed to raise the standards in Scotland's schools by giving new powers to Scottish Ministers and new duties to education authorities and schools. Education authorities were to extend their duty, established under the Education (Scotland) Act 1980, to provide adequate and efficient provision, such that they were to have regard for the development of the individual child. The Scottish Ministers were to set 'national priorities' and to define and publish 'measures of performance'. Education authorities and schools were to create development plans which should be formulated in consultation with parents and pupils respectively. The inspection of schools in Scotland had remained with HMI, there being no Scottish equivalent of Ofsted, and this legislation extended their inspection powers to include the school education functions of education authorities and pre-school education centres resourced from public funds.

The Education Act 2002 implemented the proposals set out in the White Paper *Schools – Achieving Success* (DfES) published in 2001. The legislation further increases the powers of the Secretary of State to intervene in schools and LEAs that have serious weakness but it is also a bold attempt to enable innovation in the education sector. It gives the Secretary of State and the National Assembly of Wales (NAW) the power to modify legislation, suspend legislative requirements or confer new powers if this will facilitate experimental pilot projects that will make the curriculum more suitable to particular needs. Such projects would have to ensure that children still received a broad and balanced curriculum and that pupils with special educational needs were not disadvantaged. They were to be time limited, subjected to rigorous evaluation, and what had been learnt and achieved by the project was to be widely disseminated. Similarly, a school that satisfies prescribed criteria can apply for exemption from certain aspects of the National Curriculum. Details of why and how this might be done were later circulated in the booklet *Disapplication of the National Curriculum (Revised)* (DfES 2003a).

The Act enabled the creation of a new kind of school to be known as an Academy. Providing that the same safeguards were in place as above, the Academy is permitted to have an emphasis on a particular subject area or areas. This legislation also extended to the range of schools that could be involved in EAZs and the inspection powers of Ofsted were further increased to include a duty to report on the management and leadership of schools.

Significantly the legislation separates Key Stage 4 of the National Curriculum from the preceding three stages. This gives the Secretary of State the powers to amend the subjects studied in this stage or to abolish this stage altogether. This is consistent with the desire expressed in the White Paper to 'create space for the 14–16 curriculum to allow students to pursue their talents and aspirations', to have 'high quality, widely recognised vocational options available to students of all abilities' and to remove 'structural barriers to a coherent 14–19 phase' (DfES 2001: Ch. 4). A similar desire to loosen the National Curriculum straitjacket on primary schools is evident in a recent document that exhorts teachers to take ownership of the curriculum and capitalise on the freedom that is already available to them (DfES 2003b).

Further radical reform to the secondary system was announced by the Government in early 2003 when the Secretary of State set out the four key principles that would underpin further changes to the sector. All schools would be encouraged to innovate in the way they teach and organise themselves and this would be built on strong leadership. Teachers would be relieved of some of the more routine tasks which could be undertaken by trained classroom assistants and new partnerships would be created beyond the classroom (Clarke 2003). Each of these can have massive impact on the system of schooling with the introduction of Higher Level Teaching Assistants (TTA 2003) creating a step-change in the definition of a teacher's role. The observations of Docking in relation to the first administration of the current Government seem just as apposite today in that:

> While continuing to rely on the dual strategies of competitive forces and central intervention, the Government has shifted the balance more towards the latter with an explicitly evangelical flavour and sense of mission to its drive to improve levels of achievement in schools.
>
> (Docking 2000: 35)

A terminus point

The concluding point for any history of developments in schooling has to be an arbitrary choice. For this account, it is the beginning of the twenty-first century and the state system of education is probably in as great a state of flux as it has ever been. In its second term of office the New Labour Government continues to seek the 'third way' through policies that are a mix of ideologies packaged in the wrappings of pragmatism. Power (2002) has suggested that:

> The Blair government has claimed to be developing policies on the basis of 'what works' rather than being driven by any one ideological approach. Yet it remains unclear whether the current mixture of apparent discordant strategies can succeed in delivering the claimed benefits of devolution and choice while also overcoming prevailing patterns of inequality.
>
> (Power 2002: 63)

The National Curriculum applied only to England and Wales while Scotland had the 4–16 Guidelines which were not compulsory but were adopted as practice whenever possible. The National Curriculum is still thought of as in need of revision although it is now clearly more manageable and child/teacher-friendly. With calls for relevance reaching back to a time before Callaghan's landmark speech, it may be surprising and disappointing that an eminent educationalist should observe in the *Guardian* education supplement that 'Most subjects have grown out of the secondary elitist tradition and are aimed at producing specialists. So what we have is a fine academic curriculum, which is fine if you want to be a geographer, historian or scientist' (White 2003). In 1994 Lawton suggested that 'Education policy since 1991 has seemed to be lurching from one disaster to another' (Lawton 1994: 92) and an observer in 2004 might be hard pressed to see conspicuous sure-footedness.

The pace and diversity of change over the past 25 years has been unprecedented at any other time in the development of state schooling in Britain. Much of its effect has been to create the paradox of increasing control being taken by the centre while simultaneously shifting responsibility and accountability to the edges. Gone are the days when a primary school teacher needed a good-sized car boot to carry home her National Curriculum documents but central control remains pervasive and detailed with promise of more to come. Education will always need to be a forward-looking and dynamic aspiration for the nation but we would be wise to heed the reservations of Gregory (2002) who suggests that:

> It cannot be good for a liberal society that the tentacles of central government reach so far into our schools as they work to provide education for the young. We need to find ways to revitalize educational debate. Education is too important to be left to teachers. But, as importantly, it is too important to be given over to central government.
>
> (Gregory 2002: 100)

Suggested further reading

The study of historical events is a continual fascination as they can be approached from so many different perspectives and this is particularly so for education as it permeates just about every aspect of human life. For a detailed socio-economic view of the formative years of state schooling there is much stimulation in Stephens (1998) who manages to cover a vast expanse in a small volume. He, together with Silver (1983), Gordon and Lawton (1978), Wardle (1974) and Simon (1965), considers some of the early controversies in education, e.g. compulsory attendance and the education of girls, that are now taken-for-granted elements of a modern educational system.

For access to original material Maclure (1973) is a rich source of early information on England and Wales in particular. For a specifically Scottish perspective readers should consult the second volume of Scotland's (1969) work which covers the period 1872 to the late 1960s or the book by Clark and Munn (1997) for a contemporary discussion. The full text of Acts of Parliament for England and Wales since 1988 and for Scotland since 2000 are now readily available on the Internet (http://www.hmso.gov.uk/acts.htm).

The intimate involvement of Government in the details of schooling that began in the Thatcher era is well illustrated in Barber (1996), while the controversies of more recent developments are thoroughly explored in Chitty and Dunford (1999), Docking (2000), Phillips and Furlong (2001) and Whitty (2002). The roots of unresolved debates, such as selective education or national identity in educational provision, can also be found in these works as well as in Green (1991) and Hurt (1979).

References

Ball, N. (1983) *Educating the People: a documentary history of elementary schooling in England, 1840–1870*. London: Maurice Temple Smith.

Barber, M. (1996) *The Learning Game – Arguments for an Education Revolution*. London: Gollancz.

Batho, G. (1989) *Political Issues in Education*. London: Cassell.

Blair, T. (1996) Speech given at Ruskin College, Oxford, 16 December. http://www.ruskin.ac.uk/original/archives/blairsp.htm.

Brighouse, T. (1999) 'Home and School', in B. O'Hagan (ed.) *Modern Educational Myths: The Future of Democratic Comprehensive Education*. London: Kogan Page.

Bryce, T. G. K. and Humes, W. M. (1999) 'Scottish Secondary Education: Philosophy and Practice', in T. G. K. Bryce and W. M. Humes (eds) *Scottish Education*. Edinburgh: Edinburgh University Press.

Callaghan, J. (1976) 'The Ruskin College Speech', in J. Ahier, B. Cosin and M. Hales (eds) (1996) *Diversity and Change: Education, Policy and Selection*. London: Routledge/Open University.

Children and Their Primary Schools (The Plowden Report) (1967) Report of the Central Advisory Council for Education (England) under the Chairmanship of Lady Plowden. London: HMSO.

Chitty, C. (1996) 'The Changing Role of the State in Education Provision', in J. Ahier, B. Cosin and M. Hales (eds) (1996) *Diversity and Change: Education, Policy and Selection*. London: Routledge/Open University.

Chitty, C. and Dunford, J. (eds) (1999) *State Schools: New Labour and the Conservative Legacy*. London: Woburn Press.

Clark, M. and Munn, P. (eds) (1997) *Education in Scotland: policy and practice from pre-school to secondary*. London: Routledge.

Clarke, C. (2003) *A New Specialist System*. Speech, 11 February.

Curriculum and Examination in Secondary Schools (The Norwood Report) (1943) Report of the Board of Education Examinations Council Committee under the Chairmanship of Cyril Norwood. London: The Board of Education.

Dearing, R. (1994) *The National Curriculum and its Assessment: Final Report*. London: SCAA.

Dearing, R. (1996) *Review of Qualifications for 16–19 Year Olds*. London: DfES.

Department for Education and Employment (1997) *Excellence in Schools*. London: HMSO.

Department for Education and Skills (2001) *Schools – Achieving Success*. London: HMSO.

Department for Education and Skills (2003a) *Disapplication of the National Curriculum (Revised)*. London: HMSO.

Department for Education and Skills (2003b) *Excellence and Enjoyment: A Strategy for Primary Schools*. London: DfES Publications.

Department for Education/Welsh Office (1992) *Choice and Diversity*. CM2021. London: HMSO.

Department of Education and Science (1965) *Organisations of Secondary Education*. Circular 10/65. London: HMSO.

Department of Education and Science/Welsh Office (1985) *Better Schools*. London: HMSO.

Devine, J. (2000) 'A Lanarkshire Perspective on Bigotry in Scottish Society', in T. M. Devine (ed.) *Scotland's Shame? Bigotry and Sectarianism in Modern Scotland*. Edinburgh: Mainstream.

Devine, T. M. (1999) *The Scottish Nation 1700–2000*. Harmondsworth: Penguin.

Docking, J. (ed.) (2000) *New Labour's Policies for Schools: Raising the Standards?* London: David Fulton Publishers.

Dunford, J. (1999) 'Inspection: From HMI to Ofsted', in C. Chitty and J. Dunford (eds) *State Schools: New Labour and the Conservative Legacy*. London: Woburn Press.

Education of the Adolescent (The Hadow Report) (1927) Report of the Board of Education Consultative Committee under the Chairmanship of Sir William Hadow. London: Board of Education.

15–18 (The Crowther Report) (1959) Report by the Central Advisory Council for Education (England). London: HMSO.

Gordon, P. and Lawton, D. (1978) *Curriculum Change in the Nineteenth and Twentieth Centuries*. London: Hodder and Stoughton.

Green, A. (1991) *Education and State Formation: The Rise of Education Systems in England, France and the USA*. London: Palgrave.

Gregory, I. (2002) 'Policy, Practice and Principles', in I. Davies, I. Gregory and N. McGuinn *Key Debates in Education*. London: Continuum.

Half Our Future (The Newsom Report) (1963) Report of the Central Advisory Council for Education (England) under the Chairmanship of J. H. Newsom. London: HMSO.

Hurt, J. S. (1979) *Elementary schooling and the working classes 1860–1918*. London: Routledge.

Hyndman, M. (1978) *Schools and Schooling in England and Wales: A Documentary History*. London: Harper & Row.

Infant and Nursery Schools (The Hadow Report) (1933) Report of the Board of Education Consultative Committee under the Chairmanship of Sir William Hadow. London: Board of Education.

Knox, J., Douglas J., Row, J., Spottiswoode, J., Willock, J. and Winram, J. (1560) *A First Book of Discipline*. np: Edinburgh.

Lawton, D. (1994) *The Tory Mind on Education 1979–94*. London: Falmer.

Limond, D. (2002) 'Locality, Education and Authority in Scotland: 1902–2002 (via 1872)', *Oxford Review of Education*, 28(2), 359–71.

Maclure, J. S. (1973) *Educational Documents England and Wales 1816 to the Present Day*. London: Methuen.

Matheson, D. (2003) 'Education in Scotland', in R. Griffin and C. Brock (eds) *Education Systems of the British Isles*. Saxmundham: John Catt.

Millet, A., Dillon, J. and Adey, J. (2001) 'Inspection', in J. Dillon and M. Maguire (eds) *Becoming a Teacher* (Second edition). Buckingham: Open University Press.

O'Leary, J. and Owen, G. (2001) 'Blair to axe "bog standard" state schools', *The Times*, 13 February.

Palmer, J. A. (ed.) (2001) *Fifty Major Thinkers on Education*. London: Routledge.

Phillips, R. (2001) 'Education, the State and the Politics of Reform', in R. Phillips and J. Furlong (eds) *Education, Reform and the State: Twenty-Five Years of Politics, Policy and Practice*. London: Routledge/Falmer.

Phillips, R. and Furlong, J. (eds) (2001) *Education, Reform and the State: Twenty-Five Years of Politics, Policy and Practice*. London: Routledge/Falmer.

Power, S. (2002) 'Devolution and Choice in Three Countries', in G. Whitty, *Making Sense of Education Policy*. London: Paul Chapman.

Primary Education in Wales (The Gittens Report) (1967) Report of the Committee under the Chairmanship of Professor Gittens. London: HMSO.

The Primary School (The Hadow Report) (1931) Report of the Board of Education Consultative Committee under the Chairmanship of Sir William Hadow. London: Board of Education.

Riley, K. A. (1998) *Whose School Is It Anyway?* London: Falmer.

Scotland, J. (1969) *The History of Scottish Education*. London: University of London Press.

Sharp, P. and Dunford, J. (1990) *The Education System in England and Wales*. London: Longman.

Silver, H. (1983) *Education as History*. London: Methuen.

Simon, B. (1965) *Education and the Labour Movement: 1870–1920*. London: Lawrence and Wishart.

Simon, B. (1994) *The State and Educational Change: Essays in the history of education and pedagogy*. London: Lawrence and Wishart.

Stephens, W. B. (1998) *Education in Britain 1750–1914*. Basingstoke: Macmillan.

TTA (2003) *Professional Standards for Higher Level Teaching Assistants*. Teacher Training Authority, September 2003.

Wardle, D. (1974) *The Rise of the Schooled Society: The History of Formal Schooling in England*. London: Routledge & Kegan Paul.

White, J. (2003) quoted in 'Revision Period' by John Crace. *Guardian Education*, 4 November.

Whitty, G. (2002) *Making Sense of Education Policy*. London: Paul Chapman.

Comparing educational systems

Trevor Corner and Nigel Grant

The nature of things is more securely and naturally deduced from their operations out upon another than upon our senses. And when by the former experiments we have found the nature of bodys, by the latter we may more clearly find the nature of our senses.

(Isaac Newton, *Questiones*, 1664)

Introduction

THE FIRST PROBLEM THAT needs to be dealt with in comparative education is in deciding what it is for, both generally and in terms of the individual considering making use of it. It is an inherent part of the work of Government bodies, national and international agencies, and senior managers in education to take evidence of the relevant experience of others to illuminate their own problems.

Comparative studies in education are based on a body of methodological research work which has enabled it to evolve over the past 100 years (Holmes 1981; King 1979; Watson 2001). Most students who study comparative or international education (or both) are not specialists in the field themselves. Quite properly, they are looking to the study to give them comparative insights into some other field, whether it be a teaching subject, the curriculum, educational policy or management. This is just as well, for the capacity to provide this perspective is one of the strengths of the subject's appeal, namely its value to the non-specialist.

This raises fundamental questions about approaches to the subject. Methodological discussions are concerned with finding the most effective ways of explaining the behaviour of educational systems, and it is in this light that the relative merits of the various approaches – national case studies, cross-cultural thematic studies, the construction of models and typologies, and the search for valid generalisations – have to be considered. For the purposes of research, there is general agreement that the study of comparative education has to progress from accurate *description* to *analysis*, and from that to the forming of *generalisations* about the working of educational systems. There are strong disagreements about the best ways of achieving this (Crossley 2001), but little dispute about the broad aims themselves. But when one considers the position of the non-specialist student, other criteria must be thought of as well; and these will influence the way in which the subject is presented.

Comparative perspectives

What, then, can non-specialist students gain from the study of comparative education? To say that they can develop a 'comparative perspective' on their own special fields, while true enough, needs further elaboration. Leaving aside particular interests, one might suggest that a comparative perspective can offer the following elements at least.

1. Awareness of the differences between systems and their policies and practices in various countries

Whether these are more important than the similarities is arguable; but the point needs to be made that educational problems, and the ways of tackling them, can differ considerably from those with which we are familiar.

2. Similarities between systems also have to be made clear

If only the differences are dealt with, the impression may be conveyed that the experience of other countries is irrelevant to one's own, and the main point of pursuing such study at all is lost.

3. The importance of the context within which the educational process functions has to be stressed

It is crucial to realise that education does not work in a vacuum, but is profoundly influenced by the geographical, demographic, historical, economic, cultural and political aspects of the society that it serves. At the same time, lest the impression be conveyed that the relationship between education and society – any society – purely reflects the context, the influence of the system *on* its context also has to be examined. It has to be understood that no educational system operates in isolation, but has a complex and dynamic relationship with its natural and social environment.

4. The relevance of other countries' experiences to one's own follows logically from this

Otherwise, it may be felt that comparative study, fascinating though it may be for the specialist, has little to offer anyone else. Not that one would argue for the direct *application* of other systems' practices to one's own country; this may be feasible sometimes, but involves serious dangers. The experience of other systems can contribute to an understanding of one's own; indeed, it can be argued that this is the most valuable contribution of comparative education to the non-specialist.

Strategies in comparative education

If, then, these are acceptable as learning objectives, we can go on to consider various approaches as *strategies* of study. One popular method is the 'themes' approach, which starts by taking particular topics such as the curriculum, primary schools, vocational training, educational planning and so forth, and comparing them across a number of selected systems, with the aim of formulating valid generalisations about the behaviour of educational systems in particular circumstances. An important alternative, the 'systems' approach, examines complete educational systems as functioning units in their particular societies. These are not really disagreements about where the study should be going, but about the most effective starting point.

The *themes approach* has the advantage of coming to grips with the real stuff of comparative education – comparison and analysis – right from the start. But it presents great difficulties for those without much knowledge of other educational systems, for there are many temptations to make comparisons out of context and thus fall into some serious errors. The possibility of such error is large, but a few examples will serve.

1. Education does not necessarily mean the same thing in all societies

It may have quite different aims, operate under different conditions and be assessed by different criteria. The differences are not absolute, or comparative study would lose much of its point. But there is much to be said for emphasising the differences, as these are likely to be overlooked or misunderstood if we go directly into cross-cultural comparison. For example, politicians and even senior managers in education are fond of reinforcing their arguments with assorted pieces of evidence from the experience of other countries. Many advocates of comprehensive schooling in the United Kingdom seek comfort in vague statements about European reforms and higher financial investment in schools; their opponents were equally fond of dire warnings of what they thought had been happening in the Soviet Union or, perversely, what continues to happen in the United States. Such arguments often ignore the constant American debates on school choice, charter schools, private religious schools and the merits or otherwise of restructuring one or other of the state systems (Good and Braden 2000). That much of this 'evidence' may be wrong is not really the point; even when the information was accurate, it could easily be used with little appreciation of the differences between the other systems and one's own (Grant 1968).

Advocates of greater emphasis on lifelong learning in the UK make use of the Scandinavian countries, the United States or France as models or as inspiration, while supporters of bilingualism in Scottish, Welsh, Irish or English schools point to Canada, Catalonia, Israel, Finland and the Faeroes (Haugen *et al.* 1980; Baker 2001). Again, this is not to say that the comparisons are invalid, let alone the causes. The situation in the Faeroes or Catalonia, where there is a strong numerical base for the language and vigorous institutional support, does not easily transfer to the circumstances of the Gaels of the Western Isles or the Punjabi-speakers of Glasgow, Birmingham or London where the languages are penetrated to some degree by the use of English. The purpose, expectations and effectiveness of using the language may not be only through education:

> The ownership of two languages has increasingly become seen as an asset as the 'communication world' gets smaller. As swift communication has become possible in recent decades ... so the importance of bilingualism has been highlighted.
>
> (Baker 2001: 417)

This applies to some extent to all the countries that now have to deal with the implications of the Internet and its role in promoting or demoting the use of languages (Naughton 1999). In this post-colonial age the sense of *loss* of language is widespread, extending from nationalist sensitivities in the older 'colonies' of England – Scotland, Wales, Ireland – to ethnic minority migrants such as Sikhs, Kurds, Berbers, being as it is a choice they have to make when facing the daily imperative of mastering the host language, English, French, Arabic (Davies 2003).

The differences between systems can be quite profound. The very word 'education' can have different connotations in different societies. Indeed, some languages are unable to make the distinctions which others find essential. In English, for example, the single word 'education', although constantly doing battle with 'training', 'pedagogy' or 'lifelong education', normally has to fulfil all the functions of *Bildung, Ausbildung* and *Erziehung* in German, *éducation, instruction* and *enseignement* in French, while Russian has a whole battery of words. But even when the same word is used, the associations that go with it may be different. A good example of this may be seen in comparisons between the United States and the United Kingdom; these were particularly common during discussions in the 1960s on the comprehensive reorganisation of schools in the UK, and especially in England, where the issue can still arouse more controversy than in Scotland or Wales. Years of devolution to the Scottish and Welsh Assemblies (the Northern Ireland Assembly is regularly in abeyance) has further enlivened the debate on the extent of the British systems growing apart. Interestingly, little serious evidence has yet come about to indicate different standards of achievement developing across the kingdom when all relevant social factors have been taken into account (Phillips 2000)

It is more difficult to generalise about school standards (or anything else) in the United States than in England. American education is more decentralised, and its financing is much more dependent on the resources of the particular areas where the schools are located. Standards in American schools therefore vary greatly from state to state, and within each state, and *any* generalisation thus has to be hedged about with qualifications.

But just suppose, for the sake of argument, that even broadly equivalent groups – those following academic courses to proceed to higher education – do show a marked disparity in standards (as many American educationists would readily concede). What exactly are we comparing? Debates on the range of scholastic attainment as measured by examinations are common on both sides of the Atlantic though few American teachers, parents or students would accept this as the only criterion of what the school is trying to do. American schools devote a great deal of time to socialisation, to the preparation of the student for life in American society, stressing the development of social and communication skills. It may be that the outward manifestations of this – the patriotic rituals, the varied social events, the morale-boosting sessions for the school football team and so on – would strike English teachers as faintly comical. But the same could be said of a German *Gymnasium* teacher's impression of the games and character-building by which some remaining grammar schools still set such store. The German final school certificate, the *Abitur* or *Reifeprüfung* (test of maturity), the Danish *Studenterexamen* and *Højere Forbedelsereksamen* and many of the European final school certificates taken mostly between 18 and 20 years of age are both broader and academically ahead of the English A level. Interest in a broader and deeper version of the A level has actually been helped by comparisons with the American Students Aptitude Tests (SAT) and the International Baccalaureate which is now offered in an increasing number of English schools.

These are examples of how even the meaning of 'education' can be affected by different sets of priorities. But many other factors determine what education is, what it can do and how its aims are defined; these have to be considered if any useful comparisons are to be made. In countries like the USA, France, Spain or Britain, for example, it is at least *possible* to consider leaving the choice of textbooks to the schools and the open market; the *actual* decision can be taken on a variety of grounds. But in the Baltic States, the Faeroes or Iceland, decisions are severely constrained by the small numbers speaking the national languages, whatever policy the authorities might prefer.

Again, the existence of substantial linguistic minorities in Russia, India, Belgium, Spain and a host of other countries raises problems that now have to be considered by the relatively homogeneous countries like England or Denmark where the settlement of immigrants and their descendants had confirmed their development into multicultural societies too. As for matters like distance and difficulties in communication, these are not *major* factors in Denmark, Ireland, the Netherlands or most of the United Kingdom, but they are in a huge country like Russia and they were in the United States when the pattern of educational organisation was taking shape, and are in India and China. The increased power of international agencies over education policy and practice worldwide has increased cross-cultural transfers shown by the impact on the post-Soviet Union countries in Europe or Asia where curricula, policies and the very purpose of education have been through considerable transformation (Crossley and Watson 2003).

Climate, demographic patterns and economic circumstances raise needs or impose severe constraints that do not occur in the developed world. UNESCO highlights those situations in developing countries where there are insufficient means to guarantee even universal primary education and where population growth or war can nullify every hard-won advance. These background conditions are so important for the functioning of education – and even for defining it – that they must be taken into account if we are to make any sense of the systems themselves.

2. The parts of any educational system are interdependent and have to be examined in relation to the whole

Many attempts to make international comparisons across several countries fall into the trap of assuming that things with the same name must have the same function. They may, but there can also be substantial differences. 'Primary school', for example, means in England and Wales a school for children between the ages of five and 11; but in Scotland it is from five to 12, and in the Republic of Ireland usually from four to 12. This is within an area, the British Isles, with close past or present political links; elsewhere, the difference can be greater. What is usually translated as 'primary school' or '*école primaire*' or '*Grundschule*' can cover the ages of seven to 16 in Denmark and in Sweden. Rapid change in developed countries in pre-school education has, in practice, led to most children having some form of schooling experience from three years of age and often earlier. Various systems organise their structures differently, preferring in some cases to make the main division of primary/secondary at mid-adolescence, the end of compulsory schooling, and in others at the point of transition from undifferentiated to subject specialised teaching.

Similarly, the term 'secondary school' may mean the entire stage from pre-adolescence onwards (as in the systems of the British Isles or the United States), or it may be only the stage entered *after* compulsory school, as in Scandinavia. But this does not apply everywhere; in some countries, only *certain* post-compulsory schools – generally those leading to higher education – are designated as 'secondary', thus distinguishing them from vocational or trade schools (Bell and Grant 1977).

Many common schools in Central and Eastern Europe provide the whole course from six to 17; and when this happens, the term 'secondary' is applied to the *entire* school, *including its primary section*. There were, and still remain in some of these countries, 'secondary specialised schools' which can be entered after completion of the *general* secondary school. Further, changes may take place but old titles may remain in use. Even on official notices, they use the formal title, with the informal and old-fashioned title, which is what everyone says and had a different structure, in brackets, as in Germany where unification of East and West has fundamentally affected the direction of reforms after 1990 (Wilde 2002). It is a dangerous business, especially when translation is involved, to pull institutions with similar-sounding titles out of context for separate examination.

Opportunities for misunderstanding do not end there. Schools and students in England, Wales and Scotland are often compared unfavourably with those elsewhere. School effectiveness and outcomes have been used, often in official publications, to suggest a crisis of falling standards, especially in English schools, with a perceived inability to stand up to global competition. Where evidence of widening participation and increasing pass rates of school-leaving examination is discussed this is countered by suggestions of lowering standards. The Third International Mathematics and Science Study (TIMSS) has done one of the most extensive comparisons of pupil achievements in maths and science and is regarded as providing some of the most convincing evidence for the relative failure of schools in England and Wales. However, various reasons, such as different age participation and response rates from participating schools, make even these comparisons in subjects seen as 'culture-free' somewhat flawed. A common view of education during the twentieth century has focused on its underachievement, inequality and a perceived fall in standards, perhaps due to the fact that more is expected from education by each succeeding generation.

In England (as in most European countries) the end of secondary schooling is still quite a reasonable point at which to consider what standards have been achieved. Enough of the age group stay on to make the judgement worthwhile, but with widening access to higher education there is increasing differentiation of standards for entrance. But this is even more so in the USA where something like four-fifths of the age cohort proceeds to tertiary education. Some take only short-cycle courses, some of these transfer to full higher courses, others enter longer ones from the start but drop out, and some of these drop back in again, making it difficult to keep track of any particular age group, but a reasonable estimate would be that about a half eventually complete first degrees.

Admittedly, the standard of American degrees varies considerably and with the advent of league tables for UK universities disparity of degree standards is increasingly questioned. Some American universities and colleges (public and private) can easily stand comparison academically with any higher educational institutions in the world, while others award degrees too mediocre to be recognised in other countries (or in the United States itself); and in between can be found almost every imaginable variety, from the admirable to the abysmal. But, with very few exceptions, even the worst could be reckoned to come up at least to English A-level standard and, of course, most go well beyond that. It follows, therefore, that in the United States a higher proportion of the population reaches at least A-level standard than was ever admitted to grammar school in England in the heyday of selective schooling. Even by the narrowest scholastic criteria more get there in the end; and unless we postulate some mystic law whereby certain standards must be attained by a fixed age, American education appears to perform more creditably than its detractors (on both sides of the Atlantic) would allow. To attempt an adequate assessment of a system, we have to look at all of it, not just a part. A similar point could be made about the age of starting primary school and the relevance of pre-school provision.

Nor need such considerations be confined to the formal school system, for other organisations can attend to 'curricular enrichment', as the Pioneers did in the former Soviet Union. That is all gone now, but there are some parallels in China and Cuba, and of course the *folkehøjskoler* in Denmark and the various Church organisations in some countries, particularly in Latin America, fulfil some needs for 'public enlightenment', especially for young adults. Many countries have youth and adult organisations in the cultural, linguistic, nature and athletic areas. The limitations of most of these are that they often lack adequate support and finance; they also tend to be fragmented too so that they touch few of the young people or children they are aimed at. But they are there, and sometimes function as a vital adjunct to the normal experience of formal schooling (Webber and Liikanen 2001).

There are other examples, but these should make the general point: *educational systems have to be examined as wholes, and in their contexts*, before cross-cultural studies can be expected to yield much benefit. Objective data on particular institutions can seem quite precise; but unless they are seen in relation to other institutions in the same system, and unless that system is examined in the light of the factors that make it what it is, we are in danger of misunderstanding how it works. Further, since the most common use of evidence out of context is to back up educational arguments at home, there is the additional danger that such misunderstandings may simply reinforce misunderstanding of one's own system. This is not what comparative education is for.

What, then, is it for? What, particularly after all these warnings about the importance of context, is the relevance of education in other countries to our own problems? And what is its usefulness for teachers?

Part of the answer has to do with *informing educational policy*. Individual teachers rarely feel they have much of a role to play here, but they often have more influence on the success or failure of policies than they may be aware of. In some countries they have considerable discretion in the choice of subject matter, method and even organisation, and therefore have an obligation to make thoughtful and informed choices rather than fall back on precedent or hunch. They are also involved in the larger issues in their capacity as citizens. Unless teachers are to be reduced to functionaries, the uncritical executors (however efficient) of decisions taken by someone else, wider understanding of the options available in the educational process is not only desirable but, at a time of constant educational change, necessary.

This could be said for educational theory in general, or any of its contributory disciplines. What benefits, then, can be expected for the thoughtful teacher from this particular kind of educational study?

Borrowing ideas

The possibility of borrowing ideas is usually the first that comes to mind and is often held to be the main purpose of comparative education. Governments are all too often limited in their view of its possibilities to seeing it (if at all) as a method of identifying practices that could be transplanted to their own country. But great care is needed here. Quite apart from the risk that the other countries' practices may be misinterpreted anyway, they may be too closely bound up with their specific contexts to be applicable anywhere else.

Certainly, the exportation of practices has often had unfortunate effects. After the Second World War, for example, the new communist governments in Eastern Europe drew heavily on Soviet models. This was hardly surprising, in view of the political hegemony of the USSR; the newly established regimes were not only inclined to display political loyalty, but also trying to reform their traditional systems along Marxist-Leninist lines, and at that time the USSR was the only country with experience of this.

Unfortunately – but, given the political atmosphere of the time, unsurprisingly – the remodelling on Soviet lines was quite uncritical. History was taught from a Russocentric viewpoint, textbooks were modelled on their Soviet counterparts (and sometimes were straight translations), even degrees were often renamed to correspond to Soviet practice, and of course policy was modelled on that of the USSR, sometimes even to the wording, whether appropriate to local conditions or not (Grant 1982; Grant 2000).

The former British and French colonial empires are clearer illustrations of the effects of uncritical borrowing. Most ex-colonial countries still retain their inheritance of British or French-style school systems with examinations linked to assumptions about the relationship between paper qualifications and job expectations that are wildly out of keeping with these countries' needs and conditions. The damage caused is not so much by the persistence of inappropriately Europeanised curricula, which are changing anyway; it is rather caused by the expectation that going to school will provide certificates leading to white-collar jobs in the city, when the vast majority are certain to be disappointed at some stage. Large numbers of young Africans thus receive just enough schooling to make village life unacceptable, but not enough to fit them for anything else – an explosive situation due in part to an educational system devised in London or Paris that makes little allowance for conditions in Lagos or Bamako, let alone a tribal village (MacIntosh 1971).

We continue to see the adoption of European and American models over much of the developing world. These systems differ greatly, of course, but they have all been devised to meet the needs of relatively affluent and highly industrialised societies, quite different from the low-income agrarian countries to which they have been exported. We have seen something of this in post-colonial Africa, but it is not just from former colonial powers that inappropriate models are received, but from the industrial world in general. It has become increasingly obvious that these models do not serve the needs of the 'Third World' countries, even if they could afford them; but as long as they offer such great advantages to those lucky enough to go through the whole process successfully, they make it difficult to devise other and more suitable models.

This is not to say that importation can never be valuable. For all the uncritical borrowing from the USSR in Eastern Europe, there were *some* valuable innovations, such as the development of systems of adult education and the breaking down of some of the more rigid class barriers between different kinds of school. On a more limited scale, there is the spread of Folk High Schools across the Scandinavian countries, and even some influence on adult education in Germany and Great Britain (Korsgaard 2002).

Again, for all the unfortunate effects of over-hasty and uncritical adoption of American progressive methods, their positive contribution has to be recognised as well. 'Progressivism' may have run its course by now, but it has left its mark on practice. Whenever a primary teacher teaches capacity by getting children to pour water into cans rather than recite tables, s/he is using what at first were American 'progressive' methods. That this is rarely apparent is an indication of how far these methods have been naturalised. The adoption by the Open University and the modern universities in the United Kingdom of a credit system owes much to American practice and has created a degree of flexibility hitherto lacking in British higher education. But this has not been a straight copy, rather an adaptation of an American procedure to the rather different needs of part-time students in the UK, which still managed to avoid some of the problems in the USA. It could be added that the Open University in its turn has had a considerable impact on higher education in many other countries, especially the United States.

There are many other examples of effective borrowing, with one thing in common: they were taken from systems sufficiently like the importing ones to fit in, or were adapted to do so. This, possibly, is one of the most valuable contributions of comparative studies: not only can they set forth a range of alternative ideas and practices but, intelligently applied, they can help distinguish what can reasonably be imported from what can not; and by examining educational practices in context can help indicate the kind of adaptation needed to fit them into another system.

Educational policy and analysis

Comparative education can render a particularly valuable service by providing a background of contrasts against which to examine our own problems. If our horizons are bounded by our own system, many of its practices may seem natural or inevitable; yet they may have arisen in circumstances that no longer obtain, and may now be unnecessary, arbitrary or even harmful. It is not impossible to examine one's own system critically from the inside, but it is more difficult without a comparative perspective. The very existence of other assumptions and practices can provide a necessary challenge to some of our own. It does not automatically follow that we *have* to change; even if we are alone in this practice or that, it may still fit our own circumstances. But the existence of alternatives obliges us to justify rather than assume, so that if we do adhere to something, there is a chance of knowing why we do it.

An example can be seen in the horizontal and vertical divisions within the school system. In most of the United Kingdom it is taken for granted that the division between primary and secondary school at 11 or 12 reflects a qualitative and necessary change in pedagogical styles, and even that it has some natural sanction. Sensible and convenient it *may* be but it is not inevitable. The break at this point is also found in the USA, Italy, France and some German states; but in Denmark, Sweden, Spain and some countries of Eastern Europe (and in all of them before the system collapsed) the main division, and the main point of differentiation, is at 15 or 16.

The same variation applies to *vertical* division into parallel schools for the same age group, as was common throughout Great Britain before comprehensive reorganisation. Segregation of this kind was regarded as quite unacceptable in the former USSR but as absolutely essential in most German states where nearly two-thirds of young people receive their post-secondary vocational education covering over 350 state-regulated and recognised occupations (Idriss 2002). In the USA, the common school is taken for granted, but so is *internal* division (known as 'tracking'). In every case, the matter is open to argument; and here the existence of alternatives can be a useful corrective to the widespread habit of taking one's own practice as the norm.

Comparative studies can also clarify our ideas of what is possible, a useful step before deciding whether something is *desirable*. International practice is frequently evoked over some of the more emotive issues like school uniforms or sexual differentiation, but they are often not the best examples, as they are closely bound up with a broader complex of social expectations and pressures. It would be rash, for instance, to attribute too much of the disorder in many American schools to the schools themselves; there are too many other forces in operation. But curriculum policies, for example, can profitably be looked at with an eye to what is being done elsewhere, as in the debate in the UK on specialisation versus generalisation, or the relation between school and work.

To take one example, little is expected in the English-speaking countries of average or below-average pupils in the learning of foreign languages. In the British systems, languages were formerly largely confined to the 'academic' schools or streams, and although there are an increasing number of language secondary schools, many teachers are still convinced that trying to teach languages to any but the top third of the ability range is a waste of time. Whether it is desirable that they should do so is, of course, another argument; but international evidence does not support the idea that the average child has some inherent linguistic incapacity. Bilingual and multilingual communities are common throughout the world; and even school-based learning can be extremely effective. In Scandinavia, for instance, all children learn at least one foreign language (usually English), and many learn at least one more besides; the levels of competence vary, but are generally high. Unless we believe in some kind of inborn incapacity among the Americans and British, we have to reject the idea that 'languages for all' is *impossible*. Discussions of the *desirability* of such a policy has a chance of being considered on its own merits, then, without unnecessary presuppositions.

But an international perspective can also provoke re-examination of some of our educational concepts (or slogans) like 'standards', 'discipline', 'indoctrination', 'excellence', 'leadership', 'freedom of choice', 'general culture' and so on. We are not always clear, however, just what we mean by them; and one incentive to clarify our definitions is seeing how different they are elsewhere. For example, 'democratic education' would mean maximum curricular choice and grass-roots control to most Americans, but would suggest a centrally determined uniform curriculum to the French, on the grounds that the child must be free of the chances of local circumstance. 'Leadership' has positive connotations in England, but in Scandinavia is still regarded with suspicion outside the Business Schools.

Teachers and academics in most countries have a fairly clear notion about what is meant by (say) 'university standard', but usually have difficulty in defining this. 'Indoctrination', in the sense of a deliberate inculcation of values, may be more obvious to someone looking at a system from outside than to someone actually in it; 'indoctrination' may turn out to be something that *other* people do, but which we prefer to call something else – 'moral education', perhaps, or 'citizenship'. Unless we are prepared simply to dismiss other interpretations as 'wrong' just because they are different, their very existence requires us to attempt a definition of *our* terms. We may, once again, decide that they are valid and useful, but at least we should have a better idea of what we are talking about.

Conclusion

Comparative education thus has the capacity to do in space what educational history does in time; it can provide the opportunity to understand better the workings of the educational process by giving us a wider view than the here and now. At a time when everyone in contemporary educational systems is faced with unprecedented challenges, as crises of resource and direction loom ever larger, and as the need to educate for future uncertainty becomes more urgent, the importance of clear and radical thinking could hardly be more obvious. This is not to say that *everything* is on the agenda for change; tribal customs may after all have their place, but it does not help to confuse them with laws of nature.

Comparative education cannot, of course, pretend to offer any uniquely valid set of answers, but can claim to be one useful tool for the better understanding of the educational process in general and one's own system in particular. While it uses big ideas over the global scale, it is rooted in precise observation of the particular. It will continue to have a role in informing Government policy just as Governments will continue to have a vital interest in their educational systems. Some new tasks are providing practical and purposeful goals for advising Governmental educational reforms, investigating the role of public and private agencies in education, and analysing changing structures and forces such as private education, partnerships, e-learning and the Internet (Corner 2000).

Suggested further reading

In comparative education, publications age very rapidly and for this reason the journals are the best source for up-to-date articles. Some well-established journals in the UK are *Comparative Education*, *Compare* and *Oxford Studies in Comparative Education*. Internationally, the principal journals in English are *Comparative Education Review*, the *International Review of Education*, *The European Journal of Education* and *Harvard Education Review*. Various other international journals exist within particular domains in education and will often carry articles of a comparative nature.

References

Baker, C. (2001) *Foundations of Bilingual Education and Bilingualism* (Third edition). Clevedon: Multilingual Matters.

Bell, R. E. and Grant, N. (1977) *Patterns of Education in the British Isles*. London: Allen and Unwin.

Corner, T. (2000) 'Education and the Third Wave', in C. Matheson and D. Matheson (eds) *Educational Issues in the Learning Age*. London: Continuum.

Crossley, M. (ed.) (2001) 'Comparative Education for the 21st Century: An International Response', *Comparative Education*, 37 (4).

Crossley, M. and Watson, K. (2003) *Comparative and International Research in Education: Globalisation, context and difference*. London: RoutledgeFalmer.

Davies, A. (2003) *The Native Speaker: Myth and Reality*. Clevedon: Multilingual Matters.

Good, T. and Braden, J. (2000) *The Great School Debate*. London: LEA Publishers.

Grant, N. (1968) 'Comparative education and the comprehensive schools', *Scottish Educational Studies*, 1 (2), 16–23.

Grant, N. (1982) 'Work experience in Soviet and East European schools', in J. Eggleston (ed.) *Work Experience in Secondary Schools*. London: Routledge and Kegan Paul.

Grant, N. (2000) 'Tasks for Comparative Education in the New Millennium', *Comparative Education*, 36 (3), 309–17.

Haugen, E., McClure, V. and Thomson, D. S. (eds) (1980) *Minority Languages Today*. Edinburgh: Edinburgh University Press.

Holmes, B. (1981) *Comparative Education: some considerations of method*. London: Allen and Unwin.

Idriss, C. (2002) 'Challenge and Change in the German Vocational System since 1990', *Oxford Review of Education*, 28 (4), 473–90.

King, E. (1979) *Other Schools and Ours* (Third Edition). New York: Holt Rinehart and Winston.

Korsgaard, O. (2002) 'Learning and the changing concept of enlightenment: Danish adult education over five centuries', *International Review of Education*, 46 (3), 305–25.

MacIntosh, J. (1971) 'Politics and citizenship', in J. Lowe, N. Grant and T. D. Williams (eds) *Education and Nation-Building in the Third World*. Edinburgh: Scottish Academic Press.

Naughton, J. (1999) *A Brief History of the Future: The Origins of the Internet*. London: Weidenfeld and Nicolson.

Phillips, D. (ed.) (2000) *The Education Systems of the United Kingdom*. London: Symposium Books.

Watson, K. (ed.) (2001) *Doing Comparative Education Research: Issues and Problems*. London: Symposium Books.

Webber, S. and Liikanen, I. (eds) (2001) *Education and Civic Culture in the Post-Communist Countries*. London: Palgrave.

Wilde, S. (2002) 'Secondary Education in Germany 1990–2000: one decade of non-reform in unified German education?' *Oxford Review of Education*, 28 (1), 39–51.

Psychology in education

Graham Mitchell

Can there be a psychological science that is about the best things in life? Can there be a classification of the strengths and virtues that make life worth living? Can parents and teachers use this science to raise strong, resilient children ready to take their place in a world in which more opportunities for fulfilment are available?

(Martin Seligman 2002, *Authentic Happiness*, p. 29)

Introduction

THIS CHAPTER EXAMINES THE contribution psychology makes to the study of education. There are six sections that address different themes and topics about psychology in education. The first section introduces the principal perspectives in psychology and these are then referred to throughout the rest of the chapter. In the following three sections we see psychology's role in measuring traits and abilities, in learning and in motivation. The fifth section looks at developmental disorders, and how psychology can help with diagnosis and remediation. The final section examines the more recent work of positive psychology.

Psychological perspectives

Psychology contributes to the study of education through different perspectives or approaches. The behaviourist approach emphasises the role of conditioning in human behaviour. Pavlov's research on salivation in dogs is well known. By associating a neutral stimulus like a light with food, the light alone eventually became sufficient to elicit salivation. This is called 'classical conditioning'. We can see immediate application for this in education. Neutral stimuli like classrooms, books and teachers are commonly associated with pleasurable or unpleasant experiences. Watson and Raynor demonstrated how fear could be learnt through classical conditioning with a small boy named Albert (Thorne and Henley 1997). Positive and negative associations in classroom settings may then be responsible for some of our educational likes and dislikes.

Skinner investigated operant conditioning with a box in which rats and pigeons learnt to press a lever repeatedly to receive a food reward. The reward reinforced the lever-pressing behaviour. Skinner also showed how complex behaviours could be taught by reinforcing the behaviour's subcomponents separately. This is called 'shaping' and could be applied to more complex skills like writing. The use of praise and correction in educational settings can be thought about in terms of operant conditioning. Schools' behaviour management systems tend to follow behavioural principles. We do need to question, however, whether simple stimulus-response animal models can be used to explain the complexities of classroom behaviour.

Social learning theory proposes that we learn by modelling the behaviour of others and noting the consequences of observed behaviour. Bandura advanced this theory to explain why some behaviours are developed without any apparent reinforcement (Durkin 1995). Social learning is not limited to childhood and can provide a lifelong source of learning experiences.

The cognitive approach is concerned with mental processing. The cognitive state of the student is studied, rather than thinking simply in terms of stimulus-response units of behaviour. Laboratory experiments, computer modelling and the study of deficits following brain damage are all methods used to examine processes such as attention, perception, learning, memory and language.

The psychodynamic approach places an emphasis on unconscious motives and early childhood experiences. Bowlby examined the attachment of young children to their mothers. Although we may not subscribe fully to Bowlby's original views today, the presence of significant others in a child's life is seen to be important for facilitating future social interactions and for providing resources for coping with stressful situations (Durkin 1995). Catch-up effects can occur for children with impoverished attachments, but these will depend on the quality of subsequent relationships with others.

The biological approach seeks to explain human behaviour by referring to genetic and physiological mechanisms. Brain functioning and chemical activities are seen to be relevant to an understanding of learning processes. Brain imaging can be useful when looking at the physiological causes for conditions like dyslexia.

The humanistic perspective became popular in the mid-1950s. Whereas other approaches seem to emphasise determinism by examining environmental, cognitive, psychic and physiological influences on human behaviour, the humanistic approach places an emphasis on free will. Maslow and Rogers helped to introduce this far more optimistic psychological perspective in which individuals could gain a sense of ownership of processes of growth and development. Maslow proposed a hierarchy of needs (Franken 1998). Only when basic physiological needs were satisfied would it be possible to meet higher needs including the experience of self-actualisation. Self-actualisation is related to peak experiences, reaching our potential and gaining self-fulfilment. Student motivation and classroom procedures can be thought about in terms of a hierarchy of needs. It is also worth considering to what extent the pupil or student should experience ownership of the educational process. More recently Csikszentmihalyi (2002) has extended such ideas with the notion of flow. Flow is experienced when we are so engrossed with an activity that we lose a sense of time, something relevant to student motivation. Do we always have to coerce learners into activity when some ownership of the learning process could lead to better-motivated behaviour?

The social constructionist approach invites us to see that the way we interact with our social world will affect our development and current feelings. We are embedded in a particular culture, and our sense of self is socially constructed as we engage in social relations and patterns of language. Rather than taking traditional modes of thinking and behaviour for granted, we can adopt a critical stance when viewing educational institutions and society's educational values.

Traits, abilities and attainments

Why is it that some people seem more capable of learning than others, or are more predisposed to study a particular subject? Where do traits and abilities come from? We can frame these questions within a nature-nurture study, and recognise that we result from the interaction between inherited and environmental influences. Monozygotic twins, reared together and reared apart, have been used to examine the role of biological factors in determining intelligence. This is a controversial area. Rose, Lewontin and Kamin (1984) have criticised a general willingness to accept that intelligence is hereditary, whereas others argue for this acceptance (Pinker 2002). Genetic and environmental determinism can limit our expectations of others in an educational setting. Early theories of development placed an emphasis on child development and viewed the adult as a stable fixed consequence of what had occurred in childhood. In lifespan development, we view development as proceeding throughout life. With this view we may be more optimistic about anyone's future progress because development is never finished, and future growth and positive change are always possible.

This does not mean that we should never look at a person's past. Recognising developmental correlates of current traits and abilities can be valuable. An awareness of the psychological and social factors that influence development can inform intervention decisions and help to promote optimal development. The child's social, emotional and intellectual worlds will all contain factors that influence development.

Can we, however, measure the consequences of a person's genetic background and past experiences? Psychometrics attempts to objectively measure constructs such as intelligence and personality. Individuals are scored using questionnaires, inventories and test sheets; but these need to be fit for purpose. A measure is only declared trustworthy when we can demonstrate that it is reliable, valid and standardised (Rust and Golombok 1999).

Reliability refers to the extent to which a measure is capable of delivering consistent findings. There are several different ways to measure reliability. Test-retest reliability involves repeating the test with the same participants and establishing the extent to which there is a correlation between the two sets of test scores.

Validity refers to the extent to which a test measures what it is claimed to. Reliable findings are insufficient if they fail to inform us about the measure we are interested in. A test claiming to measure creativity should be measuring exactly that and not something else. There are several types of validity.

A test needs to be standardised so that the performance of any particular sample of students can be compared to other students of similar age or educational level in the general population. We would therefore be able to judge, for instance, a pupil's intelligence relative to others in their own age group.

We are particularly interested in measuring traits, abilities and attainments, and it is important that we can distinguish between these three categories of measurement. Traits are the characteristic patterns of behaviour and thinking that we engage in. These are our signature attributes. Personality measurement has received much attention over the past few decades, but perhaps the classification that has received most attention is the five-factor model associated with two researchers, Costa and McCrae (Larsen and Buss 2002). The five factors can be summed up with the acronym OCEAN: Openness to experience, Conscientiousness, Extraversion, Agreeableness and Neuroticism.

Abilities can be thought of as measures of cognitive performance that may facilitate future attainment levels (Cooper 2002). We might be interested, for example, in measuring different facets of intelligence, such as verbal or spatial intelligence. The measurement of intelligence is problematical, even though the statistical basis is sound. Intelligence tests may be culturally, racially and gender-biased. We are nevertheless able to administer recognised tests in classrooms, record children's scores and then establish where that child is positioned relative to the population of children the child is drawn from. An Intelligence Quotient (IQ) is the ratio of mental age to chronological age, expressed as a percentage. Popular intelligence tests for assessing ability in schoolchildren have included the Stanford-Binet and the Wechsler Intelligence Scale for Children (WISC). A general intelligence factor or thinking ability factor called 'g' can be measured with psychometric tests, and intelligence differences do remain relatively stable over a lifetime (Deary 2003). Such differences are associated with later attainment in education and work, even health and longevity. Whalley and Deary (2001) provide data showing that high childhood IQ scores are associated with reduced mortality through to age 76. Intelligence testing has nevertheless been criticised (Gould 1981). Problems with intelligence testing become apparent when we examine the effects of positive and negative labelling. Rosenthal and Jacobson's (1966) work has sensitised us to the limiting and empowering influence of different contexts of expectation. Eighteen schoolteachers were told that particular children in their class had been identified with an unusual potential to make intellectual gains. Even though these children were randomly selected, IQ gains made during the year by the 'bright pupils' were higher than those in the control group. Findings from this study have been used to argue that positive expectations can influence intelligence test results. Chaikin, Sigler and Derlega's (1974) work also indicates that positively labelled children receive preferential treatment from teachers. Intelligence tests can also be used to determine who is entitled to educational resources. We may decide to assess ability at key stages in a person's life, and allocate educational resources in accordance with test results. This occurred with the British 11+ examination system, with successful children being allocated to better-resourced grammar schools and the unsuccessful to secondary modern schools with poorer resources.[1]

Gardner popularised the view that intelligence was much broader than previously defined. He proposed eight intelligences, namely verbal/linguistic, logical/mathematical, visual/spatial, bodily/kinaesthetic, musical, interpersonal, intrapersonal and naturalist (Gardner 1998). Gardner's multiple intelligence approach has proved popular and today provides the basis for many classroom learning-style initiatives (Gilbert 2002). Gardner's work nevertheless has received criticism for the marketing of well-established ideas about abilities in the guise of something new (Cooper 2002).

Goleman (1995) questioned whether IQ scores are always associated with later earning power, career advancement or interpersonal aspects of life. Sensitivity to other people's emotions and being in control of one's own emotions were claimed to be far more important qualities. Goleman's work has proved popular and some academic researchers have embraced his notion of emotional intelligence. Cooper (2002) argues, however, that additional work should be carried out before we can determine whether emotional intelligence has real value. These more recent concepts of intelligence have served to challenge views that academic success is the only real expression of intellectual worth (Rust and Golombok 1999). Different

---

[1] The 11+ applied to all parts of the United Kingdom other than Scotland where the Qualifier served a similar purpose. The Qualifier was a sort of 12+ examination, to take account of the transfer to secondary school at 12 in Scotland, and was used to filter pupils into senior secondary school for the more academically minded and junior secondary for the rest.

intelligence measures may nevertheless be useful for monitoring progress and for diagnosing educational problems.

The beliefs that we hold about intelligence may be important in determining motivation levels and achievement. Dweck (2000) conducted some research into two theories of intelligence. The entity theory holds that intelligence is stable, lifelong and difficult to change; whereas the incremental theory holds that intelligence is dynamic and subject to change. Within a challenging educational setting, those students holding an incremental theory performed better. Dweck has also demonstrated that students' theories of intelligence can be changed. We will return to student self-belief later.

Attainment can be measured through assignments, tests and examinations. Both coursework and end-of-course examinations provide information on individuals' academic attainment. Attainment figures are commonly used to assess individual student progress, identify learning difficulties, and evaluate the work of individual teachers and schools. Concern has recently been generated at the frequent testing of school students.

Ability–achievement discrepancy analyses are conducted to establish whether someone's expected attainment, as measured by an IQ test, is matched by actual attainment. Such tests can be of use when diagnosing conditions such as dyslexia, but inherent in such procedures is the assumption that IQ scores are capable of predicting attainment levels.

Learning

In identifying ways to encourage learning, it is helpful to consider three areas: the processes, the learner and the teacher. There are different approaches to the study of learning processes. We might be interested in the neuronal and chemical changes that occur when we learn something new. This biological approach can help to establish how a poor diet can limit learning, by investigating the rate, nature and stability of such brain changes.

The information processing approach of the cognitive perspective permits us to examine learning and memory. Craik and Lockhart (1972) argued that material could be recalled more easily when the original encoding of information took place at a deeper level of processing. A deeper level might involve a more enriching learning experience where additional mental processing of the learnt material takes place. Since memory is so important to processes of learning, full advantage can be taken of this idea in the classroom. It has immediate application because it causes us to think about the nature of the encoding process and the experiences of the student.

If we turn our attention to the student, we can think of learning in terms of units of stimulus-response conditioning, but this may reduce children's learning to a too mechanistic level. Bruner has argued against this approach, maintaining that attention must also be focused on the cognition of the student (Fontana 1995). The student can subjectively interpret stimuli in order to construct internal models and hypotheses, which in turn lead to expectations and predictions about the world.

In the 1960s and into the 1970s Piaget's theory of cognitive development was highly influential in educational studies and in developmental psychology (Byrnes 2001). Piaget proposed that cognitive development in children proceeds by passing through four qualitatively distinct stages, becoming more abstract and logical as the child develops. This theory suggests that children need to interact with their world to advance through the stages and to eventually experience higher-order thinking. Although Piaget is sometimes criticised for providing a too rigid structure of cognitive development, and for not taking sufficient account of environmental and cultural effects, his work has made a huge contribution to an understanding of child development. Classroom arrangements can provide children with the opportunity to actively interact with their surroundings, discovering and reflecting on their findings. The Piagetian account causes us to recognise that thinking skills develop gradually in children and teaching approaches should reflect the stage of development of the child.

Vygotsky provided another account of cognitive development, which placed an emphasis on language and discourse as mediators of the development of cognitive functioning. This is a social constructionist approach, viewing knowledge as socially constructed by and distributed among people in society. Learning therefore involves an interaction with others in social groups. The role of the teacher is important in helping the child to learn new tasks that are within their capabilities. This range of attainable but, as yet, unlearnt tasks is called the zone of proximal development (ZPD). The zone for each teacher–child interaction shifts, covering different and increasingly demanding tasks and activities. The help that teachers provide in giving cues, prompting action or generally offering support is known as scaffolding. Higher-order thinking for Vygotsky is when there is a transfer of control from the environment to the child (Byrnes 2001). Vygotsky argued that to focus on the ZPD is preferable to the assessment of current IQ scores.

Finally we will look at the teacher. What is it that makes a teacher effective? Lepper and Woolverton (2002) identified a number of common traits that were effective in bringing about stable positive changes in students' motivation, learning and progress across a variety of situations. The acronym INSPIRE has been used to capture seven common characteristics of effective teachers.

Intelligent   Effective teachers were intelligent and knowledgeable about their subject and teaching approaches.

Nurturant   They were nurturant, warm and supportive; attentive to their students' needs and expressing confidence that they would succeed.

Socratic	A more Socratic and questioning approach was used as opposed to a didactic approach.
Progressive	A progressive approach was used in the way that students were exposed to challenges and problems. Lessons were well structured with regard being paid to student learning pathways.
Indirect	Errors were identified, but teacher interventions involved cues and tips, permitting students to recognise and correct their own errors. Recognition of student achievement was made and positive behaviour was reinforced without using effusive praise.
Reflective	Some priority was given to student understanding rather than just the accumulation of factual knowledge, by encouraging students to reflect on the issues they were studying.
Encouraging	Effective teachers helped to maintain high motivation levels by encouraging students to feel confident and sense mastery of their developing skills.

Teaching approaches cannot be based on simple formulas, but such findings may help teachers to reflect on their own practices and to consider the adoption of additional strategies, styles and approaches.

Motivation

What are the causes for varying levels of motivation and what can be done to improve pupils' motivation and enjoyment of learning? Students have their own views about themselves. Some self-beliefs are liberating and empowering, whereas others serve to constrain and limit progress. So often in education we keep our eye on external factors, but there is also the need to focus on internal, cognitive resources. Pajares and Schunk (2002) consider that teachers should pay regard to pupils' self-belief as much as their achievement record, on the grounds that self-belief will influence motivation and, in turn, future academic attainment. Many of the self-belief variables that we measure are reasonably stable and behave like traits. Tests are available for a number of constructs including self-esteem, self-efficacy, optimism and explanatory style.

Self-esteem refers to our sense of worth and sense of competence (Mruk 1999). We can distinguish between global self-esteem, the way people generally view themselves, and specific self-esteem, the way people view themselves in a particular domain of life, such as academic self-esteem. Whereas global self-esteem seems more important when considering overall psychological well-being, academic self-esteem correlates better with academic achievement (Rosenberg *et al.* 1995). Although some significant correlations have been found between self-esteem and academic performance (Skaalvik 1983), this in no way proves that high self-esteem improves achievement or that achievement can be improved by boosting the self-esteem of students (Baumeister *et al.* 2003). It is just as likely that self-esteem is derived from academic performance.

Praise given with the intention of boosting self-esteem can sometimes be counterproductive (McLean 2003). A mastery approach to learning, in which students value effort and personal improvement, seems preferable to a performance approach, in which students wish to gain favourable judgements for their work (Anderman, Austin and Johnson 2001). Praising ability rather than effort can encourage students to emphasise performance over mastery. Also when failure eventually occurs, students may attribute their failure to lack of ability and become less confident as a result. Praise can also be toxic when it is given indiscriminately and for accomplishments requiring little effort. Under such circumstances the teacher's low expectations may well lead to reduced motivation.

Another related self-belief measure is self-efficacy. This refers to a sense of capability in a specific domain of life (Gaskill and Hoy 2002). In an academic setting, self-efficacy may provide a precursor for self-concept development (Bong and Skaalvik 2003). Self-efficacy can be derived from a sense of competence based on past experience (mastery experiences), seeing how other people perform their tasks (vicarious experiences), noting one's state of anxiety or enthusiasm (emotional and physiological arousal) and from the validation of one's own efforts by significant others (verbal persuasion) (Bandura 1997). Evidence suggests that self-efficacy is associated with task performance (Bandura 1997). Students with high self-efficacy scores are more likely to engage with more demanding tasks, and expend more effort and persist longer with tasks. Such student qualities are welcome in any classroom. Bandura also argues that self-efficacy plays a significant mediation role in academic achievement for factors such as gender, attitudes to school, prior attainment and cognitive ability. He implicates self-efficacy in the development of motivation, intrinsic interest and the resilience needed to buffer the negative effects of academic anxiety. This last point is relevant since school students face demands to perform well in examinations. Failure can elicit disapproval from those around and block intended career progression routes.

Confidence and higher levels of motivation can seem to grow with the experience of success, but the opposite effect is also at work. Maier and Seligman (1976) conducted behavioural research in which dogs were conditioned to avoid electric shocks. This might represent the way we adopt strategies to avoid unpleasant experiences in life. In a second stage to this work, some of the conditioned dogs were harnessed to prevent them avoiding the shock. The dogs could still put out effort, but it was wasted. The shock avoidance was now no longer contingent on the effort expended. Most dogs gave up and developed a state called 'learned helplessness', an effect we are familiar with in educational practice. It affects our confidence, our moods and emotions. It involves the loss of hope and motivation, even in bright, gifted pupils.

Explanatory style has emerged from learned helplessness research and refers to the characteristic way that we explain our failures and successes. The reformulation of the attributional style concept by Abrahamson, Seligman and Teasdale (1978) resulted in three self-belief dimensions (internality/externality, stability/instability and globality/specificity).

With a pessimistic explanatory style, setbacks are explained in terms of internal, stable and global causes. A student attributing an examination failure to lack of intelligence is providing such an explanation. There is something wrong with me (internal), the problem will persist (stable) and it will affect other aspects of life (global). Blaming a hard examiner for failure is an example of an optimistic explanatory style. There is something wrong with the examiner (external), it is unlikely to happen again (unstable) and it will only affect this examination (specific). Peterson and Barrett (1987) looked at the explanatory style of first-year university students and found that an optimistic explanatory style was associated with higher grades. The measure has been refined more recently, but explanatory style remains a useful additional self-belief measure in motivation research.

Self-handicapping strategies are more likely when self-belief resources are limited. Lack of effort can be used as a protective strategy. Trying to succeed may be too risky when failure is attributed to lack of ability. It may be preferable to preserve the belief that 'I could have succeeded had I tried.' Under these circumstances we may feel the safest approach is not to try (Dweck 2000). Self-belief, then, is an important study area when considering motivation in the classroom.

The humanistic approach points to the satisfaction of needs as the basis for motivation. This may provide a helpful perspective for the encouragement and maintenance of motivation in the classroom. Behavioural models suggest that current motivation levels are derived from our past conditioning. Effort is more likely when the association between effort and reward has been learnt. Experiences and rewards can be linked to intrinsic motivation with the mastery approach to learning, or to extrinsic motivation if there is concern with praise and the approval of others.

We can also investigate motivation by examining the social world of the child. The social constructions of gender identities are worth considering with the much-publicised 'underachievement of boys', particularly at GCSE level. If boys perceive schoolwork to be a feminised activity, they may be less likely to work or to report they are working (Francis 1999).

When things 'go wrong'

The area of developmental psychopathology examines psychological problems that affect educational progress. Development-related disorders include intellectual deficits, social behaviour deficits, learning deficits and attention deficits.

Prompt identification of intellectual deficits with intelligence tests helps remediation procedures to be initiated. There are, however, some disadvantages as well. Negative labelling can be most unhelpful to children identified as mentally retarded. Intelligence test results may not reflect innate learning potential as much as adjustment to the challenges of formal schooling (Peterson 1996). Halgin and Whitbourne (2003) catalogue a number of brilliant and well-known individuals who were labelled as being dull while at school. There are likely to be genetic and environmental contributions to mental retardation. Phenylketonuria is a metabolic disorder that can lead to intellectual impairment. Treatments have to be determined by a consideration of the causes of the condition, and will range from enrichment of the child's environment through to drug treatment and behavioural interventions.

With social behaviour deficits, children may display challenging behaviour that may have arisen through operant conditioning. Such behaviour may permit the child to exercise some control over the environment, by attention-seeking and influencing classroom procedures (Bennett 2003). Behavioural and cognitive-behavioural interventions can be effectively employed to reshape some dysfunctional behaviour.

Autism not only involves social behaviour deficits, but other problems such as those related to communication. Whereas most children will quickly develop non-verbal communication skills, this is not the case with autism and so social interactions suffer. There are several different types of autism, but it is common for the child to possess a limited understanding of what others might be thinking or feeling. Autism is associated with biological factors such as a higher incidence of seizure disorders by adolescence and increases in brain cerebral cortex size (Nolen-Hoeksema 2001). Drugs and behavioural therapy are used to reduce the intensity of the symptoms.

Dyslexia is a learning disorder, affecting both reading and writing. It is, however, a disorder with very wide-ranging symptoms, including spatial ability problems. Other spatial skills and aspects of creativity are, however, enhanced by dyslexia. In common with autism, there appears to be a diagnosis bias in the direction of boys. This may be because boys are more active and disruptive in the classroom, and therefore are more likely to be noticed. Dyslexia manifests itself at a behavioural level in the classroom, but cognitive and biological processing are both implicated in its cause. Brain scanning can be helpful in determining whether characteristic brain structure features are present. Remediation strategies include behaviour therapy, drugs and reading strategies.

Attention deficit/hyperactivity disorder (ADHD) is perhaps the most well known of the attention disorders. Children with ADHD are unable to pay attention to instructions and they are also hyperactive. Poor school performance and some degree of social isolation are common consequences. Some children with ADHD grow into normal adults and become symptom-free, whereas others are affected into adulthood (Peterson 1996). Environmental factors, such as family disruption, and biological factors, such as poor frontal lobe development, are linked to this condition. Both drugs and behaviour therapy are used to treat ADHD.

Psychology can make two distinct contributions to developmental psychopathology. The first is concerned with identifying the specific nature of the problem, which makes effective remediation more likely. The second relates to the treatment and monitoring of the condition. Both clinical and educational psychologists may be involved in managing these disorders.

Positive psychology and education

Seligman and Csikszentmihalyi (2000) have argued that psychology has focused on repairing the damage caused by disease and has neglected the process of building fulfilled individuals. Positive psychology focuses on positive cognitions about the future, such as optimism and hope. It has similar notions to those of the humanistic thinkers of several decades ago, when self-actualisation and peak experiences were being debated.

Having examined the problems caused by learned helplessness, we see that more constructive cognitions are likely to pave the way to improved motivation and success in school. Can we help children to develop beliefs that are protective and that increase resilience in the face of the many challenges life provides?

Hope will affect motivation levels and the extent to which educational experiences can be enjoyed. The Children's Hope Scale (CHS) has been developed to measure levels of hope in children (Snyder *et al.* 1997). Hope is associated with higher self-esteem, higher self-efficacy and lower levels of depression (Roberts *et al.* 2002). Interventions to build hope have involved activities ranging from the reading of hopeful stories and subsequent discussions, to the use of a summer day camp for children with psychosocial problems. It has been demonstrated that children's hope scores will tend to rise following these interventions (Roberts *et al.* 2002).

Because positive expectations can be self-fulfilling, there is reason to treat optimism as an asset. Peterson (2000) reviews a number of benefits of optimism including positive mood, good morale, perseverance, effective problem solving and academic success. The Life Orientation Test is one measure of optimism for adolescents and adults (Scheier and Carver 1985). This measure provides a score reflecting the overall global optimism of the person. Attributional style questionnaires can be used to establish optimism by measuring the explanatory style of the person. The Children's Attributional Style Questionnaire (CASQ) is one example of this (Seligman 1998).

Based on the notion that pessimism is a predisposing factor for depression, intervention projects have been devised to influence a child's cognitions, particularly with regard to explanatory style and social problem-solving skills. Roberts *et al.* (2002) point out that such interventions are beneficial, and this supports the notion that optimism can be taught.

It seems that positive interventions can be made in a child's early life to help develop resilience and coping skills, in preparation for future challenges. Psychology has much to offer the study of education. The reader is now encouraged to select additional study material from the extensive amount of psychological research work related to educational processes.

Suggested further reading

Fontana (1995) and Santrock (2001) provide comprehensive reviews of psychological issues relevant to education. Seligman's work gives a useful account of helplessness and optimism research.

References

Abrahamson, L. Y., Seligman, M. E. P. and Teasdale, J. D. (1978) 'Learned helplessness in humans: Critique and reformulation', *Journal of Abnormal Psychology*, 87, 49–74.

Anderman, E. M., Austin, C. C. and Johnson, D. M. (2001) 'The development of goal orientation', in A. Wigfield, and J. S. Eccles (eds) *Development of achievement motivation*. London: Academic Press.

Bandura, A. (1997) *Self-efficacy: The exercise of control*. New York: W. H. Freeman and Company.

Baumeister, R. F., Campbell, J. D., Krueger, J. I. and Vohs, K. D. (2003) 'Does high self-esteem cause better performance, interpersonal success, happiness, or healthier lifestyles?' *Psychological Science in the Public Interest*, 4 (1), 1–44.

Bennett, P. (2003) *Abnormal and clinical psychology*. Maidenhead: Open University Press.

Bong, M. and Skaalvik, E. M. (2003) 'Academic self-concept and self-efficacy: How different are they really?' *Educational Psychology Review*, 15 (1), 1–40.

Byrnes, J. P. (2001) *Cognitive development and learning*. London: Allyn and Bacon.

Chaikin, A., Sigler, E. and Derlega, V. (1974) 'Non-verbal mediators of teacher expectancy effects', *Journal of Personality and Social Psychology*, 30, 144–9.

Cooper, C. (2002) *Individual Differences*. London: Arnold.

Craik, F. I. M. and Lockhart, R. S. (1972) 'Levels of processing: A framework for memory research', *Journal of Verbal Learning and Verbal Behavior*, 11, 671–84.

Csikszentmihalyi, M. (2002) *Flow: The classic work on how to achieve happiness*. London: Rider.

Deary, I. J. (2003) 'Ten things I hated about intelligence research', *The Psychologist*, 16, 534–7.

Durkin, K. (1995) *Developmental social psychology: From infancy to old age*. Oxford: Blackwell.

Dweck, C. S. (2000) *Self-theories: Their role in motivation, personality, and development*. Hove: Psychology Press.

Fontana, D. (1995) *Psychology for Teachers*. London: Palgrave/BPS.

Francis, B. (1999) 'Lads, Lasses and (New) Labour: 14–16-year-old students' responses to the "laddish behaviour and boys' underachievement" debate', *British Journal of Sociology of Education*, 20, 355–71.

Franken, R. E. (1998) *Human motivation*. London: Brooks/Cole Publishing Company.

Gardner, H. (1998) 'A multiplicity of intelligences', *Scientific American Presents*, 9 (4), 18–23.

Gaskill, P. J. and Hoy, A. W. (2002) 'Self-efficacy and self-regulated learning: The dynamic duo in school performance', in J. Aronson (ed.) *Improving academic achievement: Impact of psychological factors on education*. London: Academic Press.

Gilbert, I. (2002) *Essential motivation in the classroom*. London: Routledge-Falmer.

Goleman, D. (1995) *Emotional intelligence: Why it can matter more than IQ*. London: Bantam Books.

Gould, S. J. (1981) *The mismeasure of man*. Harmondsworth: Penguin Books.

Halgin, R. P. and Whitbourne, S. K. (2003) *Abnormal psychology: Clinical perspectives on psychological disorders*. London: McGraw-Hill.

Larsen, R. J. and Buss, D. M. (2002) *Personality psychology*. London: McGraw-Hill.

Lepper, M. R. and Woolverton, M. (2002) 'The wisdom of practice: Lessons learned from the study of highly effective tutors', in J. Aronson (ed.) *Improving academic achievement: Impact of psychological factors on education*. London: Academic Press.

Maier, S. F. and Seligman, M. E. P. (1976) 'Learned helplessness: Theory and evidence', *Journal of Experimental Psychology: General*, 105, 3–46.

McLean, A. (2003) *The motivated school*. London: Paul Chapman Publishing.

Mruk, C. (1999) *Self-esteem: Research, theory and practice*. London: Free Association Books.

Nolen-Hoeksema, S. (2001) *Abnormal psychology*. London: McGraw-Hill.

Pajares, F. and Schunk, D. H. (2002) 'Self and self-belief in psychology and education: a historical perspective', in J. Aronson (ed.) *Improving academic achievement: Impact of psychological factors on education*. London: Academic Press.

Peterson, C. (1996) *The psychology of abnormality*. London: Harcourt Brace & Company.

Peterson, C. (2000) 'The future of optimism', *American Psychologist*, 55, 44–55.

Peterson, C. and Barrett, L. C. (1987) 'Explanatory style and academic performance among university freshmen', *Journal of Personality and Social Psychology*, 53, 603–7.

Pinker, S. (2002) *The blank slate*. London: Penguin Books.

Roberts, M. C., Brown, K. J., Johnson, R. J. and Reinke, J. (2002) 'Positive psychology for children', in C. R. Snyder and S. J. Lopez (eds), *Handbook of positive psychology*. New York: Oxford University Press.

Rose, S., Lewontin, R. C. and Kamin, L. J. (1984) *Not in our genes: Biology, ideology and human nature*. London: Penguin Books.

Rosenberg, M., Schoenbach, C., Schooler, C. and Rosenberg, F. (1995) 'Global self-esteem and specific self-esteem: Different concepts, different outcomes', *American Sociological Review*, 60, 141–56.

Rosenthal, R. and Jacobson, L. (1966) 'Teachers' expectancies: Determinants of pupils' IQ gains', *Psychological Reports*, 19, 115–18.

Rust, J. and Golombok, S. (1999) *Modern psychometrics*. London: Routledge.

Santrock, J. W. (2001) *Educational psychology*. London: McGraw-Hill.

Scheier, M. F. and Carver, C. S. (1985) 'The Self-Consciousness Scale: A revised version for use with general populations', *Journal of Applied Social Psychology*, 15, 687–99.

Seligman, M. E. P. (1998) *Learned Optimism*. London: Pocket Books.

Seligman, M. E. P. (2002) *Authentic Happiness*. London: Free Press.

Seligman, M. E. P. and Csikszentmihalyi, M. (2000) 'Positive psychology: An introduction', *American Psychologist*, 55, 5–14.

Skaalvik, E. M. (1983) 'Academic achievement, self-esteem and valuing of the school – some sex differences', *British Journal of Educational Psychology*, 53, 299–306.

Snyder, C. R., Hoza, B., Pelham, W. E., Rapoff, M., Ware, L., Danovsky, M., Highberger, L., Rubinstein, H. and Stahl, K. J. (1997) 'The development and validation of an individual-differences measure of hope', *Journal of Pediatric Psychology*, 22, 399–421.

Thorne, B. M. and Henley, T. B. (1997) *Connections in the History and Systems of Psychology*. New York: Houghton Mifflin Company.

Whalley, L. J. and Deary, I. J. (2001) 'Longitudinal cohort study of childhood IQ and survival up to age 76', *British Medical Journal*, 322, 819–22.

'Race' and education

John Stanley

'*Please*. Do me this one, great favour, Jones. If ever you hear anyone, when you are back home ... speak of the East,' and here his voice plummeted a register, and the tone was full and sad, '*hold your* judgment. If you are told "they are all this" or "they do this" or "their opinions are these", withhold your judgment until all the facts are upon you. Because that land they call "India" goes by a thousand names and is populated by millions, and if you think you have found two men the same among that multitude, then you are mistaken. It is merely a trick of the moonlight.'

(Zadie Smith 2000)

Introduction

SINCE THE EDUCATION ACT of 1944, a major concern for education has been with pursuing social justice, improving life chances for all children and enriching their lives. Studies on inequalities in education have revealed forms of discrimination at all levels of the education system, indicating that the desired improvement and enrichment of children's lives has not been fairly distributed. Social class, gender and 'race' are factors that, in combination, influence educational outcomes for all children. 'Race' is one of the categories used to explain educational inequality, though education is only one of a number of sectors where it is influential. It is, of course, an important social and political issue across the modern, globalised world. 'Race' is a broad social phenomenon and carries an overbearing presence in all modern societies, like the UK, which are structured along racial lines. To understand the phenomenon of 'race' in the context of education requires an appreciation of its meaning in the discourse of social relations. It is also important to be clear what is meant by the related concept of ethnicity. Aiming for a working definition of 'race' in a field where there is still considerable debate and disagreement has its pitfalls, as Cornell and Hartmann point out:

> We have to wrestle with the definition of race ... it is common in contemporary society to talk about races, race relations and racial conflict as if we had a clear idea of what

constitutes a race and where the boundary falls between one race and another. Race, however, is as slippery a concept as ethnic group.

(Cornell and Hartmann 1998: 21)

'Race' – origins and definitions

Although ideas about race can be traced back through ancient history, the categorisation of people based on the modern idea of 'race' became common in the late eighteenth and early nineteenth centuries. The acts that supported the doctrine of race were seen in the enslavement of millions of African peoples and their transportation as slave labour to the Americas. Equally, the European exploration, colonisation and imperial domination of much of the world stimulated and reaffirmed racial ideas about the inferiority of black Africans and the association of certain forms of behaviour with particular racial groups. The idea that different groups of people have different natures and that there is a clear line of distinction between them became generally accepted.

What are often called 'scare quotes' are generally used with the word 'race'; this indicates that there are some fundamental conceptual problems connected with the use of this word. The term has been used to categorise different groups of people across the globe using physical/genetic features, e.g. skin, hair, physique, facial features, and subsequently to make assumptions about their characteristics and behaviour. Such a connection is false, although a case has been made by some commentators who claim that intelligence is determined by genetics, and the low educational achievement of black pupils is due to lower, inherited intelligence. The assertions of Jensen (1969; 1973) in the USA and Eysenck (1971) in the UK were subjected to intense criticism, and the myth was exploded when the unreliability of the data was established. Kamin (1977) and Mabey (1981) have convincingly repudiated the work on genetic influence. More recently, Herrnstein and Murray's (1994) book, *The Bell Curve*, claimed that black people were genetically inferior to white people because of lower IQs. Once more the weakness of the research procedures and processes, to say nothing of the inadequacy of the conceptualisation of the research problem, meant the case fell apart. Science suggests that there is not a species type difference between peoples. 'Race' is not a social category which can identify groups of people, relying on their physical appearance to predict characteristics, behaviour and educational achievement (see Nei and Roychoudhury 1983). Indeed, there are strong and reliable claims that genetic variability is found between individuals generally, and not between the so-called different 'races'. Classifying people into 'races' is a social product rather than a biological reality. The continuing development of the science of genetics seems likely further to confirm the unreliability of the concept of 'race':

Here we have a concept which refers to a false perception: that the only legitimate use of the term 'race' is as a device for recognising that people categorise and behave differently towards one another on the basis of the significance attached to physiological differences, not the physiological differences themselves.

(Foster, Gomm and Hammersley 1996: 51–2)

However, even after establishing that the category of 'race' is invalid, that it has no scientific basis, the problem that it engenders does not disappear. The designation of inferiority which goes with the term 'race' serves to rationalise people's social position, achievements and treatment. Denying its validity will not remove it from the discourse of people and institutions. Even where it is denied, it has tended to be replaced by an equally difficult concept, namely ethnicity. The contemporary tendency has been to refer to a person's ethnicity rather than 'race'. This can result in the production of cultural stereotypes which mislead, oversimplify, categorise and, again, result in injustice. Reference to the ethnic origins of people from minority groups leads to a reification of ethnic categories and promotes an ethnic absolutism which often refers to extended kinship groups residing in another part of the world, or else static cultures. The emphasis is still on difference between groups of people and the danger is that the connotations about the specificity of human groups carried in the notion of 'race' get reconfigured under the label of ethnicity:

We should never forget that 'race' is not a spontaneously given product of perception and experience. It is an idea built up (and slowly at that) from elements which equally well might be physical traits as social customs, linguistic peculiarities as legal institutions, lumped together and homogenised according to the precepts that they must ultimately all be biological phenomena.

(Guillaumin 1995)

National statistics – minority ethnic population

The Office of National Statistics (1996) has as principal ethnic minority groups in the UK: Black Caribbean, Black African, Black other, Indian, Pakistani, Bangladeshi. These groups make up 80 per cent of the minority ethnic population of the United Kingdom.

Pathak (2000) provides useful information to fill 'a range of gaps' on information about 'race'/ethnicity. The paper uses evidence from research, statistics and evaluation studies to define the place of different ethnic groups in education, training and the labour market.

- Ethnic minorities make up 6.6 per cent of the working age population in the UK, i.e. 2.3m; 6.5 per cent of the UK population comes from a minority ethnic group.

- Indian is the largest minority ethnic group, followed by Pakistani and Black Caribbean.

- The minority ethnic population has a much younger age structure than the white population. Eleven per cent of pupils in state schools are ethnic minority.

- Minority group people live mainly in the major cities of the UK, e.g. half live in Greater London.

- Over 40 per cent of Bangladeshi people live in Inner London. Overall, Bangladeshis live in the most deprived wards, followed by a smaller proportion of Pakistanis and Black Caribbeans.

- Indians live in areas of greater deprivation than African Asians.

- On entry into pre-school, children of white UK heritage have the highest mean score in cognitive skills (verbal and non-verbal), with the lowest scores being recorded for Pakistani children. Differences in scores between ethnic groups are reduced when factors such as parents' educational and occupational status is taken account of.

- Bangladeshi, Black and Pakistani pupils perform less well than other pupils in the early key stages. Pupils from these three ethnic groups also tend to achieve significantly less well by the end of compulsory education.

- Staying on in full-time education after compulsory schooling is more common among ethnic minority people (over 85 per cent) than white people (67 per cent). However, a higher proportion of young people are in full-time employment (10 per cent) and Government-supported training (12 per cent) than their ethnic minority peers (3 per cent in full-time; 4 per cent Government-funded training).

- Ethnic minorities as a whole are over-represented in higher education, making up 13 per cent of undergraduate students.

- Ethnic minority students are disproportionately studying at the new (post-1992) universities. White working-class students have a similar experience.

- Thirty-seven per cent of ethnic minority students get a first or upper second degree compared with 53 per cent of white graduates.

(derived from Pathak 2000)

Operationalising the concepts on 'race' and education

One of the major difficulties in interpreting any kind of research is in understanding how the researcher is operationalising the concepts s/he is using. Two regular features of research into 'race' and education have been: 1) the allocation of individuals into groups, and 2) the issue of inequality in education. Research that investigates 'race'/ethnicity and education with this operationalisation of concepts will come up with evidence relating to achievement among different ethnic groups. A weakness of this work is that it has used simplistic categories, e.g. African-Caribbean, Asian, white British, other. An attempt to overcome the difficulty of operationalising 'race'/ethnicity by using a range of indicators, or by reference to self-categorisation, has been one way of trying to overcome the tendency to label whole groups of people who sometimes have little in common. A comparison of the achievements of black children with those of white children, for example, can provide misleading information. Similarly misleading is an investigation of the educational performance of pupils which does not take account of gender and social class. The indicators used in operationalising key concepts will determine in large measure what information is uncovered.

Ethnicity and difference

From the late 1980s, educators have tended to prefer to work with the notion of ethnic differences, and the Swann Report (DES 1985) gave support to and confirmation of teachers' choice of the concept of ethnicity. The social construct of 'race' leads to much disadvantage for some groups in society. The notion of 'race' is generally used in deprecating analyses of people's behaviour and potential, and where seemingly positive judgements are made they convey a mixed blessing – the association of black people with athletics and steel bands is dubious praise, since it carries with it the implication that academic achievement will not be very good.

By using the term 'ethnicity', instead of 'race', teachers feel that they are focusing on matters that directly affect education, namely identity and culture. The notion of 'new identities' (Hall 1988) and that of 'multiple identities' (Rex 1991) by focusing on the changing identities of people counters the stereotype of the homogenous ethnic group, but the idea of the changing identity should not take attention away from the need to challenge and get rid of racist behaviour and attitudes. There is the danger, however, that in ignoring 'race' teachers may be unaware of negative, unjust educational experiences which stem from prejudiced responses to skin or other physical features. Those negative educational experiences can involve violent behaviour and bullying as well as attitudes and practices based on racial differences.

Studies of 'race' discrimination in education have uncovered institutionalised racism as well as other processes responsible for producing or reproducing disadvantage. The term 'ethnicity' then, though used by people with good intentions and promoted enthusiastically in schools, can lead to a stereotyping of people by both anti-racists and racists. The danger lies in the assumption that tolerance will naturally be generated by knowledge of other cultures; this ignores the possibility that complex societies can be caricatured into neat, homogenous communities which defy reality. Secondly, it ignores the malignant nature of racism. Professed racists have been able to describe alien ways of life, by making reference to food, dress, family values and religion, as a threat to the long-established 'British way of life'. Barker (1981) claimed that racism had changed to an emphasis on cultural differences rather than inherited superiority. Racists now have two demons: the cultural and the biological. There is no doubt that focusing on differences between people can, even with the best of intentions, lead to a dangerous stereotyping of those whose lifestyles are defined and to a potential misuse of information.

Difference can also be used, particularly in political agendas, to promote exclusion and incite racist behaviour. Where there is, for instance, a shrinking labour market reducing job stability, extreme right-wing groups can exaggerate ethnic difference by claiming that the presence of ethnic minorities creates a threat to jobs and a social burden on the public budget. The activities of the British National Party and the support for the extreme right in France, Austria, Belgium and Holland in recent times are examples of the way that cultural difference is used to promote racist campaigns of hate and exclusion. Racism is thus developed with reference to ethnic difference. There is considerable intellectual support for this relativist position. It is seen first in the work of Nietzsche, and later the post-modernist/post-structuralist work of Lyotard, Foucault and Derrida. The problem with a relativist position is that it can deconstruct the principle of equality. Flecha (1999) provides a good example of this where the retention of the traditional identity and culture of the gypsies is regarded as more important than that they should experience equality of opportunity in their lives:

> Gypsy cultures have frequently prevented female teenagers from attending school because their tradition includes a key family role for women that begins in adolescence. From the relativist position, one could argue that Gypsies should not be expected to adhere to the European concept of equal educational rights for men and women ... Gender equality is presented as a European imposition rather than a basic human right ... Such analyses focus on the negative aspects of schooling and ignore the positive ones ... Gypsy women [can now] ... use schooling to exercise a professional option formerly unobtainable ... For relativists these educational opportunities are evidence of the destruction of Gypsy culture rather than of their evolution through change.
>
> (Flecha 1999: 161)

As educators seek to combat racism in their work, under whatever label it figures, it is worth recalling Guillaumin's (1995: 107) caution that though scientists have shown that 'race' does not exist, 'millions of human beings have died as a result of their race, and millions of others are now dominated, excluded and repressed for the same reason.'

Research on 'race' and education

The race relations legislation of the 1970s made some impact at the institutional level in that it called for some official response, but it made little impact on the educational experiences of children, and so the 1980s produced numerous interpretive studies on schooling and 'race'/ethnicity which studied a range of responses by pupils and teachers in multiracial and all-white schools.

Early research on educational achievement and minority ethnic group pupils is summarised in a review by Tomlinson (1980) of 33 studies of educational attainment of ethnic groups in schools. Twenty-six of these studies revealed African-Caribbean pupils were getting lower scores than white pupils on tests of performance. Moreover, the same defined group was over-represented in the category of 'Educationally Sub-Normal' and under-represented in the higher school classes. Among the findings of the Swann Report (DES 1985), looking at the educational attainments of most minority ethnic groups, was that racism, mainly unintentional, influenced underachievement. The incidence of underachievement was not so prevalent for some Asian groups who were thought to experience the negative effects of stereotyping to a lesser degree than other groups. In the continuing search for explanations of minority group underachievement, Smith and Tomlinson (1989) showed that investigations revealed school differences in educational achievements by minority group children. The various research teams argued that the differences stemmed not from differing abilities so much as different qualities of teaching and learning. Schools could make a difference to the educational achievement of pupils, whatever their ethnic origin.

As a result of research on pupil–pupil and pupil–teacher interactions (Wright 1986, 1992; Mac an Ghaill 1988; Gillborn 1990; Mirza 1992; Green 1985) the operationalisation of the concept of 'race'/ethnicity changed its focus. Wright's (1986) classroom study found black boys and girls constructing an anti-school subculture as they reached the fourth and fifth years of schooling. Similarly, Mac an Ghaill (1988) and Fuller (1980, 1983) found that girls from ethnic minority groups, though they disliked school, used it to acquire much needed educational qualifications which would enable them to escape the double disadvantage of both 'race' and gender. Gillborn and Gipps (1996) examining research conducted in the 1970s, 1980s and 1990s found that teachers who expressed a commitment to equality were still likely to work with negative representations of African-Caribbean pupils.

What is evident in the foregoing studies is what is called 'institutional racism'. Gillborn's (1990) study uses this notion and spells out the process clearly. He uses the idea of the 'ideal client' which teachers apply to their pupils. This concept carries a picture of 'appropriate pupil behaviour'; it has dimensions of class, 'race' and gender. The behaviour of African-Caribbean pupils confirmed for teachers the myth about the way the pupils' behaviour and attitudes represented a challenge to authority. The school then became a site of contestation as institutional disciplinary practices were applied by the school. 'Almost any display of African-Caribbean ethnicity was deemed inappropriate' (Gillborn 1990: 29). Gillborn (1995), while suggesting that teachers are not practising institutional racism deliberately, sees them contributing, generally unintentionally, to 'the processes that structure the educational opportunities of minority students' (Gillborn 1995: 42). Gillborn and Youdell (2000) further examine the issue of institutional racism looking at African-Caribbean pupils' experiences and achievements. Their conclusion is that there existed an institutional discourse of 'race' and ability which denied African-Caribbean students any chance of success in school. Youdell (2003) sets out further to investigate how 'the minutiae of everyday life in schools constitutes African-Caribbean students as undesirable learners.' Her conclusion is that in the ordinary conversation of school life the identities of African-Caribbean pupils are 'constituted as undesirable, intolerable, far from "ideal", within the hegemonic discourses of the school organisation'. The 'discursive constitution' of African-Caribbean identities which takes place in 'the apparently trivial moments of everyday life' is the seemingly innocuous way identities are constituted. Guillaumin similarly draws attention to the unconscious confirmation of racism when she claims that:

> Negations are not recognised as such by our unconscious mental processes. From this point of view, a fact affirmed and a fact denied exist to exactly the same degree and remain equally present in our affective and intellectual associative networks. Just talking about race means that it will always be there in residue. 'Race' is about the least conceptional, cold and abstract of notions, so it appeals from the start to the unconscious side of the mechanisms we have for acquiring knowledge and relating to other human beings.
>
> (Guillaumin 1995: 105–6)

All can achieve

The idea that minority ethnic group experience of schooling is all bad news is misleading. There are numerous examples to contradict the view that the educational experience of all minority ethnic group children is of failure. The more recent studies of 'race' and ethnicity and educational achievement do show some educational success for certain minority ethnic group children. Gillborn and Mirza (2000) in their synthesis of research evidence on 'race', class and gender have used a broader range of ethnic group categories than earlier commentators. These categories may still hide much valuable evidence, but there has to be some sort of classification if monitoring of educational achievement is to take place, and the year 2000 amendment to the 1976 Race Relations Act insists that it must. Gillborn and Mirza use the categories white, black, Indian, Pakistani, Bangladeshi. This study also attempts to establish:

> on the basis of the best available evidence, the relative significance of 'race' and ethnicity alongside other factors, especially gender and social class background, so as to clarify an agenda for racial equality in education.
>
> (Gillborn and Mirza 2000: 5)

The study quoted above is called *Educational Inequality*, and it acknowledges that minority communities should not be regarded as homogenous, but seen as they truly are: stratified by class and gender. The idea of a single, definitive cultural or ethnic experience is unacceptable. The reality is that educational experience and achievement can only be reliably judged at the conjunction of racial, social and gendered experience. Unfortunately, there are few other studies that take these three variables together. Gillborn and Gipps' (1996) earlier study, which was undertaken on behalf of Ofsted, was one that attempted to take account of 'race'/ethnicity, class and gender. Looking at GCSE Grades A–C in England and Wales in 1995, the highest averages went to pupils from advantaged backgrounds, and girls fared better than boys when socio-economic background was the same (Gillborn and Gipps 1996: 17). The Youth Cohort Study (DfEE 1999) referred to by Gillborn and Mirza (2000) addresses the variables of 'race', class and gender together; this is another rare example. Some interesting though 'tentative' conclusions are available:

- No group has been completely excluded from the improvement in GCSE attainments during the late 1980s and 1990s.

- By 1995 the gender gap was present within each ethnic group regardless of social class background.

- Ethnic inequalities persist even when simultaneously controlling for gender and class.

- When comparing like with like, in terms of gender, class and ethnic origin, consistent and significant ethnic inequalities of attainment remain clear.

The performance of African-Caribbean pupils has tended to lag behind that of white pupils, though there was an instance where, in the years 1992 and 1994, at Key Stage 1, African-Caribbean pupils in Birmingham were ahead of white pupils as recorded on national assessment tests (Gillborn and Gipps 1996). The general conclusion, however, ran true to form with the attainments of ethnic minority pupils generally lagging behind those of white pupils. As pupils moved through the junior years, that is Key Stage 2, the gap tended to widen. There are cases of

African-Caribbean boys doing better at Key Stage 1 than their white counterparts, but this advantage is soon lost as school careers develop. The declining achievements of African-Caribbean pupils is explained by Gillborn and Gipps as the product of a situation of conflict created between teachers and schooling and African-Caribbean pupils. As a consequence of this seemingly unintentional outcome, levels of achievement of African-Caribbean pupils suffer. As pupils' educational careers proceed through secondary school, to the point where they take GCSE examinations, their achievements are in comparative decline, the average difference being that African-Caribbean pupils are five points lower than white peers. Nonetheless, Gillborn and Gipps reject the idea of total black underachievement since black African pupils invariably get better results than African-Caribbean pupils.

Turning to GCSE grades A–C, which was the benchmark for a pass comparable with the old GCE 'O' level examination, Afro-Caribbean pupils are gaining less than half the national average. The results for pupils of Bangladeshi and Pakistani origin are more encouraging since they make up some of the leeway on national averages at 11 to perform in some local education authorities at or above the national average (Commission on the Future of Multi-ethnic Britain 2000).

A snapshot of variations in achievement

Notwithstanding the foregoing reservations, the consistency of much of the data from research projects suggests that the educational underachievements of many minority ethnic group pupils is an outcome of the way the schools deal with these pupils. Gillborn and Mirza's study provides a complex picture of ethnic minority educational performance, in the first place by claiming that 'all can achieve' – that is 'of the six ethnic minority categories analysed, each one is in the highest attaining category in at least one LEA' (Gillborn and Mirza 2000: 9). Hence the writers' claim that their study is looking at new evidence 'on how different groups share in the rising levels of attainment at the end of compulsory schooling' (p. 5).

There is still some improvement to be made in the monitoring of the educational achievement of minority ethnic groups and the writers express concern that a number of LEAs applying for the Ethnic Minority Achievement Grant (EMAG) could not give a figure for minority attainment in Year 11. This criticism of the monitoring of ethnic minority achievement has further support in Osler and Morrison's (2000) report for the Commission for Racial Equality (CRE) which claims that Ofsted informed neither schools nor contracted inspectors of Ofsted's responsibility for monitoring schools' procedures for preventing racism. Such strategies were recommended in the report of the Stephen Lawrence Inquiry (Macpherson 1999). Further weaknesses which Gillborn and Mirza (2000) point out are that only six LEAs provided baseline to GCSE performance by ethnic origin; and that LEAs had never produced data on performance by ethnic group before and therefore some of their returns were less than adequate. This finding sits well with the Ofsted (1999) report on LEA programmes for raising the levels of minority ethnic group attainments. Less than one-quarter of LEAs involved in that survey could provide a clear plan for improving the attainment of minority ethnic groups.

The Gillborn and Mirza study (2000) is mapping attainment at local level in a number of select LEAs. This leads to local variability and cannot provide a national picture. However, it does give 'a unique glimpse of variation between localities' (p. 8). The data relate to attainments in the summer of 1998. The report concentrates first on 'local variability' and shows that 'of the six minority ethnic categories ... analysed, every one is the highest attaining of all in at least one LEA' (p. 9). And 'Black pupils are capable of high achievement. In one in ten authorities that monitor GCSE results by ethnicity, pupils in all recorded Black groups are more likely to attain the benchmark than their white peers' (p. 10). Pakistani pupils have been recorded as a low attaining group, but 'In four out of ten LEAs that monitor for ethnic origin, Pakistani pupils are more likely to attain this benchmark than white pupils locally' (p. 10). Again Bangladeshis, who at national level lag behind white averages, do at local level in many cases reverse this pattern. However, this 'snapshot of variations' (p. 11) notwithstanding, 'significant and consistent inequalities of attainment emerge for many of the principal minority groups' (p. 11). Although members of each of the principal minority groups are more likely to gain five higher GCSE grades than ever before, it must be borne in mind that African-Caribbean, Pakistani and Bangladeshi pupils are 'markedly less likely to attain five higher graded GCSEs than their white and Indian peers nationally' (p. 12). Gillborn and Mirza (2000) conclude that ethnic inequalities are 'consistently visible' and that social class and gender differences though 'associated with differences in attainment ... [cannot] ... account for persistent underlying ethnic inequalities: comparing like with like, African-Caribbean, Pakistani and Bangladeshi pupils do not enjoy equal opportunities.' The writers draw attention to the fact that the situation is not static and that for African-Caribbean and Pakistani pupils inequalities have increased particularly in GCSE attainments.

The changing nature of educational achievement of minority ethnic pupils, while showing improvements for some groups, persistently leaves other groups disappointed. Berliner (2003) reporting in the *Education Guardian* on a recent report by Simon Warren of University of Birmingham and Professor David Gillborn of Institute of Education, London says that Birmingham LEA – 'a leader in the field of race equality in education' – is still employing a strategy which is not resulting in equality of opportunity in all schools, this in particular for African-Caribbean children. Gillborn and Warren suggest that setting, and booster groups, to help children reach targets in tests, could be working against black pupils. Typically, girls of all ethnic groups do better than boys.

The *Aiming High* national strategy, reported in the *Guardian* (Muir and Smithers 2003), is the Government's new national strategy to raise achievement levels of minority ethnic pupils and specifically black pupils who they see as one of the main underperforming groups in the country. Central to the strategy is focused work in 30 secondary schools. Each school will receive a support package including support and advice from an experienced consultant. The National College of School Leadership will also contribute, and lessons learnt will be spread throughout the country. The new strategy will involve bringing greater accountability and visibility to the issue. Inspections will deliberately focus on minority group experience, and the school and LEA will publish achievement data by ethnic group and LEA. There will be training for primary school teachers to help them support bilingual pupils. There will also be monitoring of bilingual pupils from foundation stage to secondary school.

School exclusions

School exclusions have a long history. Bernard Coard's (1971) short book with the long title, *How the West Indian Child Is Made Educationally Sub-normal in the British School System*, drew attention to the disproportionate numbers of African-Caribbean children who were being diverted from mainstream schooling into schools for the educationally subnormal. Another early report by the Commission for Racial Equality (CRE) (see Bourne *et al.* 1994), looking into pupil suspensions in Birmingham schools, discovered that from 1974 to 1980 it was recorded that black pupils were four times more likely to be excluded than white pupils. This problematic experience of schooling was further confirmed by Ofsted in a report in 1993 which discovered that the number of African-Caribbean pupils excluded from schools was disproportionately high and that similar numbers attended the referral units which LEAs have to provide for permanently excluded pupils. Osler (1997) claims that the relatively excessive exclusions of African-Caribbean pupils produces an 'educational crisis' since following exclusion there is only a 15 per cent chance that a child will be reinstated in mainstream education. Exclusion is not the same problem for girls as it is for boys, except in the case of African-Caribbean girls who constitute 9 per cent of female exclusions, and yet only just over 1 per cent of all girls in schools.

Although permanent exclusions from school are much lower than they were six years ago, the numbers of pupils thus excluded has risen for the second year

TABLE 6.1 Percentage of permanent exclusions

Ethnic Group	1997/1998	1998/1999	1999/2000	2000/2001	2001/2002*
White	83.8	84.4	82.9	83.0	82.0
Black	10.2	9.7	9.8	8.5	8.1
Of whom:					
Black Caribbean	*6.2*	*5.7*	*5.5*	*4.2*	*4.2*
Black African	*1.7*	*1.5*	*1.7*	*1.7*	*1.7*
Black Other	*2.3*	*2.5*	*2.6*	*2.6*	*2.2*
Asian	3.2	2.7	2.8	2.2	3.2
Of whom:					
Indian	*0.9*	*0.7*	*0.6*	*0.5*	*0.6*
Pakistani	*1.8*	*1.6*	*1.6*	*1.2*	*1.8*
Bangladeshi	*0.5*	*0.4*	*0.6*	*0.5*	*0.8*
Chinese	0.1	0.1	0.0	0.0	0.1
Other group	2.7	3.1	3.5	2.8	3.3
Group not known	0.0	0.0	1.0	3.2	3.3
Total	100	100	100	100	100

*estimate

running, according to figures provided by the Department for Education and Skills (DfES 2003).

The total number of exclusions has risen for the second year running, though it is considerably lower than it was in 1997/1998. Black Caribbean pupils continue to have the highest exclusion rate among the minority ethnic groups. Chinese pupils have the smallest percentage. This exclusion from full-time mainstream education of a disproportionate percentage of black young people, and African-Caribbean in particular, shows that little has changed for this group of young people. The Commission for Racial Equality has expressed concern on many occasions about what appears to be unfair treatment. There are concerns that the needs-oriented approach recommended in the Warnock Report (1978) is still being overlooked. A further strong criticism is that the Conservative Government's Education Reform Act of 1988 did nothing for the educational interests of young black pupils on a number of counts. The neo-liberal Act created the 'market' for school places, giving parents the opportunity to choose schools; white parents were thus able to avoid schools with appreciable numbers of black pupils. The competition between schools for potentially able pupils to enhance league table positions has taken priority in state education over the aims of equal opportunities for all pupils. An equally important concern is the content of the National Curriculum. Gundara claims that the 'National Curriculum, and the Anglo-centric values under-pinning it, diminishes the right to knowledge for all Britons in a multicultural society' (Gundara 2000: 39).

Adjustments to the National Curriculum subsequent to the 1988 Education Reform Act have done little to address the criticism that schooling is in the main 'white, English, Christian'. The formal curriculum of schools, together with the hidden curriculum of schooling, is seen by many writers as creating an environment where black pupils are likely to fail (Mac an Ghaill 1988; Gillborn 1990; Osler 1997; Hatcher 1997). As Gillborn and Mirza (2000) and Youdell (2003) among others claim, institutional racism is still a significant influence on the educational achievement of African-Caribbean pupils.

Race relations law

Discrimination against people on the grounds of race, colour or ethnic origin was made unlawful in the 1976 Race Relations Act. The action was unlawful whether it was direct or indirect. The Commission for Racial Equality produced a code of practice which included the elimination from all schools of racial discrimination in education (CRE 1989). The code of practice sets out to protect people who have drawn attention to unlawful practices, to identify segregation on racial grounds and to protect those who have alleged that racial discrimination has taken place. A range of practices are identified as unlawful; these include assessment, admissions, allocation to teaching groups, exclusions, careers advice, grants (pp. 12–13). This legislation has to some degree combated racism in schools, but there is still considerable evidence of violence, bullying and institutionalised racism, perpetuating both educational disadvantage and racial harassment.

The Race Relations Act of 1976 has been amended by the Race Relations (Amendment) Act 2000 which makes it unlawful to discriminate against anyone on grounds of race, colour, nationality (including citizenship), or ethnic or national origin. Public bodies must also take distinct steps to promote racial equality and good race relations. Schools must now publish a race equality policy, and monitor and assess how their policies affect minority ethnic pupils, staff and parents. Of particular importance is the monitoring of pupils' achievements. The amended Act requires public authorities to publish the results of their consultations, monitoring and assessments.

Consequences of the neglect of 'race'

Developments in 'race' and education from the Education Reform Act of 1988 were strongly influenced by the neo-liberal ideals of the Thatcher Government; this meant letting economic growth and the market provide racial equality rather than deeming that to be the responsibility of civil rights legislation and state intervention. In this way of thinking, it is the individual rather than the rights of groups that predominate and legitimate (Ben-Tovim 1997 in Modood and Werbner: 210). This move towards the freedom of the individual has pervaded all educational policy post the 1988 Education Reform Act. Particularly in relation to race/ethnicity and education, the pressure of state influence on schools to develop and pursue 'positive action' strategies to undermine racism in education has declined. In their place has been substituted a reassertion of 'English' and 'Christian' values in the National Curriculum (Troyna 1992). As the Berliner report stressed, the emphasis on individual achievement, competition and league tables has directed attention away from principles of fairness, justice and equality.

It is remarkable that the vital issue of 'race' should be neglected in this way, especially since numerous disturbing incidents were taking place in the late 1980s. The influence of the racism in the world outside school was felt inside schools too. There was the occasion when parents of children at Headfield Primary School in Dewsbury kept their children at home because the majority of pupils in the school came from Asian families. Burnage High School in Manchester, a boys' school in a largely working-class catchment area, had a number of difficult racist incidents despite its anti-racist policies. In September 1986, a 13-year-old pupil of Asian origin (Ahmed Iqbal Ullah) was stabbed to death in the playground by a white pupil of similar age. The subsequent Burnage Report (see Runnymede Trust Summary 1989) was critical of certain types of 'doctrinal anti-racism' that failed to take account of other problems which result from social inequality. Anti-racist education was taken to be a form of left-wing extremism. The tabloid press interpreted this criticism as pointing the finger of blame at the school's anti-racist policies. Instead, what the committee was criticising was policies that appeared to ignore white working-class pupils. The Burnage Committee saw this as a seedbed of division and polarisation in a context of anti-racist policies.

The hostility towards strategies to combat racism, seen in the tabloid press reporting of the Burnage stabbing, is still about. Nick Seaton, of the Campaign for Real Education, claims that a Qualifications and Curriculum Authority (QCA) call for a National Curriculum which values cultural diversity and the prevention of racism is addressing an issue that is nothing more than political correctness (Campaign for Real Education 2003). The aim of the QCA (2003) guidance materials, called *Respect for All*, is to respond to the recommendations of a report made by the committee which looked into another racist murder, that of Stephen Lawrence.

The Stephen Lawrence Inquiry Report (Macpherson 1999) was first concerned with the poor response of police officers to the murder of Stephen Lawrence, a black London teenager. However, the Macpherson Report went on to claim that racism was present in all institutions. The need for some radical thinking and a determined response to tackle institutionalised racism in all public services, especially in areas of family life and education, was stressed. Clearly the treatment of racism in schools is a persistent issue and ridding schools of racism, either institutional or personal, is still some way from being achieved. Indeed the role of education in transmitting racism is well documented. Among the many recommendations made by the Stephen Lawrence Inquiry to counter racism, some were specifically directed at education. The first of these recommendations is that the National Curriculum should incorporate the prevention of racism and the promotion of cultural diversity among its objectives. Secondly, that local education authorities and school governors should be obliged to implement strategies to combat racism including recording racist incidents, reporting such incidents to involve the pupils' parents, governors and LEAs, publications of racist incidents each year, school by school, publication of pupil exclusions on an annual and school-by-school basis. Finally, Ofsted inspections should be required to check the implementation of the anti-racist strategy of each school inspected.

The revised National Curriculum in 2000 included citizenship which involves introducing pupils to the diversity in 'national, regional, religious and ethnic identities ... and the need for mutual respect and understanding'. Sivanandan (2000) in *Macpherson and After* is very critical of the commitment seen in remarks like 'respecting cultural differences'. Other direct action stemming from the Macpherson Report was the setting up of the Advisory Group on Raising Ethnic Minority Pupil Achievement and the Race, Education and Employment Forum, both coming from the DfEE. The CRE (2000) issued a paper intended to focus on action in schools to promote equality and cultural diversity. The focus here is on distinct aspects of school life such as: leadership and management, curriculum, admissions, exclusions, parent and community involvement. There is an attached audit sheet to enable schools to monitor their standards.

Conclusion

The concept of 'race' has no scientific basis. However, even when the validity of 'race' is denied and the word 'ethnicity' is substituted, it does not remove the association of difference and inferiority where social position, achievement and treatment are concerned. Careful clarification of a working definition of 'race' and ethnicity is an important starting point for study and research in 'race' and education. In research studies, the way in which concepts are operationalised will significantly influence what is found out about 'race'/ethnicity and education. A searching study and analysis of issues may well uncover apparently good intentions or misguided ones. An instance of the latter is seen in Flecha's (1999) case of the education of gypsies, or Youdell's (2003) investigation of the 'minutiae' of life in school which makes African-Caribbean students 'undesirable ... intolerable within the hegemonic discourses of the school organisation'.

The need to monitor educational achievement by ethnic group is stressed in the work of many commentators, and the reluctance of some local education authorities to carry out routine monitoring has been addressed by the Race Relations Amendment Act 2000. The picture of minority ethnic group achievement is changing in some cases, but in others an endemic record of failure persists; this may be better addressed when consistent, reliable records are kept.

Despite the passing of almost 30 years since the 1976 Race Relations Act, education's mission to enrich children's lives is still not fairly distributed and the barrier to success created by 'race'/ethnicity is still a serious problem. Moreover, the harassment and victimisation of children on racial grounds, both inside and outside school, shows that expelling the evil of racism from schools and society is still a long way from being realised.

Suggested further reading

The Oxford Readers volume on *Racism* (Bulmer and Solomos 1999) provides a wide-ranging critical overview of both the historical development and the contemporary focus on ideas about racism. These papers introduce the reader to the broad parameters of 'race' as a field of study. The way in which 'race' affects children's life chances is shown by Gillborn and Gipps (1996) when they draw attention to the mounting incidence of racial harassment and violence; this together with an increased number of school exclusions. Gillborn and Gipps (1996) and Connolly and Troyna (1998) provide a comprehensive overview of research into 'race' and education. The virulent nature of racism is shown in Connolly (1998) when racism is seen in children at a very early age. Troyna and Hatcher (1992) sound a similar warning when they reveal institutionalised racism and individual racism interwoven in the lives of children in three 'mainly all-white primary schools'. The importance of taking account of gender and social class in conjunction with 'race' is seen in Gillborn and Gipps (1996). Gaine and George (1999) also address the interaction of 'race', class and gender. Mirza (1992) is a good example of an interpretative study where young African-Caribbean women show that their aspirations are different from black boys and white girls. Gillborn and Mirza (2000) provide a synthesis of recent research evidence on educational experience and achievement which again emphasises the interaction of racial, social and gendered experience. Useful journals include *Multicultural Teaching*; *Race and Class*; and *Race, Ethnicity and Education*.

References

Barker, M. (1981) *The New Racism*. London: Junction Books.

Ben-Tovim, G. (1997) 'Why "Positive Action" Is "Politically Correct" ', in T. Modood and P. Werbner (eds) *The Politics of Multiculturalism in the New Europe*. London: Zed Books.

Berliner, W. (2003) 'Gifted, but black', *Education Guardian*, 14 October, p. 2.

Bourne, J., Bridges, L. and Searle, C. (1994) *Outcast England: How Schools Exclude Black Children*. London: Institute of Race Relations.

Bulmer, M. and Solomos, J. (1999) *Racism*. Oxford: Oxford University Press.

Campaign for Real Education Newsletter, No. 49, spring 2003.

Coard, B. (1971) *How the West Indian Child Is Made Educationally Sub-Normal in the British Education System*. London: New Beacon Books.

Commission for Racial Equality (CRE) (1989) *Code of Practice for the Elimination of Racial Discrimination in Education*. London: CRE.

Commission for Racial Equality (CRE) (2000) *Learning for All: Standards for racial equality in schools*. London: CRE.

Commission on the Future of Multi-ethnic Britain (2000) *Report on the Future of Multi-ethnic Britain* (Parekh Report). London: Profile Books.

Connolly, P. (1998) *Racism, Gender Identities and Young Children*. London: Routledge.

Connolly, P. and Troyna, B. (eds) (1998) *Researching Racism in Education*. Buckingham: Open University Press.

Cornell, S. and Hartmann, D. (1998) *Ethnicity and Race: Making Identities in a Changing World*. Thousand Oaks, CA: Pine Forge Press.

Department for Education and Employment (DfEE) (1999) *The Youth Cohort Study*. London: HMSO.

Department for Education and Skills (DfES) (2003) *Exclusions 1997–2002*. www.dfes.gov.uk.

Department of Education and Science (DES) (1985) *Education for All* (The Swann Report). London: HMSO.

Eysenck, H. (1971) *Race, Intelligence and Education*. London: Temple-Smith.

Flecha, R. (1999) 'Modern and Post-Modern Racism in Europe', *Harvard Educational Review*, 69 (2), 150–71.

Foster, P., Gomm, R. and Hammersley, M. (1996) *Constructing Educational Inequality*. London: Falmer Press.

Fuller, M. (1980) 'Black girls in a London comprehensive school', in R. Deem (ed.) *Schooling for Women's Work*. London: Routledge and Kegan Paul.

Fuller, M. (1983) 'Qualified criticism, critical qualifications', in L. Barton and S. Walker (eds) *Race, Class and Education*. London: Croom Helm.

Gaine, C. and George, R. (1999) *Gender, 'Race' and Class in Schooling: A New Introduction*. London: Falmer Press.

Gillborn, D. (1990) *'Race', Ethnicity and Education*. London: Unwin Hyman.

Gillborn, D. (1995) *Racism and Antiracism in Real Schools*. Buckingham: Open University Press.

Gillborn, D. and Gipps, C. (1996) *Recent Research on the Achievement of Ethnic Minority Pupils*. London: HMSO.

Gillborn, D. and Mirza, H. (2000) *Educational Inequality: mapping, 'race', class and gender – a synthesis of research evidence*. London: Ofsted.

Gillborn, D. and Youdell, D. (2000) *Rationing Education: Policy, practice, reform and equity*. Buckingham: Open University Press.

Green, P. (1985) 'Multi-ethnic teaching and the pupils' self-concepts', *Annex B* in the Swann Report.

Guillaumin, C. (1995) 'The Changing Face of "Race" ', in M. Bulmer and J. Solomos (eds) *Racism*. Oxford: Oxford University Press.

Gundara, J. (2000) *Interculturalism, Education and Inclusion*. London: Paul Chapman.

Hall, S. (1988) 'The toad in the garden: Thatcherism among the theorists', in C. Nelson and L. Grossberg (eds) *Marxism and the Interpretation of Culture*. Illinois: University of Illinois Press.

Hatcher, R. (1997) 'New Labour, school improvement and racial equality', *Multicultural Teaching*, 15 (3), 8–13.

Herrnstein, R. J. and Murray, C. (1994) *The Bell Curve: Intelligence and Class Structure in American Life*. New York: Free Press.

Jensen, A. (1969) *Environment, Heredity and Intelligence*. Cambridge, MA: Harvard Educational Review.

Jensen, A. (1973) *Educability and Group Differences*. London: Methuen.

Kamin, L. (1977) *The Science and Politics of IQ*. Harmondsworth: Penguin.

Mabey, C. (1981) 'Black British Literacy', *Educational Research*, 23 (2), 83–95.

Mac an Ghaill, M. (1988) *Young, Gifted and Black*. Milton Keynes: Open University Press.

Macpherson, W. (1999) *The Stephen Lawrence Inquiry: Report of an inquiry*, London: HMSO.

Mirza, H. S. (1992) *Young, Female and Black*. London: Routledge.

Muir, H. and Smithers, R. (2003) 'Ethnic minority pupils get more help', *Guardian*, 23 October.

Nei, M. and Roychoudhury, A. K. (1983) 'Genetic relationship and evolution of human races', *Evolutionary Biology*, 14.

Office for Standards in Education (Ofsted) (1999) *Raising the Attainment of Minority Ethnic Pupils: School and LEA Responses*. London: Ofsted.

Office of National Statistics (1996) *Social Trends*, 30. London: HMSO.

Osler, A. (1997) 'Exclusion drama turns into a crisis for blacks', *Times Educational Supplement*, 10 October.

Osler, A. and Morrison, M. (2000) *Inspecting Schools for Racial Equality: Ofsted's Strengths and Weaknesses*. Stoke on Trent: Trentham Books.

Pathak, S. (2000) *Race Research for the Future: Ethnicity in Education, Training and the Labour Market*. London: Department for Education and Employment.

QCA (2003) *Respect for All: guidance materials for PSHE and citizenship*. Available from http://www.qca.org.uk/ages3-14/inclusion/1590.html.

Rex, J. (1991) *Ethnic Identity and Political Mobilisation in Britain*. University of Warwick: Centre for Research into Ethnic Relations.

Runnymede Trust (1989) *Racism, Anti-racism and Schools: A summary of The Burnage Report*. London: The Runnymede Trust.

Sivanandan, A. (2000) *Macpherson and After*. London: Institute of Race Relations.

Smith, D. and Tomlinson, S. (1989) *The School Effect: a study of multi-racial comprehensives*. London: Policy Studies Institute.

Smith, Z. (2000) *White Teeth*. London: Penguin Books.

Tomlinson, S. (1980) 'The educational performance of ethnic minority children', *New Community*, 8 (3).

Troyna, B. (1992) 'Can You See the Join? An historical analysis of multicultural and anti-racist education policies', in D. Gill *et al.* (eds) *Racism and Education*. London: Sage.

Troyna, B. and Hatcher, R. (1992) *Racism in Children's Lives*. London: Routledge.

Warnock, M. (1978) *Report of the Committee of Inquiry into the Education of Handicapped Children and Young People*. London: HMSO.

Wright, C. (1986) 'School processes: an ethnographic study', in J. Egglestone, D. Dunn and M. Anjali (eds) *Education for Some: The Educational and Vocational Experiences of 15–18 Year Old Members of Minority Ethnic Groups*. Stoke on Trent: Trentham Books.

Wright, C. (1992) *Race Relations in the Primary School*. London: David Fulton Publishers.

Youdell, D. (2003) 'Identity Traps or How Black Students Fail: the interactions between biographical, sub-cultural, and learner identities', *British Journal of Sociology of Education*, 24 (1), 2–20.

Gender in education

Jane Martin

The education system is not primarily an agent for the promotion of greater choice among students. It can only be said to provide equality of opportunity for people to fulfil the expectations which the dominant group in society has already laid down. It is when students conform to these expectations that inequality is perpetuated. While the prevailing belief is that women are inferior, and while this is taught within education with all the 'massaging' of the evidence that such teaching requires, women will continue to find themselves devalued, in the lowest paid, least skilled jobs, with least power to change those conditions.

(Spender 1980: 31)

THE FIELD OF GENDER and education has shifted dramatically since Dale Spender wrote these words for the collection of essays entitled *Learning to Lose*. Now, what is considered to be of concern with regard to gender equity (and inequality) in the British education system is the apparent 'underachievement' of boys. To understand this shift of emphasis demands that we place it in perspective. My purpose in this chapter is to adopt a longer time frame, to tease out the way in which debates about gender in education have been framed historically. To map this terrain I shall outline briefly the history of post-war education policy in England and the influence of social and cultural changes, particularly as they have affected gender distinctions.

The chapter is divided into three parts. It begins with a discussion of historical perspectives on gender and education, before moving on to more recent concerns, considered in their policy context. Overall, in the post-Second World War period, traditional expectations and roles meant the great majority of girls were trained for domesticity, even at the expense of academic ability. Nonetheless, gendered inequality did not come under scrutiny as an educational issue until the early 1970s. Then, feminist practitioners began to play a role in the gender policy-making process, acquiring a wide range of knowledges, strategies and understandings which helped them mount forceful challenges to schooling (Weiner 1994). However, the 1990s saw a redefinition of established debates about the relationship between gender and schooling triggered by the annual publication of national statistics charting the performance of boys and girls in taking and passing public examinations. Widely discussed in the English media, the insinuation is that girls' success has been at the expense of boys' failure. As a consequence, public debate and policy are now dominated by concerns about the education of boys. Indeed, popular and policy discussions about the issues have been couched in such a way as to obscure the fact that not all boys are underachieving and not all girls are succeeding in education. It is concluded that we need to see gender as relational, to critique the overly simplified and populist focus on gender binaries and direct attention to the differences that exist among groups. The interrelations of gender, 'race', sexuality, special needs and social class are important, as are individual biographies.

1944 to the early 1970s: the myth of meritocracy?

Under the influence of wartime radicalism, the passing of the Education Act 1944 provided free secondary education for all. But this did not mean 'that all children now received what had before the Act been described as secondary education' (Thom 1987: 131). The Labour Governments of 1945–51 ratified selection procedures on the lines of 'age, ability and aptitude', as recommended in the Norwood Report and the White Paper, *Educational Reconstruction* (both published in 1943). Ellen Wilkinson and George Tomlinson, her successor as Minister for Education, were both committed to the idea of three types of school which were intended to cater for three different 'types' of child. In their view, the process of selection, resting upon children's performance in the 11+ examination, provided the basis for opening up educational opportunities to the working classes. Discussion on equality did not deal with gender, however. State policy endorsed the view that women are different from men, not only biologically but also intellectually, psychologically and socially. Thus, for example, while Norwood interspersed the word 'child' with 'boy', criteria particular to girls' schooling featured in a lengthy chapter on domestic subjects. Idealised notions of 'the nation' and family culture were used as a rationale for welfare state development in the post-Second World War period, sustaining the belief of a woman's place as in the home (Deem 1981).

While many in power saw the domestic role of women as crucial for the construction and rehabilitation of social harmony and cohesiveness, the development of employment policies during the post-war labour shortage increasingly made other roles possible. Rhetoric and reality had not always cohered as the removal of the marriage bar in 1945 and the introduction of Government recruitment programmes aimed specifically at attracting experienced women workers into a number of occupations, including domestic service, nursing, teaching and textiles, show. At the same time, large numbers of women workers who had done men's jobs during the war were made redundant and working mothers had to return to the home due to the reduction in state day nursery provision. Many others responded to the influential writings of John Bowlby on the dangers of 'maternal deprivation' for normal child development (Riley 1983). This was consistent with the notion of companionate marriage popularised in the 1940s and after. Men were still intended to be the main breadwinners and women the main carers, using their equal-but-different talents to promote the common good of family members. When mediated by Government policies, the invoking of official ideologies about maternity and motherhood was never benign for women for it structured much of the thinking that went into the development of policies, sustaining the belief of a woman's place as in the home. Part-time employment for married women was one way to reinforce gender divisions in paid work and the need to accommodate men who had served in the military services was applied to limit the entry of girls into higher education. In 1946, for instance, the Minister of Labour, George Isaacs, persuaded the vice-chancellors of British universities not to admit female school-leavers 'except where they are of exceptional promise' (cited in Briar 1997: 97). This was an example of overt discrimination. Other gendered inequalities were more covert and largely overlooked during this period.

Throughout the 1940s and 1950s girls had to do much better than boys to obtain a place at a selective grammar school (Thom 1987). At the time, policy and theory around educational practice suggested that boys mature later than girls and it would be unfair to exclude them from grammar schools on the basis of test results at the age of 11 (Epstein *et al.* 1998). Because the achievement of girls was seen as a problem for boys, local authorities either adjusted boys' scores upwards or added new tests to skew the results. Ironically, in many areas it was the girls who were disadvantaged as the single sex grammar schools had more places for boys. In another bequest from the past, conjectures about male potential were reinforced by the messages contained in the discourse of overstrain and the figure of the 'healthily' unconcerned boy. Cohen (1998) points out that in nineteenth-century English culture the elite male was supposedly distinguished by his 'natural' mental superiority. Such a view of scholarly achievement means that hard work is a sign of *lack* of ability and this 'contributed to producing the underperformance of boys as an index of their mental health' (Cohen 1998: 27). In contrast, too much intellectual work was construed as detrimental for typically 'diligent' and 'industrious' girls who were seen as susceptible to overstrain. Medical practitioners warned school girls of the risks and as late as the 1930s it was claimed that a girl who worked hard might get brain fever (Rendel 1997). So, when it came to male–female 11+ result patterns, common sense and social observation suggested the difference 'is not real because it does not last, it is not a phenomenon produced by the test, it is a phenomenon produced by "Nature" ' (Thom 1987: 141). Adjustments to ensure that boys were not disadvantaged continued into the 1970s and beyond, with many local authorities still using the test results not as a qualification for entry to grammar school but as a selective filter to fill the places available (Miller 1996).

It is against this background that we need to make visible the role schools play in the process of gender identity construction, offering interpretations of what it means to be 'male' or 'female'. Messages about gender values may be revealed in various ways, across a diversity of areas, including the formal and hidden curriculum, the ethos of the school and the educational objectives defined as important. It is very obvious, however, when the purposes and content of education are discussed.

In a book entitled *The Education of Girls*, published in 1948, John Newsom, then Chief Education Officer for Hertfordshire, attacked the academic grammar schools for ignoring domestic skills and placing too much emphasis on public examinations and obtaining professional careers. Yet even here the cult of motherhood and domesticity was still prevalent. When the girls' grammar school attended by Mary Evans debated the issue that 'A Woman's Place Is in the Home', she remembered:

> The school decided this was certainly the case. Women should be at home, waiting for us to come home and ready to ferry us about to dancing class or whatever else. If women did not do this, and accept this way of life, then their only alternative fate was to be an unmarried schoolmistress. In the late 1950s this career did not look attractive and the dichotomy between employed woman and wife and mother remained absolute.
>
> (Evans 1995: 64)

Newsom insisted that it was wholly inappropriate for 99 per cent of girls to share either the curriculum or the ethos of boys' schools because 'The fundamental common experience is the fact that the vast majority of them will become the makers of homes' (1948: 110). The overwhelming significance of this has been graphically described by many. In the modern schools catering for about 70 to 75 per cent of secondary pupils, housecraft and mothercraft were championed as an integral part of the curriculum for the 'less able', predominantly working-class girls (McCulloch 1998: 120–6). But there were some who deplored this view. In *Marriage Past and Present*, published in 1938, Margaret Cole, politician, historian, journalist and author, foresaw the ever-increasing numbers of women engaging in paid work (even after marriage). She tried to challenge the assumption that domestic subjects were especially suited for less academic girls, wanting them to become status subjects and win parity with subjects like geometry. She saw no contradiction in the dual aim of preparing girls for both home and work, but ultimately it was the perceived incompatibility between the two that was visited upon the schools (Hunt 1987).

Educationally the result was a school curriculum sharply divided into 'masculine' and 'feminine' areas contributing to differentiation of treatment and opportunity. For the young female population leaving school at 15, the Ministry of Education continued to point to that special curriculum for girls, organised around familial concerns. Hence the Crowther Report, *15 to 18*, produced by the Central Advisory Committee for Education in 1959, repeated the common refrain that in the modern schools: 'The prospect of courtship and marriage should rightly influence the education of the adolescent girl … her direct interests in dress and personal appearance and the problems of human relations should be given a central part in her education' (quoted in Riley 1994: 37). The 1959 Report on Early Leaving indicated that grammar school girls were much more likely to leave school before taking national exams (Deem 1981). Jackson and Marsden's (1962) in-depth study of 88 working-class children in Huddersfield who passed for grammar school and stayed on into the sixth form, showed that working-class girls were even less likely than working-class boys to go from grammar school to university, especially a prestigious one. Cultural attitudes and material provision all worked towards encouraging girls to train as teachers which cost £255, compared to £660 a year for undergraduates – mainly white, middle-class men. That being the case, teaching was the favoured career goal of many female grammar school pupils and nearly half of the girls Jackson and Marsden researched went to colleges of education: by 1958 there were 100 teacher training colleges for women, 18 for men and 18 co-educational institutions (Heward 1993: 23–4). Ultimately, when universal student grants became available in the early 1960s 'women represented on average 25 per cent of the university population in Britain: in Oxford they were 15 per cent and only 10 per cent in Cambridge' (figures from the Robbins Report quoted in Dyhouse 2003: 173). Gendered attitudes also meant that relatively little use was made of women's skills and qualifications, despite economic concerns about a shortage of skilled workers. Consequently, women graduates were much more likely to have to accept non-graduate employment than male graduates and 'the proportion of women workers in jobs classed as skilled continued to decline in this period, having fallen from 15.5 per cent in 1951 to 13.9 per cent in 1961' (Mackie and Patullo 1977: 99).

By the 1960s a radical restructuring of English state education opened up new possibilities for change. In 1964, when the Labour Party was returned to office, it took the opportunity to promote a national policy of comprehensive education in place of the class-divided grammar/secondary modern system. It did so by means of a circular, 10/65, requesting local authorities to choose a development scheme and start the planning process. While admitting that gendered equality was not much discussed in this wider campaign, the gradual implementation of comprehensive schooling increased the number of children educated in mixed-sex state secondary schools. This meant a changing balance of power among women and men staff in senior and managerial positions. However, the accepted norm was that co-education was preferable to single-sex education both on academic and social grounds (Deem 1984). Simply put, it was hoped that the presence of female pupils would provide incentive and emulation for boys to work harder. As Arnot (1984: 50) noted, 'never it would seem has the argument been reversed.'

In theory, Deem (1981) maintains the expansion of the secondary school curriculum should have been 'helpful' to girls. Overall, the removal of barriers to female success in the 11+ examinations inevitably benefited some, predominantly middle-class girls, but in general terms that advantage did not extend to all girls. Continuity from earlier tripartite patterns of provision was especially striking in relation to gendered curriculum assumptions. In practice, Benn and Simon (1972) found that very few schools offered a common curriculum to all their pupils in the early days of the comprehensive reform. Home economics, metalwork, needlework and woodwork were still explicitly, or by default, separate subjects for girls and boys and the 1975 report on curricular differentiation noted a resilient pattern of students making stereotyped subject choices. Selection and streaming on the basis of academic ability echoed the former grammar/secondary modern divide and a tendency for girls to be channelled into arts subjects exacerbated differences in life outcomes. For the first time since the Second World War there were uncertainties in the jobs market which had major implications for the school–work transition. Young people were particularly affected by the decline of vocational apprenticeships and industrial jobs with release for college training, cutbacks in teacher training and fierce competition for university places in arts courses. In this context, oppositional gender constructions continued to impact on lives, despite the feminist challenge and the increasing numbers of women participating in paid work.

1975 to the mid-1990s – equal opportunities?

At a policy level the Sex Discrimination Act of 1975 made direct and indirect discrimination on the grounds of sex and marital status illegal in a number of spheres of public life, including education. Demands for reform of the law were first expressed formally in 1967 by two women MPs, the Conservative Joan Vickers and Labour Lena Jeger. Unsuccessful on this occasion, pressure gradually produced results. When Labour regained power in 1974 the support of the elected Minister, Roy Jenkins, helped to overcome the opposition of some Home Office officials, although the then Department of Education and Science was unenthusiastic (Rendel 1997). In the field of education the legislation applied only to maintained and not to independent schools. It covered admissions, curricular and non-curricular facilities, and extra-curricular activities, rules regarding pupils' dress and appearance, school discipline, standards of discipline and careers guidance, and set up the Equal Opportunities Commission (EOC).

In the sociology of education literature a wide range of feminist perspectives began to highlight the gendered nature of schooling. There was criticism of gender differentiation across a variety of areas as studies began to show the ways in which patriarchal relations are deployed and used in schools. Teaching styles were challenged to avoid a tendency to encourage competition between the sexes in sports, academic learning and examinations. Attention also turned to management hierarchies within schools. Most were dominated by male teachers and the proportion of women holding senior posts in secondary schools was highest in such female 'spaces' as home economics and girls' games. Further, although the 'female' atmosphere of primary schooling was seen to undermine the performance of boys, it seems that even here sexual divisions were constantly reinforced. For instance, Clarricoates (1980) found that many primary school teachers readily clustered behaviour and attitudes into two categories, one for boys and another for girls, drawing on exaggerated notions of masculinity and femininity. Such findings were backed up by research undertaken by Stanworth (1986) and Riddell (1989) in a mixed further education college and two rural comprehensive schools in the south-west of England respectively. In both studies teachers' typifications of male and female pupils were found to accommodate traditional gender codes as did pupil resistance to schooling. In one maths lesson observed by Riddell, for example, a girl produced a large make-up kit, 'spread out the cosmetics on the desk top as if it were a dressing table' and proceeded to apply the make-up. 'Amazingly, the male teacher completely ignored what was going on' (1989: 193). Writing about her single-sex grammar school, Irene Payne (1980: 15) has similarly shown how some girls used a feminine preoccupation with appearance in order to position themselves 'in opposition to the "masculinity" of school rules about appearance. I can remember bouffant hairstyles, fish-net stockings, make-up and "sticky-out" underskirts being the hallmarks of rebellious girls.'

Feminist studies of mixed comprehensive schools undertaken in the 1980s were particularly concerned with ways in which girls were steered away from traditionally 'masculine' subjects. Hence, Griffin (1985: 78–9) found that girls who pursued such subjects 'were either presumed to be interested solely in flirting with the boys or discounted as unique exceptions'. Riley (1994: 60) illustrated how gender differences can be perpetuated by teachers with particular reference to subjects traditionally perceived as male. Hence the male head of design and technology tried to ensure the limited places in technical drawing were filled by boys. Finally, Riddell (1989) found some teachers drew on a laddish construction of masculinity to appeal to certain pupils with history lessons dedicated to gory details of trench warfare during the First World War and English lessons privileging texts with male characters and often dealing with the problems of the male adolescent. One teacher, Mr Stanhope, explained Queen Mary's (1516–58) persecution of Protestants in terms of her 'unfulfilled life' since she had to sacrifice her social role as wife and mother 'for political reasons' (Riddell 1989: 196). The girls were asked to imagine her situation: 'You may have a career and you may want to return to it afterwards, but still at the heart of your lives will be getting married and having children. It's the most natural thing in the world' (*ibid.*).

Alongside all this, feminist educators worked hard to introduce classroom practice with which to challenge patterns of gender-segregated achievement. In Manchester, one of the best-known projects of this kind was initiated to encourage female interest in the sciences. Working within the action research framework, the Girls into Science and Technology Project (GIST, 1980–4) 'worked directly with teachers, attempting to reduce gender-stereotyping on the part of pupils and teachers, and promoting "gender-fair" interaction in classrooms' (Weiner 1994: 86). Other groups such as Girls into Mathematics (GAMMA) extended the focus on contact and communication networks both for support and for knowledge dissemination, producing films, exhibitions, teaching and in-service packs to encourage innovation and reform. Discussion of strategies to challenge gender inequalities in education demands attention to the meaning of equality explored by Hughes (2002) who asks, does equality mean 'the same' and if so, what measures of sameness should be used? Do you argue for women's rights on equal terms with men or should feminists be arguing that women's difference is at the root of their equality? The implications are evident in debate over the introduction of national curricula in England and Wales, following the 1988 Education Reform Act (broadly the same, but with the Welsh language incorporated in the Welsh schemes).

Feminist educators supported the notion of a common curriculum experience, albeit one that encompassed the hidden curriculum of schooling and *not* one posited on a male paradigm. Based on a far more sophisticated reading of the political, social and cultural climate, this position is very different from equal opportunities approaches that fail to address power differences embedded within the teaching and learning of school subjects. The National Curriculum logic is that all students are entitled to develop the same learning skills and experience the same areas of knowledge. Initially mathematics, science and English were defined as core up to 16 years, together with seven foundation subjects – art, geography, history, music, physical education, technology and a modern foreign language (after age 11). Since 1988, however, the compulsory elements have been reduced and more choice has been reintroduced at 14 plus. Yet feminist research has verified the ways in which the assumed knowledge base of the new curriculum structures embody gendered understandings, besides a need to consider the modes of curriculum delivery that shape the teaching and learning of school subjects (Paechter 1998). As Raphael Reed (1998: 62) suggests, one consequence of increasing demands to make the curriculum more relevant in content to boys' interests (e.g. greater use of computers and interactive learning, using football scores to teach mathematics) is a 'further masculinization of teaching styles and classroom environments'. Stereotypically male subjects are being privileged over other ideas or sets of knowledges and old differential subject choice patterns have re-emerged with the trend towards increased flexibility at Key Stage 4 and the disapplication of the National Curriculum.

Nonetheless, contemporary schoolgirls have greater access to education and training and increasing educational success generally. Analysing school statistics for the years 1985 to 1994, Arnot *et al.* (1996) found that more girls were entered for school-leaving examinations, more girls than boys were gaining five GCSEs grades A*–C, but girls in single-sex schools seemed to be at a substantial advantage. However, boys continued to achieve higher performances in relation to their entry than girls in nearly all subjects. It is also the case that interactions based on class and/or ethnicity remain crucial for both sexes. Within the GCSE results, for example, groups such as middle-class white boys and Indian and Chinese boys continue to achieve highly whereas white working-class, African-Caribbean and Bangladeshi boys tend to underachieve in the British education system (Gillborn and Gipps 1996).

Contexts, changes and continuities – underachieving boys?

We turn now to a necessarily brief consideration of current policy debates to contextualise the discussion of changes and continuities in gender and achievement in the new millennium. The instigation of a quasi-market in education by the Conservative government of the 1980s cast pupils and students as educational clients, within a framework of parental involvement and parental power. Examination and assessment performance league tables and a more stringent school inspection process (set up in 1992) all serve as mechanisms to 'measure' educational standards and performance, with an unprecedented emphasis on the phenomenon of the failing school. These new regimes have had a dramatic impact on schools, parents and pupils with a policy of local management of schools, open enrolment and a pupil-led funding formula crucial to the strategic processes of school choice. Ball and Gewirtz (1997: 214) point to the accretive value of 'successful' girls in their study of the marketing, selection and recruitment strategies in 14 case study schools. Not only do they become 'a valuable and sought after resource' but 'their presence in school normally conveys positive impressions to parents about ethos and discipline.' This should not surprise us, for it rests firmly on popular conjecture about the civilising influence of girls. It now becomes necessary to review aspects of contemporary debates about gender achievement.

Girls' improved educational performance has produced a furore of concern over threats to male breadwinning, the association of men and crime, the collapse of family life and the crisis of fatherhood. Yet Gorard *et al.* (1999: 442) demonstrate that a tendency to confuse percentage points with percentages has led to a misrepresentation of the GCSE results. Their analysis of the figures for all pupils at school in Wales from 1992 to 1997 shows girls doing better at Key Stages 1 to 4 in English and Welsh, at Key Stage 4 in languages, some design subjects and humanities, no achievement gaps in mathematics and science, with gaps at other levels either static or declining. On the basis of these research findings the researchers speculate that the educational phenomenon of the 'growing gender gap' does not actually exist. Acknowledging that the picture is far from simple, the problem needs to be well understood given the implications for participants and policy-makers. A number of points will be made.

Literacy has been at the centre of debates about gender and achievement, especially in the primary schools, but it is important not to forget that girls have traditionally excelled at language-based subjects. The opening statement of the 1993 Ofsted report, *Boys and English*, was unequivocal: 'Boys do not do as well as girls in English in schools.' On the other hand, classroom-based research suggests boys' greater show of interest in the new forms of technology (film, computer and CD-ROMs) may be a better preparation for changing world literacy than may often be the case for girls (Marsh 2003). Moreover the patterns of achievement change at the post-compulsory level since the few young men who enrol on A level courses in English literature are more likely to outperform their female counterparts. With regard to mathematics, data from the Leverhulme Numeracy Research Programme – a longitudinal study of teaching and learning in English primary schools between 1997 and 2002 – highlighted girls not doing as well as boys in mathematics overall (Lucey *et al.* 2003). At GCSE, the tendency to play safe with examination entries of girls in mathematics means more girls than boys achieve grade C from the Intermediate tier, but mathematics departments in schools only encourage continuation with a B or C grade gained from the Higher tier. It is salient that more boys got A* grades in GCSE mathematics, biology, chemistry and physics in August 2003 and more boys took the elite single science subjects of physics and chemistry than either biology or the balanced science associated with state schools (http://educationguardian.co.uk accessed 29 October 2003).

In terms of further qualifications, there has been a swift acceleration both in the proportion of 18-year-olds achieving A level over the last 20 years and the number of entries from females. But subject choice is still heavily influenced by gendered views of future adult work. Fewer young women opt for business studies, computing, economics, mathematics, physics and technology, whereas the reverse is true of biology, French, history, home economics, psychology and sociology. Yet it is the case that those who make non-traditional choices excel compared with their fellows, presumably as a result of their being exceedingly able. Vocational qualifications are even more gendered than their academic counterparts. While the overall numbers of young men and women entering the Modern Apprenticeships scheme (launched in 1994) are now almost equal, young men predominate in engineering manufacturing (96 per cent), motor industry (97 per cent), construction (99 per cent) and information technology (67 per cent). Young women predominate in hairdressing (92 per cent), health and social care (89 per cent), childcare (97 per cent) and travel service (86 per cent). In the words of the EOC, 'these vocational choices and channelling make an almost immediate impact on earning potential and are a contributing factor to the 20% pay gap which exists between men and women' (EOC 2001).

In a speech at the 11th International Conference for School Effectiveness and Improvement, then Schools Standards Minister Stephen Byers argued that 'the laddish anti-learning culture' was impeding boys' achievement (*Guardian*, 6 January 1998). As a result of these concerns each local authority was required to address the issue of male disadvantage in drawing up its Education Development Plan. But the preoccupation with masculinities is not new. Early sociological investigations into the educational experiences of adolescent boys in the secondary school document the ways in which boys construct their masculine identities in the classroom. Influenced by neo-Marxist ideology, Willis's (1983) study focused on a group of anti-school working-class 'lads' who rejected the legitimacy of schooling because it had no relevance for the type of unskilled manual jobs that they wanted/expected to get on leaving school. These male students linked their counter-school culture to that of the factory floor. In so doing they asserted definitions of masculinity that positioned mental work and having girls as friends as effeminate. Similarly, in *Schooling the Smash Street Kids*, Corrigan (1979) used the analogy of a 'guerrilla struggle' to represent the ability of white, working-class, heterosexual boys in the north-east of England to monopolise space in the classroom, despite the 'occupying army' of teachers. While these studies are useful in drawing attention to the articulation of social class as a variable in the construction of gender difference, they have been criticised by feminists for their neglect of gender-power dynamics and the variety of masculine forms that exist across a spectrum of difference (Skelton 2000).

More recent work on gender identity construction in education addresses these concerns. For instance, Connell (1995) outlines four versions of masculinity which he calls hegemonic, subordinate, complicit and marginalised. While these categories are helpful in that they enable us to take account of gender as a lived social practice as Francis (2000) notes, the flip side of this explanatory framework is the suggestion of a hierarchy of 'types'. This may imply something more fixed than it really is, besides the problems such categorisations pose for the very concepts of masculinity and femininity. So, Francis argues instead that 'there are different strategies of constructing oneself as masculine, or feminine, rather than different types of masculinity and femininity' (2000: 16). Boys/men negotiate and take up a variety of masculinities and some of these confer power and prestige, while others are stigmatised and subordinate.

Significantly, dominant constructions of masculinity have implications for the broader topic of special educational needs (SEN). This is particularly clear among young boys positioned as slow learners, poor at sport, and lacking physical strength and skill, who may resort to overtly challenging behaviour which may, in turn, make them liable to being classified as having special needs. Benjamin (2003) also highlights the need to take other underlying social inequalities into account. So, for example, African-Caribbean children of both sexes are more vulnerable to exclusion from school than their white peers (Osler and Vincent 2003); working-class boys are found in greater numbers in 'less acceptable' categories of emotional and behavioural difficulties and moderate learning difficulties; and middle-class boys dominate the non-stigmatised category of specific learning difficulties.

At the other end of the spectrum, figures for the degree finals in 2001 show that more men than women gained firsts in percentage terms, but as 54 per cent of those taking finals were women, a greater number of women got top marks (*Guardian*, 16 January 2001; 13 April 2002). However, if you take the figures for firsts and upper seconds together they show that more women achieved one of the two top classes, 59.9 per cent compared with 51.8 per cent of men. So, how can we make sense of this educational success story? As Mahony (1998: 39) points out, in the 1970s and 1980s perceptions of the differential abilities of boys and girls triggered a very different reaction to concerns about schoolgirl attainment in maths and science. Consequently, 'it took a good deal of persuasion by (mainly) feminists before policy-makers would look beyond the innate capacities of girls themselves for explanations.' In contrast, the perception of boys as innately clever continues. Conversely, so does a tendency to imply that girls' academic attainment is the result of compliant hard work: even though there was no corresponding decline in female performance after the reduction of coursework in GCSEs in the mid-1990s (Arnot *et al.* 1999). Moreover, deep connections between knowledge and power mean girls' good performance in a particular subject may affect its status and perceived difficulty, as well as its place in contemporary society. Despite media reports of betrayal and the idea that schools have neglected boys' learning needs (*Independent*, 27 November 2003), men are still over-represented both in top jobs and in the most powerful positions in society. Also, it is deeply ironical that evidence once used to help explain the underachievement of girls, like the issue of boys' laddish attitudes, is being used across time to signify different conclusions. Female school performance *has* improved but there is plenty of evidence to support the argument that this is *despite* the continuing male dominance in the classroom, the playground, curriculum content and greater demands on teacher time and energy (Francis 2000).

Conclusion

To come full circle and return to the quote with which we started, it remains the case that gender constructions have consequences in the workplace and in society. Despite any early learning disadvantage, top jobs continue to go to men. Female graduates can expect to earn 15 per cent less than their male equivalents by the age of 24 and it is mostly men on very high salaries who comprise the new elite in the financial and multinational sectors. The counterpoint to this is that professions like law and medicine are losing much of their traditional power and status just at the time when large numbers of women are coming into them (Walkerdine *et al.* 2001).

In many ways, media talk of 'troubled masculinities' is masking another story. In this story, the script is one of rising assessment performance of boys *and* girls over the past 50 years, making the phenomenon one of relative rates of improvement for both sexes. But this is absent from the dominant discourses that Epstein *et al.* (1998) see played out in the public debates about boys and achievement. And more worryingly, the 'poor boys' discourse, the 'failing schools failing boys' discourse and the 'boys will be boys' discourse have all achieved a common-sense status within which female success is socially constructed as pathology. Contemporary schoolgirls may have greater career ambition, they may show an awareness of the gender-discriminatory nature of the adult workplace, plus inequality of housework and childcare, all of which may have provided new motivation for educational achievement as Francis (2000) suggests, but where will the exam results get them? Will this new generation of girls have the power to change conditions and which girls are we talking about? Working-class girls with few or no qualifications are hardly ever mentioned. Middle-class girls may go on to resolve the contradiction of 'career' and 'motherhood' by employing other women. As the authors of *Growing Up Girl* conclude: 'the much hyped girl power and female future looks decidedly unsteady and, for most, extremely difficult' (Walkerdine *et al.* 2001: 216).

Suggested further reading

Lessons for Life: The Schooling of Girls and Women 1850–1950 edited by Felicity Hunt (1987) provides an enjoyable and accessible introduction to the history of the education and socialisation of women. *Growing Up Girl* (2001) by Valerie Walkerdine, Helen Lucey and June Melody provides a fascinating exploration of the interrelations of gender and class since the 1980s. For an example of recent work that sees gender as relational, read *Boys, Girls and Achievement* (2000) by Becky Francis.

References

Arnot, M. (1984) 'How shall we educate our sons?' in R. Deem (ed.) *Co-education Reconsidered*. Milton Keynes: Open University Press.

Arnot, M., David, M. and Weiner, G. (1996) *Educational Reforms and Gender Equality*. Manchester: Equal Opportunities Commission.

Arnot, M., David, M. and Weiner, G. (1999) *Closing the Gender Gap: postwar education and social change*. Cambridge: Polity Press.

Ball, S. J. and Gewirtz, S. (1997) 'Girls in the Education Market: choice, competition and complexity', *Gender and Education*, 9 (2), 207–22.

Benjamin, S. (2003) 'Gender and special educational needs' in C. Skelton and B. Francis (eds) *Boys and Girls in the Primary Classroom*. Maidenhead: Open University Press.

Benn, C. and Simon, B. (1972) *Half Way There: Report on the British Comprehensive-School Reform*. Harmondsworth: Penguin.

Board of Education (1943) *Educational Reconstruction*. Cmd. 6458. London: Board of Education.

Board of Education (1943) *Curriculum and Examination in Secondary Schools (The Norwood Report)* London: Board of Education.

Briar, C. (1997) *Working for Women? Gendered Work and Welfare Policies in Twentieth-century Britain*. London: UCL Press.

Clarricoates, K. (1980) 'The importance of being Ernest ... Emma ... Tom ... Jane. The perception and categorization of gender conformity and gender deviation in primary schools', in R. Deem (ed.) *Schooling for Women's Work*. London: Routledge and Kegan Paul.

Cohen M. (1998) 'A habit of healthy idleness: boys' underachievement, schooling and gender relations', in D. Epstein, J. Elwood, V. Hey and J. Maw (eds) *Failing Boys? Issues in Gender and Achievement*. Buckingham: Open University Press.

Cole, M. (1938) *Marriage Past and Present*. London: J. M. Dent and Sons.

Connell, R. W. (1995) *Masculinities*. Cambridge: Polity Press.

Corrigan, P. (1979) *Schooling the Smash Street Kids*. London: Macmillan.

Deem, R. (1981) 'State Policy and Ideology in the Education of Women, 1944–1980', *British Journal of Sociology of Education*, 2 (2), 131–43.

Deem, R. (1984) *Co-education reconsidered*. Milton Keynes: Open University Press.

Dyhouse, C. (2003) 'Troubled Identities: gender and status in the history of the mixed college in English universities since 1945', *Women's History Review*, 12 (2), 169–93.

Epstein, D., Elwood, J., Hey, V. and Maw, J. (eds) (1998) *Failing Boys? Issues in Gender and Achievement*. Buckingham: Open University Press.

Equal Opportunities Commission (EOC) (2001) *Gender Issues in Modern Apprenticeships*. Manchester: Equal Opportunities Commission.

Evans, M. (1995) 'Culture and Class', in M. Blair and J. Holland, with S. Sheldon (eds) *Identity and Diversity: Gender and the Experience of Education*. Clevedon: Multilingual Matters.

15–18 (The Crowther Report) (1959) Report by the Central Advisory Council for Education (England). London: HMSO.

Francis, B. (2000) *Boys, Girls and Achievement*. London: Routledge-Falmer.

Gillborn, D. and Gipps, C. (1996) *Recent Research on the Achievements of Ethnic Minority Pupils*. London: Ofsted.

Gorard, S., Rees, G. and Salisbury, J. (1999) 'Reappraising the apparent under-achievement of boys at school', *Gender and Education*, 11 (4), 441–54.

Griffin, C. (1985) *Typical Girls? Young Women from School to the Job Market*. London: Routledge and Kegan Paul.

Heward, C. (1993) 'Men and women and the rise of professional society: the intriguing history of teacher education', *History of Education*, 22 (1), 11–32.

Hughes, C. (2002) *Key Concepts in Feminist Theory and Research*. London: Sage.

Hunt, F. (ed.) (1987) *Lessons for Life: The Schooling of Girls and Women 1850–1950*. Oxford: Basil Blackwell.

Jackson, B. and Marsden, D. (1962) *Education and the Working-class*. London: Routledge and Kegan Paul.

Lucey, H., Brown, M., Denvir, H., Askew, M. and Rhodes, V. (2003) 'Girls and boys in the primary maths classroom', in C. Skelton and B. Francis (eds) *Boys and Girls in the Primary Classroom*. Maidenhead: Open University Press.

Mackie, L. and Patullo, P. (1977) *Women Who Work*. London: Tavistock.

Mahony, P. (1998) 'Girls will be girls and boys will be first', in D. Epstein, J. Elwood, V. Hey and J. Maw (eds) *Failing Boys? Issues in Gender and Achievement*. Buckingham: Open University Press.

Marsh, J. (2003) 'Superhero stories', in C. Skelton and B. Francis (eds) *Boys and Girls in the Primary Classroom*. Maidenhead: Open University Press.

McCulloch, G. (1998) *Failing the Ordinary Child? The theory and practice of working-class secondary education*. Milton Keynes: Open University Press.

Miller, J. (1996) *School for Women*. London: Virago.

Newsom, J. (1948) *The Education of Girls*. London: Faber and Faber.

Ofsted (1993) *Boys and English*. London: HMSO.

Osler, A. and Vincent, K. (2003) *Girls and Exclusion: rethinking the agenda*. London: RoutledgeFalmer.

Paechter, C. (1998) *Educating the Other: Gender, Power and Schooling*. London: Falmer Press.

Payne, I. (1980) 'Sexist ideology and education', in D. Spender and E. Sarah (eds) *Learning to Lose*. London: The Women's Press.

Raphael Reed, L. (1998) ' "Zero tolerance": gender performance and school failure', in D. Epstein *et al.* (eds) *Failing Boys? Issues in Gender and Achievement*. Buckingham: Open University Press.

Rendel, M. (1997) *Whose Human Rights?* Stoke-on-Trent: Trentham.

Riddell, S. (1989) 'Pupils, resistance and gender codes: a study of classroom encounters', *Gender and Education*, 1 (2), 183–98.

Riley, D. (1983) *War in the Nursery: theories of the Child and Mother*. London: Virago.

Riley, K. A. (1994) *Quality and Equality: Promoting Opportunities in Schools*. London: Cassell.

Skelton, C. (2000) *Schooling the Boys*. Buckingham: Open University Press.

Spender, D. (1980) 'Education or Indoctrination?', in D. Spender and E. Sarah (eds) *Learning to Lose*. London: The Women's Press.

Stanworth, M. (1986) *Gender and Schooling: A Study of Sexual Divisions in the Classroom*. London: Hutchinson.

Thom, D. (1987) 'Better a Teacher Than a Hairdresser? "A Mad Passion for Equality" or, Keeping Molly and Betty Down', in F. Hunt (ed.) *Lessons for Life: The Schooling of Girls and Women 1850–1950*. Oxford: Basil Blackwell.

Walkerdine, V., Lucey, H. and Melody, J. (2001) *Growing Up Girl: psychosocial explorations of gender and class*. Basingstoke: Palgrave.

Weiner, G. (1994) *Feminisms in Education*. Buckingham: Open University Press.

Willis, P. (1983) *Learning to Labour: How Working-class Kids Get Working-class Jobs*. Aldershot: Gower.

Social class and school

Richard Hatcher

The social class you are born into exerts as powerful an influence now as it did 50 years ago. It is the best predictor of who will gain high qualifications and the most prestigious jobs.

(*Changing Britain, Changing Lives*, Ferri *et al.* 2003)

THE RELATIONSHIP BETWEEN social class and school has long been, and still is, one of the central debates in the study of education. It is not just a matter of academic debate. In large part the history of education, at least for the past century and a half, can be written in terms of the movement to achieve equality for the working class or in terms of the educational benefits enjoyed by the middle class. For most of this period the main aim was equality of access, first to free elementary schooling, then to secondary school and thus to university education. The introduction of comprehensive education in the 1960s, largely replacing the previous selective system, seemed to be a turning point, but although the comprehensive school enabled a much larger number of children from working-class backgrounds to achieve qualifications that had previously been the prerogative of the middle class, substantial social class inequalities in school attainment remained. The state school system continued, and still continues today, to serve the interests of the middle class much better than it does those of the majority of children from working-class backgrounds. (Meanwhile, of course, the privileged position of most children of the upper class continues to be safeguarded by the elite private schools.)

The real but limited success of the comprehensive reform raised a number of new questions which went far beyond issues of structure and access. How can we understand the relationship between social class, home and school? Why do working-class children tend to do less well than middle-class children, even in the same school? Is the school an instrument of working-class opportunity, increasing social mobility and perhaps even reducing inequality in society, or is it an institution that tends to reproduce patterns of social inequality? If providing equality of access is not enough, what other reforms are needed in order to tackle educational inequality? Class seemed to affect every aspect of the school: what it taught, how it taught it, how it organised its teaching groups, the language that teachers and pupils used, the relationship between school and home. Meanwhile, parallel questions were being raised around issues of racial and gender equality in school, cross-fertilising those around class.

In the late 1980s the issue of class inequality, like that of gender and 'race', was subsumed into the discourse and policies of a general raising of standards. Under the Conservatives, one key element was the creation of market competition among schools, and the main battleground on which the debate around class equality took place became the extent to which the quasi-market in education was a mechanism of class differentiation. Under the current Labour Government we have seen the continuation of the agenda of raising standards and 'school improvement', combined with the quasi-market, but with the addition of a number of initiatives aimed specifically at raising achievement among lower-achieving and socially disadvantaged pupils and schools.

In this chapter I will examine the implications of Labour's education policies in terms of social class. But first I need to set the scene in terms of the extent of social class inequality in Britain today.

Social class and economic inequality

There are different conceptions of social class. In 'official' discourse 'class' has often been replaced by terms such as 'socio-economic status' or 'social advantage and disadvantage'. The criteria of social classes are generally either income and wealth or occupation. In school education the most common criterion is eligibility for free school meals (FSM). My aim here is to examine the distribution of income and wealth in Britain today and then relate it to educational attainment.

Economic inequality is very substantial in Britain and it is increasing. The latest figures from the Inland Revenue on the distribution of marketable wealth (which includes rent and dividends) show that the richest 1 per cent of the population had 20 per cent of the nation's wealth in 1996 and 23 per cent in 2001. The poorest half of the population had 7 per cent in 1996 and 5 per cent in 2001, after the first four years of the Labour Government (Foot 2003). Of particular relevance to school is the extent of child poverty. One in three children are in families that fall below the poverty line, but according to the Ethnic Minority Foundation the figure is significantly higher for Pakistani and Bangladeshi children (nearly 70 per cent), black Caribbean children (41 per cent) and Indian children (36 per cent) (Sarda 2003).

A recent study published by the Joseph Rowntree Foundation shows that the Government could meet its target of reducing child poverty by one-quarter in 2004 (one million children), but it would need to substantially increase redistribution of wealth towards the poorest families if it is to meet its long-term target of halving child poverty by 2010 (Sutherland *et al.* 2003).

What prevents this redistribution is the market. There is a contradiction at the heart of Government policy between its attempts to reduce poverty by a range of anti-poverty measures and its commitment to the market, which functions to increase inequality. The national minimum wage has made little impact on inequality because of high pay rises at the top. Pensions and benefits have risen much less than top income, which remains low taxed. Inequality is greater now, in Labour's second term of office, than it was under Margaret Thatcher. The Gini coefficient, a measure of inequality, has increased from an average of 29 points under Thatcher to 35 points in 2001–2 under Blair (Waugh 2003).

Class inequality in education

These massive differences in the economic status of families have massive consequences for the education of their children. There is a strong correlation between the social class of families, defined in terms of socio-economic status, and their children's attainment at school (West and Pennell 2003). According to the *Education and Child Poverty* report, published in March 2003 by the End Child Poverty group, the attainment gap between poor and better-off children is evident at just under two years of age and widens during school, until at GCSE poorer children are one-third as likely to get five A*–C GCSEs (Smithers 2003).

After school the pattern continues, with young people from unskilled backgrounds being five times less likely to enter higher education than those from professional backgrounds (Smithers 2003). Universities themselves are increasingly class-divided, with the 'new universities' having a much higher proportion of working-class students than the elite universities.

The report *Changing Britain, Changing Lives* by Ferri, Bynner and Wadsworth, published in February 2003, compared cohorts of adults born in 1946 and 1970. In spite of overall improvements in income, health and housing, people without qualifications are more excluded from society and live in greater poverty than 50 years ago. Family income for those with degrees was almost twice as high as those with no qualifications in the cohort born in 1970. For the 1946 cohort the gap was 30 per cent. In short, according to the study:

> The social class you are born into exerts as powerful an influence now as it did 50 years ago. It is the best predictor of who will gain high qualifications and the most prestigious jobs.
>
> (Quoted in Sanders 2003)

How does poverty affect school attainment?

Up to now I have spoken of the effect of social class background on whole sections of the school population. Beneath the generalisations are the lives of individual children and young people, and of course at the individual level not all pupils from poorer backgrounds achieve less well at school and not all pupils from well-off backgrounds do better. So although social class is a powerful overall determinant, it works through a complex of mediating processes which generate differences at the individual level. Some of these mediations are material factors. Lack of money may mean less private space in the home to study, fewer books, less access to a computer, less time because of the demands of looking after siblings or having a part-time job, less chance of holidays abroad or no chance of private tutoring to boost exam grades.

Class is also mediated by cultural factors. They revolve around the meaning of knowledge in the lives of families. More specifically, they concern the meaning of academic knowledge, the sort of knowledge that is valued in school, as against the everyday knowledge that comes from the working-class workplace, the community or the street in class cultures. Researchers have shown how children and young people from different class cultures tend to have different relationships to knowledge. (I have discussed this in Hatcher 2000.) By 'school knowledge' I mean two things. One is its intrinsic meaning: the extent to which it engages the pupil's interest and becomes internalised in the pupil's mental structures and integral to how the child understands the world. The other is its extrinsic meaning: the extent to which it is seen by the pupil as having instrumental value, in particular in terms of gaining qualifications which provide access to future career and education destinations after school. Middle-class homes are more likely to engender a positive relationship to the sorts of knowledge that are validated by school. They are more likely to provide the sort of cultural experiences, ranging from shared reading activities to music tuition and involvement in clubs and other activities outside the home, which have significant benefits in terms of success at school. Middle-class parents, almost by definition, have themselves succeeded in the education system and provide role models for their children of the causal link between school success and career.

One crucial area of knowledge and its meaning in relation to success at school concerns language, spoken and written. School success depends on the ability to understand and use 'academic' forms of language. The spoken language of the home may be linguistically similar in register to that of the school, facilitating learning, or linguistically distant, a barrier to learning. Reading and writing are the fundamental skills that determine subsequent school success. It is not simply mastery of the technical skills, it is also the meaning of reading and writing for the child. Homes where children have few books and seldom see their parents reading or writing tend to generate a different orientation to literacy, a different cultural predisposition, from ones where reading and writing, and in particular the sorts of texts that demand language skills similar to those required for school success, are everyday activities.

There is another form of knowledge that is also significant for school success and which also tends to be the prerogative of the middle class. I mean instrumental knowledge about how to succeed in the education system. For example, knowledge about how to choose a school; knowledge about how to negotiate with teachers, in order perhaps to secure a place for one's child in a higher set; knowledge about how to effectively support one's child's homework or assessed coursework; knowledge about curriculum choices and their likely subsequent benefits; knowledge about how to apply to university and choose an appropriate course. In short, the knowledge, communication skills and confidence that middle-class parents tend to have and use to maximise their positional advantage in education.

Empirical evidence for this argument is provided by an analysis of the 2001 PISA data by Nash (2003). PISA (the Programme for International Student Assessment) measures how well 15-year-olds perform in English, maths and science in 43 countries. There is a high correlation between family socio-economic situation (SES) and the number of books in the home, and between family SES and the child's reading attainment. Family SES and reading attainment both correlate closely with pupils' job aspirations. Nash argues that the evidence supports the claim that there are class differences in the development in the early years of 'effective cognitive skills'. He employs two concepts developed by the French sociologist Pierre Bourdieu – 'cultural capital' and 'habitus' – which have been found particularly useful in understanding these mediating processes between social classes in society and the individuals who comprise them. 'Cultural capital' refers to the forms of knowledge that are legitimised and validated by those holding power within particular social fields. In the context of the school, some forms of knowledge are recognised and valued; others are not. 'Habitus' refers to the 'systems of dispositions', the ways of thinking and feeling, conscious and unconscious, that are generated within particular social fields and which give rise to tendencies to act in particular ways. So, for example, the middle-class family provides a habitus which tends to develop in the child the sorts of ways of thinking, feeling and acting that are favourable to success in school.

What can schools do about class differences in attainment?

There are two opposite and equally mistaken common responses to the relatively low attainment of pupils from poorer working-class backgrounds at school:

to underestimate what schools can do to compensate or to overestimate what schools can do. In the first view, children's paths through school are socially pre-determined and teachers can do little to make a difference. This view takes two forms. One is a sort of sociological fatalism in which only fundamental changes in society can make any difference to the attainment of working-class pupils. The other is 'deficit theory' – the belief that poor working-class parents are to blame because they are incompetent and irresponsible.

In the second view, schools can overcome social factors and if they do not it is the school's fault. Again, this view takes two forms. One underlies the Government's 'school improvement' agenda:

> Poverty is no excuse for failure. We have many examples of teachers, pupils and schools who are succeeding against the odds in deprived rural and urban areas.
>
> (David Blunkett, Secretary of State for Education, in 1997, quoted in Gold 2003)

Nash calls this 'state-sponsored impossibilism' (Nash 2003: 79). Ironically, the con-clusion is shared by those critics who, in rejecting 'deficit theory', tend to idealise working-class cultures and place all the blame on the school for social inequalities in education.

The position I take is that working-class cultures are shaped by class society in ways that tend to create habituses that do not generate the cultural capital needed for school success. Schools alone cannot compensate, but they can potentially make some significant difference, even in a profoundly unequal society. Whether they do so depends upon the policies they pursue. The policies currently pursued are largely determined by the Government's education agenda for schools and I turn now to an examination of its implications for equality.

Labour education policy

It is possible to argue that although Labour's economic and social policies have done little to reduce inequality in the wider society, Labour's education policies are a powerful countervailing force. How true could this be?

David Miliband, the Schools Minister, said in January 2003 that 'The evidence is clear ... that schools serving similar types of pupils achieve dramatically different results' (quoted in Gold 2003). The Government claims that this shows that poverty cannot be an excuse for low performance. All these underperforming socially deprived schools have to do is to imitate high-performing socially deprived schools. But is it true that the Government is comparing like with like? The Government has refused all requests to make the data available for independ-ent analysis. It does not differentiate between schools with over 35 per cent free school meals and it will not give information on types of schools (e.g. single-sex) or social composition (e.g. ethnic composition). The *Times Educational Supplement* carried out its own survey, which showed that in schools with 50 per cent or more FSM attainment was lower than in those between 35 per cent and 50 per cent, showing the peer group effect (*Times Educational Supplement*, 7 March 2003). Most poor schools performed about the same. Of the high-performers, most had some special intake advantage, such as being all girls, selecting on religious grounds or having extra funding from specialist status. The same argument applies to many of the case studies of higher-attaining schools in socially disadvantaged areas in the 'school improvement' literature.

Government policies to tackle class in school

In the foreword by David Blunkett, at the time the Secretary of State for Education, to *Excellence in Schools* (DfEE 1997), the Labour Government's first major policy document on education after it was elected, he stated that one of the Government's principal objectives was 'to eliminate, and never excuse, underachievement in the most deprived parts of our country' (p. 3). The Government claims that its policies are successfully raising standards. But raising standards does not necessarily reduce inequality. Overall standards can rise, including those of lower-achieving pupils, while the class inequality gap widens, and this is what is happening. It is the difference between 'polarising improvement' and 'equalising improvement'. Ofsted research shows that since 1996, the year before Labour took office, the gap in attainment between rich and poor students has narrowed in primary schools but widened in secondary schools. The Chief Inspector for Schools, David Bell, recently reported that inner-city secondary schools are falling even further behind affluent schools in the suburbs (Slater 2003a).

The major Government policy that is aimed at tackling low educational achievement in socially deprived areas is *Excellence in Cities* (DfEE 1999). EiC was launched in 1999, now covers 58 local authorities and will be extended to one in three of all state secondary schools by 2004. It has seven main elements: learning mentors, learning support units, the 'Gifted and Talented' programme, city learning centres for IT, beacon and specialist schools, and action zones where clusters of schools work together.

How successful has EiC been? According to an Ofsted report on EiC published in June 2003, the percentage of young people achieving five or more A–Cs rose at the same rate as the national average in the four years from 1998 to 2001, and faster than the national average in 2002 (Shaw 2003). The results in Key Stage 3 maths and English tests have improved faster in EiC areas than nationally in the past four years. But the report notes that EiC is not the only reason for improvement. According to David Bell, the Chief Inspector for Schools:

There are rapid improvements in some schools but this is offset by disappointing progress, or even decline, of others. You've got to be realistic about what such schemes can achieve ... they can have a positive impact on pupil attainment ... But there is still a substantial gap in achievement [between] excellence in cities and education action zones and pupils across the country.

(quoted in Woodward 2003)

However, although the improvement in GCSE five A–Cs in EiC schools in 2002 was above the national average, the improvement in the average GCSE points score was below the national average. The explanation is that there is a process of polarisation among schools within EiC areas. A minority of schools are improving above the national average and another group of schools are improving but less than the national average or even not improving at all. So there is a widening gap between EiC secondary schools. An analysis of the figures from Birmingham, England's largest LEA, bears this out. In 2002 there were 13 mixed comprehensive schools where less than 25 per cent of pupils achieved five or more GCSEs at grades A*–C. Nine of the 13 schools did worse in 2002 than 2000. Of the seven mixed comprehensive schools scoring above 60 per cent at grades A*–C in 2002, five had improved since 2000.

How Labour education policies reinforce class inequalities

The consequences for social class in schools are not determined just, or even mainly, by Government policies aimed specifically at areas of social deprivation. EiC policies are just part of a much broader policy agenda for schools. There is evidence that the tendency of its modernisation programme is to reproduce rather than to ameliorate patterns of social inequality. In short, there is a contradiction at the heart of Labour education policy between its concern, reflecting its working-class electoral base, for reducing the effects of social disadvantage in education, exemplified by the Excellence in Cities programme (however effective it may or may not be), and the overall effects of its education policies, and in particular the way in which differentiation of provision acts as a mechanism of social class selection.

'Diversity and choice'

One of the main themes of Labour Government policy has been to attack the notion of the comprehensive school (itself only partly achieved within the English school system) and to encourage different types of state schools (Chitty and Simon 2001). Three reasons are offered. Children have different aptitudes and these require different types of schools; diversity provides greater scope for innovation in the system, leading to improved effectiveness; and choice of school is an extension of democracy, and the greater the diversity of schools the more meaningful choice becomes. Labour has exacerbated the existing historical divisions within the British school system. Spearheading the policy of differentiation is the creation of specialist schools – secondary schools which provide the National Curriculum but also specialise in a curriculum area. Specialist schools receive substantial extra funding. Critics argue that it is creating a two-tier school system. Government policy is that eventually all secondary schools should become specialist schools, though it seems unlikely that the additional funding will extend to all.

Parents are able to exercise some choice about which school to send their children to. The intended basis of choice is provided by the publication of regular national tests of pupils and inspection reports of schools. The combination of Government-sponsored diversity and an element of parental choice perpetuates patterns of social class inequality, favouring middle-class families because middle-class parents have the social capital to be able to 'play the system' more successfully (Gewirtz *et al.* 1995; Ball 2003).

The Government's claim that 'diversity and choice' are the best way both to raise standards and to reduce inequality contradicts recent evidence from the PISA study. The UK performs well overall but has one of the largest attainment gaps between rich and poor students in the developed world. The PISA report demonstrated that comprehensive school systems are more effective at reducing inequality. (See 'Literacy skills for the world of tomorrow – further results from Pisa 2000', published by the OECD and UNESCO, www.pisa.oecd.org.) It praises Finland, which performed best in the study, for its comprehensive system and for giving teachers a high degree of responsibility and autonomy. Andreas Schleicher, head of the OECD's educational indicators and analysis division, says there are no advantages to selection: 'The trade-off between quality and equity does not exist in reality.' This finding contradicts the policies of specialist schools, which disproportionately attract middle-class pupils, and of selection via parental choice, which undermines the social mix which is important in raising standards for all (Slater 2003b).

Ability grouping

Social class differentiation between schools is paralleled by differentiation within schools. The Labour Government has encouraged the grouping of pupils by 'ability' in secondary and even primary schools. The evidence for the consequences for social class equality is unclear, but some studies have suggested that ability grouping tends to reproduce patterns of social inequality. Hallam (2002), reviewing the research evidence, found that pupils in the lower ability groups tended to be taught a reduced curriculum and given repetitive work that offered no challenge or stimulation. They often became demoralised and disaffected and fell behind, further widening the equality gap.

14-plus curriculum

The separation of pupils from different social classes into different pathways through school which lead to different destinations after school is shown most clearly in the Government's proposal to end the National Curriculum at age 14, from when foreign languages and the humanities (including history and the arts) would be optional. A survey by the TES in 2002 (Ward 2002) found that it is mainly schools in working-class areas that will abandon the teaching of modern languages, while they remain an indicator of academic success in middle-class schools.

Testing

According to research commissioned by the National Union of Teachers, pupils may take up to 75 external tests and exams during their school careers. The test regime not merely identifies differences in attainment, it reinforces them by focusing resources on those pupils most 'profitable' for the school in terms of test results, who are disproportionately from better-off families (Gillborn and Youdell 2000). This testing regime is a powerful factor in creating different class identities among pupils, as research by Diane Reay has shown:

> The paradox of our contemporary English test regime is that, while the stated aim is to raise the achievement of all children, one consequence of the growing preoccupation with testing and assessment is the fixing of failure in the working classes.
>
> (Reay 2003: 113)

A culture of performativity

During the 1970s and early 1980s a flowering of teacher-led innovation to tackle educational inequality took place, exemplified in numerous school working groups, LEA-based initiatives and publications based on teachers' work. This has now virtually disappeared under the pressure of a culture of performativity designed to produce a new professional identity for classroom teachers as of skilled technicians, 'delivering' (the word is significant) syllabuses devised elsewhere geared to Government-imposed pupil attainment targets. The resulting intensification, extensification and regulation of teachers' work has inhibited their ability to innovate in order to tackle inequality, partly by marginalising it as a priority and partly simply by sapping the energies required.

Why does Labour adopt class policies in school?

Up to now I have discussed class in terms of the unequal distribution of educational success to children from different social backgrounds, as measured by economic status. Now I need to introduce a different perspective on class. The state school system does not just function to reproduce the advantages of the middle class over the working class. It has a more fundamental purpose, which is to help to reproduce the conditions of existence of capitalist society as a whole. By capitalist society I mean a society based on a market economy, where the production of goods and services is primarily determined by profit. In this context the principal function of the school is to produce the sorts of future workers the economy needs, its 'human capital'. Labour's rationale for its education reforms makes it clear that the most important function of the education system is its contribution to economic competitiveness (see, for example, the White Paper, *Schools: Achieving Success*, DfES 2001).

From this perspective, the dominant class interests that drive education policy are not those of the middle class, although they benefit at the expense of the working class, but those of the dominant class itself, the employers, the rich, the ruling class.

Labour's 'human capital' argument is that economic competitiveness in the new knowledge economy depends on a highly educated labour force. This is a dangerous half-truth. Certainly the economy requires a layer of highly educated workers, but it also requires a substantial layer of less-qualified workers for low-skill jobs, many of them in the expanding service sector, and a pool of unemployed and semi-employed who can be moved into and out of the labour force as needed. A school system geared to these stratified labour needs inevitably reproduces educational inequality rather than countering it.

Whose curriculum?

The school curriculum is a particular selection of knowledge and skills. As Bob Connell says:

> Each particular way of constructing the curriculum (i.e. organizing the field of knowledge and defining how it is to be taught and learned) carries social effects. Curriculum empowers and disempowers, authorizes and de-authorizes, recognizes and mis-recognizes different social groups and their knowledge and identities.

> (Connell 1994: 140)

I have said that the fundamental function of school is to help to reproduce the conditions of existence of capitalist society. That provides the principle that governs the selection of knowledge to be taught in the school curriculum. Of course, some areas of knowledge, such as maths or the principles of science, are independent of class interests, but their contexts and applications are not, and subjects such as English and history have evoked fierce contention over which social interests are privileged. The official curriculum tends to reproduce the dominant world-view and marginalise the voices of subordinate social groups. In that broad context, Labour's particular concern for the formation of human capital has determined the priorities of the curriculum as it is today: 'basic skills' in the primary school and curriculum differentiation in the secondary school, especially from age 14 onwards, into vocational and academic tracks in order to create a stratified future workforce corresponding roughly to the differential requirements of the economy.

Up to now I have discussed social class interests in terms of attainment as measured by test scores and exam results. But the class interests of working people and their children in education are not limited to ending 'underachievement' in the present system, they also encompass changing the curriculum, and indeed school itself, in order to provide an 'education for emancipation', an education that helps pupils to understand and challenge the inequalities of society. Schools have made some progress in this direction, albeit limited, around issues of race and gender, but seldom around the issue of class.

Labour's electoral interests

In addition to Labour's conception of the aims of education, its electoral interests as a political party militate against tackling class inequality in education. It has to convince the dominant class that its policies will meet their economic needs for an appropriately skilled, stratified and socialised workforce. But it also has to win enough votes to remain in power. New Labour built itself by occupying the 'middle ground' in British politics and attracting middle-class votes away from the Conservatives. It is determined to retain that support by avoiding egalitarian reforms which might undermine the privileged position of middle-class families in the education system.

Three agendas for change

The school system is a site of class struggle. School is an institution in which different social interests meet and conflict. But even in our present unequal market-based society, school can be more responsive to working-class interests or less so. I want to outline three agendas for change. One can be called a defensive or oppositional agenda. It is based on opposition to the key policies which sustain inequality, such as opposition to SATs, league tables, specialist schools, the spread of ability grouping, the socially divisive post-14 curriculum and the remaining grammar schools. It also tends to give a high priority to increased funding for schools in poor areas, a demand recently echoed by David Bell, the Chief Inspector (Slater 2003a).

The second agenda can be called the 'best practice' agenda. It aims to identify those schools that seem to be most effective in tackling inequality and raising standards in socially deprived areas as models which other schools can learn from. It is exemplified by numerous books about 'school improvement' (see for example National Commission on Education 1996 and Maden 2001) and Government publications such as *Excellence in Cities* (DfEE 1999).

These two agendas only partly overlap. The 'best practice' advocates seldom refer to the damaging effects of key Government policies, which, as we have seen, are a major factor in perpetuating the inequalities and low standards of attainment which the 'school improvement' movement wishes to address. This Government policy framework (only slightly alleviated by the relaxation of control in primary schools permitted by *Excellence and Enjoyment*, DfES 2003) severely restricts the innovative measures schools are able to take to tackle inequality. In that sense, in spite of some valuable lessons which can be learnt from effective schools in poor areas, the 'best practice' agenda is a conservative agenda. It is underpowered for the task of tackling social class inequality.

The third agenda encompasses the demands of the first, and includes some of the successful practices identified in the second, but goes further. Class affects every aspect of schooling, and an effective programme of change requires an equally comprehensive response. But I began by defining the core of the problem of the education of pupils from working-class backgrounds in terms of relationships to knowledge, and it is difficult to believe that an alternative can really be effective unless it places at its centre a radical rethinking of the curriculum and how it is taught. The issue is exemplified by the disaffected school students in a recent research study by Riley and Rustique-Forrester (2002):

> A common feeling expressed by many of the students we talked to was that 'learning' was boring ... Almost uniformly, students found few connections between what they encountered in school and what they were experiencing, or were likely to experience, outside of it.
>
> (p. 34)

> Examples of teaching enjoyed by disaffected young people, and perceived as effective by them, included those experiences where pupils were able to connect learning to their own lives and their expectations about their futures.
>
> (p. 72)

The issue is not a curriculum restricted to popular experience, but one in which 'academic' knowledge and popular experiences and meanings are interwoven, and mutually and critically illuminate each other. One in which 'school knowledge' infuses and informs the purposes and actions in the life-worlds of children and young people, and teachers and pupils have the means to develop pedagogic relations of quality. To find examples of this approach we need to look beyond the UK to countries where there is more freedom to innovate.

One of the striking features of the 'school improvement' agenda is that it is not based on, nor even acknowledges, distinctive and emancipatory theories of education, only on apparently all-purpose content-free theories of institutional change. Perhaps the best-known educationist in the emancipatory tradition is Paulo Freire. The most large-scale application of his approach is the programme of education reform that has been implemented by the Workers Party Government of the state of Rio Grande do Sul in Brazil (with a population of ten million) and by the city council of its capital Porto Alegre, a city of 1.3 million. The making of education policy takes place through processes of participatory democracy based on popular assemblies. The resulting policy is based on the Freirean theory of the dialectical relationship between knowledge and social practice. I will quote from one of its policy documents:

> We understand the Dialectic Conception of Knowledge as a way to interpret, analyse and know reality in order to transform it, through the coherence between theory and practice. It implies putting into practice a knowledge of reality, a theory of the production of knowledge as a social, collective and participatory process. It also implies the analysis of the existing conflicts in our practice and understanding them as expressions of the social, economic, political and cultural contradictions of the society in which we live … In this way, the study of the reality lived by the group and the perception of this reality constitute the point of departure and the raw material of the educational process.
>
> (Rio Grande do Sul State Department of Education 2000: 35–7)

> For the Popular Government, democratising means constructing in a participatory way an education project of Social Quality, transformative and liberating, in which the school is a practical laboratory for the exercise and conquest of rights, of the formation of historical, autonomous, critical, creative individuals, full citizens, identified with ethical values oriented to the construction of a solidaristic social project. It is also about forming individuals who place at the centre of their concerns the practice of justice, liberty, human respect, fraternal relations between men and women and harmonious coexistence with nature. In this vision we reaffirm our commitment to the deeply humanist character of the public school, in opposition to the vision, which is today hegemonic, of submission to the values of the market, whose sole concern is to create consumers and customers and to turn education into a commodity subordinated to the logic of

entrepreneurialism, naturalising individualism, conformism, competition, resignation and, in consequence, exclusion.

(Rio Grande do Sul State Department of Education 2000: 95–7)

My second example of a school that illustrates an emancipatory approach comes from the United States. Central Park East Secondary School is a public school belonging to the New York City Board of Education. It started in 1985 and has 450 students in grades 7–12. Its non-selective intake comes mainly from one of the poorest areas of the city, East Harlem; 85 per cent are African-American or Latino. More than 20 per cent are eligible for special needs support. But the school achieves high academic success: 97.3 per cent graduate from high school and of them 90 per cent go on to college (Meier and Schwarz 1999). The school is guided by the principles of the Coalition of Essential Schools:

> The fundamental aim of CPESS is to teach students to use their minds well, to prepare them for a well-lived life that is productive, socially useful, and personally satisfying. The school's academic programme stresses intellectual achievement and emphasizes the mastery of a limited number of centrally important subjects. This programme goes hand-in-hand with an approach that emphasizes learning how to learn, how to reason and how to investigate complex issues that require collaboration and personal responsibility.

(Meier and Schwarz 1999: 31)

There is a common core curriculum in grades 7–10 organised around two major fields – maths/science for half the day and humanities (art, history, social studies and literature) for the other half. Grades 11–12 spend more time in off-site learning – courses in colleges and museums, internships. The curriculum is based on five principles of critical enquiry:

1 How do you know what you know? (Evidence)

2 From whose viewpoint is this being presented? (Perspective)

3 How is this event or work connected to others? (Connections)

4 What if things were different? (Supposition)

5 Why is this important? (Relevance)

(Meier and Schwarz 1999: 36)

In terms of assessment, the high school diploma is based on the presentation of 14 portfolios to a graduation committee – which comprises at least two teachers plus an adult of the student's choice and a student member. Accountability is ensured through a range of external 'critical friends', including university staff.

Because the relationship between the student and the curriculum is mediated by the teacher, the quality of the relationship between the teacher and the students is regarded as crucial. No teacher teaches more than 40 students in the week, because the school regards that as the maximum number with whom it is possible to establish a personal relationship of quality. In grades 7–10 each lesson is two hours long and each teacher teaches two lessons a day. Small classes are the priority: the maximum class size is 20. Each teacher has a 'tutorial group' of under 15 students for two years, meeting for several hours each week, with close links between tutor and families.

Conclusion

Transforming the educational prospects of working class pupils means *transforming the educational experience schools offer them*. If we are to challenge class inequality in education we need to create and popularise a richer vision of schooling as a common transformatory and emancipatory education of quality. That means radically rethinking the curriculum and the whole experience of school from a working-class point of view. So there is a dual aim: an education that enables working-class pupils to get the exam results that give access to good jobs and higher education, but also what I have called an 'education for emancipation', one that gives them the knowledge, skills and values to challenge the injustices of our present society.

Suggested further reading

For readers wishing to find out about policy that flows from the analysis in this chapter, then the following should be useful: Beane and Apple (1999), Ball (2003), Chitty and Simon (eds) (2001), Connell (1993) and Hatcher (2000).

For a wider discussion of education policy, see Gillborn and Youdell (2000), Freeman-Moir and Scott (2003) and Maden (2001).

References

Ball, S. J. (2003) *Class Strategies and the Education Market*. London: Routledge Falmer.

Beane, J. A. and Apple, M. W. (1999) 'The case for democratic schools', in M. W. Apple and J. A. Beane (eds) *Democratic Schools*. Buckingham: Open University Press.

Chitty, C. and Simon, B. (eds) (2001) *Promoting Comprehensive Education in the 21st Century*. Stoke on Trent: Trentham Books.

Connell, R. W. (1993) *Schools and Social Justice*. Philadelphia: Temple University Press.

Connell, R. W. (1994) 'Poverty and education', *Harvard Educational Review*, 64 (2), 125–49.

DfEE (1997) *Excellence in Schools*. London: The Stationery Office.

DfEE (1999) *Excellence in Cities*. London: Department for Education and Employment.

DfES (2001) *Schools: Achieving Success*. London: Department for Education and Skills.

DfES (2003) *Excellence and Enjoyment*. London: Department for Education and Skills.

Ferri, E., Bynner, J. and Wadsworth, M. (2003) *Changing Britain, Changing Lives*. London: Institute of Education, University of London.

Foot, P. (2003) 'Adding up to much less', *The Guardian*, 26 November 2003.

Freeman-Moir, J. and Scott, A. (eds) (2003) *Yesterday's Dreams*. Christchurch: Canterbury University Press.

Gewirtz, S., Ball, S. J. and Bowe, R. (1995) *Markets, Choice and Equity in Education*. Buckingham: Open University Press.

Gillborn, D. and Youdell, D. (2000) *Rationing Education*. London: Routledge.

Gold, K. (2003) 'Poverty is an excuse', *Times Educational Supplement*, 7 March.

Hallam, S. (2002) *Ability Grouping in Schools*. London: Institute of Education, University of London.

Hatcher, R. (2000) 'Social Class and School', in M. Cole (ed.) *Education, Equality and Human Rights*. London: Routledge Falmer.

Maden, M. (ed.) (2001) *Success Against the Odds – Five Years On*. London: Routledge Falmer.

Meier, D. and Schwarz, P. (1999) 'Central Park East Secondary School: The hard part is making it happen', in M. W. Apple and J. A. Beane (eds) *Democratic Schools*. Buckingham: Open University Press.

Nash, R. (2003) 'Dreaming in the Real World: Social Class and Education in New Zealand', in J. Freeman-Moir and A. Scott (eds) *Yesterday's Dreams*. Christchurch: Canterbury University Press.

National Commission on Education (1996) *Success Against the Odds: Effective Schools in Disadvantaged Areas*. London: Routledge.

Reay, D. (2003) 'Reproduction, Reproduction, Reproduction: Troubling Dominant Discourses on Education and Social Class in the United Kingdom', in J. Freeman-Moir and A. Scott (eds) *Yesterday's Dreams*. Christchurch: Canterbury University Press.

Riley, K. A. and Rustique-Forrester, E. (2002) *Working with Disaffected Students*. London: Paul Chapman.

Rio Grande do Sul State Department of Education (2000) *Principles and Directives for State Public Education/Principios y Directrices para la Educación Pública Estatal*. Porto Alegre: CORAG.

Sanders, C. (2003) *Times Higher Educational Supplement*, 28 February.

Sarda, K. (2003) *Guardian*, 17 December 2003.

Shaw, M. (2003) 'Ofsted finds little action in city zones', *Times Educational Supplement*, 6 June.

Slater, J. (2003a) 'City schools need boost', *Times Educational Supplement*, 21 November.

Slater, J. (2003b) 'Class segregation holds Britain back', *Times Educational Supplement*, 4 July.

Smithers, R. (2003) 'Report points up extent of class divide in British education', *The Guardian*, 25 March.

Sutherland, H., Sefton, T. and Piachaud, D. (2003) *Poverty in Britain: The impact of government policy since 1997*. York: Joseph Rowntree Foundation.

Ward, H. (2002) 'French: strictly for the bourgeoisie?' *Times Educational Supplement*, 22 November.

Waugh, P. (2003) 'Poverty levels have grown under Labour', *The Independent*, 12 May.

West, A. and Pennell, H. (2003) *Underachievement in Schools*. London: Routledge Falmer.

Woodward, W. (2003) 'Aid for city pupils has mixed success', *The Guardian*, 2 June.

Special educational needs and inclusion in education

Mary Kellett

I am part of an oppressed group of people who need to challenge the cultural barriers that stop them being able to reach their full potential.

(Simone Aspis, the first person with a learning difficulty to be appointed as a national spokesperson for a British political party, Green Party Press Office 2001)

Introduction

THE FOCUS OF THIS chapter is special educational needs and inclusion. Both terms are in common usage at the time of writing and the relationship between them is one of the issues explored, along with an examination of the principal ideological and pedagogical debates. Before that, the historical origins of special education are explained in order to assist better understanding of how special educational needs and inclusion have evolved into their present form. Attention is paid to important legislation that has shaped the course of special education over time and pedagogical approaches such as behaviourist and interactive teaching methods that were developed. The final part of the chapter looks at inclusion, beginning with the social model it is built upon, how it is developing, and the impact it is having both at policy level and in the grass roots of the classroom.

The origins of special educational needs

We pick up the historical trail in the nineteenth century when discourses on education produced the 'medical' and 'charitable' models of disability. The medical (sometimes known as 'deficit') model viewed children's behaviour in terms of *internal* biological differences, categorising 'syndromes' and 'conditions' as defects within the child. This perspective disregarded any *external* factors such as poverty, health or life experience as having any bearing on the nature of the disability. The charitable model saw disabled children as tragic figures, deserving of pity. This was a disempowering perspective, viewing disabled children as passive recipients of philanthropy. Once again, the fault was seen to lie within the child – disability was a personal deficiency. Because of the dominance of these discourses, when basic education for most children was established – (Forster's 1870 Education Act and the 1872 Education (Scotland) Act) – no provision was made in these Acts for disabled children or children with learning difficulties.

Doctors could diagnose four levels of special 'condition': *idiot, imbecile, feeble-minded* and *moral-defective*. The Departmental Committee on Defective and Epileptic Children (1898) investigated whether the education system could be adapted for any of these children. The committee concluded that *imbeciles* were best placed in an asylum, the *feeble-minded* and *moral-defectives* could attend special schools but *idiots* were deemed ineducable and excluded from the education system altogether. The differentiation of these categories was not clearly defined and School Boards were required to appoint a medical officer to decide a child's 'condition' and educational placement (1913 Mental Deficiency Act). In Scotland, the Education of Defective Children (Scotland) Act 1906 gave School Boards the ability to cater for defective children in special schools or classes. Those incapable of learning were, as in England, assigned to institutions by their local parish councils.

The 1921 Education Act required that numbers of 'feeble-minded' and 'backward' children within each local authority were recorded so that separate education could be provided. This maintained a powerful link between the diagnosis of a category and the allocation of a particular type of education. It was this impetus that led to the development and rapid adoption of the intelligence test (Burt 1937) as a diagnostic tool to determine degrees of special educational need.

The 1944 Butler Act heralded a radical reappraisal of the education system (Stakes and Hornby 1997). The use of the terms 'subnormal', 'remedial' and 'maladjusted' became common. Educationally subnormal children were identified as those retarded by more than 20 per cent for their age but who were not so low grade as to be ineducable. This accounted for approximately 10 per cent of the child population, 1 per cent of whom attended special schools or hospitals, the remainder being taught in small groups within the umbrella of a school. An increasing number of special schools were opened between the 1950s and 1970s and the number of hospital special schools also grew.

Behaviourist teaching

The 1970 Education (Handicapped Children) Act and the 1974 Education (Mentally Handicapped Children) (Scotland) Act finally brought all children into the framework of education irrespective of their disability or degree of learning difficulty. The absolute right to a full education for all children without exception was established and the 'ineducable' category abolished. As a consequence of this, educators began to turn their attention to better understanding ways in which children with severe and complex learning difficulties could be taught (Rose 2001). Many of the approaches adopted were based on behaviourist methods. This model assumed that many behaviours are learnt, including, for example, challenging or difficult behaviour. Rather than diagnosing a deficit the behaviourist model begins by identifying what the child needs to learn and then constructs a way of teaching this behaviour. These techniques were adapted to teach a whole range of skills in a behaviourist-based curriculum. The Skills Analysis Model (Gardner *et al.* 1983) is one such example. It advocated breaking the teaching process down into six small steps:

- Identify core areas of the curriculum.
- Subdivide these areas into their component parts.
- Write targets for each identified component.
- Prioritise the targets.
- Write a programme to teach each target.
- Assess and record whether the target has been achieved.

Although these methods achieved some modification in undesirable behaviour and acquisition of certain discrete skills, the approach was heavily criticised because it promoted learning without understanding and skills acquired in this way could not be transferred to other situations (McConkey 1981; Collis and Lacey 1996).

This new interest in special education was reflected in the setting up of the Warnock Committee (1974) to review provision in the United Kingdom. The Warnock Report (1978), and the resulting 1981 Education Act that it informed, was a watershed in the history of special education. For the first time it created the concept of a special educational 'need' and appropriate *provision* rather than a 'condition' and *treatment*. The committee regarded the terms 'educationally subnormal' (England and Wales) and 'mentally handicapped' (Scotland) as causing unnecessary stigmatisation, particularly in later life. It was decided that these would be replaced by one term, 'children with learning difficulties'.

What is a special educational need?

As described above, the idea of a special educational 'need' was first coined in the Warnock Report along with the term 'children with learning difficulties'. But what exactly do we mean by these terms? Pupils are deemed to have a special educational need when they are unable to reach their learning potential without either additional support or adaptations to their learning environment. This can be for a variety of global and/or specific reasons. There could be global cognitive delay when pupils may experience difficulty learning at the same level or pace as their typically developing peers. There may be a specific learning difficulty with reading or writing (sometimes known as dyslexia, although dyslexia is itself a large umbrella term for many specific difficulties) or numeracy. Equally there may be a specific difficulty related to attention span or memory. Emotional and behavioural difficulties can also interfere with the learning process and require special support. Equally, there are children who are very able (the current educational term for this is 'gifted and talented') and not able to reach their learning potential without adaptations to their learning environment and additional resources. It should be clear from these examples that provision for a special educational need is all about accommodating the individual learner through provisions and adaptations that *enable* rather than *disable*.

The Warnock recommendations

The Warnock Committee recommended that special educational need be seen as a continuum. A five-stage assessment procedure was established with progressively greater input from professionals at each stage along the continuum, culminating in a 'statement'. This Statement of Special Educational Need (Record of Need in Scotland) was to be produced when a child required extra educational provision. The document legally committed the local education authority to meet the child's identified special educational needs. Parents were to be involved in the process and a 'named person' would act as a key contact for them.

The Warnock Report judged that one in five children would require special educational provision at some time during their school career. Therefore a more flexible approach was required where the majority of children with special educational needs could be identified and helped within the ordinary school. Adaptations to the school building, the curriculum and teaching techniques were to be considered where this would help meet a child's 'special educational need'.

Integration (not to be confused with inclusion, which is discussed later) was encouraged by the Warnock Report (1978) and was described as a way of bringing children with special educational needs into the community of mainstream schools. This could be achieved in three different ways:

- locational integration – special units or classes set up within an ordinary school;

- social integration – children attending a special class or unit but eating, playing and socialising with other children;

- functional integration – children with special needs joining a mainstream class either on a part-time or full-time basis.

Interactive approaches

A backlash from behaviourist teaching resulted in the promotion of interactive teaching approaches (Collis and Lacey 1996; Nind 2000) and an emphasis on person-to-person interaction as a basis for learning. More attention was given to creating a responsive learning environment (Ware 1996). For pupils with severe and complex learning difficulties some of these approaches such as *Intensive Interaction* (Nind and Hewett 1994) were developed from a theoretical basis of caregiver–infant interaction with an emphasis on contingent responding and working from a child's strengths – in other words building on what a child could do rather than concentrating on what a child could not do.

The labelling culture

However laudable the abolition of inappropriate labels such as 'idiot' or 'imbecile' is, if one label is simply replaced by a different one, the potential for denigration and ridicule is not necessarily removed. The substitution of these terms by categories such as 'mentally retarded', 'educationally subnormal' and 'maladjusted' led to abusive taunts of 'retards' and 'subnormals'. It has taken a long time to learn from these early blunders and even in the 1980s and 1990s we were compounding, not lessening, the problem. One of the consequences of Warnock's 'continuum' of special educational need was that it reinforced categorisation. Along this continuum children could have a range of learning difficulties categorised as mild or moderate (ESN), severe and complex (SLD), profound and multiple (PMLD), or emotional and behavioural (EBD). Inevitably this led to increased use of the abbreviated terminology and terms such as 'EBDs,' 'SLDs' and 'PMLDs' were soon in common use among professionals. The problem with this is that the word 'child' or 'pupil' does not appear anywhere, suggesting that the category relates to something less than human. Even when the odd child acknowledgement tag was thrown in for good measure (e.g. 'our EBD kids' rather than 'our EBDs'), the child part always came after the label. Child activists felt that this put the spotlight on the disability rather than the child. A child is a child first and foremost; some children also happen to have learning difficulties. Hence, in the last decade it has become common practice to refer to children who have special needs as, for example, a child *with* severe and complex learning difficulties rather than an SLD child. This applies equally to adults as well as children, the value of the human individual being always prized above the learning difficulty.

The National Curriculum

The Education Reform Act 1988 introduced the National Curriculum in England and Wales and gave an impetus to considering how the whole curriculum could be made accessible for children with special educational needs. The relevance and importance of the National Curriculum for children with special educational needs has been controversial. Some writers have argued that it brought new opportunities to previously excluded children (Carpenter *et al.* 1996). Others saw significant parts of it as inappropriate or limiting (Fletcher-Campbell 1994). There was criticism that the prescriptive nature of the National Curriculum placed too much emphasis on product not process. National Curriculum 2000, one of a series of revisions to the original National Curriculum, went some way to redress this and offered guidance on meeting pupils' diverse learning needs.

Another concern was that the first level of attainment was so far beyond the reach of some pupils that they would have no realistic opportunity of achieving at anything (Tilstone 1991). In 1998 the Qualifications and Curriculum Association (QCA) introduced eight 'P' levels, preparatory levels of attainment leading up to level 1, but there has been criticism that even these level descriptors are too widely spaced to be meaningful for many pupils with profound learning difficulties. Assessment by level of attainment is also viewed by some as anti-inclusionary because it leads to grouping of children by ability.

Literacy and numeracy hours were introduced in England in 1998 and 1999 respectively when all maintained schools were required to follow prescribed guidelines or provide evidence that literacy and numeracy of at least equivalent duration and quality was being provided. There has been a mixed response to this latest curriculum initiative, some complaining that it is a retrograde step towards narrow prescription and others that it has made literacy and numeracy more accessible to some groups of learners.

There is still widespread debate about whether an adapted National Curriculum is appropriate for all pupils, particularly for pupils with profound and complex learning difficulties. On the one hand it is a powerful enactment of the common humanity of all children and their rightful entitlement to the same curriculum. On the other hand, a 'one-curriculum approach' may be inhibiting for some groups of children if it prevents time being spent on training for essential life skills or complementary teaching approaches and therapies that are known to be beneficial. At the time of writing, the Qualifications and Curriculum Association are clarifying their position on curricular inclusion for pupils with more severe learning difficulties. They intend to produce National Curriculum guidelines for secondary pupils whose attainment is likely to remain below level 1. They also intend to provide guidance on a range of non-National Curriculum provision, e.g. therapy, which can be made available within a pupil's individual curriculum. Ultimately, the onus is on teachers to use the National Curriculum in ways they judge to be relevant. There are many fine examples of teachers successfully including pupils, even those with very profound learning difficulties, in a meaningful way. One such example was documented by Tilstone *et al.* (2000):

> It is hard for her teachers and caregivers to know when Manjula is learning because she does not use speech or any kind of sign language. However, by including her in the visit to the cathedral they are providing her with important experiences, shared with other children. In fact, these experiences give Manjula the opportunity to show that she is aware of important things during the visit. Sitting in her wheelchair, beneath the cathedral's Rose Window, Manjula is left for a few minutes to look, listen, and feel where she is. As the sun shines through the window, Manjula smiles and wrings her hands with pleasure. Back in school, Manjula's teacher and learning support assistant help her to make a 'sensory' picture book as part of a topic on the cathedral. They make her a personal tape of the kind of organ music heard during the visit. This brings learning to life for Manjula, and brings other real benefits. Some of her classmates also enjoy the organ music and the class teacher organises a small 'listening group'. Manjula's mother and father, when they hear about this successful activity, decide to make her a tape of Buddhist chants used in their community temple. Thereafter, whenever the family visits the temple, they play the tape in the car and Manjula gets very excited with anticipation. The curriculum experience described here has been well matched to Manjula's needs, and importantly, this has been 'negotiated' on the basis of her response to an activity. She might have been left out of the visit, but instead she was included and showed her educators, friends and family that she was developing a seemingly new awareness that could help her develop valuable choice-making skills.
>
> (p. 14)

Resourcing special educational needs

The Education Act 1993 placed a duty on the Secretary of State to issue a Code of Practice and the power to revise it from time to time. The first Code of Practice came into effect in 1994 (DfEE) and was updated in 2001 (DfES). It provides practical advice to local education authorities, maintained schools, early education settings and others on carrying out their statutory duties to identify, assess and make provision for children's special educational needs. In this respect it maintains an approach that looks for individual difficulties rather than developing a whole-school approach, but the involvement of pupils themselves in this process was at least one step towards empowerment and the wider emphasis on children's rights.

In the past, special educational needs were entirely funded from local educational authorities. Since the introduction of the local management of schools more and more of these funds have been devolved to schools themselves. The most recent ruling on this relates to the Standards and Frameworks Act (1998) requiring local authorities in England and Wales to delegate at least 80 per cent of their overall education budget directly to schools. The remaining 20 per cent is used to support advisory services and fund provision for pupils with statements of special educational needs. With a large portion of direct funding coming to individual schools, *head teachers* have been able to appoint more Special Educational Needs Coordinators, or SENCOs (many schools now refer to these as Inclusion Coordinators, or INCOs) to oversee the organisation and management of special educational needs. However, the majority of the funds are spent on employing assistant teaching staff to support the children's learning and for ongoing staff training.

Inclusive education

The drive towards inclusion grew out of the social model of disability. This perspective views society as being disabling rather than a particular condition associated with an individual. In other words it is society's failure to adapt the environment to accommodate an individual's condition that is the disabling factor. In educational terms this translates as mainstream schools needing to adapt their physical environment, teaching styles and curricular provision where necessary to meet the diverse needs of all pupils.

The context for inclusion is situated within a human rights' discourse predicated by the United Nations Convention on the Rights of the Child (1989) and a standpoint of equality. Segregation of children from their peers is seen as a denial of those human rights. Inclusion and participation are essential to human dignity and to the enjoyment and exercise of human rights. The UNESCO Salamanca Statement (1994) called on the international community to endorse the approach of inclusive schools by implementing practical and strategic changes. The Centre for Studies on Inclusive Education (2002) emphasised that this statement was a clear commitment to 'education for all' within the mainstream system. The concept of inclusion extends beyond special educational needs and disabilities to the wider embracement of human diversity: of gender, ethnicity, sexuality, cultural heritage and religion.

In 1997 the United Kingdom's commitment to inclusion was underlined by the Green Paper *Excellence for All* (DfEE). The paper supported the move from segregated to mainstream education for more children. Special schools were to have a more flexible role, part of which would be to provide active support for children moving to mainstream schools and act as a source of training and information for mainstream staff.

If schools are to educate a diverse range of learners in one and the same classroom then a variety of different teaching approaches need to be considered. This may involve physical changes to the learning environment, sometimes additional adult support and invariably adaptations to the curriculum. The emphasis on 'diversity' steers thinking towards the total learning environment rather than individual 'need' or 'difficulty'. Some argue that inclusion involves accessing specialist teaching skills (e.g. Hornby and Kidd 2001) whereas others claim that no special set of methods or pedagogies are needed to teach children with diverse learning experiences (e.g. Thomas and Loxley 2001). These opposing viewpoints illustrate deep-rooted tensions that exist among professionals in their different approaches to inclusion and this will now be examined further.

The inclusion debate

The road towards inclusion has not been entirely smooth. While there have been few ideological objections to inclusion, there have been many concerns raised about its feasibility in practical terms. There has been some resistance from teachers who worry that they do not have the skills to teach children with learning difficulties or children with emotional and behavioural difficulties and are concerned about the impact inclusion will have on other typically developing pupils in their classes (Florian 1998). Some even argue that children with severe learning difficulties may actually be worse off because they will not get the specialist teaching they have received in the past nor the small classes that typically populate special schools. One of the difficulties appears to be that inclusion moved too quickly, before mainstream schools and mainstream teachers had enough time to adapt. Pupils began to move out of special schools and into mainstream but the specialist teaching skills did not move with them. Specialist teachers stayed with the remainder of the pupils left in special schools and the Government's aim for this expertise to be used to support children in mainstream and provide training for mainstream staff did not wholly materialise. However, there is evidence that this situation is beginning to change with initiatives such as the Barnado's special school that successfully transformed itself into an inclusion advisory service (Bannister *et al.* 2003).

A major concern for teachers is that inclusion will only work if properly resourced. Children with diverse and multiple disabilities need more staff to be able to accommodate their needs – sometimes on a one-to-one full-time basis. Despite increased recruitment of assistants to support classroom teachers, insufficient numbers and insufficient training remain major obstacles. Clough and Nutbrown (2002) in their exploration of early years educators' attitudes to inclusion found mixed responses:

> A lovely idea – inclusion – and when it's good, it's great! I have been able to have children in the nursery with Down's syndrome and children with various emotional difficulties – abused children – but when they [the LEA] asked us to take in a child with autism, well, we had to say 'no'. Too risky – I was frightened that if we did – something terrible would happen and it would be my responsibility. So yes, lovely idea – but it really is an ideal that will never be achieved – total inclusion is impossible.
>
> (Janie, nursery teacher – cited in Clough and Nutbrown 2002)

It is noteworthy that this early years teacher thinks in terms of 'being asked to *take in*' a child with autism as if the child is somehow 'outside' the frame. There is no apparent conception of the child's entitlement to be included as of right, or of the nursery's obligation to adapt its provision in order to accommodate all children, whether autistic or not. The other point that is evident from this quote is that many teachers are clearly receiving neither the training that would help them to know and understand autism nor the support and resources required.

The Special Educational Needs and Disability Act (2001) has caused many schools to reconsider their attitude to inclusion. Schools can refuse a child only if their admission would harm the education of other pupils in the school. The Act places education within the remit of the Disability Discrimination Act and therefore it is illegal to discriminate against a student because of his or her disability. LEAs and schools (and post-16 education providers in due course) are required to develop access for disabled pupils to premises and the curriculum.

Some schools encountered difficulties in the transition towards greater inclusion and one of the initiatives that served as a self-help tool was the *Index for Inclusion* (Booth *et al.* 2000). The *Index* provided a set of materials to guide schools through the inclusion process promoting the building of supportive communities to foster high achievement for all pupils.

> The *Index* involves a process of school self-review on three dimensions concerned with inclusive school cultures, policies and practices. The process entails a progression through a series of school development phases. These start with the establishing of a coordinating group. This group works with staff, governors, students and parents/carers to examine all aspects of the school, identifying barriers to learning and sustaining and reviewing progress. The investigation is supported by a detailed set of indicators and questions which require schools to engage in a deep and challenging

exploration of their present position and the possibilities for moving towards greater inclusion.

(Booth *et al.* 2000: 2)

It is at the grass roots level of the classroom where much of the inclusion debate is played out. We have already considered some of the training and resourcing issues above, and we now examine some of the practical and pedagogical issues related to everyday classroom management. Most support for pupils who have learning difficulties is provided by teaching assistants and a primary pedagogical concern is whether this support should be provided 'in' or 'out' of the classroom. In the past it was common practice for pupils to be taken out of their classroom and supported on a one-to-one or small group basis. From an inclusive perspective this is seen as problematic as an inclusive ideology adapts the learning environment to the pupil's needs rather than creating a separate 'exclusive' learning environment. Moreover, there are consequences for the social and cultural dimensions of learning if support is provided outside the classroom. Increasingly, the preferred scenario is for teaching assistants to work alongside pupils within the classroom context. There are some tensions inherent in this provision as some teachers still feel that pupils would benefit from the kind of focused one-to-one support that could be provided outside the classroom.

Inclusion has not evolved without its critics. Such criticisms (e.g. Farrell 1997; Wilson 1999) focus on the tension that exists between the philosophical principle of inclusion and a continuing level of support for specialist segregation (Croll and Moses 2000). Although critics embrace inclusion as an educational ideal, they discuss the need for a pragmatic response. They suggest that special schools still have a role to play with regard to children with severe learning difficulties and emotional and behavioural difficulties and question the capacity of mainstream schools to meet their needs and the problem of inadequate resources and funding.

Inclusion on the international stage

Since the United Nations Convention on Children's Rights (1989) and the UNESCO Salamanca Statement (1994) there has been a consistent move towards inclusion on an international scale, particularly in Europe, America and Australia. This provides a rich source of evaluative and comparative research data that we can draw on within the inclusion debate. For example, Forlin's (2001) study in Australia investigating potential stressors for 571 teachers implementing inclusion has been informative in identifying where appropriate training and resources might alleviate stress. Forlin found that a major source of stress for teachers was their concern that they were inadequately trained to cope with teaching pupils with learning difficulties and that their anxiety to get this right was reducing their overall ability to teach other pupils in the class. Lack of time and resources were also high stress factors, whereas some of the least stressful factors related to the actual interaction with the 'included' pupils and their parents. This would suggest that teachers in Australia are not opposed to the ideology of inclusion but feel inadequately trained and resourced to be as effective as they would like to be. Similar scenarios can be found in schools across the UK and the stark message seems to be that for inclusion to work properly it has to be appropriately funded. Thomas and Loxley (2001) claim that we cannot construct inclusion without first deconstructing special education, not least because the single funding pot is having to support both systems simultaneously resulting in crises of funding, training and resourcing.

Exclusion

Despite the laudable ideology of inclusion there are still a great many pupils who are excluded from schools, not because they are deemed 'ineducable' in the historical sense but because they are judged to be 'too difficult'. Most of these pupils fall into the special need category known as 'emotional and behavioural difficulties'. In such cases, pupils are passed out to special schools or Pupil Referral Units, some of which are residential. In principle these 'referrals' are for an agreed fixed term with the aim being to reintegrate pupils back into mainstream schools. In practice this does not always happen as often as the ideology suggests and placement becomes all but permanent. Visser *et al.*'s research (2002) on pupils with emotional and behavioural difficulties concluded that not enough was being done to encourage schools to become more open, positive, diverse communities that are 'barrier-free' to pupils with emotional and behavioural difficulties.

Conclusion

As you will have gathered from reading this chapter, special educational needs and inclusion are complex and hotly debated issues. When we see inclusive education in the context of history, we see how the thinking behind it is evolving. One of the aims of this chapter has been to explore where different arguments about inclusive education are mutually supportive and where there is tension and conceptual confusion. There tends to be agreement at the moral stage of defining inclusive education, but when we move on to enact inclusion in practice the ideological unity becomes more fragmented (Clough 2000). This is partly because it is relatively early in the inclusion time line and we are still working hard to get it right. Valuing diversity is at the centre of these efforts. Any attempt to define the difference between 'special education' and 'inclusive education' centres on this crucially important aspect of diversity. 'Special education' might be defined in terms of 'separate but equal' whereas 'different but equal' more aptly describes 'inclusive education'. Looking back over the historical origins of special education that have been charted in this chapter readers may be tempted to think that inclusive education is going to be just another phase that will pass. What persuades me otherwise is the ideology of human rights that underpins it. As such, I see the task ahead not so much as mapping the dots but joining them up.

Suggested further reading

For those interested in the ideological thinking around inclusion, a good read is Thomas and Loxley (2001). Alternatively Peter Clough (2000) or Croll and Moses (2000) are also very informative about theoretical frameworks. For readers wanting more on the pupil perspective and the transition process from special to mainstream school, turn to Julie Allan (1999), a very accessible book that charts the personal experiences of 11 pupils with special educational needs. Thomas *et al.*'s (1998) book about one school's journey to inclusion has become widely accepted as a classic. A good article that explores the challenges of educational inclusion for pupils who are perceived as the most difficult to include is Visser *et al.* (2002). Readers who would like to find out more about the practical aspects of inclusion at ground level should look at Booth *et al.*'s (2000) *Index for Inclusion* and an evaluation of its use in early years classrooms that was undertaken by Clough and Nutbrown (2002). Rose (2001) focuses on special education in the primary age range and for readers interested in a more international perspective, I would recommend Forlin (2001). If you want to find a good 'dip-in' text with short, readable chapters on a wide range of issues relating to inclusion then Nind *et al.* (2003) have recently edited two excellent companion books. The first volume looks at learners and learning contexts and explores examples of good practice. The second volume compares and evaluates different approaches to inclusion within the education sphere. The chapters in both volumes draw on a particularly diverse group of authors and provide multiple perspectives on inclusive education.

References

Allan, J. (1999) *Actively Seeking Inclusion: pupils with special needs in mainstream schools*. London: Falmer.

Bannister, C., Sharland, V., Thomas, G., Upton, V. and Walker, D. (2003) 'Changing from a special school to an inclusion service', in M. Nind, K. Sheehy and K. Simmons (eds) *Inclusive Education: Learners and Learning Contexts*. London: David Fulton Publishers.

Booth, T., Ainscow, M., Black-Hawkins, K., Vaughan, M. and Shaw, L. (2000) *Index for Inclusion: developing learning and participation in schools*. Bristol: CSIE.

Burt, C. (1937) *The Backward Child*. London and Aylesbury: University of London Press Ltd.

Carpenter, B., Ashdown, R. and Bovair, K. (1996) *Enabling Access*. London: David Fulton Publishers.

Centre for Studies on Inclusive Education (2002) *The UNESCO Salamanca Statement (1994)*. Available from http://inclusion.uwe.ac.uk/csie/slmca.htm.

Clough, P. (2000) 'Routes to inclusion', in P. Clough and J. Corbett (eds) *Theories of Inclusive Education: A Students' Guide*. London: Paul Chapman.

Clough, P. and Nutbrown, C. (2002) 'The Index for Inclusion: Personal perspectives from early years educators', *Early Education*, spring issue.

Collis, M. and Lacey, P. (1996) *Interactive Approaches to Teaching*. London: David Fulton Publishers.

Croll, P. and Moses, D. (2000) 'Ideologies and utopias: education professionals' views of inclusion', *European Journal of Special Needs Education*, 15 (1), 1–12.

Department for Education and Employment (1994) *The Code of Practice on the Identification and Assessment of Children and Special Educational Needs*. London: DfEE.

Department for Education and Employment (1997) *Excellence for All Children: Meeting special educational needs*. London: DfEE.

Department for Education and Skills (2001) *Special Educational Needs Code of Practice*. London: The Stationery Office.

Education Act (1870). London: HMSO.

Education Act (1921). London: HMSO.

Education Act (1944). London: HMSO.

Education Act (Handicapped Children) (1970). London: HMSO.

Education Act (1981). London: HMSO.

Education Reform Act (1988). London: HMSO.

Education Act (1993). London: HMSO.

Farrell, P. (1997) 'The integration of children with severe learning difficulties: a review of the recent literature', *Journal of Applied Research in Intellectual Disabilities*, 10 (1), 1–14.

Fletcher-Campbell, F. (1994) *Still Joining Forces? A follow up study of links between ordinary and Special Schools*. Slough: NFER.

Florian, L. (1998) 'An examination of the practical problems associated with the implementation of inclusive education policies', *Support for Learning*, 13 (3), 105–8.

Forlin, C. (2001) 'Inclusion: identifying potential stressors for regular class teachers', *Educational Research*, 43 (3), 235–45.

Gardner, J., Murphy, J. and Crawford, N. (1983) *The Skills Analysis Model*. Kidderminster: BIMH Publications.

Hornby, G. and Kidd, R. (2001) 'Transfer from special to mainstream – ten years later', *British Journal of Special Education*, 28 (1), 10–17.

McConkey, R. (1981) 'Education without understanding', *Special Education: Forward Trends*, 8 (3), 8–11.

Mental Deficiency Act (1913). London: HMSO.

National Curriculum (2000) http://curriculum2000.co.uk/new_curriculum.htm.

Nind, M. (2000) 'Teachers' understanding of interactive approaches in special education', *International Journal of Disability and Education*, 47 (2), 183–99.

Nind, M. and Hewett, D. (1994) *Access to Communication: Developing the Basics of Communication in People with Severe Learning Difficulties Through Intensive Interaction*. London: David Fulton Publishers.

Nind, M., Rix, J., Sheehy, K. and Simmons, K. (eds) (2003) *Inclusive Education: Diverse Perspectives*. London: David Fulton Publishers.

Nind, M., Sheehy, K. and Simmons, K. (eds) (2003) *Inclusive Education: Learners and Learning Contexts*. London: David Fulton Publishers.

Rose, L. (2001) 'Primary school teacher perceptions of the conditions required to include pupils with special educational needs', *Educational Review*, 53 (2), 147–56.

Special Educational Needs and Disability Act (2001). London: The Stationery Office.

Stakes, R. and Hornby, G. (1997) *Change in Special Education Provision: What Brings It About?* London: Continuum.

Thomas, G. and Loxley, A. (2001) *Deconstructing Special Education and Constructing Inclusion*. Buckingham: Open University Press.

Thomas, G., Walker, D. and Webb, J. (1998) *The Making of the Inclusive School*. London: Routledge.

Tilstone, C. (1991) (ed.) *Teaching Pupils with Severe Learning Difficulties*. London: David Fulton Publishers.

Tilstone, C., Lacey, P., Porter, J. and Robertson, C. (2000) *Pupils with Learning Difficulties in Mainstream Schools*. London: David Fulton Publishers.

UNESCO (1994) (Salamanca Statement) World Conference on Special Educational Needs: Access and quality. Paris: UNESCO.

United Nations (1989) *Convention on the Rights of the Child*. New York: United Nations.

Visser, J., Cole, T. and Daniels, H. (2002) 'Inclusion for the difficult to include', *Support for Learning*, 17 (1), 23–6.

Ware, J. (1996) *Creating a Responsive Environment*. London: David Fulton Publishers.

Warnock, M. (1978) *Special Educational Needs. Report of the Committee of Enquiry into the Education of Handicapped Children and Young People*. London: HMSO.

Wilson, J. (1999) 'Some conceptual difficulties about inclusion', *Support for Learning*, 14 (3), 110–12.

10

Early childhood education in the United Kingdom

J. Eric Wilkinson

It should be noted that children at play are not playing about; their games should be seen as their more serious-minded activity.

(Montaigne 1533–92)

Introduction

THE ORIGINS OF EARLY childhood education in Britain go back nearly 200 years to the time of the social reformer Robert Owen. As part of his model village in New Lanark, Scotland, he established the very first nursery, reputably in the world, for young children with working parents. The emphasis was on a stimulating child-centred curriculum based on play, exploration, singing and dancing. Unfortunately, after Owen left in 1825 to establish New Harmony in America, the nursery was discontinued, largely as a result of the greed for profit generated by the industrialisation of Britain in the nineteenth century.

In recent times, much attention has been given to education in the early years, a trend that is evident in most Western countries. There are three main reasons for this. Firstly, research has demonstrated the all-round psychological and social benefits to the child that high quality early childhood education offers. Secondly, it has been shown that a good early years experience has positive effects on subsequent educational achievement. Thirdly, early childhood services contribute to meeting the objectives of a healthy and prosperous society by promoting a more effective labour force and a more supportive family environment.

The findings of research on the effects of early childhood education on children's psychological and social development are now well established. Studying the effects of childcare on language development, McCartney (1984) identified that the degree of verbal responsiveness of staff in nurseries affected the language development of children in their care. One of the seminal studies that highlighted the significance of childcare quality on the social development of children was reported by Phillips *et al.* in 1987. The ability to establish co-operative relationships was significantly affected by a good nursery experience. In reviewing the literature Clarke-Stewart (1991) identified several indicators that impinge on children's development. These are: a well-organised and stimulating physical environment, a responsive and trained care-giver, a balanced curriculum, relatively small groups of children and relatively generous adult–child ratios.

Turning to the impact of pre-school education on subsequent educational achievement, a review of the relevant literature was undertaken by Sylva and Wiltshire (1994). They concluded:

> When pre-school education is of high quality it leads to lasting enhancement of educational performance and later employment. It does this through encouraging high aspirations, motivation to learn and feelings of task efficacy, especially for children from disadvantaged backgrounds.
>
> (Sylva and Wiltshire 1994: 47)

This finding was echoed by Ball (1994) in the report of the Royal Society of Arts: *Start Right: The Importance of Early Learning*.

There is also evidence that early childhood education can help to raise attainment in the formal school sector. Shorrocks (1993) undertook a systematic follow-up study of children at the age of seven, half of whom had pre-school experience, in which she controlled for socio-economic background. Her study showed:

- There were significant differences in favour of those with nursery experience in both English and mathematics, but not for science.

- Children with pre-school experience scored significantly higher in reading and writing.

- In mathematics, the picture was less clear: many of the attainment targets showed similar differences, but interestingly not those concerned with number work.

- In science, there were significant differences in many of the attainment targets, but not in the one concerned with the processes of scientific thinking.

(Shorrocks 1993 : 4)

As far as the impact of early childhood education and care on wider social issues is concerned, it is now recognised that nursery provision counteracts poverty by facilitating parental economic activity, it provides the main care-giver (usually the mother) with temporary relief from constant vigilance and can provide employers with continuity in valued personnel if provision for very young children is readily accessible.

Parents are now more economically active than during the Second World War. But is this trend for more working parents good for children? Some would argue that the 'demand' on mothers to work places them in a very invidious position. At times children are neglected. In such situations early childhood education and care have a vital role to play. In countries where it is the cultural norm for parents to work (for example, in Denmark) the state provides extensive early childhood services to suit the needs of the parents. There is no evidence to suggest that children are disadvantaged in such circumstances.

Not until fairly recently has it become widespread in the UK for mothers with young children to work. This has been particularly pronounced in families with children under three years of age. In sustaining the attitude that children under the age of three are better off with their mothers rather than in a nursery or with a childminder, the work of Bowlby (1952) on the psychological impairment for children as a consequence of maternal deprivation has been tantalisingly influential, despite more recent work that demonstrates that young children are quite capable of appropriate bonding with a range of adults (Schaffer 1977). However, the issue about whether working mothers can have detrimental effects on their child's well-being still remains unresolved. The work of Belsky (2001) in the USA supports the view that, if a child is placed in childcare outside the home for more than 20 hours per week when the child is under one year of age, there may be some detectable negative effects.

However, given the convincing evidence in support of pre-school education, writers such as David (1990) and Moss and Penn (1996) have consistently argued that quality early childhood education should be made universally available to families with young children. The Government responded robustly to these arguments by introducing a policy of free pre-school places, albeit part-time, for all four-year-olds whose parents wish it from 1999 and for all three-year-olds from 2001 (DfEE 1998a; SO, 1998). The publication in 1998 of the Government's policy for the early years entitled *Meeting the Childcare Challenge* (DfEEa, subsequently referred to as the Childcare Strategy) represented a sea change in the relationship between the state and the family with young children such that the state was set to take a much more proactive role in the provision of early years services.

Pre-school education and national childcare strategies

The common features of the Childcare Strategy for all parts of the UK were:

- raising the quality of care
- making childcare more affordable

- making childcare more accessible by increasing the number of places and improving information.

The strategy is based on five principles: quality, affordability, diversity, accessibility and partnership.

The key element of the Government's approach is that early childhood services should be based on 'partnerships' between the local authorities and the different types of provider within a mixed-economy model of services. The partnerships between the local authorities, the private and voluntary sectors should:

- Ensure that the plan enhances the care, play and educational experience of young children and the care and play experience of children up to age 14, including those with special educational needs and those with disabilities.

- Bring together the maintained, private and voluntary sectors in a spirit of co-operation and genuine partnership, based on existing good practice.

- Be directed by the diverse needs and aspirations of children locally, and of their parents, and pay attention to the support of families.

- Be further directed by the requirements of the local labour market and the needs of local employers, seeking advice from the local Training and Enterprise Council as appropriate.

- Generate genuine partnership and debate between all providers and others, and seek agreement about how needs can best be met.

- Recognise that the private and voluntary sectors have particular strengths.

- Recognise that these sectors often give support to, and in turn are supported by, parents.

- Understand the reality of the constraints on the local authority, both financial and other.

- Pay regard to value for money, taking both cost and quality into account, including recognition that the majority of childcare provision normally will be, or will become, financially viable within a short period (DfEE 1998b).

Partnership with parents

While the Government's policy of promoting partnerships between the different providers of pre-school education and local authorities is welcome, the partnership that individual nurseries have with parents is crucial. Attending a nursery is often the first step to independence for most children. Parents must have confidence that by sending their child to a nursery their child must be well cared for and be helped to learn. It must not be forgotten that the home environment in general is richly educative (Tizard and Hughes 1984).

In their relationship with parents, different nurseries operate different models of partnership. In the independent sector (where parents often have full-time employment) partnership depends on effective and efficient communication, whereas in the voluntary sector, parents take an active involvement in the delivery of a caring and stimulating environment.

Most nurseries now recognise the importance of continuity between home and nursery, often interpreting their role as helping parents to provide complementary experiences at home to those in nursery, for example, reading stories, responding to questions etc. Many nursery teachers and nursery nurses now regard it as part of their job to communicate with parents about the progress of individual children.

Early childhood services in the UK

There are three main categories of provision for children under five years of age in the UK: local authority services, voluntary services and private services.

As far as local authority provision is concerned, this consists of two subdivisions: *education*-based services and *social (work)* services. Of the specifically educational provision there are three types: nursery schools, nursery classes attached to primary schools and (with the exception of Scotland) reception classes in primary schools. These types of provision are staffed by both nursery teachers and nursery nurses. Of the social (work) services there are day nurseries, family centres and children's centres staffed largely by nursery nurses. With the exception of reception classes, the differentiation between these two types of nursery is being eroded, largely as a result of the pioneering work on integration in Strathclyde Region in Scotland in the late 1980s (Penn 1992; Wilkinson 1995).

In the voluntary sector, playgroups run by local mothers, assisted by a playgroup leader, are the most common, though most of the places in these groups are for one or two short sessions each week with a small charge being levied for each session. Less prevalent are mother and toddler groups and crèches.

In the private sector, provision varies widely from childminders (who look after children in their own homes) through private nurseries (very similar to local authority nursery schools) to nursery classes in fully independent schools. Childminders and private day nurseries are available to address the needs of working parents who are willing to meet the costs of these services, which vary between £100 and £200 per week.

Moss and Penn (1996) have undertaken an extensive and useful comparison of the different types of provision and clearly demonstrated substantial shortcomings of the current system. Despite the implementation of the Childcare Strategy there is still wide variation in 2004 in cost, staffing and opening times of early childhood services in the UK resulting in a complex piecemeal system (see Table 10.1). While implementation of the Childcare Strategy has resulted in significant improvement in access to early years services, there are still major concerns as to whether the services are meeting the diversity of family needs.

As far as the organisation of services is concerned the vast majority of places are part-time, attendance being for half a day, either mornings or afternoons. In 2002, of those three and four-year-olds attending nursery schools and classes, 85 per cent did so on a part-time basis. Most nursery schools and classes close for school

TABLE 10.1 Differences between education and care for young children

	Daycare	Education
Main aims	• various: supporting parents, promoting quality, caring for children, providing stable and safe environment	• promoting children's learning • preparation for primary school
Curriculum	• of peripheral concern: basic play materials, rough groupings of materials	• central: extremely sophisticated: eight basic areas, subdivided into many parts, each with many ideas about practice
School	• little contact with primary school	• dovetailed with National Curriculum
Staff	• two-year vocational training in nursery nursing • multi-role job description	• staff formally qualified to teach in primary school sector following four-year BEd course • main task to teach, any other tasks a distraction from teaching
Children	• focused on children aged 0–5 • view of children's paramount need to feel safe and secure	• focused on children aged 3–5 • view of child's paramount need to learn and master basic linguistic and numerical tasks
Style of learning	• meaningful learning, diffuse, occurs throughout day, in many situations	• meaningful learning, intense, concentrated into short periods in educational setting
Staff accountability	• through staff support, supervision and managerial oversight	• through written development planning, individual or team-based
Effectiveness	• mainly measured by child/parent satisfaction	• mainly measured by children's developmental outcomes

(Penn and Wilkinson 1995)

holidays. In addition, there is a professional distinction between nursery nurses and nursery teachers resulting in differentiation of status, remuneration and promotion prospects.

In ideological terms there is still a widespread view among parents and some professionals in the UK that very young children (i.e. under three years) could be seriously impaired unless they are reared by their mothers. This means that in the UK there is very little educational provision for under-threes in the local authority sector, despite comparative evidence that many other European countries provide extensive and successful facilities for under-threes. However, this attitude is now being challenged. Provision for under-threes is being taken seriously by respective Government departments. For example, in Scotland, guidelines have been issued to those professionals working with very young children (Learning and Teaching Scotland 2003) and provision for under-threes is improving though largely in the private and voluntary sectors. In addition, the Government's Sure Start programme is beginning to impact on those children deemed to be in vulnerable circumstances.

Since 1998, the number of children experiencing early childhood education and care in the UK has increased dramatically. Table 10.2 shows the percentage of three and four-year-old children in England by type of provider in 2000 and 2003 (provisional estimates). The proportion of children accessing early years services in England has virtually doubled since the mid-1990s. In 1998 the estimated proportion was in the range 50 to 60 per cent; while in 2003 the figure for three and four-year-olds has risen to nearly 100 per cent. In terms of the difference between the two age groups, the proportion of three-year-olds accessing services was 93 per cent in 2003 while for four-year-olds it is now universal.

TABLE 10.2   Proportion of three and four-year-olds by type of early years education provider in England 2000–2003

Form of early years provision	2000 (%)	2003 (%) (provisional)
Private and voluntary providers	30	38
Independent schools	4	5
Nursery and primary schools	59	59
Nursery schools and classes	30	28
Infant classes in primary schools	29	31
All providers	93	102

Source: DfES web site www.dfes.gov.uk/statistics/DB/SFR/
Notes   1. Percentages are given as percentages of the three and four-year-old population.
          2. Several children access more than one type of provider.
          3. The percentage in infant classes in primary schools include children in reception and other classes not designated as nursery classes.

In Scotland, the pattern of provision is somewhat different to that in England and Wales. There is no equivalent of the reception class. Where available, parents choose to send their children to a nursery school, nursery class, day nursery, playgroup and/or private nursery. However, the dramatic increases in the number of three and four-year-olds accessing early years provision witnessed in England has also been replicated in Scotland (SE 2003a).

Theoretical perspectives

The theoretical basis of pre-school provision is both complex and extensive. It is complex not only because it is intricately interwoven with several academic disciplines but because the different types of provision give different emphasis to different theories. It is extensive because the field has received much research attention from a wide variety of domains and individuals. The design, restructuring and revision of institutional systems for the education and care of young children is inherently based on an understanding, whether implicit or explicit, of this theoretical background.

The principal theoretical strands that inform and shape provision for families with children under five are:

- *ideology* of childcare and child rearing
- *psychology* of child development
- *the nature* of education and care of children.

Childcare is inextricably bound up with the realisation of equal opportunities and the relief of disadvantage. As such it is immersed in ideology and is a matter of public responsibility. 'Childcare makes a contribution to the relief of disadvantage and the promotion of equality' (Cohen and Fraser 1991: ii).

How childcare affects children and families is a critical feature of developmental psychology:

> Far from disrupting the family by taking over some of its childcare functions, day care services ought to be seen as providing experiences that complement those obtained at home, with corresponding advantages for child development.
>
> (Schaffer 1990: 153)

Equally, the kind of learning experiences, activities, knowledge and values children are expected to engage with as part of their upbringing and induction into the world are also critical. 'But what do we mean by education for under-fives, what form should it take, what methods should be employed, and what role do adults need to adopt?' (David 1990: 5)

The pre-school curriculum

Since the time of the first nursery in New Lanark, 'play' has been a central feature of nursery activities. It was not until after the Second World War, however, that governments began to take an interest in the activities inside the nursery. In Scotland, the 1950 Primary Memorandum published by the then Scottish Education Department defined the aim of nursery education:

> The aim of nursery school education is to provide the right conditions for growth, and so to ensure the harmonising of the whole personality of the child. Whenever reference is made to aspects of development, whether physical, mental, emotional, spiritual, or social, it must not be forgotten that these are all inter-dependent aspects of a unity.
>
> (SED 1950: 127)

The Memorandum went on to state:

> The value of the physical aspect is perhaps the most obvious. In general, the term covers medical care, adequate rest and sleep, balanced diet, play within doors and in the open air, suitable clothing, and training in hygienic habits.
>
> (SED 1950: 127)

In other words, it was the health care aspect of nurseries that was stressed by central government in the post-war period. This stress on health was the dominant influence in nurseries for some 30 years, many nurseries being under the direct supervision of the Ministry of Health (DES 1967). In day nurseries, health care was paramount; children had to be protected from disease and squalor. It was not until the 1970s that a change took place when attention was paid to children's intellectual needs. In *Before Five* (SED 1973), the aim of nursery education was broadened into activities aimed at child development:

> The ideal educational environment in these years will afford opportunities for the child to develop his physical, intellectual, social and emotional capacities.
>
> (SED 1973: 1)

For the first time, priority was to be given in early childhood education to a child's broad developmental needs. In 2000 the then Department for Education and Employment in England established the 'foundation stage' as a distinct period in the English education system (DfEE 2000).

The foundation stage is defined as that period in a child's life from age three to the end of the reception year, i.e. age five. To offer guidance on appropriate learning experiences for children at this stage, the Qualifications and Curriculum Authority (QCA) in England issued a set of curriculum guidelines referred to as *Curriculum Guidance for the Foundation Stage* for professionals working with children in the age range three to five (DfEE 2000). The guidance specifies six areas of development as the framework within which detailed learning outcomes, referred to as 'early learning goals', are stipulated. These areas are:

- personal, social and emotional development;
- communication, language and literacy;
- mathematical development;
- knowledge and understanding of the world;
- physical development;
- creative development.

To help practitioners in planning early years activities, the guidance issued by the QCA identifies the concept of 'stepping stones' that show the knowledge, skills, understanding and attitudes that children need to learn during the foundation stage in order to achieve the desired early learning goals. In each curriculum area specified the guidance outlines four progressive steps a child needs to take in order to reach the specified early learning goals and hence be in a position to benefit from more formal education in a primary school setting. An example of such a progression in the area of creative development is shown in Figure 10.1.

In Scotland, the then Scottish Consultative Council on the Curriculum, in its report *A Curriculum Framework for Children 3–5* (SO 1999) defined the aims of early childhood education as to:

- Provide a safe and stimulating environment, in which children could feel happy and secure.
- Encourage the emotional, social, physical, creative and intellectual development of children.
- Promote the welfare of children.
- Encourage positive attitudes to self and others and develop confidence and self-esteem.
- Create opportunities for play.
- Encourage children to explore, appreciate and respect their environment.
- Provide opportunities to stimulate interest and imagination.
- Extend the children's abilities to communicate ideas and feelings in a variety of ways.

To help achieve these aims, the Curriculum Framework document outlines curriculum guidelines in terms of planned learning experiences based on five aspects of children's development and learning. The only difference between the Scottish

What does the practitioner need to do?	Progression from age three
• Be interested in and participate in children's play • Model the pretending process, supporting children's understanding of the ways in which one object can be used to represent another	↓
• Ensure that there is enough time for children to express their thoughts, ideas and feelings in a variety of ways, such as in role play, by painting and by responding to music • Provide appropriate materials, and extend children's thinking through involvement in their play, using questions thoughtfully and appropriately	↓
• Pay particular attention to children who are less confident • Be aware of the link between imaginative play and children's ability to handle narrative • Introduce language that enables children to talk about their experiences in greater depth and detail	↓
• Be aware of what fires children's imagination • Support children's ideas through the provision of appropriate materials • Model techniques and teach skills that will enable children to do what they have planned successfully • Extend children's experience and expand their Imagination through pictures, paintings, poems, music, dance and story • Support children's developing understanding of the ways in which paintings and pictures and dance express different ideas, thoughts and feelings • Regularly introduce new vocabulary to enable children to talk about their experiences and feelings and describe their actions	Early learning goals for imagination

Source: DfEE (2000)

FIGURE 10.1   The foundation stage early learning goals for the development of imagination in the curriculum area creative development

guidelines and the English guidance, in terms of curriculum areas, is that in the English guidance mathematical development forms a discrete area, while in the Scottish guidelines mathematical development is integrated into knowledge and understanding of the world.

Thus, for the first time in the 200-year history of nursery education in the UK, Government has specified the parameters of children's learning. The drivers for this policy are based on raising standards of educational achievement in the compulsory school years and facilitating parents to be more economically active. Reports such as *World's Apart* (Ofsted 1996), which compares educational achievement internationally, have had a major impact on successive Governments' policy despite evidence to show that performance in external examinations such as A levels and Highers has improved. Nevertheless the present Government's emphasis on early childhood education, which forms a key element of its Childcare Strategy, is to be warmly welcomed.

Although definition of the curriculum by central Government agencies is generally accepted among early childhood professionals (Wilkinson 2003), its delivery and impact on children's general well-being is more controversial. With the influx of young children into reception classes in England and Wales, which have inferior child–teacher ratios compared to nurseries, formalisation of the pedagogy for such children has taken place in a number of settings. Some four-year-olds in reception classes no longer enjoy a spontaneous, play-based, caring and stimulating environment associated with good nurseries. Instead they are subject to school pressures to conform and engage with formal, highly structured learning. While there is much to be said for stimulating children intellectually from an early age, excessive rigidity can have undesirable psychological consequences.

> The informality of the nursery must be preserved – it is just as important for children to develop socially, emotionally and physically as it is to understand the world.
>
> (Wilkinson 1992: 8)

Introduction of the foundation stage with its associated curriculum guidance is intended to reinforce a more child-centred pedagogy, which has its roots in the writings of Jean Jacques Rousseau in the eighteenth century in France.

Quality of the nursery experience

Defining quality

Of paramount importance in pre-school education is the pursuit of quality, partly motivated by 'value for money' in public sector services, but also motivated by the now well-established relationship between quality and children's progress. The importance of quality in early childhood services was raised in the Rumbold Report (DfES 1990). Since then, various organisations (e.g. European Childcare Network 1991, 1996) and several local authorities have recognised that quality matters. However, defining quality in early childhood services is not straightforward. The complex problems of definition have been discussed at length (Elfer and Wedge 1992; Watt 1994; Moss and Pence 1994; Abbott 1994; Dahlberg, Moss and Pence 1999). To reach a universal definition of quality is not feasible – definitions vary according to the perspective of a particular stakeholder group.

As claimed by Dahlberg *et al.* (1999) it is more fruitful to examine the different meanings attributed to quality by the various influential stakeholders. They identify two categories of meaning: one descriptive and relative, the other evaluative and quasi-objective. In the former category of meaning, referred to by Moss and Pence as the 'inclusionary paradigm', the process of reaching a common understanding between the various immediate stakeholders is central. The primary purpose in this paradigm is to deliver a service to children and families that both professional educators/carers and parents mutually agree is worthwhile. Clearly such an approach contributes to the development of a dynamic early years setting. Unfortunately it ignores the political realities associated with funding and accountability – features with which recent Governments are concerned.

In the second category of the meaning attributable to quality, that is, the evaluative meaning, the primary purpose is to assess how well a service performs and/or meets its aims and objectives. In order to do this a benchmark of quality is usually stipulated in advance against which judgements can be made. Very often this is the paradigm used by researchers in this field (e.g. Harms and Clifford 1980; Sylva *et al.* 1999). While the strength of this approach affords some degree of comparative analysis (see, for example, Stephen and Wilkinson 1995), the weakness is that context, culture and choice are ignored.

In moving the debate forward it seems not unreasonable to explore the possibility of combining the two paradigms into a unified process of quality definition and quality assessment. Such an arrangement would initially draw on the evaluative tradition by establishing a broad quality framework through mutual agreement between a number of stakeholders. The framework would then be used in such a way as to give individual nurseries the opportunity to describe their practice and generate supportive evidence which would be available for external scrutiny (Wilkinson and Brady 1990). In their work with the Scottish Independent Nurseries Association (SINA), Wilkinson and Stephen (1998) specified such a framework based on defined standards in six key areas:

- the learning environment
- partnerships
- management

- the social experience
- staff
- accommodation and resources.

Drawing on a range of literature, Wilkinson and Stephen identified a wide range of indicators for each of the six key areas. In the case of Key Area 1 (the learning environment) the indicators covered curriculum, record-keeping/ assessment, planning, promoting learning, special needs and equal opportunities. This approach to quality assurance has now been adopted by the Centre for British Teachers in its scheme *Quality Matters* (CfBT 2000).

Quality assessment

Two approaches to the assessment of quality can be identified in practice. The qualitative approach relies on the professional judgement of teachers, nursery nurses and others, while the quantitative approach is based on 'objective' measurement often using pre-specified scales. The former approach, which characterises inspections by Her Majesty's Inspectorate of Schools, has the advantage of being more comprehensive and detailed but is open to potential bias and possible dispute. It is also only feasible to undertake intensive inspections at lengthy intervals of time (in the case of Ofsted inspections, every five to six years at the time of writing). The latter approach to quality assessment is potentially more rigorous and quasi-objective but necessarily depends on a more rigid definition of 'quality'. Such an approach is being used in the longitudinal research study being undertaken at the London Institute of Education in the Effective Provision of Pre-school Education (EPPE) Project. This is a five-year longitudinal study which began in 1997. Among other matters, the study aimed to compare and contrast the developmental progress of 3,000+ children selected from a wide range of social and cultural backgrounds in six local authorities in England which have differing pre-school experiences (Sylva *et al.* 1999). Using the revised edition of ECERS (Harms, Clifford and Cryer 1998) and its English Extension (ECERS-E), comparisons were made between the different types of provider – public, private and voluntary. On the vast majority of indicators, nursery schools and classes were rated highest while playgroups in the voluntary sector were rated lowest, a finding not consistent with quality of provision in Scotland for these services in partnership with a local authority.

> This study shows clearly that well-resourced pre-school centres which had a history of 'education' (including a more substantial number of trained teachers, LEA in-service training, Ofsted 'Section 10' rather than 'pre-school Section 5' inspection) were providing the highest quality of care and education. The centres from the 'care' tradition, despite their more favourable ratios, were offering a different level of care and education.
>
> (Sylva *et al.* 1999: 19)

Sylva *et al.* concluded in their interim report, however, that the standard of education and care in pre-school provision in England was adequate in the vast majority of settings.

Until very recently, the assessment of the educational progress of young children has been overwhelmingly concerned with the teaching and learning process either to help in pedagogical planning (Wolfendale 1993) or in screening children for special educational needs (Lindsay and Pearson 1981). Blenkin and Kelly (1992) make out a strong case for the primacy of the pedagogical purpose in assessment:

> We have throughout this book advocated those forms (of assessment) we consider most conducive to the promotion of educational growth in pupils – those which are formative, holistic, emphasising strengths rather than weaknesses, judgmental rather than metric.
>
> (Blenkin and Kelly 1992: 165)

Since the introduction of national testing by the last Government, a sea change has taken place in the purpose of assessment (Blatchford and Cline 1994; Burgess-Macey 1994). Information from assessment is now required to evaluate the effectiveness of different educational institutions, principally schools.

No longer is it accepted that all schools are doing a good job. For example, in one local authority, Hackney, the Government has taken direct action in the management of its schools in order to improve national standards. Further, accountability and new management practices have heralded the concept of 'value-added'. Head teachers, Directors of Education and HMIs are all interested, for different reasons, in evaluating the effectiveness of particular schools.

> Schools feel the need to prove that they are teaching children effectively and that the learning that a child can demonstrate by the age of the Key Stage 1 tests of assessment has in fact been facilitated by the school. Without baseline assessment on entry to school the value-added component of a child's later performance cannot be calculated.
>
> (Burgess-Macey 1994: 48)

Inventing the concept of 'value-added' was in recognition of the fact that different schools have to conduct their business with children from different socio-economic groups. It has long been recognised that a relationship – albeit complex – exists between educational attainment and social class. It is therefore unreasonable to expect all schools to educate their children to the same level of achievement irrespective of the social factors external to the school.

However, it is not only the 'value-added' requirements that have prompted the use of assessments for evaluative purposes. The present Government's policy of raising education standards partly through its programme of Early Intervention also plays an important role. In order to assist the process of raising standards, considerable investment is now taking place in the early stages of a child's education. Various schemes are being put in place to identify children 'at risk' and to offset any possible subsequent learning difficulties. Evaluative questions are being asked about the effectiveness of such intervention. Answers to these questions are increasingly being located in the assessment of children's progress.

Lindsay (1997) identified seven purposes of assessment in two main categories: those which are child-focused and those which are school-focused. In the child-focused category he includes such matters as screening, monitoring and pedagogy while in the school-focused category he locates resource planning and accountability.

There is considerable debate in the literature (Drummond 1993; Lindsay 1997) as to whether any one scheme for assessing four and five-year-old children – sometimes referred to as 'baseline assessment' – can adequately address each of the purposes. Wolfendale (1993) identified a number of concerns and dilemmas which are 'an amalgam of technical educational and socio-political issues'. Despite what Wolfendale refers to as 'a long list of objections to Baseline Assessment – at every level – theoretical, ideological, practical and financial' she concludes:

> Paradoxically in fact there does appear to be a consensus, based on reality principles, that a form, or forms, of on-entry to school assessment is a viable idea.
>
> (Wolfendale 1993: 33)

However, considerable concern has been expressed about the purpose and practice:

> Early years educators need to treat the issue of assessment very carefully. We need to be clear about which purposes of assessment we are working towards, and which models of the early years curriculum and of children's learning underpin our models of assessment. We cannot uncritically adopt a model handed down from the National Curriculum and assessment procedures.
>
> (Burgess-Macey 1994: 48)

Similarly, Lindsay concluded: 'Baseline assessment is potentially a very useful addition to the education system – but only if developed and used wisely' (Lindsay 1997: 26). Several baseline assessment schemes now in use throughout the UK use formative procedures where information about a particular child's learning is generated on the basis of the professional judgement of those involved with the child (Black and Willan 1998). It is now regarded as good practice in early childhood education that assessment information can play a vital role in ensuring that all children engage with the learning process as effectively as possible (Wilkinson et al. 2001).

Recent developments

It is increasingly recognised that early childhood education is inextricably bound up with childcare. No longer are education and care separate processes. All the experiences children encounter make an important impact on their well-being, not only in the early years but in subsequent stages, even into adulthood. That early childhood services are critical to future well-being has been recognised in the Government's Green Paper *Every Child Matters* (Chief Secretary to the Treasury 2003) which followed a similar publication in Scotland *For Scotland's Children* (SE 2001). These Green Papers set out a framework for services for children and young people from birth to 19, the main purpose of which is:

> to reduce the number of children who experience failure, engage in offending or antisocial behaviour, suffer from ill-health or become teenage parents.
>
> (Chief Secretary to the Treasury 2003: 5)

The key to delivering such social goals are the arrangements for accountability and integration of services and the reform of the wide range of professionals who work with young children and their families.

In Scotland the Childcare Strategy is in the process of being superseded by the new Integrated Learning Strategy (SE 2003b). This strategy identifies the need for health professionals, education professionals and social work professionals to work much more collaboratively in the delivery of specific targets in the following areas:

- To improve children's health
- To improve children's social and emotional development
- To improve children's ability to learn
- To strengthen families and communities
- To reduce barriers to employment.

In order to bring about such ambitious goals the work of early childhood educators and other professionals who engage with young children needs to be remodelled in structured terms:

> The challenge is to indicate and foster in young children a mind-set that internalises such attributes so that children's routine day-to-day behaviour reflects a more sophisticated level of awareness of the need to be meaningfully engaged with the process of self-improvement. As such, the task facing educators of young children – whether they be teachers, nursery nurses, playleaders or parents – is daunting.
>
> (Wilkinson 2004: 285)

Conclusion

Early childhood education has come a long way since the days of Robert Owen. Although much of the original informality has been retained, there is a more formal definition of children's early years experience. It is now considered to be one of the most important sectors of education. Rapid expansion of provision has thrown into sharp focus the debate about the nature of experiences most beneficial to young children. It is now accepted that exposure to a formal pedagogy too soon can have detrimental effects on children's subsequent education. In many European countries – particularly in Scandinavia – formal school does not begin until children are over seven years old. Children's experiences prior to this are firmly rooted in experiential learning – exploration, play, music and social activities. In Scotland much of this spontaneity is also in evidence. In England and Wales, however, the situation has been far from ideal. During the 1980s and early 1990s too much emphasis was placed on formal learning. Only with the introduction of the foundation stage is the situation beginning to change for the better.

An all-rounded, quality nursery experience has untold benefits for children, parents and the wider society. It is fundamental not only to the subsequent schooling process but to the promotion of a more tolerant and understanding society. The challenge now facing early years professionals is to find an appropriate mechanism where more effective collaboration is pursued. As the recent Green Paper states:

> We want to put children at the heart of our policies, and to organise services around their needs. Radical reform is needed to break down organisational boundaries.
>
> (Chief Secretary to the Treasury 2003: 9)

Suggested further reading

The literature in this field of education is vast. However, readers are recommended to explore the following texts. For further debate on promoting learning see Anning and Edwards (1999); for a very readable discussion on young children's personal, social and emotional development see Dowling (2000). For a challenging critique on nursery education see Moss and Penn (1996) and for a thoughtful analysis of the quality debate, see Dahlberg *et al.* (1999). For an up-to-date account of policy developments in Scotland since 1997 see Wilkinson (2003). This book raises a number of important tensions between the need to protect vulnerable children and the necessity to give all children a challenging learning experience. Readers will also find useful the book by James, Jenks and Prout (1998) which provides a modern sociological dimension to the early years debate.

References

Abbott, M. (1994) 'Introduction: The search for quality in the early years', in L. Abbott and R. Rodger (eds) *Quality Education in the Early Years*. Buckingham: OU Press.

Anning, A. and Edwards, A. (1999) *Promoting Children's Learning from Birth to Five: developing the new early years professional*. Buckingham: Open University Press.

Ball, C. (1994) *Start Right: The Importance of Early Learning*. London: Royal Society of Arts.

Belsky, J. (2001) 'Developmental Risks (Still) Associated with Early Childcare', *Journal of Child Psychology and Psychiatry*, 42 (7), 845–59.

Black, P. and Willan, D. (1998) *Inside the Black Box*. London: School of Education, King's College.

Blatchford, P. and Cline, T. (1994) 'Baseline Assessment: Selecting a Method of Assessing Children on School Entry', *Education*, 3 (13), 10–15.

Blenkin, G. M. and Kelly, A. V. (1992) *Assessment in Early Childhood Education*. London: Paul Chapman.

Bowlby, J. (1952) *Maternal Care and Mental Health*. Geneva: World Health Organisations.

Burgess-Macey, C. (1994) 'Assessing Young Children's Learning', in P. Keel (ed.) *Assessment in the Multi-ethnic Primary Classroom*. Stoke-on-Trent: Trentham Books.

Centre for British Teachers (2000) *Quality Matters*. Reading: CfBT.

Chief Secretary to the Treasury (2003) *Every Child Matters*. Norwich: The Stationery Office.

Clarke-Stewart, A. (1991) 'Day Care in the USA', in P. Moss and E. Melhuish (eds) *Current Issues in Day Care for Young Children*. London: HMSO.

Cohen, B. and Fraser, N. (1991) *Childcare in a Modern Welfare System*. London: IPPR.

Dahlberg, G., Moss, P. and Pence, A. (1999) *Beyond Quality in Early Childhood Education and Care*. London: Falmer Press.

David, T. (1990) *Under Five – Under Educated?* Buckingham: OU Press.

Department for Education and Employment (1998a) *Meeting the Childcare Challenge*. London: HMSO.

Department for Education and Employment (1998b) *Early Years Development and Childcare Partnerships – Planning Guidance 1999–2000*. Sudbury: DfEE Publications.

Department for Education and Employment (2000) *Curriculum Guidance for the Foundation Stage*. London: QCA.

Department of Education and Science (1967) *Children and their Primary Schools (The Plowden Report)*. London: HMSO.

Department of Education and Science (1990) *Starting with Quality. The Report of the Committee of Inquiry into the Quality of Educational Experience Offered to Three- and Four-year-old Children (The Rumbold Report)*. London: HMSO.

Dowling, M. (2000) *Young Children's Personal, Social and Emotional Development*. London: Paul Chapman.

Drummond, M. J. (1993) *Assessing Young Children's Learning*. London: David Fulton Publishers.

Elfer, P. and Wedge, D. (1992) 'Defining, measuring and supporting quality', in C. Pugh (ed.) *Contemporary Issues in the Early Years: working collaboratively for children*. London: Paul Chapman and National Children's Bureau.

European Childcare Network (1991) *Quality in Services for Young Children*. Brussels: Commission of the European Communities.

European Childcare Network (1996) *Quality Targets in Services for Young Children*. Brussels: Commission of the European Communities.

Harms, T. and Clifford, R. M. (1980) *Early Childhood Environment Rating Scale*. New York: Teachers College Press.

Harms, T., Clifford, R. M. and Cryer, D. (1998) *Early Childhood Environment Rating Scale* (Revised edition). New York: Teachers College Press.

James, A., Jenks, C. and Prout, A. (1998) *Theorizing Childhood*. Oxford: Polity.

Learning and Teaching Scotland (2003) *Care and Learning for Children Birth to Three*. Dundee: L&T Scotland.

Lindsay, G. A. (1997) *Baseline Assessment: A Positive or Malign Initiative?* Coventry: Institute of Education, University of Warwick.

Lindsay, G. A. and Pearson, L. (1981) *Identification and Intervention: school based approaches*. Oxford: TRC.

McCartney, K. (1984) 'Effect of Quality Day Care Environment on Children's Language Development', *Developmental Psychology*, 20(2).

Moss, P. and Pence, A. (1994) *Valuing Quality in Early Childcare Services*. London: Paul Chapman.

Moss, P. and Penn, H. (1996) *Transforming Nursery Education*. London: Paul Chapman.

Ofsted (1996) *World's Apart. A Review of International Surveys of Educational Achievement Involving England*. London: HMSO.

Penn, H. (1992) *Under Fives – The View from Strathclyde*. Edinburgh: Scottish Academic Press.

Penn, H. and Wilkinson, J. E. (1995) 'The future of pre-five services in the United Kingdom', *Early Child Development and Care*, 108, 147–60.

Phillips, D., McCartney, K. and Scarr, S. (1987) 'Child Care Quality and Children's Social Development', *Developmental Psychology*, 23(4).

Schaffer, H. R. (1977) *Mothering*. Glasgow: Fontana.

Schaffer, H. R. (1990) *Making Decisions about Children*. Oxford: Basil Blackwell.

Scottish Education Department (SED) (1950) *The Primary School in Scotland*. Edinburgh: HMSO.

Scottish Education Department (SED) (1973) *Before Five*. Edinburgh: HMSO.

Scottish Executive (SE) (2001) *For Scotland's Children*. Edinburgh: Scottish Executive.

Scottish Executive (SE) (2003a) 'Summary Results of the 2003 Pre-School and Daycare Census', *Statistical Bulletin*, 29 July.

Scottish Executive (SE) (2003b) *Integrated Strategy for the Early Years Consultation*. Edinburgh: Scottish Executive.

Scottish Office (SO) (1998) *Meeting the Childcare Challenge – A Childcare Strategy for Scotland*. Edinburgh: The Stationery Office.

Scottish Office (SO) (1999) *A Curriculum Framework for Children 3–5*. Dundee: Scottish Consultative Council on the Curriculum.

Shorrocks, D. (1993) 'Seven year olds assessed', *Concern*, Autumn.

Stephen, C. and Wilkinson, J. E. (1995) 'Assessing the Quality of Provision in Community Nurseries', *Early Child Development and Care*, 108, 99–114.

Sylva, K. and Wiltshire, J. (1994) 'The impact of early learning on children's later development', *Education Section Review*, 18 (2), 47.

Sylva, K. *et al.* (1999) *Characteristics of Pre-School Environments*. Technical Paper 6a, Effective Provision of the Pre-school Education (EPPE) Project. London: Institute of Education.

Tizard, B. and Hughes, M. (1984) *Young Children Learning*. London: Fontana.

Watt, J. (ed.) (1994) *Early Education – The Current Debate*. Edinburgh: Scottish Academic Press.

Wilkinson, J. E. (1992) 'Young Children Thinking', in *Reflections on Curriculum Issues – Early Education*. Dundee: SCCC.

Wilkinson, J. E. (1995) 'Community Nurseries: Integrated Provision for Pre-Fives', *Early Child Development and Care*, 108, 1–106.

Wilkinson, J. E. (2003) *Early Childhood Education – the New Agenda*. Edinburgh: Dunedin Academic Press.

Wilkinson, J. E. (2004) 'Reflections on new policies for Early Childhood Education and Care in Scotland', *Education in the North*, 11.

Wilkinson, J. E. and Brady, J. (1990) 'Pre-Five Evaluation Research in Strathclyde', in *The School and its Community*. Edinburgh: SCRE.

Wilkinson, J. E., Johnson, S., Watt, J., Napuk, A. and Normand, B. (2001) 'Baseline Assessment in Scotland: an analysis of pilot data', *Assessment in Education*, 8(2), 171–92.

Wilkinson, J. E. and Stephen, C. (1998) 'Collaboration in Pre-School Provision', *Early Years*, 19 (1), 29–38.

Wolfendale, S. (1993) *Baseline Assessment: A Review of Current Practice, Issues and Strategies for Effective Implementation*. Stoke-on-Trent: Trentham Books.

11

Compulsory education in the United Kingdom

Estelle Brisard and Ian Menter

It is time to realise that 'compulsory education' is impossible. You can compel children and adolescents to 'go to school'. If you use more draconian discipline than most of us would now wish to see, you may, in theory, be able to compel all of them to sit quietly at their desks. But if they do not wish to learn, they will not learn.

(William Whitson, Letter to *The Herald*, 5 January 2004)

Introduction

COMPULSORY EDUCATION – a simple phrase, but what does it mean? For a child born a thousand years ago, it would have meant very little. The emergence of education as a social system only started – and then only in Western Europe and for a small proportion of children – during the middle ages. Few children born in England or Scotland in 1600 would have received 'an education'. By 1800, a boy born to the landed classes or into a clerical family might well have been compelled to attend school and a girl of the same background might have received an education from a private governess. However, by the year 1900, every child born in Britain was required by law to attend school to the age of 14. Exemptions from this rule were possible only where the child possessed a certificate that they had reached the educational standard required by the local by-laws (DfES 2003).

By the 1990s, not only was attendance at school compulsory for the majority of children from the age of five until the age of 16, but for much of the time spent there, the content of the curriculum had also become compulsory – at least in England, Wales and Northern Ireland. By the year 2000, the majority of children in England aged between five and 11 were compelled to attend school, compelled to follow a defined curriculum and compelled to be taught for part of the day through a centrally determined method – the literacy and numeracy strategies. Those who were not compelled to attend school were nevertheless to be educated 'otherwise' (see below) and those attending private schools were not required to follow the National Curriculum or the national strategies.

In this chapter we trace the apparent steady encroachment of the state, through its education system, on the 'freedom of the child', from the nineteenth century through to the present. The first half of the chapter examines these historical developments in more detail and seeks to explore what were the intentions and motivations behind each element of compulsion. In the later part of the chapter we describe and critically examine the current situation across the four countries that comprise the UK. There is a sense in which it is helpful to judge developments in other parts of the UK as responses to English developments – sometimes accepting and adopting similar policies and sometimes reacting against and developing alternative policies.

The development of compulsory education in the UK

The emergence of state education

Green (1997) has noted that the education system developed after the formation of the British state. Therefore, by contrast with several other European countries the education system played a less significant part in the formation of national identity. Rather, the way in which the education system developed may be seen as a reflection of the existing 'settlement' of national identity. As we shall see, the notion of national identity in the context of Great Britain or of the United Kingdom is far from settled. 'British' has often been confused with 'English' – particularly by the English and by people from outside the UK.

In tracing the emergence of state education systems we can see the strong influence of a 'voluntary' sector. Green (1997) goes so far as to suggest that:

> Both in the eighteenth and nineteenth centuries this voluntary approach was held to be morally, and educationally, superior to compulsory schooling schemes in continental Europe. These were associated with despotism and subservience, in contrast to the freedoms enjoyed by British citizens, which were seen as being essential to British character. Voluntarism ... meant freedom for pupils from compulsory attendance, and freedom for schools from state interference.
>
> (p. 94)

Towards the end of the nineteenth century this voluntaristic ideology started to be in considerable tension with some other strong emergent beliefs. There was a powerful belief in the rights of all children to be educated to a basic level of literacy in order to engage with the modern world. There was also a separate but often related belief in the development of society through education. But thirdly and most powerfully of all was the belief that in the interest of maintaining morality in society, all people should be able to read – in order to have personal access to the messages contained in the Bible.

Thus it was from the outset that the churches played a major role in the provision of schooling. Even before elementary schooling was made compulsory in 1880, a very large majority of children were attending some form of schooling for at least a year or two, with a strongly Christian dimension. The quality of provision was very variable and few stayed beyond the age of 11. In 1893 the leaving age was set at 11, but by 1900 it had been raised to 14.

Driving the development of schooling and its emergence as a state system was the motor of the industrial revolution. The nineteenth century saw both an enormous expansion of the population in Britain (almost doubling in 50 years from 1821 to 1871, to an estimated 26 million) but also very large increases in the proportion of that population who were children and of the proportion who were living in urban settlements.

Provision of secondary education during the nineteenth century was even more uneven than that of elementary schooling. Secondary schools existed largely as foundations established to provide entry into the higher professions, often via one of the universities, and the pupils were largely children from middle and upper social classes, although even at this time, it was possible for a small number of pupils from poor backgrounds to gain admission. It was not until 1902, with the creation of local education authorities in England and Wales, that a national system of secondary education began to emerge. The Board of Education had been established in 1899 and by 1904 it had defined a four-year secondary programme leading to a certificate.

These developments of elementary and secondary education, together with major developments in university education, effectively established – by the end of the nineteenth century – the framework for education in Britain that still exists today.

It is possible to understand the way in which state education developed in its compulsory form as a continuing struggle between different interest groups in society. Raymond Williams (1961) offered a very interesting account along these lines in his influential book *The Long Revolution*. The revolution of Williams' title was the gradual emergence by the second half of the twentieth century of social democracy in Britain. He examines the way in which transformations in a number of social and cultural institutions, including the press, broadcasting, fiction and drama, have played a part in the creation of this society.

In his account of the development of education, Williams identifies three groups who each played a part in the way in which state education was constructed in the late nineteenth century, but who, he also argues, could still be identified at the time he was writing, in the second half of the twentieth century. The three groups he identified were:

- the public educators – who argued that 'men had a natural human right to be educated, and that any good society depended on governments accepting this principle as their duty';

- the industrial trainers – who 'promoted education in terms of training and disciplining the poor, as workers and citizens';

- the old humanists – who promoted 'a liberal education, in relation to man's health as a spiritual being'.

(pp. 162–3)

As we trace compulsory education through the twentieth century it is not difficult to see these three groups continuing to argue their cases, sometimes in co-operation with each other and sometimes in opposition.

The development of state education in the twentieth century

The legacy of the nineteenth century for elementary schools was a tightly defined and – in the light of subsequent developments – narrow, knowledge-based curriculum. This was broadened, at least in theory, when the Revised Code was published in 1904 (see, for example, Heller 1904). The purpose of elementary schools was 'to form and strengthen the character and develop the intelligence of children, and ... assist both girls and boys, according to their different needs, to fit themselves, practically as well as intellectually, for the work of life' (quoted by Ross 2000: 21). As secondary schools developed in the early part of the twentieth century, however, their curriculum was based very much on subjects, including English, Latin, geography, history, mathematics and science, drawing, manual work, physical exercises and housewifery (in girls' schools) (see Ross 2000).

So both in the emerging primary and in the secondary curriculum we can see the influence of Williams' industrial trainer strand and of the public educator strand. The old humanist strand is there too, in the commitment to particular forms of intellectual knowledge, but this came increasingly to the fore as the century progressed, through the development of a child-centred philosophy which emphasised the individualism of each human being, and, drawing on ideas from the burgeoning discipline of psychology, as well as some traditional philosophical strands, educationists argued for an approach that was based on the individual needs of the child. This way of thinking was especially prevalent in relation to younger children and was clearly articulated in the Hadow Reports of 1927, 1931 and 1933.

The Second World War had a major impact on the development of the 'welfare state'. It was recognised that families whose young people had served the country so bravely in wartime deserved the kind of social support that should now be affordable, at least once post-war reconstruction was fully under way. So it was that the National Health Service and the social security system both emerged at this time. In education the coalition Government of the day supported the development of the 1944 Education Act, under the leadership of the Secretary of the Board of Education, R. A. Butler. The significant achievement of this legislation was to establish the provision of universal secondary education for the first time. This was achieved through creating a two-stage approach to compulsory education, bringing in a transfer from primary to secondary education at the age of 11.

A further 'achievement' of the Act was to introduce and legitimate differentiation into secondary schooling, a feature that was the subject of considerable contestation throughout the rest of the twentieth century and indeed continues in different form to this day. The idea which underpinned this policy was that children could be classified by their ability to benefit from different forms of education. It was believed that some children were capable of greater intellectual development than others, according to their supposedly innate – and therefore fixed – level of intelligence. So it was that children could legitimately be channelled into either a grammar school, a secondary modern school or a technical school. The channelling (actually selection) was largely achieved through the administration of a public examination, the 'eleven plus', as it became known. Sociological studies carried out during the 1950s and 1960s claimed to show how this system severely curtailed opportunity for children from working-class backgrounds, which led the Labour Party to commit itself to the provision of 'comprehensive education' in 1965, a universalist approach to compulsory schooling, which aimed to see all children attending their local neighbourhood school. This goal was only partially achieved during the later part of the century and, under 'New Labour', around the recent turn of the century, we have witnessed the emergence of a new discourse of specialisation, through which secondary schools are encouraged to develop a profile in a particular area of the curriculum and pupils can be selected, in part, through their aptitude in this field, whether it be the arts, sport, languages or whatever other field the school claims strength in.

The private schooling sector (of which some schools are confusingly described as 'public schools') has continued its parallel existence throughout the whole historical period, effectively ensuring that a sector of society, mostly those with sufficient wealth to have the choice, is removed from the state school population. Schools in the private sector are not required to offer the National Curriculum, nor to administer national tests. There is a further group of students who are not educated in school at all but may be taught at home, often by one or both of their parents. For those parents who are against schooling as a form of education or who believe their children will not benefit from institutional provision, it remains possible to opt out. However, both the private sector and home schooling are subject to legal requirements, designed to ensure that the education, health and welfare needs of children are met.

The legal dimension to the compulsion in school attendance – or education otherwise – has been given added significance over recent years because of two factors. Firstly, there has been the increased emphasis on 'parental choice' of the school their children will attend. The discourse of choice was very much a part of the Conservative Government's approach to the marketisation of education. 'Open enrolment' was a phrase derived from their 1988 Education Reform Act, which imposed on schools the requirement to admit children who wished to attend. This requirement could not be entirely open-ended, however, for very practical reasons, including the physical size of a school and the need to organise pupils into viable class units. So what was the parent who could not secure a place for their child at their chosen school meant to do? Although there were appeal procedures and parents were often offered a range of alternatives, in the end the law required them to ensure their child was educated. As Harris (1993) says:

> The basic legal duty on a parent to ensure that his or her child receives an efficient full-time education suitable to his or her age, ability and aptitude, 'either by regular attendance at school or otherwise', has not changed since the Education Act 1944.
>
> (p. 43)

The second factor which has increased the significance of compulsion is the increased attention that has been paid to truancy. This has been a high priority under both Conservative and Labour Governments. Truancy rates (actually more positively described as 'attendance rates') have been a key performance indicator for schools since the development of published profiles and performance tables during the 1980s. It was the Labour Government, however, that introduced new legislation aimed at bringing the parents of frequent truants to court. In fact, few cases have reached the courts and those that have, have usually resulted in some embarrassment for the LEA concerned, if not the Government, as they have tended to appear as vindictive attacks on very needy, poor and often dysfunctional families.

In the development of compulsory education in the United Kingdom over the past hundred years or so, England can be seen as having been the main driving force – because of its size and the locus of power in Westminster – at least until devolution in the late 1990s. However, it is often said that education is more highly valued in each of the three smaller parts of the UK than it is in England. Certainly, Scottish identity has a strong element of pride in its education provision. This stems in part from the success of the ancient Scottish universities in the stimulation of the 'invention of the modern world' (see Herman 2001). Since the creation of the uneasy union between England and Scotland in 1707, education together with the church and the legal system have been seen as the triumvirate of Scottish distinctiveness. Among those who have written about the separate development of the Scottish education system, Humes and Bryce (2003) have described its distinctiveness in terms not only of organisational differences (which are described below) but also of national culture and identity, including a particular set of values (see also Paterson 2003).

The particular distinctive elements of the provision of compulsory education in Wales and Northern Ireland are discussed in the next section of this chapter.

Compulsory education in the twenty-first-century UK

Organisation

As noted in the first section of this chapter, currently all pupils aged between five (or four in Northern Ireland) and 16 must receive full-time education either at school or through alternative arrangements approved by the state. Education is free at the point of delivery in each of the 22,800 state-maintained primary schools and the 4,306 secondary schools of the UK, and statutory education is organised as a continuous progression between primary and secondary education with very slight variations in the age of transfer to secondary education between the four countries (Figure 11.1).

It can be argued that, over the last 50 years, compulsory education in the UK, and in England more particularly, has been characterised by the two seemingly conflicting trends of *rationalisation* and *diversification* of its provision. Table 11.1

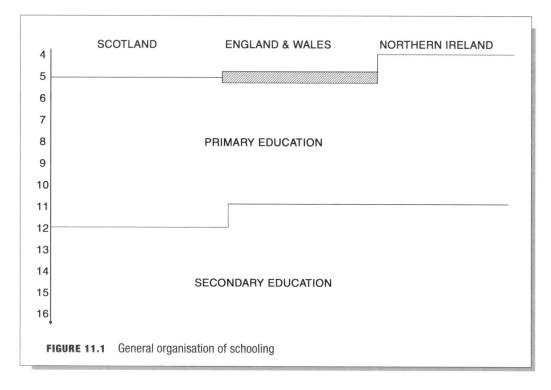

FIGURE 11.1 General organisation of schooling

TABLE 11.1   Primary and secondary schools in the UK

	WALES	ENGLAND	NORTHERN IRELAND	SCOTLAND
PRIMARY SCHOOLS	*Public sector:* (1,624) ■ *Infant* (4–7) ■ *Junior* (7–11) ■ *Combined infant & junior* (5–11) *27% Welsh-medium schools* **In some parts:** *Preparatory schools (5–12/13)*	*Public sector:* (17,985) ■ *Infant* (4–7) ■ *Junior* (7–11) ■ *Combined infant & junior* (5–11) **In some parts:** *First schools* (5–8) *Middle schools* (9–14)	*Public sector:* (920) ■ *Infant* (4–7) ■ *Junior* (7–11) ■ *Combined infant & junior* (5–11) **In some parts:** *Preparatory departments of grammar schools* (4–12)	*Public sector:* (2,271) ■ *Gaelic-medium schools* (58) ■ *New Community school*
SECONDARY SCHOOLS	***Comprehensive and non-selective*** *Public sector:* (227) ■ *Welsh-medium schools* (14) *Non-maintained* (56)	***Mostly comprehensive, some selection*** *Public sector:* (3457) ■ *State-maintained comprehensive:* (2,886) ■ *Grammar schools* (161) ■ *Modern* (130) ■ *Middle deemed secondary* (300) ■ *Specialist schools* (685) *Non-maintained* (2,206)	***Selective*** *Public sector:* (235) ■ *Grammar schools* (71) ■ *Secondary intermediate* (164) ■ *Irish language schools* (3) ■ *Integrated schools* (40+) *Non-maintained* (25) ■ *Irish language schools* (5) ■ *Integrated schools* (11)	***Comprehensive and non-selective*** *Public sector:* (387) ■ *Gaelic-medium schools* (19) *Non-maintained* (122)

presents a complex system of state-maintained, selective and independent schools together with more recently introduced schemes such as grant-maintained schools (now foundation schools). There has also been a number of distinct national initiatives, such as the emergence of *integrated schools* in Northern Ireland, the introduction of *New Community schools* and *Learning Communities* in Scotland, and the setting up of *Education Action Zones* with associated *Beacon* and *Specialist* schools in areas of underachievement in England. Finally, the increasing number of *Welsh-medium* and *Gaelic-medium* schools in Wales and Scotland respectively is an indication of the ongoing debate, fuelled by devolution, around issues of national identity, the place of indigenous languages such as Welsh, Scots, Gaelic and Irish in the education system, and that of education generally in the process of nation building.

The first rationalisation move was a result of the 1944 Education Act in England and Wales and the 1947 Education Act in Northern Ireland which abolished the former division between elementary and higher education and established three phases of education with the first two – primary (5–11) and secondary (11–15, and later 16) – being compulsory. This generally resulted in the construction of new schools as well as the progressive reorganisation of primary and secondary schools in accordance with the new pattern. Currently, in England and Wales most primary schools are maintained by local education authorities, and are divided into infant schools (5–7), junior schools (7–11) and combined infant and junior schools which cater for both age groups. In some parts of England, a three-tier system still exists which can consist of first (5–8), middle (9–14) and then high schools. In Scotland and Northern Ireland, primary schools cover the whole seven years of primary education from Primary 1 to Primary 7 and are funded by the Local Authority Education Departments in Scotland and the Education and Library Boards in Northern Ireland. Some children are educated in the preparatory department of grammar schools in Northern Ireland. Despite the establishment of national schools in the nineteenth century on the principle of non-denomination, Northern Ireland education has developed historically along the line of religious segregation. At primary level, there are three main categories of schools: controlled primary schools, which can be considered to be Protestant schools; voluntary or maintained voluntary primary schools, which can be considered to be Catholic schools; and grammar preparatory schools.

At secondary level, a second rationalisation occurred in 1965 with the generalisation of comprehensive schooling mentioned earlier that would cater for all children regardless of their ability. The number of grammar schools and secondary modern schools declined rapidly in the 1970s and 1980s. Currently, there are no grammar schools in Wales and Scotland but there remain some in certain parts of England. Whether at primary or secondary level, the majority of Welsh pupils (97 per cent) attend comprehensive schools. In Scotland and England the figures are 95 per cent and 89 per cent respectively (Croxford 2000). The remaining pupils attend selective schools in the public sector or fee-paying independent schools. One of the main characteristics of secondary schooling in Northern Ireland remains segregation by religion, as mentioned above, but also by ability (its system being selective) and often gender (there remain many single-sex schools) (Dunn 1999: 88). Seventy per cent of children aged 11 take the 11+ transfer procedure, which involves tests in mathematics, English and science, to gain entry to one of the 70 grammar schools, but less than 40 per cent succeed. The others attend one of the 166 free secondary intermediate schools which again are divided

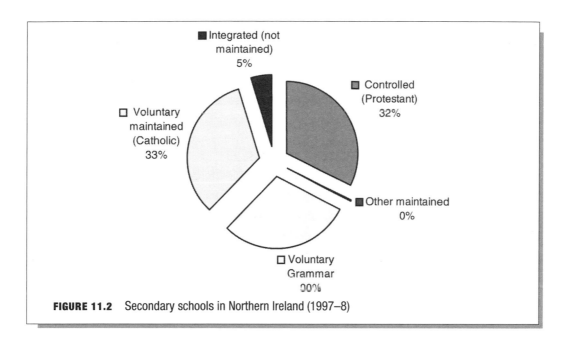

FIGURE 11.2 Secondary schools in Northern Ireland (1997–8)

between controlled (including grant-aided integrated schools) and voluntary maintained schools (Figure 11.2). Croxford (2001) has investigated the implementation and impact of compulsory schooling in the UK. She reports that in Scotland 'the change from selective to comprehensive schooling between 1965 and 1975 led to an increase in the average attainment of all pupils but especially those with low prior attainment and girls' (p. 1). Talking to the Northern Ireland Association for Headteachers in secondary schools, Croxford argued that because Scotland has embraced a comprehensive system more wholeheartedly than England and Northern Ireland, comprehensive education has been more successful in Scotland in reducing social inequality. It has also resulted in a reduction in extremes of low and high pupil attainment which, she argues, are reinforced by less uniform or more selective schooling provision, such as that currently existing in England and Northern Ireland respectively. She points out, however, that, through parents' choice of school or use of subject specialism, hidden forms of selection can be found in both Scotland and England.

Since the late 1980s, compulsory education in the UK has been characterised by an increasing diversity of provision between its four components. In Northern Ireland, the Department of Education (DENI) has encouraged initiatives to try to reduce religious segregation at school which have led to the introduction of two curricular themes called *Education for Mutual Understanding* and *Cultural Heritage* in the Northern Ireland curriculum (Table 11.2, p. 198) and to the creation of mixed-faith schools, known as *Integrated schools*, many of which are now grant-aided.

The establishment of *New Community schools* (NCSs) at national level in Scotland and of *Learning Communities* by Glasgow City are two examples of recent initiatives that seek to encourage the integration of the provision of school education with social work and health education. The aim is to raise children's educational achievement through the improvement of the child's wider social, physical and familial condition. In the case of the NCSs, extra funding is provided to either single schools or clusters of schools to allow the integration and expansion of the range of services offered to young people in disadvantaged areas (SEED 2003). *Learning Communities* are local clusters of schools situated in the East end of Glasgow and which typically consist of a secondary school and its associated primaries and pre-five establishments. Only six learning communities have been created so far with only a limited amount of funding from Glasgow City (SCRE 2001).

Diversity of provision in the UK is nowhere more marked than in England where a concern for diversity and parental choice resulted in the introduction of Grant-Maintained (GM) schools and City Technology Colleges in the late 1980s by the then Conservative Government (see Clough *et al.* 1991; Docking 2000a). The changes made to the schooling provision in England differ in their nature from those implemented in the Scottish system whose 'strong egalitarian and universalistic tenor … has proven resistant to attempts to devolve governance to institutions and to use competition to improve performance' (Ozga and Lawn 1999: 228). From the mid-1990s in England, the New Labour Government took up the Conservative commitment to diversity while reasserting at the same time a somewhat conflicting rationalisation agenda thereby seeking to introduce 'co-operation within a system designed for competitiveness' (Jackson 2000: 178). The School Standards and Framework Act 1998 renamed all state-maintained schools *Community schools, Voluntary* or *Voluntary-aided* schools and *Foundation* schools. The Act effectively abolished the former GM schools which were reintegrated within local authority control as Foundation schools for the sake of enhancing coherence and co-operation by re-establishing equal funding (if not powers) between all maintained schools.

Raising standards through co-operation and partnership is the main theme of New Labour policies for schools which underpin initiatives like the Education Action Zone partnerships which enable clusters of schools located in areas of disadvantage to use a number of support initiatives as well as additional funding for three years to improve the quality of their provision (Jackson 2000). The EAZ scheme is itself associated with the Excellence in Cities strategy, one aim of which is to force LEAs to co-operate on a range of issues, such as school disaffection, truancy or else catering for gifted and talented pupils. In this aim, LEAs and schools can call upon designated centres of excellence, called Beacon schools, to share good practice with them. They can also benefit from the expanding programme of specialist schools which the Government claims will provide challenging, well-resourced learning environments in nine different curricular and vocational areas. Schools designated by the Department of Education to become Beacon schools receive additional funding for their work with cluster schools. Likewise, a successful bid to become a specialist school will ensure significant funding (£100,000 +) for the school for a period of four years. At the heart of this vast funding campaign is the Government's attempt to instigate a partnership culture in the profession through externally imposed and financially rewarded co-operation. The bidding process to gain specialist status and secure extra funding is very competitive, however, and threatens to run counter to the promotion of a genuine partnership between schools. It also raises the question of whether the change of culture currently initiated by New Labour policies will be sustainable once funding decreases or ceases altogether.

Curriculum

The system of compulsory education in England, Wales and Northern Ireland as we know it today is the result of the state's unprecedented intervention in education from the late 1980s. It has already been noted at the beginning of this chapter that historically education forms a single system in England and Wales (Green 1997) and over the last 20 years, the organisation and content of compulsory education in England and Wales has been the object of a significant number of Government initiatives aiming at raising standards and allowing the UK to compete in world markets.

Through the 1988 Education Reform Act and the introduction of a National Curriculum the Conservative Government effectively took away from the teaching profession their responsibility for deciding what should be taught to pupils of compulsory school age in all state schools in England and Wales. The new statutory document also set out attainment targets for learning and provided a specific framework for the assessment, monitoring and reporting of pupils' learning (see *Assessment*, below). Similar curricula already existed in other European countries such as France or Germany where education historically played a much more prominent role in the construction of the state, but in England and Wales, this initiative was perceived as having 'fundamentally and probably irreversibly transformed the nature of state education' (Bash and Coulby 1991: 1). The curriculum was implemented between 1989 and 1996 in England and Wales and a number of changes were introduced during that time by the Secretary of State in each country. The Qualifications and Curriculum Authority (QCA) in England and the Qualifications, Curriculum and Assessment Authority for Wales (ACCAC) are the statutory bodies responsible for the reviews of curriculum and assessment arrangements in each country. The last review of the National Curriculum for England and Wales took place in 2000 and aimed to promote *clarity*, *coherence* and *continuity* and to reduce requirements generally.

The Education Reform Act 1988 does not apply to Northern Ireland and Scotland, both of which have their own separate curriculum arrangements (Table 11.2). However, in all four countries:

> curricula are formulated in terms of aims and objectives, including 'general teaching requirements' or 'common requirements' and educational cross-curricular themes, programmes of study, targets of attainment and exemplary schemes of work.
>
> (Le Métais *et al.* 2001: 9)

In Northern Ireland, a compulsory school curriculum was established by the Northern Ireland Order 1989 and was introduced into schools in 1990. The order was reviewed in 1993 and 1996 and the responsibility for the curriculum and assessment procedures lies with the Northern Ireland Council for Curriculum, Examinations and Assessment (CCEA). Between the ages of four and 16, all pupils attending publicly financed schools follow the NI Curriculum and study ten compulsory subjects and six compulsory cross-curricular themes. Those educational themes are not taught separately but woven through the main subjects of the curriculum. Pupils' academic entitlement varies according to the school years which are divided into four key stages, as in England and Wales. The Northern Ireland Curriculum is currently undergoing a review, the process of which originated in a perceived need to increase curriculum *relevance* and to move towards the *development of important life skills* (Smith 2003: 4). The revised framework will be implemented in September 2004 for primary schools and at KS4, with KS3 changes being introduced in September 2005 only.[1] The content of the 14–16 curriculum was particularly criticised by the CCEA Chief Executive Gavin Boyd in 2001 as being 'too rigid, too narrow and too academic, with vocational and technical qualifications often seen as second best' and therefore failing to prepare pupils for the challenge of the twenty-first century (CCEA 2001a). A proposal for a new statutory curriculum at Key Stage 4, *Their Future in Our Hands*, was therefore published in February 2001 (CCEA 2001b) and aimed to increase flexibility and move away from a content-led curriculum and towards a more skill-based, broad, balanced and liberal education for 14 to 16-year-olds. The new arrangements, to be phased in after September 2003, will offer pupils provision for:

- Key skills
- Personal development
- A scientific and technological component
- A creative component
- A work-related component

(CCEA 2001b: 4)

[1] Information available at www.ccea.org.uk

In a similar way to England and Wales, where one major development following the 2000 review was the introduction of Citizenship in September 2002, in Northern Ireland, it resulted in a proposal to include Local and Global Citizenship in the NI Curriculum. In Scotland, Education for Citizenship is one of the five cross-curricular aspects which aim, through the 5–14 programme, to prepare pupils for life in a rapidly changing society.

Scotland, unlike the three other components of the UK, does not have a National Curriculum but has devised, over the period 1987–93, a non-statutory 5–14 programme which sets out guidelines for teachers and local authorities on what should be taught to pupils of compulsory education age. The 5–14 curriculum originated in a need for consensus in teaching and learning at compulsory level and for the reconciliation of primary and secondary approaches to the curriculum and particularly the challenge of the 'fresh start' philosophy in the first year of secondary education (Adams 2003; Boyd 1997). Advice on the structure and balance of the curriculum 5–14 were published in 1993 and reviewed in 2000. In Scotland, the underpinning principles of the 5–14 curriculum are reinforced in the reviewed document; these are *progression, continuity* and *coherence* – especially so in the transition from primary to secondary education – as well as *balance* and *breadth*. In addition to the non-statutory status of the 5–14 programme, Adams (2003) identifies two main differences with the National Curriculum for England and Wales: the first one is that the Scottish curriculum does not separate between the primary and the secondary stages of education, and its longer time span (5–14) aims to encourage continuity of experience. Thus in Scotland, the curriculum and the assessment procedures (see below) reflect a commitment to:

- the importance of continuity in a child's education;
- children's differing rates of development;
- the importance of avoiding treating each subject as if it were a self-contained entity.

(Clark 1997: 37)

Contrastingly, the National Curriculum for England and Wales is divided into Key Stages 1 and 2 (for primary) and Key Stages 3 and 4 (for secondary). It also makes a distinction between three 'core' subjects which constitute a prescribed 'basic' entitlement and six foundation subjects at Key Stage 2 plus one at Key Stage 3 while no core statutory subjects exist in the Scottish document (Adams 2003: 374).

Scottish pupils aged 14 embark on a two-year course of study in which they will generally study seven or eight subjects selected from the Standard Grade curriculum framework. McKinnon and Statham (1999) point out that:

> The education of children over 14 is influenced by the fact that Scotland, unlike England, has only one examination board, and so pupils throughout the country who are taking its Standard [Grade] examination follow the same syllabus.

(p. 171)

TABLE 11.2 Curriculum arrangements in the UK

Curriculum	ENGLAND	WALES	SCOTLAND	NORTHERN IRELAND
Name and Nature	National Curriculum (Statutory)	National Curriculum (Statutory)	5–14 Guidelines 14–16 Standard Grade Curriculum (Advisory)	Northern Ireland Curriculum (Compulsory)
Time span	5–16 4 Key Stages KS1: 5–7 KS2: 7–11 KS3: 11–14 KS4: 14–16	5–16 4 Key Stages KS1: 5–7 KS2: 7–11 KS3: 11–14 KS4: 14–16	5–14 No Key Stages + 14–16	4–16 4 Key Stages KS1: 4–8 KS2: 8–11 KS3: 11–14 KS4: 14–16
Subjects and/ or curricular areas/themes	Core subjects Maths, English, science Fewer compulsory subjects at KS4 Foundation subjects Technology, history, ICT, geography, music, art, physical education and from KS3, a modern foreign language Other legal requirements Religious education, sex education	Core subjects Maths, English, ICT, science, Welsh Fewer compulsory subjects at KS4 Foundation subjects Technology, history, geography, music, art, physical education, Welsh (in schools where it is not a core subject) and from KS3, a modern foreign language	Curricular areas (5–12) Language, mathematics, environmental studies, expressive arts and physical education, religious and moral education with personal and social development and health education 14–16 subjects (12–14) English, mathematics, history, geography, modern studies, science, MFL, art and design, PE, technology, RME, music, drama, social and personal development, computing	Compulsory subjects Religious education, English, maths, science and technology, creative and expressive studies, language studies (Irish in Irish-medium schools only) Compulsory cross-curricular themes from KS1 Education for mutual understanding, cultural heritage, health education, information technology From KS3 Economic awareness, careers education

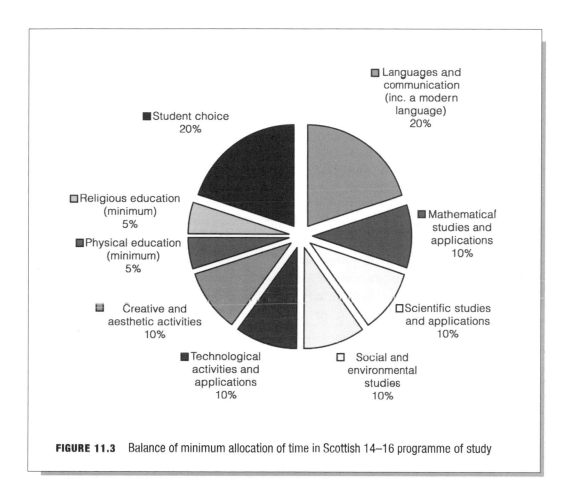

FIGURE 11.3 Balance of minimum allocation of time in Scottish 14–16 programme of study

As Figure 11.3 shows, the allocation of study time differs between subjects in S3/S4 (age 14–16). In practice, pupils' freedom of choice is limited by the range of subjects available in their school (Gavin 2003: 463).

The most recent reviews of school curricula in the various parts of the UK all appear to have been an opportunity for the curriculum authorities to articulate what the purpose of education should be for their society. Smith (2003) points out that 'the curriculum can still be regarded as the clearest statement by any society on the purpose of education, the values it holds most dear and an expression of what the society strives to be' (p. 2). Yet this statement was not necessarily made explicit in the curricular documents mentioned previously which set out a framework for compulsory education in the four countries.

For the first time, however, the revised National Curriculum 2000 for England and Wales sets out the aims and values of the school curriculum (DfEE and QCA 2000). It also lays down what the purpose of this national framework is:

- To establish a learning entitlement for all pupils, regardless of their socio-economic background, their culture, race and gender and their ability.
- To establish standards for the performance of pupils.
- To promote continuity and coherence of pupils' learning experience.
- To promote public understanding of the work of schools and teachers.

Likewise, the Scottish Guidelines published in 2000 include a previously absent rationale for the 5–14 curriculum and in Northern Ireland, Smith (2003) welcomes the ongoing curriculum review as an opportunity to do just that. All three frameworks link education to the development of the person and of society with clear reference also being made to the economy in the English and Scottish documents. These see teachers and schools as preparing pupils to become *active*, *productive* and generally *well-rounded adults, workers* and *citizens*. The Scottish 5–14 document clearly emphasises the promotion of humanistic values such as aesthetics and intellectualism, and focuses on the affective and creative dimensions of the learner, encouraging teachers' sensitivity to personal feelings, emotions and imagination. All three documents stress the importance of promoting the spiritual and physical development of the child, with an additional emphasis on more traditional aims of the *moral* and *cultural* development of the pupils in the Curriculum NI and the National Curriculum (England and Wales) and on their cognitive (*mental*) development in the English document as opposed to *intellectual* development in Scotland and Northern Ireland. Finally, Le Métais *et al.* point out that 'the curricula in Northern Ireland, Wales and Scotland make explicit links between the subject matter and national heritage' (2001: 14). The impact on pedagogy of the introduction of a National Curriculum in England and Wales is addressed later in this chapter.

Assessment

With the National Curriculum, the 1988 Education Reform Act also introduced a specific framework for assessment of all pupils aged five to 16 in all state schools in England and Wales. Each subject had its own set of attainment targets and pupils' progression towards the targets is assessed as part of a national programme of assessment through Standard Assessment Tasks (SATs), which take place at age seven, 11 and 14 in England and Wales, as well as through teacher assessment. Pupils in England and Wales are assessed in all core subjects by teacher assessment *only* at the end of Key Stage 1. At the end of Key Stage 2, however, they are assessed by teacher assessment and are also required to sit SATs in core subjects only. In Welsh-medium schools, Welsh language replaces English as a core subject. At the end of Key Stage 3 all pupils are assessed in both core and foundation subjects by their teacher and also through Standard Assessment Tasks.

A new statutory assessment known as baseline assessment was introduced in the late 1990s in all four parts of the UK, albeit in different ways. It refers to the assessment of four and five-year-old pupils in all or one or two of the following: reading, writing, and personal and social skills. Baseline assessment has been mandatory in England and Wales since 1997, but a new scheme of teacher observation has been introduced to replace formal testing from August 2002. In Scotland, as for 5–14 assessment generally, it remains at the discretion of the local authority, and can take the form of external tests or teacher assessment (Croxford 2003: 740–1).

At first sight, assessment arrangements in Northern Ireland are organised in a similar way as in England and Wales. In Northern Ireland, baseline assessment takes place during the first year of compulsory education, age four, through teacher assessment exclusively, and must be completed by the end of the first primary year. Thereafter, pupils are assessed at the end of each key stage, that is age eight, 11 and 14. However, pupils are not required to sit end-of-key-stage subject tests at Key Stage 1 and Key Stage 2 but compulsory assessment takes place in English and mathematics (or in Irish and mathematics in Irish schools) through teacher assessment only. At Key Stage 3, assessment then takes the form of both teacher assessment, as well as end-of-key-stage tests in mathematics, English (or Irish) and science. At the end of Key Stage 4 (age 16) a number of national qualifications are offered by a range of awarding bodies[2] to pupils in England and Wales, and in Northern Ireland. Most of them take the General Certificate in Secondary Education (GCSE) in which they can choose a range of single general or vocational subjects. The number of subjects to be taken by pupils is not regulated. Short GCSE courses and alternative specialist or vocational qualifications as well as entry level qualifications for pupils who are performing below GCSE level are now available at the end of Key Stage 4 in England and Wales and, with some restrictions, in Northern Ireland.[3]

In Scotland, each curricular area of the 5–14 curriculum possesses a set of *Attainment Outcomes*, which are broad competences that pupils are expected to develop. These are divided into strands and attainment targets differentiated in levels. These attainment targets are descriptors of attainment at various stages with A being the lowest level and F the highest one. A pupil's achievement is based on their progress between the levels and they are allowed to move from one level to the next at their own rate, with assessment only taking place when the pupil is deemed to be ready. National testing only occurs in mathematics and English (reading and writing) in Scotland, and even then there is no externally

---

[2] There are three unitary awarding bodies in England (AQA, EDEXCEL and OCR), one awarding body in Northern Ireland (CCEA) and one in Wales (WJEC).

[3] http://www.ucas.ac.uk/candq/ukquals/eng/quals.html; http://www.deni.gov.uk/teachers/circulars/latest/dc2003–06.pdf

imposed age for testing as these are used by the teacher to confirm that the pupil has reached a particular level. In practice, however, the tests can present barriers to the pupils' progression given a teacher cannot report a pupil as having achieved a particular level until they have passed the national test at that level. The validity of the reading and writing tests themselves has been questioned by teachers who feel that they do not reflect the range of curricular outcomes that have to be covered in the course; some English teachers have argued that strands like 'reading for pleasure' or 'reading aloud', for instance, simply cannot be assessed through the kind of assessment instruments used by the tests.

At the end of the last year of compulsory education (S4), pupils take a national Scottish qualification called Standard Grade, which was introduced in the early 1980s following the Dunning Report in 1977. This new system of assessment incorporates both internal and external assessment and offers three levels of difficulty called Foundation, General and Credit levels, as a way to ensure certification for all. Pupils typically take seven or eight subjects: in addition to English, mathematics and a modern foreign language which are compulsory, pupils must choose a social subject (history, geography, modern studies), a scientific subject, a creative and aesthetic subject (art, drama, music or PE) and a technology subject (computing, technological studies, home economics). This is where the principles of breadth and choice conflict, often with some implications on student motivation given there remains little real margin for choice with three compulsory subjects and then only one possible choice per curricular area.

Pedagogy

'The cultures of teaching are shaped by the contexts of teaching' (Feiman-Nemser and Floden 1986: 515); that is, what is understood as the role of the teacher and the activity of teaching is highly context-dependent. Williams' old humanist strand, such an important part of the early development of schooling in England, is associated with principles of *individualism, morality* and *specialism* (McLean 1990). A key characteristic of such *humanism* is that it is anti-rational, and hence it has been suggested that little weight is given in England to 'rational, methodical and systematic knowledge objectives' (Holmes and McLean in McLean 1990: 126). With the principles of *individualism* and *morality* the emphasis in English education is on the whole child and the development of the individual. Traditionally, Scottish secondary education has evolved differently from its English counterpart with rational-encyclopaedic elements and less emphasis on specialism and experience in the learning process (McLean 1995). In his famous book on *The History of Scottish Education*, James Scotland had argued that 'the training of the intellect' was of paramount importance in Scotland and education in the classroom was definitely more teacher-centred than child-centred (Humes and Bryce 2003). For a long time in Scotland it was thought that strong discipline and, if required, corporal punishment were *sine qua non* for effective and productive learning to take place. The 1965 report on *Primary Education in Scotland* brought about more child-centred approaches to teaching and learning and eventually led to the abolition of corporal punishment in 1981 in Scotland, later than many Western European countries but earlier than England and Wales which waited until 1986. Harrison (1997: 164) points out that in Scotland, 'child-centred educational philosophy was adopted more cautiously although perhaps more thoroughly than in England.' If the primary classroom in Scotland aspires to be a more and more 'child-centred, caring place', teaching and learning in the secondary schools remains strongly subject-oriented and examination-oriented, especially so for pupils aged 14–16.

The introduction of a National Curriculum in 1988 in England and Wales, and of national frameworks to raise the standards of numeracy and literacy in the primary school in England and also in Scotland, have had a significant impact on teachers' work in the classroom as has the setting of performance targets for schools in all four parts of the UK in the late 1990s. The impact of the National Curriculum on teaching and learning in the primary classroom in Wales has been investigated by Cox and Sanders (1994) and in England by Pollard *et al.* (1994) and by Croll (1996). The findings for both countries are remarkably similar: teachers and head teachers in both countries are generally positive about the National Curriculum, which, they claim, provides a useful framework for planning and progression (especially throughout Key Stages 1 and 2) and some clarifications of teaching and learning aims (Cox 2000). Furthermore, it has resulted in an increase in collaboration on curriculum planning within schools and therefore more coherence in pupil entitlement. Data collection for these studies took place before the first review of the National Curriculum in 1993 which slimmed down its content, and teachers expressed serious misgivings about the overloaded content and the demands placed on them by what they perceived as burdensome procedures for assessment and recording of pupils' learning. The English report stressed the predominance of work in core subjects (English and mathematics particularly) and the lack of flexibility of the framework which made it difficult for them to adapt their teaching to the children's needs (Cox 2000). Likewise, Le Métais *et al.* (2001: 22) report that 'the high profile given to English/Welsh and mathematics through the frameworks in Wales have temporarily reduced the amount of time devoted to [the foundation subjects].' Finally, the Welsh study reported evidence that the organisation of the National Curriculum in a great number of core and non-core separate subjects made it hard for teachers to retain cross-curricular activities in their teaching (Cox and Sanders 1994, quoted in Cox 2000).

With the arrival of New Labour in government in 1997, teaching methods in the primary school were to undergo yet more changes in England with the introduction of methods for teaching literacy and numeracy in the primary schools. The National Strategies for Literacy and Numeracy were originally conceived by the Conservatives who piloted them shortly before they left office (Docking 2000b). As with several Conservative initiatives, these were taken up and implemented by the Labour Government in 1998 and 1999 respectively, as a result of a controversial Ofsted report on the teaching of reading in London Boroughs (HMI 1996) and in light of evidence from international studies of pupils' achievements in English and maths, where English pupils appeared to perform less well than many of their foreign counterparts (Docking 2000a). Primary teachers' teaching of literacy and numeracy were blamed and this justified an unprecedented central intervention into teaching methods. Both strategies aim to set high expectations and challenging targets for pupils, promote active participation and engaging activities, and support teaching and learning.

Around the same time, the Scottish Office Education and Industry Department launched the Early Intervention Programme (EIP) which aimed to break the link between education failure and socio-economic advantage as acknowledged in a number of reports and research studies (see Fraser *et al.* 2001). This initiative stems from the same concern with social inclusion in Scotland which led to the implementation of the New Community School scheme and of Learning Communities in Glasgow, as mentioned earlier. The choice of a planned intervention from nursery to primary three level was advocated in the 1996 Task Force report to the Secretary of State for Scotland as a suitable way to achieve long-lasting improvements in pupils' performance (*ibid.*). The Literacy and Numeracy Strategies in England provide teachers with what can be seen as a rather prescriptive (although non-statutory) approach for the teaching of reading and writing as well as for mathematics. The Literacy Hour effectively provides the teacher with a set teaching plan for reading and writing, in which the lesson is divided into four parts of 10 to 20 minutes each and which combines whole-class teaching and groupwork. Likewise, teachers are encouraged to allocate 45 to 60 minutes to mathematics teaching every day using a three-part lesson which consists of an *oral mental starter*, a *main activity* and a *plenary*. The strategies strongly recommend that teachers spend more time on core subjects and that they use more whole-class teaching and questioning, and engage the class in interaction.

In contrast with the English initiative, a major characteristic of the Scottish EIP is its flexibility and lack of prescriptiveness with education authorities being expected to 'consider the needs of their area and devise programmes to suit' (SOEID 1999, quoted in Fraser *et al.* 2001: 18). Yet, the national evaluation of EIP in Scotland reports a 'remarkable similarity in the teaching methodologies being adopted across the 32 authorities' (Fraser *et al.* 2001: 24). The document reports evidence of significant changes to classroom practice following the implementation of the programme with an emphasis on phonic-based approaches to reading, more direct teaching of mental arithmetic involving high levels of pupil–teacher interaction, and an increased reliance on whole-class teaching generally (*ibid.*). A number of evaluations of the Literacy and Numeracy Strategies in England have been conducted, among which are some by HMI (2002) and others by an independent team of Canadian researchers (Earl *et al.* 2000, 2001, 2003). The OISE/UT evaluation (Ontario) reports that most of the teachers and head teachers interviewed felt that classroom teaching had improved considerably as a result of the strategies, with greater use of whole-class teaching, more structured lessons and improved planning. Opinions vary, however, as to the extent to which pupil learning has improved. In any case, all appear to value the Numeracy Strategy more than its Literacy counterpart in terms of pupil learning and simplicity of implementation.

Following what they considered to be the successes of the National Literacy and Numeracy Strategies in primary schools, non-statutory frameworks for the teaching of English and mathematics at Key Stage 3 were introduced in the 2001/02 academic year (Key Stage 3 Strategy), followed in 2002/2003 by similar frameworks for the teaching of science, information and communication technology (ICT), and the foundation subjects at the same level. Little evidence is available at this stage of the impact of the expansion of the original initiatives to the secondary sector and to additional subjects apart from a recent HMI report (HMI 2003).

Another initiative which was introduced throughout the UK and had a noticeable impact on teachers' work and pedagogy is the introduction of perform-ance targets for schools, otherwise known as 'target setting'. Since 1998, bench-marking information based on public examination results and SATs is provided to schools and local authorities by each Department of Education to enable them to set their own targets for improvement, mainly in relation to pupil performance. As with the national frameworks for literacy and numeracy in England and in Scotland mentioned earlier, the driver behind target setting is Government's concern with raising standards. Yet while the NLS and NNS focus on processes and transaction, the driver behind the introduction of target settings is more a concern with measurable outcomes. Measurable outcomes are linked to discourses of school *effectiveness* which are in sharp contrast with initiatives such as EIP, for instance, where the emphasis is more on school *improvement* through 'achieving changes in practice at both management and classroom level' (Fraser *et al.* 2001: 8). Currently, a main concern with target setting is that pressure on schools to achieve targets can result in assessment-driven curriculum and pedagogy and that the way teachers teach becomes increasingly determined by these initiatives (MacGilchrist 2003).

What is clear is that in England, 'policies still seem to be based on the belief that standards will not be raised without targets being set and monitored and that teachers, teacher-trainers and education authorities need to be told how to do their work' (Bines 1998). Brown (2001) has argued, however, that the same comment can increasingly be made in relation to Scottish policies. The Literacy and Numeracy Strategies, and the Key Stage 3 Strategy have not been implemented outside England. In fact, as Cox (2000) noted, in the very year that the Literacy Strategy was introduced in England, the Welsh Office published its own vision of a much more collaborative approach to raising standards in literacy in its report *National Year of Reading: getting ready*, which argues that teachers and policy-makers should work together at improving teaching and learning strategies. Despite some of the improvements that the national strategies and the centrally manufactured LEA and schools collaboration may result in, in light of more genuinely collaborative developments in other parts of the UK, one could argue with Croll (1996) that:

> The government may find a partnership model more effective in getting educational change to happen than a model based upon the view of teachers as implementers.
>
> (in Cox 2000: 80)

Compulsory education post-devolution

> The educational and legislative traditions of England, Wales, and Northern Ireland mean that they share many similarities in terms of educational and curricular structure and terminology. This convergence is reinforced by the fact that pupils from the three nations traditionally take General Certificate of Secondary Education (GCSE) and GCE Advanced Level examinations at age 15–16 and 17–18 respectively. However, the devolution of responsibility for education to the Assemblies, and the emergence of alternative forms of external accreditation of learning, may result in greater divergence over time.
>
> (Le Métais *et al.* 2001: 5)

We have seen some of this diversity in our description of provision for curriculum, assessment and pedagogy. We may also be starting to see some evidence of the smaller parts of the UK leading the way for England. For example, the relaxation of the curriculum in the early years is well under way in Wales, and in Scotland a major review of the secondary curriculum may lead to less of a subject-based framework. In England, where teachers and some parents have been calling for such moves, we may yet see similar policy developments.

Changes such as these do nothing to reduce the compulsion of attendance at school, but they may reduce the compulsion on schools and teachers to teach particular content in particular ways. Education is likely to remain high on the political agendas, not least because of the increased recognition of the linkage between economic success and education. With this being the case, we are likely to see continuing debates about the purposes of education, reflecting the continuing struggles between industrial trainers, public educators and old humanists. Indeed, there may well be a fourth key grouping now, which is a global rather than a national force. These might be called the 'global networkers', who believe that electronic communication is creating a global information society, where national boundaries are becoming increasingly irrelevant. Certainly, there are many aspects of learning and teaching that now make use of the World Wide Web. With economic activity increasingly being organised at transnational level, it would seem essential that future citizens have access to an understanding of these networks and can make full use of them in their learning.

Indeed, the very real possibility is raised that for many young people, more learning will be available through their privately owned technology than is available through formal schooling. Such a scenario could give rise to a very different view of compulsory schooling, where it was seen less as an entitlement and more as an imposition. Of course, such a scenario is also dependent on young people having access to the necessary technology and there must be very real fears that a 'digital divide' will open up between those in the UK who own the technology and those who do not. On the other hand, with careful investment, these new technologies have the potential to expand basic educational provision in a way that could not have been foreseen by those who originally argued for compulsory education.

The other developing agenda, which must call into question a simple view of compulsory education covering the early years of life, is that of lifelong learning. If we are, as is argued, living and working in a society where change is continuing to accelerate, then the idea that compulsory schooling between the ages of five and 16 can equip individuals with all of their life's needs is highly dubious. If, on the other hand, the implication of these changes is indeed that individuals will require learning opportunities throughout their lives, then why should these early years receive such priority? Certainly, we may still argue for the acquisition of a range of essential skills during one's childhood, but the promotion of particular forms of knowledge may be far less important than in the past.

Suggested further reading

Compulsory education in Scotland is very well served by the large volume edited by T. Bryce and W. Humes, *Scottish Education*, published by Edinburgh University Press. The edition published in 2003 emphasises the post-devolution view.

Information on the other three constituent parts of the United Kingdom may best be gleaned from official web sites, such as:

- Department of Education In Northern Ireland (DENI): http://www.deni.gov.uk/

- Scottish Executive Education Department (SEED): http://www.scotland.gov.uk (Topics/Education and Training)

- Department for Education and Skills (DfES): http://www.dfes.gov.uk

- The Welsh Assembly Government's Training and Education web site: http://www.learning.wales.gov.uk/

Finally, the *Factfiles UK* section of the *Information Network on Education in Europe* provides very comprehensive data on and analysis of Education in England, Wales and Northern Ireland: http://www.nfer.ac.uk/eurydice/factfiles/factfiles.asp

References

Adams, F. (2003) '5–14: Origins, Development and Implementation', in T. G. K. Bryce and W. M. Humes (eds) *Scottish Education* (Second edition, Post Devolution). Edinburgh: Edinburgh University Press.

Assessment for All (*The Dunning Report*) (1977) Report of the Committee to Review Assessment in the Third and Fourth Years of Secondary Education in Scotland under the Chairmanship of J. Dunning. Edinburgh: HMSO.

Bash, L. and Coulby, D. (eds) (1991) *Contradiction and Conflict: the 1988 Education Act in action.* London: Cassell.

Bines, H. (1998) 'Hail zero intolerance? Opinion', *Times Educational Supplement*, 22 May, p.15.

Boyd, B. (1997) 'The statutory years of secondary education: change and progress', in M. M. Clark and P. Munn (eds) *Education in Scotland.* London: Routledge.

Brown, S. (2001) *What Is Teaching For?* The General Teaching Council (Scotland) Annual Lecture, 8 May 2001.

Bryce, T. and Humes, W. (eds) (2003) *Scottish Education* (Second edition, Post Devolution.) Edinburgh: Edinburgh University Press.

CCEA (2001a) News release NR/10/01, Thursday 22 March 2001, accessed at http://www.ccea.org.uk/press/nr10.01.

CCEA (2001b) *Their Future in Our Hands. Proposals for Key Stage 4, Giving schools greater flexibility on what they teach 14–16 year olds.* Belfast: CCEA.

Clark, M. (1997) 'Developments in Primary Education in Scotland', in M. Clark and P. Munn (eds) *Education in Scotland: Policy and Practice from Pre-school to Secondary.* London: Routledge.

Clough, N., Lee, V., Menter, I., Trodd, T. and Whitty, G. (1991) 'Restructuring the Education System?', in L. Bash and D. Coulby (eds) *The Education Reform Act.* London: Cassell.

Cox, T. (2000) 'The impact of the National Curriculum upon primary education in Wales', in R. Daugherty, R. Phillips and G. Rees (eds) *Education Policy-making in Wales: explorations in devolved governance.* Cardiff: The University of Wales Press.

Cox, T. and Sanders, S. (1994) *The Impact of the National Curriculum on the Teaching of 5 Year Olds*. London: Falmer Press.

Croll, P. (1996) 'Practitioners or policy makers? Models of teachers and educational change', in P. Croll (ed.) *Teachers, Pupils and Primary Schooling*. London: Cassell.

Croxford, L. (2000) 'Inequality in Attainment at Age 16: a "Home International" comparison', *CES Briefing* No. 19, May. Edinburgh: Centre for Educational Sociology.

Croxford, L. (2001) *Comprehensive Schools in Great Britain: evidence from research. A report to the Northern Ireland Association of Headteachers in Secondary Schools*. Edinburgh: Centre for Educational Sociology.

Croxford, L. (2003) 'Baseline assessment in Scotland', in T. G. K. Bryce and W. M. Humes (eds) *Scottish Education* (Second edition, Post Devolution). Edinburgh: Edinburgh University Press.

Department for Education and Employment and Qualifications and Curriculum Authority (2000) *Disapplication of the National Curriculum*. London: HMSO.

Department for Education and Skills (2003) *School Attendance – frequently asked questions*. Available at www.dfes.gov.uk/schoolattendance/faq. Accessed 6 January 2003.

Docking, J. (ed.) (2000a) *New Labour's Policies for Schools*. London: David Fulton Publishers.

Docking, J. (2000b) 'Curriculum Initiatives', in J. Docking (ed.) *New Labour's Policies for Schools*, pp. 61–75. London: David Fulton Publishers.

Dunn, S. (1999) 'Northern Ireland: Education in a Divided Society', in D. Phillips (ed.) *The Education Systems of the United Kingdom*. Wallingford: Symposium Books.

Earl, L. *et al.* (2000) *Watching and Learning: OISE/UT evaluation of the National Literacy and Numeracy Strategies*. London: DfEE.

Earl, L. *et al.* (2001) *Watching and Learning 2: OISE/UT evaluation of the National Literacy and Numeracy Strategies*. London: DfEE.

Earl, L. *et al.* (2003) *Watching and Learning 3: Final report of the external evaluation of England's National Literacy and Numeracy Strategies*. London: DfEE.

Education of the Adolescent (The Hadow Report) (1927). Report of the Board of Education Consultative Committee under the Chairmanship of Sir William Hadow. London: Board of Education.

Feiman-Nemser, S. and R. E. Floden (1986) 'The Cultures of Teaching', in M. C. Wittrock (ed.) *Handbook of Research on Teaching* (Third edition). New York: Macmillan.

Fraser, H., MacDougall, A., Pirne, A. and Croxford, L. (2001) *More than 'An extra pair of hands'? National Evaluation of the Early Intervention Programme Final Report*. Glasgow: SCRE.

Gavin, T. (2003) 'The structure of the secondary curriculum', in T. G. K. Bryce and W. M. Humes (eds) *Scottish Education* (Second edition, Post Devolution). Edinburgh: Edinburgh University Press.

Green, A. (1997) *Education, Globalization and the State*. London: Macmillan.

Harris, N. (1993) *Law and Education: Regulations, Consumerism and the Education System*. London: Sweet and Maxwell.

Harrison, C. (1997) 'How Scottish is the Scottish curriculum: and does it matter?' in M. M. Clark and P. Munn (eds) *Education in Scotland*. London: Routledge.

Heller, J. (1904) *Heller's Annotated Edition of the Code: The New Code for Public Elementary Schools – revised to July 1904* (Forty-fourth edition). London: Bemrose.

Her Majesty's Inspectorate of Schools (HMI) (1996) *The Teaching of Reading in 45 Inner London Primary Schools*. London: Ofsted.

Her Majesty's Inspectorate of Schools (2002) *The National Literacy Strategy: the first four years 1998–2002*. London: Ofsted.

Her Majesty's Inspectorate of Schools (2003) *Key Stage 4: Towards a Flexible Curriculum*. London: Ofsted.

Herman, A. (2001) *The Scottish Enlightenment: The Scots' Invention of the Modern World*. London: Fourth Estate.

Humes, W. and Bryce, T. (2003) 'The distinctiveness of Scottish education', in T. G. K. Bryce and W. M. Humes (eds) *Scottish Education* (Second edition, Post Devolution). Edinburgh: Edinburgh University Press.

Infant and Nursery Schools (The Hadow Report) (1933). Report of the Board of Education Consultative Committee under the Chairmanship of Sir William Hadow. London: Board of Education.

Jackson, P. (2000) 'Choice, diversity and partnerships', in J. Docking (ed.) *New Labour's Policies for Schools*. London: David Fulton Publishers.

Le Métais, J., Andrews, R., Johnson, R. and Spielhofer, T. (2001) *School Curriculum Differences Across the UK*. Slough: National Foundation for Educational Research.

MacGilchrist, B. (2003) 'Has school improvement passed its sell-by date?' Professorial Lecture delivered at the Institute of Education, University of London, 14 May, Institute of Education, University of London.

McKinnon, D. and Statham, J. (1999) *Education in the UK, Facts and Figures* (Third edition). Milton Keynes: Open University.

McLean, M. (1990) *Britain and a Single Market Europe*. London: Kogan Page.

McLean, M. (1995) *Educational Traditions Compared: content, teaching and learning in industrialised countries*. London: David Fulton Publishers.

Ozga, J. and Lawn, M. (1999) 'The cases of England and Scotland within the United Kingdom', in S. Lindblad and T. Popkewitz (eds) *Educational Governance and Social Integration and Exclusion*. Uppsala: Uppsala University Press.

Paterson, L. (2003) *Scottish Education in the Twentieth Century*. Edinburgh: Edinburgh University Press.

Pollard, A., Broadfoot, P., Croll, P., Osborn, M. and Abbot, D. (1994) *Changing English Primary Schools? The impact of the ERA at Key Stage One*. London: Cassell.

Primary School (The Hadow Report) (1931) Report of the Board of Education Consultative Committee under the Chairmanship of Sir William Hadow. London: Board of Education.

Ross, A. (2000) *Curriculum: Construction and Critique*. London: Falmer.

Scottish Council for Research in Education (SCRE) (2001) 'Glasgow's Learning Communities', *SCRE Newsletter* No. 69. Glasgow: University of Glasgow.

Scottish Executive Education Department (SEED) (2003) *Key findings from the national evaluation of the new community schools pilot programme in Scotland*. Edinburgh: SEED.

Smith, A. (2003) 'Teacher Education and the Northern Ireland Curriculum Review'. Paper presented at a conference on *Teacher education in a climate of change*, organised by the Department of Education for Northern Ireland and the Department for Employment and Learning, Limavady, 28–29 April 2003.

Williams, R. (1961) *The Long Revolution*. Harmondsworth: Penguin.

Post-compulsory education 16–19

Anthony Coles

'Tis Education forms the common mind,
Just as the twig is bent, the tree's inclined.
(Alexander Pope 1688–1744)

Introduction

'Post-compulsory' education and '16–19' are terms in common use to describe the further education (FE) sector. This chapter will examine the historical background to the sector and describe the issues currently facing those who work and study in institutions often marginalised by innovation and funding reform. Finally, the future challenges will be addressed in order to establish the way forward for organisations that hold the key to this country's prosperity.

While, as we have seen in previous chapters, there is much to distinguish Scotland and England in terms of pre-16 education and while there are certainly similarities, the differences are such that the two systems are kept relatively easily apart. The same cannot be said of 16–19 education. Schools in England and Scotland offer their various national qualifications but further education demonstrates a major overlap between the two countries. This situation is of historical and ongoing significance and reflects that while Scotland's school system was never part of England's, Scotland's vocational training system was seldom apart from that of England. The situation risks confusion for the reader since, as we shall see, at various points the similar terms are used for different things. There is also the problem of precisely which body controls or exerts influence over what. Scotland may well have a devolved parliament but it is still part of the United Kingdom and must respond to the economic demands and priorities laid down by the Westminster Parliament.

The sector is characterised by its diversity. Much of the FE curriculum is delivered in school sixth forms and sixth-form colleges (and fifth and sixth years in Scottish secondary schools), these tending to focus on academic subjects and A levels, Highers and the like, but with an increasing role in delivering vocational subjects, as well as in FE colleges. Specialist colleges exist to provide training in areas such as land-based industries and art and design. Furthermore, many employers in the public and private sector are involved in work-based training in partnership with colleges and there is a significant role for the voluntary sector.

Learners in this sector are diverse in terms of social background, ethnicity, academic ability and even age; despite this chapter focusing on the 16 to 19 age range, it is not unusual to find learners as young as 14 in FE classes and those in retirement have access to the full range of provision. The curriculum in FE is extremely broad. Although it has roots in technical and vocational education, the 'adult' environment has proven attractive to learners taking academic qualifications in the form of A and AS levels following the General Certificate of Secondary Education (GCSE) and Scottish National Courses after Standard Grade. The range of vocational courses has been expanding since the introduction of General National Vocational Qualifications (GNVQs) (GSVQ in Scotland – now entitled Scottish Group Awards), which are available in subjects as diverse as business, science, and travel and tourism. Most FE colleges offer provision in craft subjects such as catering, construction trades, and hairdressing and beauty, for example.

Historical perspectives

Despite efforts to the contrary, a polarity still exists between academic and vocational pathways following the minimum school leaving age. Until the age of 16, the majority of pupils will have followed a traditional academic route, with design technology and possibly enrichment activities being the only taste of a technical curriculum. The exception is the use of information and communication technology (ICT), the one technological subject to which pupils are exposed throughout their school career. Given the distinct historical roots of academic and vocational education, it is clear why it has been so difficult to form a coherent post-16 curriculum providing equality of opportunity for those having diverse career aspirations. This has been recognised by those influencing policy-makers such as Helena Kennedy in her introduction to *Learning Works: Widening Participation in Further Education*:

> Further education suffers because of prevailing British attitudes. Not only does there remain a very carefully calibrated hierarchy of worthwhile achievement, which has clearly established routes and which privileges academic success well above any other accomplishment, but there is also an appalling ignorance amongst decision-makers

and opinion-formers about what goes on in further education. It is so alien to their experience.

(FEFC 1997: 1)

The situation described above would resonate with mid-nineteenth-century curriculum planners; during this period, the provision of science and technical education in Britain was poor when compared with other European countries. The apprenticeship was favoured as the dominant form of training for craft professions and little credence was given to the value of underpinning knowledge. The influence of the landowner class and their scepticism and mistrust of those in possession of technical knowledge has been blamed for Britain's lack of progress in providing sound vocational education; in this context 'vocational' includes science, engineering and business. Green (1999) provides a review of issues influencing the development of nineteenth-century vocational education. He draws attention to the paradox that, despite the influence of the landowner class and the Anglican Church:

> The overwhelmingly dominant values of the Victorian era were those of individualism, enterprise and *laissez-faire* liberalism, at once both tempered and sharpened by religion.
>
> (Green 1999: 48)

He continues to argue that the industrialisation of the nineteenth century progressed despite the lack of state control over technical education; the liberal hegemony considered that centralisation and state control detracted from the importance of individual entrepreneurship.

The Mechanics' Institutes were the predominant source of technical education for the working classes in the nineteenth century and the forerunners of the Workers Educational Association and later many FE colleges. The first Mechanics' Institute was opened by George Birkbeck as the Edinburgh School of Arts in 1821. Birkbeck was later involved in founding the London Mechanics' Institute in 1823 (Kelly 1957). The movement spread rapidly until several hundred were in existence by the mid-nineteenth century. Early founders debated the philosophy of the movement, with intellectual reform and emancipation of the working classes often conflicting. The Institutes were funded by individual subscription and local government grant.

The last decades of the eighteenth century saw the development of polytechnics such as the Regent Street Polytechnic (1882) and the Central Institution (1884), the latter under the auspices of the City and Guilds of London Institute which obtained funds from livery companies; another example of the reluctance of central Government to become involved in the funding of technical and vocational education.

The need for a more skilled workforce to meet economic challenges resulted in several Royal Commissions into technical education in the late nineteenth century.

The most influential of these was the Samuelson Commission on Technical Instruction (1884) leading to the Technical Instruction Act (1889). The Act enabled local authorities to organise vocational and technical classes supported by the public rate; essentially the first co-ordinated public support for technical education. The success of the scheme resulted in a need for additional funding. This was provided by a local taxation on alcohol ('whiskey money') as a result of the Local Taxation (Customs and Excise) Act of 1890. The North East Wales Institute of Higher Education in Wrexham was one of the institutions formed under this scheme with a mixture of locally relevant courses in mining, for example, though arts subjects were offered and proved popular. Local education authorities (LEAs) in England and Wales were established as the bodies controlling technical and vocational education by the Education Act 1902. The Act also enabled LEAs to form Grammar and Junior Technical Schools giving pupils a choice of an academic or vocational route after leaving school at 13. In Scotland it was the 1918 Education (Scotland) Act which created not local education authorities but rather Local Authority Education Departments and these took over technical and vocational education.

The years of the First World War diverted attention away from thoughts of technical education, often thought to be a strength of German adversaries. This was paradoxical, since the German Technical High Schools were a significant influence on the development of technical education in Britain in the late nineteenth century. Apart from the 1918 Education Act, which attempted to introduce Day Continuation Schools but failed due to funding cuts in 1922, significant developments awaited the 1944 Education Act (and the 1945 Education (Scotland) Act) following a significant increase in work-based training during the Second World War. A legacy lasting to the present day was provided by the introduction of the Ordinary and Higher National Certificates.

The 1944 and 1945 Acts established the current three-tier system of Primary, Secondary and Higher provision in addition to raising the school leaving age to 15. There was provision for technical and 'Other Further Education'. However, there was little appetite for spending large sums of money on building the technical schools and these provisions were never fully implemented. The Percy Committee on Higher Technological Education in 1945 resulted in some colleges of technology being expanded to meet specific local needs and the White Paper *Technical Education*, published in 1956, saw the introduction of a 'Diploma in Technology'. The Crowther Report (HMSO 1959) recognised the poor uptake of places in further education by school leavers and recommended the raising of the school leaving age to 16.

The involvement of employers in technical education was reinforced in 1964 with the formation of the Industrial Training Boards as a result of the Industrial Training Act. These were the forerunners of a series of employer-led organisations including the Manpower Services Commission, the Training Agency and, more recently, Training and Enterprise Councils.

The Industrial Training Boards (ITBs) were co-ordinated by the Central Training Council (Central Training Council 1965). Each had responsibilities for different industries. For example, the first to be established were involved in construction, engineering, and infrastructure such as gas and electricity. The ITBs were a further example of a reluctance of the state to become involved in funding work-based training since they were subsidised by a levy on the relevant industry. Once it became clear that some companies had robust training schemes for new and established workers, the remit of the ITBs was modified to focus on the areas of greatest need. The ITBs' influence diminished during the 1980s and they finally became Non-Statutory Training Organisations (NTSOs) in 1989.

A series of rebranding and merger exercises resulted in NTSOs becoming Industrial Training Organisations, National Training Organisations (NTOs, incorporating Lead Bodies which were responsible for setting occupational standards) and Occupational Standards Councils which co-ordinate Lead Bodies, professional organisations and providers to ensure compliance with National Vocational Qualification requirements, in addition to employers and other professional bodies. They also had a remit to co-ordinate Modern Apprenticeships (MAs). The NTOs consisted of representation from the education sector, trade unions and professional organisations. Currently, clusters of NTOs are forming Sector Skills Councils with responsibility for larger sections of the public and private sector.

Current debates

The discussion on the development of 16 to 19 education in the United Kingdom above portrays a sector in a constant state of flux. Despite many initiatives designed to provide coherent pathways for young people, whether their strengths lay in academic or vocational subjects, there were still significant skills shortages and a perception that the current system favoured those with academic strengths. This problem was tackled with renewed vigour in the 1990s in order to improve competitiveness in the face of increased global competition. Although economic factors were highly significant at this time, social inclusivity was also a major concern; it was recognised that barriers resulted in the exclusion of a significant proportion of the population from participation in academic and vocational education, and that inclusion of these individuals held the key to social and economic prosperity.

Inclusiveness and participation have been major themes in FE over the last decade. The Kennedy Report (FEFC 1997) on widening participation in FE commented on the disadvantages of institutions applying marketplace criteria to decisions on their curriculum offer:

There is also growing disquiet that the new [business] ethos has encouraged colleges not just to be businesslike but to perform as if they were businesses.

(FEFC 1997: 3)

The report stimulated the widening participation debate and prompted many institutions to reappraise their curriculum offer. Strategies were proposed based on devising frameworks for credit transfer and accumulation, an entitlement to advice and guidance, access to qualifications to NQF Level 3 (SCQF Level 7) for all, embedding widening participation in quality assurance systems and the development of value added measures in FE.

Teaching qualifications

Although staff working in FE tend to specialise in one main curriculum area, the complexity of the sector described above requires that FE teachers have a range of skills and personal qualities. Some of these are distinct from, but at least as demanding as, those required of school-based teachers. The management of diversity is a critical skill in all situations in which learning takes place, but FE teachers may, at the extreme, be faced with a class in which the learners differ significantly in terms of age, ethnicity, social background and prior experience; effective use of differentiation and individual learning plans are essential attributes under these circumstances. All teachers must bear some responsibility for the development of their learners' generic skills such as numeracy and communication, but this has become formalised in FE with the introduction of Key Skills. Staff are often required to teach and assess to NQF Level 2 (SCQF Level 5) in subjects in which they have little prior experience, or even the standard prerequisite qualification one level above that at which they teach. Effectively this means that staff teaching Key Skills in *Application of Number* should have the equivalent of A level or Higher Grade mathematics, or at least Key Skills NQF Level 3 (SCQF Level 7) in this subject. This is an unrealistic expectation which would result in huge staff shortages if implemented. This has been a serious issue following the publication of the Subject Specifications for teachers of adult literacy, numeracy and ESOL (English for Speakers of Other Languages) at Level 3 (DfES/FENTO 2002) which require teachers to be able to carry out regression analysis and solve quadratic equations.

Working effectively with the issues described above requires a well-trained and motivated workforce. Historically, formal teaching qualifications have not been required to work in the FE sector. The possession of an appropriate subject qualification was usually sufficient. In the case of academic courses such as A level, Higher Grade, GCSE and Standard Grade, this usually involved a degree. Those teaching craft subjects such as plumbing and electrical installation would normally need the appropriate trade qualification such as City and Guilds and a period of occupational experience.

TABLE 12.1   Qualifications Frameworks in the UK

SCQF level	SQA National Units, Courses and Group Awards	SVQ level	Higher Education	GCE	NQF level	NVQ level
12			Doctorates		8	
11		SVQ 5	Masters		7	5
10			Honours degree Graduate diploma		6	
9			Ordinary degree Graduate certificate		5	
8		SVQ 4	Higher National Diploma Diploma in Higher Education		4	4
7	Advanced Higher		Higher National Certificate Certificate in Higher Education	A2; AVCE	3	3
6	Higher	SVQ 3		AS		
5	Intermediate 2 Credit Standard Grade	SVQ 2		GCSE A*–C	2	2
4	Intermediate 1 General Standard Grade	SVQ 1		GCSE D–G	1	1
3	Access 3 Foundation Standard Grade					Entry
2	Access 2					
1	Access 1					

Key: GCE   General Certificate of Education
NQF   National Qualifications Framework
NVQ   National Vocational Qualification
SCQF Scottish Credit and Qualifications Framework
SQA   Scottish Qualifications Authority
SVQ   Scottish Vocational Qualification

Note: The term 'National' applies to all parts of the UK except Scotland, the Credit and Qualifications Framework for Wales and the Northern Ireland Credit Accumulation and Transfer Scheme having adopted the same nomenclature as the English.

Sources: www.scqf.org.uk (for Scotland); www.qca.org.uk (for England); www.elwa.ac.uk (for Wales); www.nicats.ac.uk (for Northern Ireland)

Traditionally, the City and Guilds 7307 qualification has been taken by aspiring FE teachers. This was a one-year part-time course at NQF Level 3 covering subjects such as teaching methods, principles of learning, producing resources and assessment. Teaching practice involved 30 hours of paid or unpaid work, usually in a local college, but occasionally in the private or public sector. Assessment was via assignments, production of a teaching file containing resources, lesson plans and schemes of work and usually three classroom observations. The majority of teachers then continued to complete a Certificate in Education ('Cert Ed') qualification involving a further year of part-time study, assignments and around 120 hours of teaching practice.

Possession of the 7307 or Cert Ed was voluntary and employers varied considerably in the extent to which they required their staff to become fully qualified. The consequence is that only 60 per cent of full-time FE teachers are qualified (DfES 2002a), though 'qualified' did not necessarily mean to Cert Ed level. Many of those who were unqualified resented the imposition of mandatory qualifications and the need to complete a training course to qualify them to do a job that they had already been doing for many years. The problem was compounded by 60 per cent of staff in FE being part-time, with only 30 per cent of part-time staff being qualified. A significant problem was that reliable data on the qualifications of staff were very difficult to obtain. Part-time staff further resisted the requirement to engage in a protracted training programme when they may have taught for a few hours each week. There was concern that mandatory qualifications would cause acute staff shortages in many areas, particularly as there was already difficulty recruiting to some disciplines such as construction, information technology and modern languages.

The picture was one of increasing demands on a poorly qualified workforce, with pay levels below those of equivalent teachers in schools. The result was poor motivation and underachievement against targets in many areas.

The skills and attributes required by FE teachers have been stipulated by the Further Education National Training Organisation (FENTO) in a set of standards which have been used to form the basis of the City and Guilds 7407 (NQF Level 4) qualification and the majority of HEI-based Certificate and Postgraduate Certificate in Education courses (FENTO 1998). It was also the intention that the FENTO Standards would be used for training, recruitment and continuing professional development.

In England and Wales, the Office for Standards in Education (Ofsted) assumed responsibility with the Adult Learning Inspectorate (ALI) for the inspection of FE provision from the Further Education Funding Council (FEFC) in 2001 as new regulations for the inspection of FE provision and the training of FE teachers came into effect (DfES 2001a, 2001b). These regulations stipulated that all permanent and fractional staff teaching in FE would need to be working towards a

FENTO-endorsed teaching qualification. In Scotland, inspection of FE remained in the hands of Her Majesty's Inspectorate of Education. At the time of writing, the Scottish Department for Enterprise, Transport and Lifelong Learning is reviewing proposals for the training of FE teachers in Scotland but there is, as yet, no indication that FE lecturers in Scotland will be obliged to undertake training for a teaching qualification.[1]

Ofsted soon realised that their experience of the FE sector was limited and embarked on a survey exercise of eight Higher Education institutions (HEIs) and 23 FE colleges (Ofsted 2003) before beginning full inspections. Though the general quality of FE teacher training by HEIs was considered to be good, a number of shortcomings of the system as a whole were identified. These came as little surprise to those involved in training. Briefly, the lack of specialist subject support and mentoring was identified as a major weakness. The FENTO Standards were considered to be inappropriate for the requirements of new teachers. Insufficient time and rigour was devoted to assessing intending teachers' abilities in the classroom and the baseline standard for the achievement of the teaching qualification lacked definition. On the same day the DfES published a consultation document outlining proposals for the reform of FE teacher education (DfES 2003a). The response to the Ofsted survey was to propose formalised subject-specific mentoring in the workplace; more robust assessment of teaching effectiveness; a review of the FENTO Standards with a view to convergence between FE and school teacher training requirements; and an appraisal of the current funding system which has consistently underfunded FE teacher training when compared with the school sector.

Most FE teacher trainers in England agreed with the findings of the Ofsted survey, but concern remained about the practicality of finding sufficient suitably qualified FE staff with the time to act as mentors. Many considered that FE teacher training would benefit from being controlled by the Teacher Training Agency, thereby facilitating convergence with the school sector. In many ways the use of the Sector Skills Council to regulate FE teacher training perpetuates the undue influence of employers over vocational education which, many would argue, has been the source of many problems over the last 150 years.

In Scotland the Further Education Development Forum was established in 1998 to oversee the initial training and the professional development of FE teachers. It is wholly funded by the Scottish Executive and answerable to the Scottish Parliament via the Department for Enterprise, Transport and Lifelong Learning. That Lifelong Learning should have been bundled with Enterprise and Transport never ceases to raise eyebrows but by adopting a consensual approach it seems to function. It does however, as in England, distance FE from the school sector. As for the initial

---

[1] The situation is in a state of flux and the reader is invited to consult www.fepdfscotland.co.uk for latest developments.

training of FE teachers, this is conducted by four of Scotland's universities, compared with seven who offer initial training for school teachers.

Qualifications framework

The framework of academic and vocational qualifications remained relatively stable during the late twentieth century following the introduction of O levels and A levels in the academic curriculum and Ordinary and Higher National Diplomas in the vocational curriculum. The most significant change for several decades was proposed by Dearing (1996) in his report *Review of Qualifications for 16 to 19 Year Olds* and the report *Qualifying for Success* (DfEE 1997): predecessors to the Curriculum 2000 initiative. Curriculum 2000 sought to broaden the 16 to 19 curriculum and achieve parity of esteem between academic and vocational qualifications. In order to achieve this, a National Qualifications Framework (NQF) was developed and formalised in the Education Act (1997), enabling a comparison to be made between the level of academic and vocational qualifications. The NQF and its Scottish homologue are summarised in Table 12.1 above.

The regulatory authority responsible for the NQF in England is the Qualifications and Curriculum Authority (QCA). QCA are currently reviewing the NQF structure. The purpose is to enable the framework to be used to communicate the relationship between qualifications to consumers. Changes include an increase in the number of levels beyond Level 3 to harmonise with policies in Wales and Northern Ireland; removal of labels such as Foundation, Intermediate and Advanced; removal of categories such as occupational and vocational to promote parity of esteem and increased compatibility with unitised and credit-based qualifications.

Significant changes to the structure of A levels were proposed and later implemented. Although it was previously possible to follow a modular route to A level, the majority of candidates still took all examinations at the end of Year 13. An AS (Advanced Supplementary) award was available, but uptake was generally low and the qualification did not represent an intermediate step to A levels. Curriculum 2000 reforms fully modularised all A level programmes and split the qualification into Advanced Subsidiary (AS) and A2. The intention was that the level of the AS would sit between GCSE and A level. The intention was that four subjects would be taken at AS level by most candidates at the end of Year 12. This would commonly be reduced to three A2 subjects completed at the end of Year 13. The qualifications carried increased coursework weighting, and academic and vocational subjects could be combined.

Although the intention of Curriculum 2000 was to broaden the post-16 curriculum and provide increased unitisation, it was a challenging process for providers, awarding bodies and learners. Providers struggled to cope with the implementation timetable and there were significant issues over funding and allocation of time to the broader curriculum in Year 12. The requirement for Key Skills also placed significant demands on institutions. Awarding bodies were faced with a huge increase in the number of examinations, partly as a result of the increased number of subjects taken, but also the higher assessment burden. For example, an A level biology examination consisted of two papers at the end of Year 13 (total 4.5 hours) and a coursework portfolio moderated during the same year. In order to pass AS and A2 biology, five examinations (total 7.75 hours) and two coursework units are required. There were considerable difficulties with the recruitment of sufficient examiners to meet the increased demand. The modular approach has advantages in terms of motivating learners and providing regular progress checks, but modules are often taken in January and June, resulting in much more time being spent on preparation and assessment.

The problems described above came to a head in 2002 when it appeared that many A2 candidates had had their coursework marks reduced by the exam board, resulting in a much lower final grade. Amid accusations of Government interference and manipulation of pass rates, the former Chief Inspector of Schools, Mike Tomlinson, was asked to report on the issue (DfES 2002a). He concluded that the Curriculum 2000 changes had been implemented too quickly with inadequate piloting. Unrealistic demands were placed on candidates by an intensive examination timetable and insufficient time to study the broader curriculum. He recommended that the relationship between QCA, DfES and the awarding bodies should be clarified, and that the administrative requirements should be reformed including more time for marking and the award process and increased use of ICT. More training for examiners and officers was also considered necessary.

Curriculum 2000 reforms also included a change in the title of Advanced GNVQs to 'Vocational A Levels'. These became available as six-unit (Single Award) and 12-unit (Double Award) qualifications and could be taken with AS and A2 qualifications. The subjects available as six-unit awards are shown in Table 12.2.

Generic skills in various guises such as Common and Core Skills have been part of most vocational qualifications such as the BTEC OND and HND for many years. The Curriculum 2000 reforms introduced the Key Skills qualification, which was intended to form an integral part of the 16 to 19 curriculum and be available as a work-based qualification. Key Skills awards were developed in Communication, Application of Number, Information Technology, Improving Own Learning and Performance, Problem Solving and Working with Others at NQF Levels 1 to 5. The intention was that learners would be able to achieve at least Level 2 in the first three of these by the end of Year 13.

Little consideration was given to how the additional workload of supporting and assessing Key Skills would be staffed, or to the additional burden placed on

TABLE 12.2   Subjects available at Vocational A Level (six-unit awards)

Art & Design
Business
Construction & Built Environment
Engineering
Health & Social Care
Information & Communication Technology
Land & Environment
Leisure & Recreation
Manufacturing
Media: Communication & Production
Performing Arts
Retail and Distributive Services
Science
Travel & Tourism

candidates already overloaded with AS and A2 assessments, particularly given the use of examinations to assess Key Skills. The result was a considerable variation in the method of Key Skills delivery, with many debates over whether they should be integrated within the existing curriculum via a mapping process supported by tutorials or treated separately with dedicated Key Skills lessons. Sufficient staff were seldom available to support the latter, while many staff were insufficiently qualified to deliver and assess Key Skills as part of their main subject. Consequently, attendance and achievement were poor, and candidate motivation was low since they often failed to see the relevance of the new qualification. Guidance was also lacking on who would be exempt from taking the qualifications as a result of possessing an equivalent such as GCSE Grade C or above.

The Key Skills Support Programme, managed by LSDA, was established by the DfES in response to the criticisms of the Key Skills implementation described above. The purpose of the programme is to provide advice and support for the delivery of Key Skills, indicative mock examination papers, teaching materials and initial diagnostic exercises.

The White Paper *21ˢᵗ Century Skills: Realising our potential* (DfES 2003b) set an agenda for the development of Key Skills, particularly in relation to work-based learning. Consultation for the White Paper indicated that employers consider that young people still lack the necessary skills for work, including communication, teamwork, self-confidence and willingness to learn. The response to this problem included a move to begin Key Skill delivery at 14 as part of Key Stage 4. This was in line with recommendations in *14–19 Opportunity and Excellence* (DfES 2002c) that work-related learning should contribute to the curriculum of all Key Stage 4 pupils. Delivery and assessment of Key Skills in the workplace, particularly as part of the Modern Apprenticeship scheme, was a major focus of the White Paper. Recommendations made in this area included an improvement in on-demand and ICT-based assessment, the incorporation of Key Skills units in NVQ programmes, web-based delivery in the workplace, and a level playing field for the funding of Key Skills in FE and via work-based providers.

There is clearly a commitment to the further development and integration of Key Skills into academic, vocational and work-based programmes, but concerns remain about the ability of staff to support these programmes in various settings. Staff delivering Key Skills at Level 2 should have at least a Level 3 qualification, though in practice many lack the Level 2 qualifications that they are teaching. Questions still remain on whether the current six Key Skills units described above fully meet employers' requirements. A single Key Skills qualification providing evidence of a wider range of skills appropriate to academic, vocational and work-based settings would simplify the process and provide opportunities to tailor programmes to individual needs.

The problems arising from the implementation of Curriculum 2000 prompted the Government to commission a wide-ranging review of the whole 14 to 19 qualifications structure chaired by Mike Tomlinson. The terms of reference included the development of a coherent range of 14 to 19 learning programmes, assessment methods and qualification structures. A central proposal was a qualifications structure based on the Matriculation Diplomas proposed in the Green Paper *14–19: Extending opportunities, raising standards* (DfES 2002d: see Figure 12.1).

The Diplomas incorporate Key Skills, existing qualifications and enrichment activities, and would be graded as pass, merit or distinction. A more detailed breakdown of achievement would be provided for higher education and employer selection purposes. The Liverpool Graduation Project was cited as an example of this Baccalaureate-style qualification. The Project involves accreditation for academic achievement, personal skill and wider experience, and is being extended to all Liverpool schools following an initial pilot. The report indicates that learners will probably be expected to follow a broader curriculum, possibly having to select subjects from arts, humanities, science and modern languages, for example.

Since 1999, Scottish qualifications for the 16 to 19 age-group have undergone a

Proposed Matriculation Diploma	Existing qualifications
Level 3 (advanced) Diplomas	AS and A Level, Level 3 NVQ, Advanced Extension Award and equivalent qualifications
Level 2 (intermediate) Diplomas	
Level 1 (foundation) Diplomas	GCSE at grades A*–C, intermediate GNVQ, Level 2 NVQ and equivalent qualifications
	GCSE at Grades D–G, foundation GNVQ, Level 1 NVQ and equivalent qualifications
Entry Level Diplomas	Entry Level Certificates

FIGURE 12.1 Comparison between current qualifications and the proposed Matriculation Diploma (Adapted from DfES 2003c)

radical restructuring. Gone is the previous regime whereby pupils either entered directly to Higher grade in fifth year (age 16/17), undertook a mixed regime of Highers in some subjects and various National Certificate modules in others or took a diet composed solely of National Certificate modules. Instead, all pupils entering fifth year now enrol on National Qualifications, their entry level being dependent on their performance at Standard Grade. This system continues into the sixth year and represents an endeavour at allowing the more academic pupils a progression route within school that is recognised for university entrance while allowing the less academic and the slower starters the chance to climb the qualifications ladder in a meaningful fashion.

The five levels with their entry requirements are shown in Table 12.3. All levels consist of three units (each of which counts as qualification – a National Unit – in its own right) and all those beyond Access culminate in a terminal examination. In terms of equivalency with England, the Universities and Colleges Admission

TABLE 12.3 Entry requirements for National Qualifications

National Qualification	Entrance qualification
Access	None
Intermediate 1	Standard Grade at grade 5 or 6
Intermediate 2	Standard Grade at grade 3 or 4
Higher	Standard Grade at grade 1 or 2
Advanced Higher	Higher grade

(Source: www.sqa.org.uk)

Service (UCAS) considers Highers to be worth slightly more than AS and Advanced Highers to be on par with A level.[2]

All this operates under the Scottish Credit and Qualifications Framework which is a partnership between the Scottish Qualifications Authority, the Quality Assurance Agency for Higher Education and Universities UK, and supported through the Scottish Department for Enterprise, Transport and Lifelong Learning. It appears to be in a more advanced state of development than its English cousin, a situation helped by there being in Scotland a single awarding body (the Scottish Qualifications Authority) for vocational education and school-level academic education. However, it suffers from many problems, not least of which concerns the understanding by employers of just what the various levels actually mean. Employers are familiar with Highers, these having been around since 1888; they feel they understand Standard Grade – although until recently they tended to do so in terms of the O-Grade which S-Grade replaced from 1988 onwards. The National Certificate modules which became National Units under the SCQF left them confused. Aware of this, SCQF has embarked on a series of awareness campaigns to attempt to explain to employers what the new Framework means.

What distinguishes SCQF from NQF is not just its state of development but the fact that it encompasses all levels of education and training, from the most very basic (Access 1) to the most advanced (Doctorate). In contrast, in England the National Qualifications Framework is separate from the Framework for Higher Education Qualifications. In principle, the single framework that the Scots enjoy will facilitate transfer without further ado between, for example, HND and degree courses, the essence of the framework being that it matters not how or where one has acquired credits, the important point is to have them and then one can move with them.

[2] See http://www.ucas.ac.uk/candq/tariff/tariff0403.doc for details.

14 to 19 issues

England and Wales

Although many of the debates discussed above have a bearing on 14 to 16-year-olds, there have been recent developments in policy particularly relating to this age group. Curriculum initiatives have tended to distinguish between the Key Stage 4 academic curriculum for pupils aged from 14 to 16 delivered in schools and the post-16 academic and vocational curriculum delivered in schools and colleges. The implication here is that the age of 16 represents a natural break with the end of compulsory schooling and the (traditional) need for young people to make a decision between a career with academic requirements and one with a vocational emphasis. Although there have been efforts to harmonise academic and vocational qualifications in terms of parity of esteem and assessment methodology, many of which have been described above, the need for younger pupils to experience vocational subjects has only been addressed relatively recently. A variety of new initiatives have had an impact on the curriculum in FE and schools. The effect has been to raise a series of debates over the readiness of both sectors to respond to rapid change once again. Discussions have centred on the skills of staff: those of schoolteachers to deliver a vocational curriculum and those of FE teachers to manage younger learners.

Recent developments in the integration of vocational subjects into the Key Stage 4 curriculum began with Part 1 GNVQs. These qualifications consisted of three units from the full Intermediate (Level 2) GNVQ and could be taken in conjunction with other traditional GCSEs. The alternative qualification perpetuated the academic/vocational divide and the qualifications were soon developed into Vocational GCSEs, which became available in 2002 in a range of subjects, including business, engineering, health and social care, and travel and tourism. The retention of the 'Vocational' title demonstrated the somewhat half-hearted attempt to achieve parity of esteem. The philosophy of Vocational GCSEs was to investigate a work-based vocational subject using a variety of teaching and learning methods from the traditional to those more commonly used with GNVQs such as projects, visits and mini-enterprise activities. Each Vocational GCSE consists of three units and is the equivalent of two non-vocational GCSEs and carries a double grade. Assessment is internal and external, the latter taking the form of tests or internally marked, externally moderated assignments.

In conjunction with the introduction of Vocational GCSEs, the Increased Flexibility Programme provided opportunities for Year 10 pupils to gain additional support for their vocational programme as a result of partnerships between their school and predominantly FE colleges, but occasionally universities or training centres. Additional opportunities were available for pupils to take qualifications other than Vocational GCSEs due to the close links with colleges. These include

BTEC First and NVQs. The latter were not previously available to those under 16, but particular subjects were designated as such under Section 96 for funding purposes. Progression to Foundation and Advanced Modern Apprenticeships was also possible. The scheme included an extended period of work placement and was funded through Learning and Skills Councils (LSCs). Initial evidence suggests wide regional variation in the success of the scheme. Concerns arose over how pupils would be selected amid fears (mostly unfounded) that the disaffected would predominate. FE teachers felt poorly prepared for teaching the younger age group (A. Coles unpublished) and issues over duty of care and responsibility arose. Disparity between the conditions of service for schoolteachers and FE lecturers also caused tensions since both groups would be working together under similar circumstances.

The Green Paper *14–19: Extending opportunities, raising standards* (DfES 2002d) proposed to formalise the stage at which vocational training enters the curriculum from 16 to 14. Three distinct phases were proposed between the ages of 14 and 19. The first would see a much more proactive role for the careers service through Connexions in conjunction with pupils, the schools and parents in devising a career plan at the end of Key Stage 3. Connexions would continue to monitor and review the plan; a significant extension of the remit for the service. The second phase would consist of a modified Key Stage 4 curriculum with a core of English, maths, ICT, citizenship, religious education, careers and physical education. There would be an entitlement to one subject from modern languages, design and technology, arts and humanities with the suspension of current disapplication arrangements. Modern Apprenticeships would gain a role in the 14 to 16 age-range and hybrid academic/vocational curricula would be encouraged with the 'vocational' title being removed from GCSEs and A2 qualifications. The final phase would involve the award of a 'Matriculation Diploma' covering Key Skills, vocational and academic qualifications, and work-based learning at three levels depending on the qualifications achieved. Flexibility on when examinations could be taken, a new 'Distinction' grade at A2 and a new role for the inspectorates in 14 to 19 provision were also proposed.

Success for All (DfES 2002b) recognised the diversity of the FE sector in terms of the learners, learning providers and models of delivery. The report suggested that the spirit of competition had led to some examples of weak provision and that local needs were not always met.

The report's recommendations focused on the need for FE provision to meet national and local skills needs identified with the LSCs playing a key role through the production of Local Area Reviews and Learning Strategies designed to identify skill shortages. Ofsted and Adult Learning Inspectorate (ALI) reports would be used to identify the strengths and weaknesses of local provision and make recommendations for alternatives where necessary. Sector Skills Councils would co-ordinate the involvement of employers. A programme of continuing professional development, including leadership training, was proposed for FE teachers, trainers, support staff and work-based trainers, including substantial support for e-learning. For several years FE teachers have felt marginalised by attempts to harmonise their training with Qualified Teacher Status (QTS) programmes, while working under poorer conditions of service and rates of pay than their school-based counterparts; a problem exacerbated by closer working relationships as a result of 14 to 19 initiatives. Recommendations made in *Success for All* ('golden hellos' and repayment of training loans) are unlikely to have a significant impact on this issue.

The need to broaden the curriculum offered to learners between the ages of 14 and 16 was recognised and recommendations were made to improve collaboration between schools, colleges, private training providers and employers. The assumption was made that colleges and college staff were prepared for an influx of younger learners; the recent reform of FE teacher education did not take this possibility into account and the result was concern among FE teachers that they lacked the skills to manage further diversity in the classroom.

Success for All drew attention to deficiencies in the support provided for basic skills and set an agenda for improvement in literacy, language and numeracy according to recommendations made in *Skills for Life* (DfEE 2001)

A radical departure in the form of the Education Maintenance Allowance (EMA), in which young people entering Year 12 would be paid to remain in further education, was piloted for several years from 2000. Different models were trialled at various locations in the UK. Evaluation indicated an increase of around 6 per cent in participation with an improvement in attendance and coursework. The impact was most significant on male learners (DfES 2002e). The model to be implemented from September 2004 involves means-tested payments of up to £30 per week for up to three years plus a bonus of £100 for remaining on the course and making good progress. The administration of the scheme has been challenging as payments are dependent on satisfactory attendance and progress; the weekly reporting system has been time-consuming for FE teachers and administrative staff, though the improvements in achievement, particularly on vocational courses, have confirmed the effectiveness of the scheme.

Scotland

In Scotland, the creation of the Higher Still programme, which led to the restructuring of post-16 school qualifications outlined above, is perhaps the most significant 14 to 19 issue. It is an attempt to recognise that a certification of achievement is possible at all levels, from those with learning difficulties whose ultimate attainment might be Access 1 to the most academic who may embrace a clutch of Advanced Highers.

The Scots still cling to the notion of breadth in their post-16 curriculum, however well founded or not this remains in reality (Matheson 1999). However, by insisting on certificating virtually all 16-year-olds, they attempt to demonstrate that academic attainment is open to all and this in a meaningful manner. The downside is, of course, that some certificates – such as grade 7 in standard science – may serve to show the outside world that the pupil has merely attended the class and failed everything. Nonetheless, there is coherence to the system and a range of progression routes are mapped out, with attempts being made to accommodate within a single structure the entire ability range, albeit at the potential price of some complicated arrangements in terms of classroom teaching.

Work-based training and the skills deficit

The treatment of FE and work-based education as separate entities, with the Government being responsible for the organisation and funding of the former and employers the latter, has resulted in the UK faring badly when compared with other countries (Keep 1996). The proportion of young people remaining in education after the school leaving age has been lower than other European countries and traditionally UK employers have been willing to employ school leavers with minimal qualifications. If full-time education is continued beyond 16, dropout rates are high at approximately 30 per cent and the current target of 50 per cent participation in higher education is lower than many other European countries. Half the number of UK workers have vocational qualifications when compared with Germany and only 5 per cent of pupils aged 15 are enrolled on vocational programmes compared with 9 per cent in France, 20 per cent in the Netherlands and 30 per cent in Germany (OECD 2001).

One of the key problems associated with ensuring an adequately trained and qualified workforce is that the system is reactive to historical data, rather than proactive in response to trends and predictions. The vocational education and training system needs to be able to respond to changes in the labour market, rather than react to crises as a result of skills shortages. Such shortages are not necessarily the result of changes in the popularity of vocational subjects, but they result from occupational mobility, retirement resulting from the ageing of the workforce, and the creation of new types of jobs in response to economic demands. For example, there is an increasing demand for technical skills and employers also require more staff with higher levels of generic skills, particularly in the IT and management sectors (Campbell 2001). In addition to the numeracy, communication and IT skills specified by Key Skill qualifications, problem solving and working with others were commonly cited, and further personal skills not necessarily addressed by Key Skills qualifications were required. These included the ability to respond to change, entrepreneurship, facilitation, ethical competencies, leadership, cultural awareness, customer handling, and meta-competencies including instinct and judgement. This is concerning since the incorporation of such skills in the pre-16 curriculum is only just being proposed (DfES 2003c).

Overall, one in four of those who are economically active lack a qualification, or have qualifications below the equivalent of NVQ Level 4 (Campbell 2001). This is not a homogenous pattern across the workforce though. Achievement at NVQ Level 2 is low among boys and ethnic minorities while girls tend to make slow progress from Level 2 to Level 3. The report makes the important point that vocational qualifications overall are in the minority of all qualifications taken in the UK, with half of the economically active population holding academic qualifications (including GCSE, Standard Grade, Higher Grade, O, AS and A level and degrees), while only a quarter of the population of England hold vocation qualifications (Figure 12.2.). In addition to a variation in the possession of qualifications across the workforce, there were regional variations in the quality of work-based training and significant differences in uptake, with those most in need (the unskilled and part-time workers, for example) receiving the least training.

The data described above set the context for the participation of those leaving school with the intention of engaging in work-based training. The current model of work-based training has its roots in a series of initiatives resulting from a response to high youth unemployment in the late 1970s. The 'new vocationalism' beginning with the Holland Report (HMSO 1977) spawned the Youth Opportunities

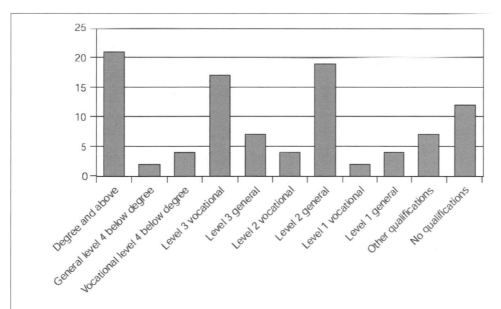

FIGURE 12.2 Highest qualification of economically active people in England in 2001 (%) (Spring 2001 Labour Force Survey, cited in Campbell 2001)

Programme (YOP) across the UK, which was based in FE colleges and designed to increase employability of 16-year-olds by providing work experience and support for work-related and basic skills. The programme was, however, seen as 'slave labour' by young people and served to reduce the pool of youth labour available. Despite few young people entering work directly from the scheme, the generic skills element was considered beneficial to long-term employability (Coles and MacDonald 1996). Soon after the start of the YOP scheme, the New Training Initiative (NTI) was launched in 1981. The NTI was designed to modernise the traditional craft apprenticeship, provide pre-entry training for intending apprentices and extend the availability of work-based training to an underskilled workforce. The scheme achieved very limited success, with craft apprenticeships left in decline and few incentives for employers to improve their training (Keep 1996).

The YOP scheme was replaced by the Youth Training Scheme (YTS) in 1983 and later by a two-year YTS2. The YTS2 scheme resulted in a large expansion of the youth training sector and caused tensions between public and private providers, rather than fostering a culture of partnership. This occurred as a result of the funding arrangements, which allowed employers to continue their own training schemes but claim subsidies associated with YTS2 (Coles and MacDonald 1996).

The YOP and YTS schemes were supported by a framework of pre-vocational courses under the umbrella of the Technical Vocational Education Initiative (TVEI), leading to the award of the Certificate in Pre-Vocational Education (CPVE). TVEI operated under the auspices of the Manpower Services Commission, a quango under the Department of Trade. Its remit extended into pre-vocational courses and modules not only in support of YOP and YTS but also more generally within schools and colleges. In England and Wales this meant the Department of Trade exerting an influence over part of the remit of the Department for Education and Science while in Scotland, for the first time, a Department which was not part of the Scottish Office could exert an influence – via offers of funding which were subject to strict conditions – on what went on in Scottish schools and colleges.

The pre-vocational courses were designed to provide support with generic and employment-related skills, including work experience for those intending to enter a vocational field. Inevitably, the emphasis on the practical resulted in TVEI having a poor image and it was seen as a second-rate curriculum for those unable to engage in the mainstream (Atkins 1984). The key issue of parity of esteem between the academic and vocational curriculum surfaced again. The validity of the vocational as valid knowledge is central to the future planning of the curriculum as discussed by Lewis (1999):

> As the British debate over the introduction of the TVEI and pre-vocationalism has shown, acceptance of the practical as valid knowledge remains firmly a matter of intense

philosophical debate. For many, what is at stake is the purity of the curriculum. They deem as invalid any claim that the practical arts belong in their own right.

(p. 139)

The TVEI was replaced by a system of Training Credits in 1996 in which those aged 17 or above received vouchers administered by the Training and Enterprise Councils in England and Wales, while in Scotland the task was shared between Scottish Enterprise and Highlands and Islands Enterprise which were to be used for vocational or academic training. The intention was to place more responsibility and choice in the hands of the trainee, yet abrogate responsibility for vocational training in favour of employers. Training Credits could be used to fund Modern Apprenticeships or NVQs at Level 2 or above.

Modern Apprenticeships (MAs) were introduced in 1993. They were intended to provide training in a specific vocational area for young people aged from 16 to 24. Trainees receive a training allowance if they are in a work placement, or a guaranteed minimum wage if they are in employment. On-the-job training is provided by the employer and this is supported by a training provider such as an FE college, which administers the training. MAs are available at Foundation and Advanced levels. The Foundation MA lasts for 12 months and is available in more than 60 vocational areas. Trainees work towards a Level 2 NVQ, Key Skills qualifications, a Technical Certificate and Employer Rights and Responsibilities. The Advanced MA lasts for two years and involves a Level 3 NVQ. Funding is provided through the LSC (Education and Learning Wales in Wales and the Local Enterprise Company in Scotland). The qualification structures are developed and maintained by the relevant employment NTO.

A recent evaluation of MAs in Wales (NCELWA 2003) indicated that employers were satisfied with the operation of MAs and would continue to be involved. Those without trainees knew little of the scheme and stated that they only recruited trained staff. Training providers were frustrated by the lack of progression from Level 2 to 3, poor completion rates and the difficulty in obtaining placements. MAs were perceived as sound by young people in the 14 to 24 age-range, but of lower status than traditional academic routes. Former trainees felt that their expectations were met, but some did not receive Key Skills support. Completion rates were considered dependent upon the quality of provision, often seen as higher in larger, better-resourced employers. The report identified that the MA programme would be improved by better marketing to enhance perceptions of the programme, improved partnership arrangements and more transparent and equitable funding.

The core qualification upon which MA programmes are based is the NVQ (SVQ in Scotland). The structure of NVQs is maintained by the National Council for Vocational Qualifications (the Scottish Qualifications Authority in Scotland). NVQs and SVQs are competence-based qualifications, assessed according to the ability of the candidate to perform a range of occupationally specific tasks and address certain specified knowledge requirements (Jessup 1991). They are associated with a range of different delivery models; some are almost entirely work-based with assessment taking place in the workplace at one extreme to those assessed in a realistic work environment, usually an FE college or private training provider. NVQs and SVQs can be studied full-time or part-time and are unit-based enabling credit accumulation. The key to their flexibility is that they can be used to accredit an initial training programme, or existing competence via accreditation of prior learning. Assessors need to hold appropriate assessor awards and the programmes are validated by awarding bodies such as Edexcel although, as mentioned previously, in Scotland only SQA validates the programmes. Their flexibility is further enhanced by the range of different types of evidence that can be offered for assessment by the candidate. This can take the form of a product, observation of a task by an assessor, witness testimony or written evidence of competence. NVQs and SVQs have contributed to sealing the academic/vocational divide to some extent due to their availability at five different levels from Entry to Level 5 (Table 12.1), thereby spanning traditional levels of vocational qualifications (Levels 1 to 3) to include higher and professional levels (Levels 4 and 5).

The main criticism of NVQs and SVQs relates to their narrow focus on a range of highly job-specific tasks to the extent that the skills accredited are not easily transferred to other occupations. The skill levels addressed by NVQs and SVQs have also been criticised as extremely low and in 'danger of producing a semi-literate underclass' (Keep 1996: 108). Keep continues to emphasise the dangers of a low skill economy resulting in competition with other low wage, low skill economies and a severe disadvantage in relation to our high skill competitors.

Conclusion

The historical perspectives discussed above indicate a long history of the academic/vocational divide. Many attempts have been made to achieve harmonisation and parity of esteem between the two routes, but each attempt has foundered through a lack of commitment to the cause. A reluctance by ministers (usually a product of the academic curriculum) to risk tarnishing the 'gold standard' – as A level is frequently termed but, interestingly, Highers are not, despite their somewhat longer heritage – academic curriculum with vocationalism has resulted in the marginalisation of the latter. The organisation and funding of work-based learning and FE teacher training has been left to employers' organisations, furthering the divide. HEIs must bear some responsibility too as they have been slow to understand and recognise the diversity of skill developed within a vocational curriculum. The interim recommendations of the Tomlinson review of 14 to 19 qualifications in England bode well for the future. The ten-year timescale should allow sufficient opportunity for proper planning and piloting, but success will depend on a willingness of Government and other stakeholders to develop a vision for education and training sufficiently flexible to respond to economic and social challenges in decades to come. This will also give us time to see if the innovations north of the Border bear the fruit that is hoped for in the rhetoric that surrounds them.

Suggested further reading

Contemporary issues relating to the development of post-compulsory education are discussed in Gray and Griffin (2000) which covers the relationship between academic and vocational qualifications. Ashcroft (1995) discusses quality assurance, staff development, course design and resource management. Collaboration and partnerships represent a critical issue in the sector and are discussed in Abramson *et al.* (1996). Moon (2001) addresses issues relating to the National Curriculum while the developmental roots of the FE sector are described in Roderick and Stevens (1972).

Journal relevant to post-compulsory education include: *Education and Training*, the *Journal of Vocational Education and Training, FE Now!, Learning and Skills Research (LSDA)*, the *Journal of Further and Higher Education* (NATFHE) and the *NATFHE Journal*.

References

Abramson, M., Bird, J. and Stennett, A. (eds) (1996) *Further and Higher Education Partnerships: The Future for Collaboration*. Buckingham: Society for Research into Higher Education and Open University Press.

Ashcroft, K. (1995) *The Lecturer's Guide to Quality and Standardsin Colleges and Universities*. London: Falmer.

Atkins, M. J. (1984) 'Pre-vocational courses: tensions and strategies', *Journal of Curriculum Studies*, 16 (4), 403.

Campbell, M. (2001) *Skills in England 2001: The Research Report*. Leeds: Policy Research Institute.

Coles, B. and MacDonald, R. F. (1996) 'From new vocationalism to the culture of enterprise', in R. Edwards, S. Sieminski and D. Zeldin (eds) *Adult Learners, Education and Training*. London: Routledge.

Dearing, R. (1996) *Review of Qualifications for 16 to 19 Year Olds*. London: School Curriculum and Assessment Authority.

DfEE (1997) *Qualifying for Success: a Consultation Paper on the Future of Post-16 Qualifications*. London: DfEE.

DfEE (2001) *Skills for Life: The national strategy for improving adult literacy and numeracy skills*. London: DfEE.

DfES (2001a) *The Post-16 Education and Training and Inspection Regulations 2001*. London: DfES.

DfES (2001b) *The Further Education Teachers' (England) Regulations 2001*. London: DfES.

DfES (2002a) *Inquiry into A Level Standards: Final Report*. London: DfES.

DfES (2002b) *Success for All*. London: DfES.

DfES (2002c) *14–19 Opportunity and Excellence*. London: DfES.

DfES (2002d) *14–19: Extending opportunities, raising standards*. London: DfES.

DfES (2002e) *Implementation of the Education Maintenance Allowance Pilots: The second year*. Research Brief No. 333. London: DfES.

DfES (2003a) *The Future of Initial Teacher Education for the Learning and Skills Sector: an agenda for reform*. London: DfES.

DfES (2003b) *21st Century Skills: Realising our potential*. London: DfES.

DfES (2003c) *Principles for Reform of 14–19 Learning Programmes and Qualifications*. Working Group on 14–19 Reform. London: DfES.

DfES/FENTO (2002) *Subject Specifications for Teachers of Adult Literacy, Numeracy and ESOL*. London: DfES.

FEFC (1997) *Learning Works: Widening Participation in Further Education*. Coventry: FEFC.

Further Education National Training Organisation (1998) *Standards for Teaching and Supporting Learning in Further Education I England and Wales*. London: FENTO.

Gray, D. and Griffin, C. (eds) (2000) *Post-Compulsory Education and the New Millennium*. London: Jessica Kingsley.

Green, A. (1999) 'Technical Education and State Formation in Nineteenth-Century England and France', in B. Moon and P. Murphy (eds) *Curriculum in Context*. London: Paul Chapman Publishing.

HMSO (1959) *15 to 18: A Report of the Central Advisory Council for Education (England)*. London: HMSO.

HMSO (1977) *Young People and Work (The Holland Report)*. London: HMSO.

Jessup, G. (1991) *Outcomes: NVQs and the emerging model of education and training*. London: Falmer Press.

Keep, E. (1996) 'Missing Presumed Skilled: training policy in the UK', in R. Edwards, S. Sieminski and D. Zeldin (eds) *Adult Learners, Education and Training*. London: Routledge.

Kelly, T. (1957) *George Birkbeck: Pioneer of adult education*. Liverpool: Liverpool University Press.

Lewis, T. (1999) 'Valid knowledge and the problem of practical arts curricula', in B. Moon and P. Murphy (eds) *Curriculum in Context*. London: Paul Chapman Publishing.

Matheson, D. (1999) 'Scottish Education: myths and mists', *Oxford Studies in Comparative Education*, 9 (2).

Moon, R. (2001) *A Guide to the National Curriculum*. Oxford: Oxford University Press.

NCELWA (2003) *Evaluation of Modern Apprenticeships and National Traineeships in Wales*. Birmingham: NCELWA.

Ofsted (2003) *The Initial Training of Further Education Teachers: a survey*. London: HMI.

Organisation for Economic Co-operation and Development (2001) *Education Policy Analysis*. Paris: OECD.

Roderick, G. and Stevens, M. (1972) *Scientific and Technical Education in Nineteenth Century England: a Symposium*. Newton Abbot: David Charles.

Post-compulsory education: further education, higher education, lifelong learning

Catherine Matheson

Next in importance to freedom and justice is popular education, without which neither freedom nor justice can be permanently maintained.

(James Garfield 1831–81)

Introduction

AS WE SAW IN THE last chapter, further education in the United Kingdom has a long history of being marginalised to a greater or lesser extent. Higher education, on the other hand and especially in the last 40 years, has moved to centre stage and remained there.

The term 'further education' seldom seems to cross politicians' lips except insofar as when mentioned as part of the seamless boundary between further and higher education. Higher education has also not only to be mentioned in relation to but to have a presence in further education colleges, thus helping make the lines between further education and higher education more and more blurred. This is in addition to further education serving as the supplier of courses designed for persons (usually aged over 21) to acquire the necessary qualifications to enter higher education.

As for higher education institutions, through their outreach and extra-mural work, they have long served as one of the mainstays of adult and continuing education across the United Kingdom. It is with these central roles in mind that I intend to develop this chapter around higher education and to branch off into the related areas of further and adult education as the need arises. It is worth mentioning that there are many other organisations that have offered and continue to offer what used to be termed 'liberal adult education' as well as community education which aim at improving quality of life and, if they happen to have a vocational application, it is more by accident than by design.

If higher education has been firmly at the centre of the political agenda since the 1990s, at the time of writing (January 2004) this is due in no small part to the current controversy over variable student tuition fees in England, better known as the 'top-up fees' issue, whereby the Government proposes that higher education institutions could impose up to a maximum fee of £3,000 (Baty 2003: 2). (Tuition fees of £1,000 were first introduced in the UK in 1998 while maintenance grants were abolished in 1999.)

The nineteenth century

At the beginning of the nineteenth century the British universities were unevenly distributed. England had only two universities, Oxford and Cambridge, while Scotland with only a tenth of the population had four: St Andrews, Glasgow, Edinburgh and Aberdeen. The Scottish universities had seen their student numbers rise sharply in the latter part of the eighteenth century and offered large lectures and a less developed tutorial system than Oxford and Cambridge. The two English universities were far more aristocratic and elitist than their Scottish counterparts and concentrated on the liberal education in the arts and humanities, providing mainly non-vocational courses for residential as opposed to predominantly local students. Although the University of Durham, founded in 1832, was based on the Oxford and Cambridge 'aristocratic' model of a collegiate university, University College London, established in 1827, was based on the Scottish model.

In the second half of the nineteenth century several of the industrial English cities established civic or 'bourgeois' universities which were locally supported, vocationally orientated, and closely related to and dependent upon local business and industry with middle-class students living largely at home (Bligh 1990). Whether aristocratic or bourgeois, university education in the nineteenth and early twentieth century was largely a privilege for the fortunate and wealthy, especially in England.

A notable exception was the University of London, created in 1836, a purely examining body and offering only external degrees until the end of the nineteenth century for courses in technical colleges and other institutions as well as correspondence courses and which thus provided an alternative route of part-time study, distance learning and franchised degrees for non-traditional entrants such as women, mature and working-class students. A relatively unknown aspect of higher education is that in the late nineteenth century part-time students constituted the majority outside Oxford, Cambridge and Durham, while residence did not become a dominant feature of higher education until the early twentieth century when the provincial colleges obtained university charters and more especially after the expansion of higher education in the 1960s (Wright 1989).

> In 1883 when a further new university college was opened in Dundee … its Principal felt able to claim that the availability of university places per head of population in Scotland at that time was exceeded only in Switzerland.
>
> (Bell 2000: 166)

Scotland's higher education experienced significant growth even before the creation of University College Dundee. In the eighteenth century the 'total student population tripled … with student numbers at Edinburgh University alone increasing from 400 in 1700 to 2,300 in 1824' (Smith 2000: 311) though few bothered to graduate. As Smith (2000) makes clear, the current divide between education and entertainment simply did not exist as we know it now. Indeed, she argues that amusement *and* instruction were a major feature of at least some Scottish higher education and that the instruction was indeed *higher* education. In this way, this eighteenth and early nineteenth-century idea of *infotainment* was not a dumbing down of higher education in order for it to appeal to a wider public. As importantly, if not more so, Smith demonstrates that until the full force of the Victorian cult of domesticity began to be felt by Scottish women, there was a major and continued growth in the opportunities afforded to wealthier Scottish women to attend courses of higher education, estimating that 'there were over 5,000 class enrolments by women at the Andersonian [Institution in Glasgow] alone, between 1796 and 1845' (Smith 2000: 326). The Andersonian would eventually become a College of Advanced Technology and then finally the University of Strathclyde in 1964.

This 'storming of the citadel' was severely hampered by the growing link from the mid-nineteenth century between university *qualification* and professional employment. Men, it seems, did not mind women educating themselves in the same manner that they minded women seeking prestigious employment. It was only from 1875 in England and 1889 in Scotland that legislation enabled universities to confer degrees on women though it took until the last quarter of the twentieth century for women in Great Britain to achieve overall parity of numbers with men in higher education.

Adult and vocational education as we know them have their likeliest ancestor in the Mechanics' Institutes of the nineteenth century. In Mechanics' Institutes, 'workers could improve their basic skills, learn new scientific and technological knowledge and broaden their minds' (Hall 1994: 3), initial job training being done on the job. The notion of broadening the mind is crucial and ties in directly with the goal of the University Extension classes, born as a direct consequence of the growth in the railway system – and the postal service. Tutors would tour the country, armed with cases of books, lodging in cheap hotels, teaching evening classes in just about every university subject imaginable (except the 'professions') to workers who had spent their day toiling in the mines or in factories. The correspondence course, for its part, had been launched in the immediate wake of the introduction of the postage stamp in 1840. Thus, in the course of the eighteenth century we see two distinct forms of learning distant from the institution concerned: on the one hand there is the correspondence course where the learner's only contact with the centre is by post – together with the occasional trip to the centre for examination; on the other there is the Extension class with the tutor travelling great distances to reach the learners. Interestingly enough, we see both in modern form in that most hi-tech of establishments, the Open University.

The literary aspect of the Extension classes is underlined in the report of the Committee on Distribution of Science and Art Grants (1896) which advised the allocation of additional grants to enable students attending evening science and art classes to gain further literary instruction through University Extension classes. As we shall see shortly, it was through the University Extension classes that one of the mainstays of adult education in the United Kingdom, the Workers' Educational Association, was born.

The late eighteenth and early nineteenth century also saw the creation of the model village. Devised by industrialists ostensibly to house the workers and their families, these were constructed at some distance from any centre of population and so quite effectively allowed the owner control over multiple aspects of the inhabitants' lives. I shall briefly discuss two such model villages, New Lanark, near the Falls of the Clyde, and Bournville, which now lies inside Birmingham. There were many more but all shared the idea of the benevolent paternalistic employer.

In 1800 Robert Owen, a Welsh entrepreneur who had made his money in the Manchester cotton trade, arrived in New Lanark to take over management of the cotton mill from his father-in-law, the social reformer David Dale (a director of the Royal Bank of Scotland). Owen realised that he could increase productivity by improving on the already high quality housing (Kreis 2002) and by educating not just the children of the workers but also the workers themselves (Donnachie 2003). We can speculate as to the true motives for this venture but the upshot is clear as Owen (1835) claims in his *A New View of Society* that by education one can give any character one wants to a community. As we saw in Chapter 10 of this volume, Owen established the first nursery school; he also set up his *Institute for the Formation of Character* which was in effect a school and a community centre.

> The three lower rooms [in the Institute] will be thrown open for the use of the adult part of the population, who are to be provided with every accommodation requisite to enable them to read, write, account, sew or play, converse or walk about. Two evenings in the week will be appropriated to dancing and music, but on these occasions, every

accommodation will be prepared for those who prefer to study or to follow any of the occupations pursued on the other evenings.

(Owen 1816)

Following in many respects the social reform trends set by Owen, George Cadbury and his brother Richard constructed Bournville in 1879 initially for key workers in their chocolate factory, only later expanding it to admit other workers. Like Owen before them, they included a school in the village but George, unlike Robert Owen, was a committed teacher who spent Sunday mornings teaching in the Quaker-run (though secular in its curriculum) Birmingham Adult School. Within the village, the Cadburys operated what might now be termed 'community education' by organising leisure activities for the inhabitants. They were incidentally among the first employers to give their workers free time on bank holidays and reputedly the first to make Saturday a half-day, instead of the usual full-day, in order to give their workers more time for other activities (Spartacus Educational 2002).

The twentieth century

From the Renaissance until the Modern Age the most insurmountable barriers to higher education had been on the grounds of gender and also very often of religious discrimination. From the late nineteenth century these were progressively removed but the financial barrier to university education was slower to disappear. At the institutional level the idea of providing scholarships to ease the way for students of limited means developed at a snail's pace. In any case, few scholarships were sufficient to allow a student without other support to attend university, although various discretionary local education authority grants had been available for teacher training since the nineteenth century. Age, whether for men or for women, was not a barrier to higher education insofar as mature students were not excluded from it and had been catered for in considerable numbers by franchised degrees from the University of London and at the provincial colleges which gained university charters in the early twentieth century (Wright 1989).

By way of comparison, let us note that in 1900 there were seven universities for an English and Welsh population of 23 million, while the US state of Ohio with 3 million citizens boasted 37 higher education institutions (Miliband 1992). At the beginning of the twentieth century, there were about 29,500 full-time students in higher education in Britain. Most of these, around 24,000, were in universities, and the rest mainly in teacher training colleges with only a very small proportion in technical colleges. By 1945 the number of full-time students in Britain had risen to about 100,000 and it nearly doubled by 1960 to about 180,000 (Edwards 1982). Two years later in 1962 it was still just under 200,000, while in 1970 it was just under

500,000 and in 1987 well in excess of 500,000. The current number of full-time students is now around 1 million and the total number of students is nearing 1.5 million (HESA 1998). There was a continual acceleration until 1955 and then a far steeper acceleration from 1955 to 1970 when the numbers increased two-and-a-half-fold followed by a plateau (while in the decade 1987–97 the number of full-time students rose sharply and nearly doubled).

Equality of opportunity

Broadly speaking, before the Second World War, university education in the UK had the function of supporting and reproducing a socio-professional elite and universities were attended and staffed mainly by people drawn from the upper-middle class. Was then the expansion of higher education the consequence of the Robbins Report of 1963, better equality of opportunity in education (the major concern of progressive politicians and educationalists since the beginning of the twentieth century), the raising of the school-leaving age in 1947 and 1973 or some other factor?

While it is difficult to determine the extent to which the raising of the school-leaving age in 1947 and then again finally in 1973 (and not in 1970 as had been previously promised) was directly linked to the explosion in student numbers, a measure such as this is unlikely to lead to a decrease in the number of students entering higher education. Indeed, a seemingly inevitable consequence of the expansion or universalisation of secondary education would be the growing pressures for higher education places. Following the same logic in order to expand even further as the present Government wishes, it is imperative that more pupils stay on at school after the school-leaving age. For precisely that reason in the late 1990s, as we have moved from elitist to mass higher education, pupils in Britain are not yet legally required but only encouraged to stay on at school until the age of 18 or even 19. In 1998 Baroness Blackstone, the Higher Education Minister, even suggested that A levels were 'too narrow and elitist' and prevented too many young people, especially those from working-class background, from going on to higher education (Clare 1998: 1).

In the case of higher education the simple question of equal participation was for a long time clouded by the substitution of the question of equality of opportunity, a very elastic term and as elusive a philosophical concept as it is a practical target, which has been taken to apply to those able and willing to make use of it. Such a concept of policy culminated with the so-called 'Robbins meritocratic principle' that anyone able to get the necessary qualifications and willing to go should find a place in higher education. Having highlighted that the proportion of middle-class children who reach degree-level courses was 'eight times as high as the proportion from working-class homes' (Committee on Higher Education 1963: 46) and had remained unchanged since the 1920s, the Robbins Committee Report, a sociological analysis of the influence of class on access to the higher levels of education, argued for a massive expansion in the provision of university places within the discourse of equality of opportunity in terms of extending educational opportunity to all those qualified and willing to participate.

While the Robbins Report recommended a massive expansion of higher education on the grounds of equality of opportunity, it did not actually generate the explosion in the number of students because this exponential growth (which has so often in Britain been attributed to the Robbins Report) actually started about seven years prior to that date and was almost exactly duplicated throughout the individual countries in Europe (Edwards 1982). The age participation rates for 18-year-olds which measures the number of entrants as a proportion to the size of the relevant 18-year-old group showed a more significant increase *before* the Robbins Report than *after*, as the rate went from 3 per cent in 1950 to 8.5 per cent in 1962, only to reach 12.7 per cent in 1977, 14 per cent in 1987, 20 per cent in 1992 and 34 per cent in 1998. In other words, the age participation rate nearly tripled in the 12 years before the Report and rose by only about a third in the course of the following 14 years; 24 years after Robbins it had not even doubled.

The 'sharp and internationally synchronous and uniform escalation of higher education post-1955 indicated that a sufficiently powerful change in the international climate of economic and social thinking could trigger off a rapid change in the demand for higher education' (Edwards 1982: 67), especially if the ground had been prepared by raising the school-leaving age in the previous decade. The rate of growth of student enrolments in the late 1950s and 1960s was not much influenced by variations in the total population of 18 to 21-year-olds because working-class children, who constituted the majority of this population, had very little involvement in higher education, unlike the children of the rapidly expanding professional and managerial class whose services were increasingly needed by employers to adapt to the growing economic demand for qualified human resources.

As a result, the sharp escalation in student numbers from 1955 to 1970 was not accompanied by any significant change in relative participation rates by social class since the great majority of the increased flow came from the same social class as before, and so in the 1970s there was still the extreme disparity of social participation to higher education in the UK. Accordingly, the liberal expansion of higher education in the 1960s led to the situation that the relative chances of young people from different background gaining access have changed only slightly and then in favour of those groups already well-off (Edwards 1980; Halsey *et al.* 1980). In the 1970s the rate of growth of higher education slowed down. However, in the decade 1968–78, the proportion of students from professional and managerial classes expanded rapidly while the much smaller proportion from the children of manual workers correspondingly declined (Edwards 1982).

The financial barrier to higher education largely remained until 1945 and then began to slowly disappear as the number of grants awarded by local authorities increased to keep up with the rise in numbers. From the early 1960s the local authorities were required to give mandatory grants to suitably qualified full-time students accepted for university first degrees. Notwithstanding a system of income-related mandatory grants instead of discretionary local authority grants, the implementation of the Robbins recommendations failed to significantly increase the relative participation of the working class and higher education remained consequently deeply inegalitarian, reflecting the class structure of society by denying opportunities to working-class people and favouring those from a middle-class background. The lifting of the financial barrier did not remove the more entrenched social class divide, perhaps because of the increasing emphasis on residence ever since the early twentieth century and more especially since the early 1960s, or perhaps simply because although the cost of the post-Robbins expansion was borne by all the taxpayers, the balance of reward favoured those who were already better-off (Williamson 1986).

Whether higher education plays an integral part in schooling's complicity in the reproduction over the generations of an unequal and hierarchical social and sexual division of labour or serves as a means of social empowerment is open to question, because, whereas the social exclusiveness of higher education was not showing many signs of being eroded, the gender exclusiveness was faring much better and seemed slowly to be being erased. The participation of women saw a steady increase from 1971 to 1981, reflecting a trend in the school system with more girls gaining qualifications to enter higher education. The percentage of full-time students in the universities in Great Britain was seven men for three women in 1971–2, six men for four women ten years later and five men for five women today (Williamson 1986).

Apart from social class and gender inequalities, additional barriers to higher education remained those of age, regional and race inequality. If the number of full-time mature students increased slowly but fairly steadily from 8,500 in 1971–2 to 10,200 in 1979–80, the proportion of mature students, however, fell marginally, although there was a sharp rise in the number of women over 25 and a fall in the proportion of men, especially those aged 21–24 (Squires 1981). Regional participation rate when known variations in social class composition were taken into account showed that Scotland, Wales and the North-West of England were doing better than expected on the basis of social class trends, while Northern England and East Anglia were doing rather worse (Williamson 1986). When social class was taken into account, 37 per cent more Scots entered university education than would have been expected on the basis of what happened in England and Wales. This much higher participation was perhaps the result of a different educational system in which the transfer from secondary to higher education takes place a year earlier and which has a broader upper-secondary curriculum. The better than expected performance in Wales and in the North-West of England was not explicable in such terms and points, particularly in the case of Wales, to the importance of general and political attitudes towards education (Farrant 1981). The extent to which this remains true is currently the subject of ongoing debate and controversy. Osborne (1999) suggests that Northern Ireland is now doing somewhat better than the rest of the UK in terms of participation by lower social classes and that Scotland is now lagging behind (Wojtas 1999), though the differences are minimal.

Widening access and increasing participation

As higher education in the UK has moved from an elite to a mass system, its overall participation rate has increased more than eleven-fold from 3 per cent in 1950 to nearing 34 per cent half a century later. The percentage of male and female participation in higher education is now more or less equal, while the age participation rate was, and still is, unequally distributed according to social class divisions and to age and, to a lesser extent, geographic situation.

Access and participation are now among the major policy issues in post-school education in the UK (Fulton 1981, 1989; Williams 1997a; Davies 1994; Parry and Wake 1990; Ainley forthcoming) and worldwide (Halsey 1992; Davies 1995). In Britain and in many industrialised countries 'the impact of the idea of access has arguably been felt most keenly in the last decade or so [since the mid-1980s] and then in the sectors of, first higher education and then, more recently higher education and training' (Tight 1996: 131).

As the concept of access to higher education has undeniable political resonances and has to do with who gets educational opportunities and who does not, it is worth bearing in mind that the question as to who should have access depends on what higher education is for and on the advantages it brings, both for the individual and for society. In the UK, the concept of wider access and increased participation in higher education is not infrequently deemed to raise fears about lowering of standards and credential inflation as well as fears that a graduated system of institutions and courses would still privilege an elite.

Because the motivations behind the major policy issue of widening access and increasing participation were both the uncertainty caused by the demographic decline and fluctuations of the traditional entry cohort of the 16 to 19-year-olds, and a desire to open up opportunities for more and different people closely related to the former, it is useful to examine how the Government and funding bodies have approached the issue of access since the mid-1970s.

Two Labour Government documents at the end of the 1970s, a 1978 Green Paper (Department of Education and Science (DES) and Scottish Education Department (SED) 1978) and a 1979 Report (DES 1979) looked at the impact of the projections of an increasing 18-year-old population in the early 1980s followed by a rapid decline in the second half of the decade which would leave the system with considerable spare capacity. The immediate concern was to prevent a too-rapid expansion in the early 1980s while attempting longer-term planning by suggesting measures against a severe pruning of higher education because of a projected demographic fall in the traditional entry cohort. Because of predictions that between 1981 and 1996 the number of people aged between 30 and 44 would increase by about 1.6 million, the number aged over 44 by about 0.3 million, and the number aged between 16 and 29 would decrease by about 0.6 million, the effect of the two Government Papers was to make many academics and institutions much more aware of the potential of mature student entry because they suggested ways of avoiding the impending fall in student numbers for the best reasons: expansion and equalisation of educational opportunities (Squires 1981).

Indeed, for many, mature students were beginning to be seen as the way to save higher education from decline in the 1990s. Although the 1978 Green Paper had suggested that a way of coping with the demographic fall was to increase the number of mature students, especially those from a working-class background, and to further increase the participation of women, there were many obstacles to the effective implementation of these ideas, not least of which was the arrival of a Conservative Government in May 1979 led by Prime Minister Margaret Thatcher.

In the summer of 1981 the Conservative Government announced a programme of cuts in public expenditure in the universities which was to reduce their income by about 20 per cent in real terms in the next two years. The Government let it be known that the major objective of the squeeze was to reduce the number of students entering higher education. The financial disincentive for not meeting target numbers had a rapid effect on institutional behaviour of the universities. Because the polytechnics were funded within a local authority system, the impact of reduced unit costs on their institutional finances was not as immediate as it was with the universities. The polytechnics consequently expanded as fast as possible, reasoning that their unit costs would have been even further reduced if other HE institutions had expanded and they had not.

The attempted squeeze of higher education provision in the first half of the decade was therefore marked by an unprecedented expansion in student number (30 per cent increase) along with reduced unit costs (25 per cent decrease) in the polytechnics and colleges which saw students denied university places flocking to them. In 1984 the funding bodies (University Grants Committee (UGC)/National Advisory Body for public higher education sector (NAB)) each produced two strategy documents as well as a joint statement which, by stressing 'ability to benefit' from higher education, raised awareness and changed for ever the climate for access and continuing education (UGC 1984a, 1984b; NAB 1984a, 1984b). The following year came the Government's response in the form of a Green Paper (DES 1985) which grudgingly accepted the 'ability to benefit' as long as it was greater than the costs and not at the expense of standards. In other words, the Green

Paper stressed efficiency and a rather elitist concept of quality (Wagner 1989). The 1987 White Paper (DES 1987) nevertheless widened the criteria for entry even further by saying that 'places should be available for all with the necessary qualities [and not qualifications] to benefit from higher education' (DES 1987: 7).

In 1989, in a speech at Lancaster University, the Secretary of State for Education and Science urged that the participation rate among the 18-year-olds should double from 15 per cent to reach 30 per cent within the next 25 years and that in the latter part of the 1990s the expansion of higher education should see an increase in participation from the conventional student age group and from the 'new patterns of recruitment among non-conventional students' (Wagner 1989: 156). By the time the 1991 White Paper (DES 1991) was published the participation rate of the 18 to 19-year-olds was one in five and the anticipation was that the number would be one in three by the year 2000. The binary divide between the universities and the polytechnics (established from 1967 onwards with the majority in the early 1970s and financed by the local education authority except in Scotland where they were funded by the Scottish Education Department (SED) but had close relationships with the local community) was removed with the 1992 Further and Higher Education Act when the funding bodies, the status of which had already been changed by the Education Reform Act of 1988 to increase public accountability, were simultaneously divided geographically according to the nations of the UK while being united across the higher education sector.

From 1964 the history of higher education has been, along with the discourse of widening access and increasing participation which followed that of equality of opportunity, one of decreased financial commitment and increased control. This is further illustrated by the fact that the whole system of mandatory grants was gradually replaced from 1990 by a part-grant, part-loan scheme, a measure already tentatively contemplated by various governments since the late 1960s. The present Government took things even further in terms of decreased financial commitment by introducing tuition fees in 1998 and in removing maintenance grants in 1999 when loans were available to part-time students for the first time. There is an apparent paradox in the Government's attitude to access. On the one hand, there are fees and loans and, on the other, the Government's acceptance of Dearing's (1997) recommendation that:

> Increasing participation [...] must be accompanied by the objective of reducing the disparities in participation in higher education between groups and ensuring that higher education is responsive to the aspirations and distinctive abilities of individuals.
>
> (NCIHE 1997: 101)

The Government's response to Dearing admitted that the current student support arrangements have not encouraged students from lower socio-economic groups to enter higher education, whether on full-time or part-time courses (DfEE

1998a). From Robbins to Dearing the issues of widening access and increasing participation have progressively become central policy concerns for a rapidly expanding and, from the late 1980s, an exploding, mass higher education system. The proposed 1998 White Paper, which was downgraded to the 1998 Green Paper *The Learning Age* in February (DfEE 1998b), aims to expand further and higher education to provide for an extra 500,000 people by 2002 and to widen participation in, and access to, learning in further, higher, adult and community education and through the University for Industry.

Adult education

Following its creation by the Rochdale Pioneers in 1844 (Holyoake 1907), the Co-operative Movement formally took education as one of its aims in 1882. 'Technical correspondence courses and junior classes were developed during the 1890s and by 1900 over 1,000 students were enrolled for courses, over 500 adults had already taken exams in industrial history, bookkeeping and citizenship and over 900 juniors' (Co-operative College 2003). Although the educational mission of the Co-op has waxed and waned over the years it has left a lasting legacy on at least two fronts. One is the continuing existence of the Co-operative College which 'aims to provide adult and lifelong learning programmes that emphasise co-operative values and principles and be a centre of excellence in training, learning, consultancy and research for the co-operative and mutual sector in the UK and internationally' (Co-operative College 2003). Another is the Workers' Educational Association (WEA).

Marsh (2002) tells us how the founder of the WEA, Albert Mansbridge, had effectively grown up in the Co-operative Movement. Mansbridge then moved on to University Extension classes where, between 1891 and 1901, he studied a wide range of subjects and later became an evening class teacher. Mansbridge recognised in the University Extension classes that they had become a haven for the middle classes. Indeed by the 1980s, it was frequently stated that adult education was dominated by white, middle-class, middle-aged women.

Mansbridge's solution was to found an organisation for the workers, run by the workers. His initial title for the organisation, reflecting the sexism of his age, was the Association to Promote the Higher Education of Working Men. This was quickly changed to the Workers' Educational Association.

The fortunes of the WEA in England and Wales are somewhat more positive than in Scotland. WEA became a major provider of adult education in the former while in the latter it was denied *Responsible Body Status* as a provider of adult education and this made its 'development heavily dependent on collaboration with the universities, local authorities and trade unions' (Duncan 1999: 106).

The University Extension classes for their part grew, developed and changed into a plethora of extra-mural courses, covering almost every subject imaginable until, in the 1990s, much of the subsidy provided to them by local government was withdrawn (Vorhaus 2002). Indeed from 1979 onwards, market forces had been steadily applied and course fees steadily increased. This is aptly illustrated by the example of a class in Danish language which in 1977 cost £2.50; by 2003 it cost £113.[1]

Nonetheless, the twentieth century saw the development and perhaps the apotheosis of the notion of lifelong learning. Especially in the period after 1972 (the year that *Learning to Be* – the Faure Report – was published by UNESCO) 'lifelong learning' became increasingly a positive term, first among academics and social activists and then among politicians. The problem was that they did not generally mean the same thing. Lifelong learning quickly became an elastic concept, one which basically meant whatever the person using it wanted it to mean, just as long as there was some notion of lifelong and some notion of learning. 'Lifelong education' came into fashion as did terms such as 'learning society' and 'learning age'. However, while the advocates of the concept from the 1970s until the mid-1990s concerned themselves principally with improving quality of life, the political advocates from the mid-1990s onwards seemed more concerned with the economic aspects of lifelong learning. The Government Green Paper *The Learning Age: a Renaissance for a New Britain* (DfEE 1998b) emphasised above all else that by continuing to seek qualifications – and not merely learning or even education – one increased one's chances of improving one's economic situation. We continue to be forever reminded of the pace of technological change and it would not take a great cynic to believe that there are conscious attempts to make workers feel threatened, and this goes beyond the notion of simply avoiding or removing complacency. It is as Cropley (1977) cited from Ohliger and Dauber: 'concomitant to lifelong education is lifelong students, condemned to perpetual inadequacy' (p. 156).

Despite all this, at ground level a locally spawned initiative appeared in a few areas directly presenting active learning as a lifelong activity. This was the admission of adult learners into secondary schools. While adults were admitted to a rare few secondary schools in England (such as the community schools in Sutton in Ashfield and Milton Keynes), in Scottish urban areas in particular, as a direct response to falling school rolls, adults were actively sought, first for leisure classes and later to study for O-grades and Highers. As I have discussed elsewhere, this meant adolescents learning alongside adults while in the school's crèche, some of those same pupils might be learning childcare with the children of some of the adults (Matheson 2000). Active learning was thus presented as something that one can do for the full length of one's life.

---

[1] See http://www.gla.ac.uk:443/departments/adulteducation/index.php?SelectedSubject=Languages &SelectedSubheading=Danish.

Access courses and alternative routes to higher education

The broad idea of wider access has different ideological roots and is not to be confused with the narrower concept of Access courses designed for mature students without formal qualifications to gain specific entry to further and higher education and which offer an alternative to established examination systems designed for adolescents, whether A levels or Highers or vocational qualifications. While some mature students follow the traditional route and return to college or school to study A levels or Highers, a steadily growing minority of students now enter university via the above-mentioned alternative routes.

Although there had always been older people studying for degrees, the admission of mature students without the conventional entry qualifications was given a boost in the mid-1970s when the grant regulations were changed to make such students, if they were studying full time, eligible to receive mandatory awards as opposed to awards at the discretion of the local education authority. In 1978 the first Government recognition of Access courses occurred when the Department of Education and Science asked seven selected local authorities to provide special courses for people who had 'special needs which cannot be met by existing educational arrangements' and who possessed 'valuable experience but lacked the qualifications required' (DES 1978). Although there is a higher drop-out rate for mature students as opposed to their younger fellow students, the performance of those who graduate is comparable to non-mature students and this whatever the entry route (Woodley 1991).

The 1985 Green Paper welcomed Access courses provided that 'the challenge of non-standard entry is to maintain a reasonable degree of openness for late developers, and for those who for whatever reason did not enter higher education earlier, while ensuring that academic rigour and standards are maintained' (quoted in Brennan 1989). The 1987 White Paper and subsequent Government pronouncements have placed increasing emphasis on extending access and have seen Access courses as playing an important role in it by recognising them as one of three entry routes, the other two being A levels or Highers and vocational qualifications. Although the number and range of Access courses has grown exponentially since 1978, they are only one of the recognised routes of access to further and higher education for mature students over the age of 21. Access to higher education by other alternative routes does also exist and includes long-standing diverse and flexible methods such as examination or assessment, through liberal adult education provision, through assessment of prior (experiential) learning, through probationary enrolment and through open entry schemes (Tight 1996).

Over the years Access courses have gained increasing recognition among politicians and others as providing an answer to problems of participation in higher education in the 1990s. Arguably, the more broadly based Access courses, which offer a closer matching of requirements than A levels or Highers because they tend to be linked to a particular institution and which emphasise continuous assessment rather than final examinations, provide an alternative, more flexible route while emphasising equality of opportunity (Stowell 1992).

Access courses are often perceived by providers and recipients as a form of positive action targeting disadvantaged minority groups and seeking to increase their representation in higher education. Yet while it is:

> undeniable that they have helped many individuals to pursue their education further than they might otherwise have been able to do, Access courses have yet to make a major impact upon the social make-up or the assumptions of higher education.
>
> (Tight 1996: 132)

This particular criticism of Access courses perhaps explains, or is perhaps explained by, the fact that they tend to overemphasise higher education as a destination and thus help sustain conventional perceptions of higher education rather than seeking to change them (Tight 1996).

Foundation degrees

The closing years of the twentieth century were marked by the creation of yet another route into higher education, the Foundation degree, a vocationally focused higher education qualification (DfES 2003a). This was designed for persons with professional experience wishing to develop their knowledge further. Indeed, in many cases, professional experience and not qualification was the deciding factor in permitting entrance to the course whose length ranged from two to three years part time. The aim of the Foundation degree is to increase the number of people qualified at higher technician and associate professional level (DfES 2003a). Possession of the Foundation degree will permit the holder either to enter the final year of an existing undergraduate course or to enter a specially created 'top-up' degree. In the case of learning support assistants or teaching assistants, it was commonly intended that the 'top-up' degree be with Qualified Teacher Status. However, at the time of writing, the existing one-year top-up degrees do not yet give QTS and a PGCE has to be undertaken afterwards in order for the students to gain QTS status.

It is too early to say what market value Foundation degrees will acquire. Neither can we be sure whether holders of 'top-up' degrees will be treated on a par with holders of traditional degrees but we need only look to the experience of holders of degrees of the Open University to see what might well occur. It is well documented that for many years following the creation of the Open University in 1970, holders of its degrees were frequently viewed with more than a little suspicion. That they had entered their course with no qualifications was frequently justification enough for this attitude; that they had done the course part-time simply added fuel to the fire. Time will tell if the Foundation degree follows a similar path. Foundation degrees are offered in a range of forms and formats by a wide range of institutions. It is too early to evaluate and comment on the influence of Foundation degrees in the higher education landscape. Foundation degrees do not yet exist in Scotland.

The twenty-first century

Paradoxically, one benefit of the funding squeeze in the 1980s and the shift in funding towards a focus on student numbers has been a greater openness on the part of many institutions to mature, part-time and other 'non-traditional' students. In 1991 a quarter of university entrants were classified as entering via 'non-traditional' routes and in 1995 one-third of undergraduate entrants were over 21 (HEFCE 1996). This has in some way reflected the desire of higher education institutions to maintain numbers during a demographic decline of the traditional cohort, but also reflects some determination to offer new opportunities to previously under-represented groups (Miliband 1992). Although the White Papers of 1987 and 1991 (DES 1987, 1991) talked less about qualifications and more about 'qualities' required to enter higher education and stressed flexibility and accessibility, they did not outline specific measures for coherent reform. Whereas the expansion of higher education in the 1980s and 1990s saw significant improvements in relative participation rates for women, most minority ethnic groups and mature students the exact position of social class is not fully known because of shortcomings in available data. Although the data is extremely problematic and tends to relate only to full-time students on first degree courses (Davies 1997), it would nevertheless seem that ratios of participation from lower socio-economic groups have remained fairly constant and there still remain a disproportionate number of students from a professional and managerial background as opposed to partly skilled and unskilled background (HEFCE 1996, 1997a, 1997b; NCIHE 1997; CVCP 1998).

A recent HEFCE (1997b) report found that young people from very high-income professional neighbourhoods in exclusive areas had a 75 per cent chance of getting to university; those from middle-class families in owner-occupied suburban semi-detached houses 35 per cent; and those from low-income semi-skilled and unskilled families living in areas of high unemployment 7 per cent (Carvel 1997). Recent figures show that 8 per cent of young people from lower socio-economic groups enter higher education compared with 16 per cent of middle-class origin and 39 per cent from managerial and professional families (Metcalf 1997). 'The expansion of higher education since 1987 has been unable to shift the balance of opportunities between most social groups' (Robertson 1997: 10).

Recent developments and key differences between higher education in England and in Scotland

Since 1992 higher education has been funded along national lines with separate funding councils for England, Wales, Scotland and Northern Ireland. As a consequence there is the likelihood that the already diverse patterns of provision and participation will increase (Cormack *et al.* 1994). Unlike the Robbins Report (1963), the Dearing Report (1997) had the advantage of having a separate Scottish Committee (Garrick) to take account of the distinctiveness of Scottish higher education. The creation of the Scottish Parliament further shaped the nature, size and direction of Scottish higher education in ways that were different from England.

The Scottish higher education system contains several features which distinguish it from that of England and the rest of the UK:

- four-year honours degree courses;
- larger and standardised provision at sub-degree level with a national framework of HNDs (Higher National Diplomas) and HNCs (Higher National Certificates) awarded by SCOTVEC (the Scottish Vocational Educational Council) which merged with the Scottish Examinations Board in 1997 to become the Scottish Qualifications Authority (SQA);
- a correspondingly large involvement of further education colleges in higher education (Schuller *et al.* 1999; Smith and Bocock 1999);
- instead of up-front tuition fees of £1,000 per year, a graduate endowment of £2,000 to be repaid once a graduate earns a salary of £16,000 (Grant 2003; Mackie 2001).

The Scottish system of close relations and easy articulation between further education and higher education was praised in the Dearing and Garrick Reports. Around a quarter of Scottish higher education is offered in further education colleges, double the proportion in England (Schuller and Bamford 1999: 2). This goes some way to providing the seamless transition from advanced school level to university level and onwards that is at the heart of the Dearing vision and that of the Learning Age. In 1997 the age participation index for the population aged 17–21 was 43 per cent against 33 per cent for England and the rest of the UK (Arbuthnott 1997). Two years later 47 per cent of the age cohort are in the tertiary sector as compared to 35 per cent in England (Bone 1999). The participation rate among young Scots increased from 47.2 per cent in 1998/99 to 47.6 per cent in 1999/00 (Scottish Executive 2001) and is by far the highest in the UK (Mackie 2001). This is due to the fact that a great number of higher education courses are offered in the further education sector. The high participation rate is largely attributed to the funding model which existed already before the (re)creation of the Scottish

Parliament (when SOE[I]D funded higher education courses instead of SHEFC as was the case for HEFCE in England) (Smith and Bocock 1999; Mackie 2001).

Paradoxically, even though the seamless transition model saw many Access courses held in higher education institutions, as well as in further education institutions as is the case in England, the university population has tended to be less mature in Scotland than in England with 41.5 per cent of Scottish students in higher education institutions being over 25 compared with 44.8 per cent in England (Schuller and Bamford 1999). As from 1998 Scottish higher education institutions have been able to waive tuition fees for part-time undergraduate students who are unemployed or on low incomes and to develop more courses tailored to their needs (SHEFC 1998). In Scotland, unlike in England, the application rate for mature students over 25 appears to have stopped dropping and even to be going up again (Mackie 2001).

Tuition fees became a key issue for the Scottish Parliament and this coincided with the (re)creation of the said Parliament in 1999. Interestingly, because of intense political pressure by the Liberal Democrats, the Cubie Committee was set up in 1999 not by the SEED (Scottish Executive Education Department) but by the Scottish Parliament itself, thus making the enterprise a more significant one (Mackie 2001). The abolition of up-front tuition fees and replacing them with a graduate endowment scheme was part of Labour's partnership deal with the Liberal Democrats. The SEED accepted Cubie's recommendations that bursaries for low-income independent students and for those with additional support needs should be reintroduced. The SEED also accepted that every student would be entitled to student loans, even those from high-income families. Finally the further education system was restructured along Cubie's lines and anomalies between the sectors removed thus reinforcing the notion of a seamless robe between further and higher education (Mackie 2001).

In practice all the above means that for students domiciled in Scotland higher education in Scotland costs less than for students domiciled in England, around £6,000 for a four-year honours degree course instead of an average of £10,000 for a three-year honours degree course. The support for students in part-time employment is also better and student retention is also higher in Scotland (Mackie 2001).

Because of the tuition fees issues, English policies to encourage wider access by way of special bursaries and by giving more money to higher education institutions for taking on students from under-represented groups were heavily criticised by educationalists for being difficult to implement and for being ineffective and based on the premise framed within an elitist discourse that under-representation is caused by the limitations of certain socio-economic groups who are not well enough informed, educated, qualified and above all motivated (Woodrow 2001; Callender 2001). Scottish policies are taken by both Scottish and English educationalists (Mackie 2001; Callender 2001) to be based on a more egalitarian premise within an inclusive discourse that under-representation is socially constructed and that the blame belongs to higher education institutions who are not well enough targeting, informing, guiding, recognising potential, recruiting, meeting post-entry needs of vulnerable students. According to Woodrow (2001) and Callender (2001) the Cubie Report offered a coherent system aiming at equity and social justice with very different aims than Blunkett-derived policies which also claim to aim at equity and social justice.

UK figures from UCAS (Universities Central Admission System) released on 11 April 2001 show that the number of people applying for higher education places is continuing to rise. There has been a 1.3 per cent increase in the number of UK applicants under 21 and a 5 per cent increase in 21 to 24-year-olds though a 1.8 per cent drop in over-25s (*Education and Training Parliamentary Monitor*, May 2001: 2). But as reported by Thomson and Wojtas (2000), higher education acceptance rates figures from October 2000 showed that in terms of entrants to higher education 'Scotland booms' whereas 'England bombs'. There was a 7.8 per cent rise in the number of Scottish students who won places at Scottish universities. This was matched by a drop of 15 per cent in the number of English students accepted to Scottish institutions. Total acceptances rose by 2.6 per cent. At English universities the acceptance rate was lower than in Scotland and climbed by just 1.7 per cent with a 2.2 per cent rise in English students. Overall, things are expected to improve in the long term as the number of young people aged 18/19 began to start rising after 2002.

The issue of access to higher education has become a topic that is rising rapidly in the Government's agenda. Access refers to expanded or increased participation or more specifically to the provision of non-standard modes of entry (Open University, Access courses, Accreditation of Prior Experiential Learning and now two-year Foundation degrees). New ways of funding students and institutions as well as performance indicators have been introduced to support not only access and expanding participation but more specifically widening participation. This has to do not just with a greater fairness in admitting students to elite institutions but attempting to overcome the far wider pattern of social exclusion of less well off and disadvantaged groups in higher education, especially students from social class 3m, 4 and 5, those from deprived geo-demographic areas, from under-represented ethnic minority groups, those with learning difficulties and disabled students (Woodrow 2001).

In 1999/2000 there were just over 1.8 million students in higher education in the UK with 78 per cent or 1,448,000 at undergraduate level. Of the full-time undergraduate students 56 per cent are female and 44 per cent are male (HESA 2001). Over a third of part-time students study either business and administration studies or education. Male students are more attracted to computer sciences, engineering and technology, physical and mathematical sciences, architecture, building and planning, and less pulled towards education, languages and paramedical subjects (HESA 2001). Female students follow the opposite trend. In terms of traditionally academic subjects, mature students are found in similar proportion to younger students in humanities and social studies. Computer sciences, social, economic and political studies are more popular with students with non-traditional qualifications, especially women (HESA 2001).

In educational research there is a keen interest in comparative perspectives in examining variations across schools in young people's transitions, especially the role played by family background and school actors in young people's educational and post-educational decisions, and the way school characteristics interact with the characteristics of young people and how this relationship affects their destinations. At the same time there is also a keen interest in examining funding issues and widening participation in higher education for young people (Callender 2001; Woodrow 2001) as well as mature students (Davies *et al.* 2002).

Conclusion

Higher education no longer means only a full-time three-to-four-year residential engagement with a narrowly focused learning experience, at the expense of the state and at the benefit of a socially advantaged elite. Many believe that it is insufficient that access to higher education be simply widened to increase participation without thinking of as well transforming higher education itself which needs to provide more short courses, part-time courses, modules and credit-based learning, facilitate a mix-and-match approach and transfer from one institution to another, take courses outside its walls and to the people, use Accreditation of Prior Experiential Learning (APEL) to select students, offer courses for professional groups, activities and learning methods for mature students. Much has been done to stimulate demand for higher education from under-represented groups through raising expectations and improving attainment by measures such as community outreach and promotion, information, advice and guidance, and development of progression routes. Higher education has opened new opportunities and diversified its provision and hence met the challenge of the twenty-first century, whereby the right of access to higher education should be available to potential learners throughout their lives. But more needs to be done to change the internal barriers that are personal inhibitions (linked to social class, gender, ethnicity, age) and the public barriers to graduate employment that are gender, ethnic and age discrimination.

Although the changes in higher education since the 1960s, and especially since the late 1980s, were embedded in a discourse, espoused by the access movement, underpinned by an ideology of social justice and equity (Williams 1997b), national policies have nevertheless seemingly tended to be driven by a preference for numerical growth and not by a concern for social justice and equity. In particular, expansion and structural changes and even the recognition of alternative routes have failed to a significant extent to challenge the culture of elitism and consequently how higher education is perceived among the under-represented groups. Now with the issue of top-up fees it may seem that despite wider access, English higher education is still a 'mass system in its public structures', but nevertheless still 'an elite system in its private instincts' (Scott 1995: 2).

Despite wider access to higher education, and despite the focus of Parliament in widening access to higher education, UK productivity lags behind other industrialised countries. American and French workers produced 26 per cent and 21 per cent respectively more for every hour worked than British workers (Brennan 2003). Since further education has a greater impact on the whole UK workforce than higher education, this means that learners in further education deserve as much support as undergraduates, and since a better skilled workforce is a more productive workforce, this means providing learners and employers with courses that meet their needs. Until now, further education colleges faced many bureaucratic difficulties in offering flexible training and qualifications and especially in gaining funding for them (Brennan 2003), but the White Paper (DfES 2003b) plans to allow greater flexibility to further education courses will hopefully help increase the skills levels for NVQ Level 2 and 3 learners, an outcome that has been desperately needed in the UK for a long time.

Lifelong Learning and Higher Education occupied centre stage in the late 1990s, but, according to Frank Coffield, Lifelong Learning died in 2003.

> She was all things to all people. The politicians loved her because in their hands she was so flexible, the practitioners loved her because they could do anything they liked in her name, and the researchers loved her because they made money recording her every twist and turn.

> (Coffield 2003: 5)

Suggested further reading

Bligh's (1990) *Higher Education* presents a very comprehensible but clear picture of the structure and history of higher education and is highly accessible and easy to read. Edwards' (1982) *Higher Education for Everyone* analyses the reasons for the continuing social stratification of higher education and sets the case for universal higher education. *Access and Institutional Change* edited by Fulton (1989) looks at the processes of selection for and exclusion from higher education and at the effect of the internal processes of higher education on 'non-traditional' students.

References

Ainley, P. (forthcoming) 'Towards a Seamless Web or a New Tertiary Tripartism? The emerging shape of post-14 education and training in England', *British Journal of Educational Studies*.

Arbuthnott, J. (1997) 'The distinctiveness of Scottish higher education', in R. Crawford (ed.) *A Future for Higher Education*. Glasgow: COSHEP.

Baty, P. (2003) 'TUC backlash over fees hike', *Times Higher Education Supplement*, 12 September, p. 2.

Bell, R. (2000) 'Scotland's Universities', *Comparative Education*, 36 (2), 163–75.

Bligh, D. (1990) *Higher Education*. London: Cassell.

Bone, D. (1999) 'Beyond Ivory Towers: The university in the community', in T. Bryce and W. Hume (eds) *Scottish Education*. Edinburgh: Edinburgh University Press.

Brennan, J. (1989) 'Access courses', in O. Fulton (ed.) *Access and Institutional Change*. Milton Keynes: The Society for Research into Higher Education and Open University Press.

Brennan, J. (2003) 'Now is the time to help people top up their skills', *Independent*, 6 November.

Callender, C. (2001) *Higher Education: A risky investment for some?* Paper presented to the CHERI Conference *Access and Retention in Higher Education*, City Conference Centre, 18 May.

Carvel, J. (1997) 'University intake startlingly biased towards the rich', *Guardian*, 19 April.

Clare, J. (1998) 'Universities told to make entry easier', *Daily Telegraph*, 18 September, p. 1.

Coffield, F. (2003) 'Epitaph for the Big L', *Times Education Supplement*, 5 September, p. 5.

Committee of Vice-Chancellors and Principals (CVCP) (1998) *From Élitism to Inclusion: Good practice in widening access to higher education*. Summary Report. London: CVCP.

Committee on Distribution of Science and Art Grants (1896) *Science and Art Grants: report of the committee appointed to inquire into their distribution, in which is included a revised edition of the Science and Art Directory embodying the recommendations of the committee*. London: HMSO.

Committee on Higher Education (1963) *Higher Education. Report of the Committee under the Chairmanship of Lord Robbins*, Cmnd 2154. London: HMSO.

Co-operative College (2003) Available at www.co-op.ac.uk.

Cormack, R., Osborne, R., Gallagher, A., Fisher, N. and Polland, M. (1994) 'Higher Education Participation of Northern Irish Students', *Higher Education Quarterly*, 48 (3).

Cropley, A. J. (1977) *Lifelong Education: a psychological analysis*. Oxford: Pergamon.

Davies, P. (1994) 'Fourteen years on, what do we know about adult students? Some reflections on national statistical data', *Journal of Access Studies*, 9 (1), 45–60.

Davies, P. (ed.) (1995) *Adults in Higher Education: International Experiences in Access and Participation*. London: Jessica Kingsley.

Davies, P. (1997) 'Number crunching: the discourse of statistics', in J. Williams (ed.) *Negotiating Access to Higher Education: the Discourse of Selectivity and Equity*. Buckingham: Society for Research into Higher Education and Open University Press.

Davies, P., Williams, J. and Osborne, B. (2002) *Mature Students Recruitment to Higher Education*. London: DfES

Department for Education and Employment (1998a) *Higher Education for the 21st Century: Response to the Dearing Report*. London: DfEE.

Department for Education and Employment (DfEE) (1998b) *The Learning Age: a Renaissance for a New Britain*. London: The Stationery Office.

Department for Education and Skills (2003a) *An Introduction to the Foundation Degree*. London: DfES. Available at www.foundationdegree.org.uk.

Department for Education and Skills (2003b) *The Future of Higher Education*. London: HMSO.

Department of Education and Science (DES) (1978) *Letter of Invitation to Chief Education Officers*. London: DES.

Department of Education and Science (1979) *Future Trends in Higher Education*. London: HMSO.

Department of Education and Science (1985) *The Development of Higher Education into the 1990s*. Cmnd 9524. London: HMSO.

Department of Education and Science (1987) *Meeting the Challenge*. Cmnd 114. London: HMSO.

Department of Education and Science (1991) *Higher Education: A New Framework*. London: HMSO.

Department of Education and Science and the Scottish Education Department (DES/SED) (1978) *Higher Education into the 1990s: A Discussion Document*. London: HMSO.

Donnachie, I. (2003) 'Education in Robert Owen's New Society: The New Lanark Institute and Schools', in *The encyclopedia of informal education*. Available at www.infed.org/thinkers/et-owen.htm. Last updated: 24 May 2003.

Duncan, R. (1999) 'A critical history of the Workers' Educational Association in Scotland 1903–1993', in J. Crowther, I. Martin and M. Shaw (eds) *Popular Education and Social Movements in Scotland Today*. Leicester: NIACE.

Edwards, E. G. (1980) 'British Higher Education: long-term trends in student enrolment', *Higher Education Review*, 12 (2), 7–43.

Edwards, E. G. (1982) *Higher Education for Everyone*. Nottingham: Spokesman.

Farrant, J. H. (1981) 'Trends in admissions', in O. Fulton (ed.) *Access to Higher Education*. Guildford: The Society for Research into Higher Education.

Fulton, O. (ed.) (1981) *Access to Higher Education*. Guildford: The Society for Research into Higher Education.

Fulton, O. (ed.) (1989) *Access and Institutional Change*. Milton Keynes: The Society for Research into Higher Education and Open University Press.

Grant, G. (2003) 'University chiefs to demand top-up fees north of the Border', *Daily Mail*, 24 December, 15.

Hall, V. (1994) *Further Education in the United Kingdom* (Second edition). London: Collins Educational/Staff College.

Halsey, A. H. (1992) 'An international comparison of access to higher education', *Oxford Studies in Comparative Education*, 1 (1), 11–36.

Halsey, A. H., Heath, A. F. and Ridge, G. M. (1980) *Origins and Destinations: Family, Class and Education in Modern Britain*. Oxford: Oxford University Press.

HEFCE (1996) *Widening Access to Higher Education: A Report by the HEFCE's Advisory Group on Access and Participation*. Executive Summary. Reference M9/96 April 1996. Bristol: HEFCE.

HEFCE (1997a) *The Participation of Non-traditional Students in Higher Education*. Summary Report. Bristol: HEFCE.

HEFCE (1997b) *The Influence of Neighbourhood Type on Participation in Higher Education*. Interim Report. Bristol: HEFCE.

HESA (1998) *Students in Higher Education Institutions 1996/7*. Cheltenham: Higher Education Statistics Agency.

HESA (2001) *Students in Higher Education Institutions 1999/2000*. Cheltenham Higher Education Statistics Agency.

Holyoake, G. J. (1907) *Self-Help by the People: The History of the Rochdale Pioneers*. London: Swan Sonnenschein.

Independent Committee of Enquiry into Student Finance (2000) *Student Finance: Fairness for the Future* (The Cubie Report). Edinburgh: Scottish Executive.

Kreis, S. (2002) *Robert Owen 1771–1858*. Available at http://www.historyguide.org/intellect/owen.html.

Mackie, D. (2001) *How do access policies compare? England, Northern Ireland, Scotland and Wales*. Paper presented to the CHERI Conference, *Access and Retention in Higher Education*, City Conference Centre, 18 May.

Marsh, C. (2002) *Mansbridge: a life*. Available at http://www.wea.org.uk/pdf/Mansbridge.pdf.

Matheson, C. (2000) 'Education in non-traditional spaces', in C. Matheson and D. Matheson (eds) *Educational Issues in the Learning Age*. London: Continuum.

Metcalf, H. (1997) *Class and Higher Education: The Participation of Young People from Lower Social Class Backgrounds*. The Council for Industry and Higher Education.

Miliband, D. (1992) 'Introduction: expansion and reform', in D. Finegold *et al.*, *Higher Education, Expansion and Reform*. London: Institute for Public Policy Research.

National Advisory Body (NAB) (1984a) *Report of Continuing Education Group*. London: NAB.

National Advisory Body (NAB) (1984b) *A Strategy for Higher Education in the Late 1980s and Beyond*. London: NAB.

National Committee of Inquiry into Higher Education (NCIHE) (1997) *Higher Education in the Learning Society: Report of the National Committee (The Dearing Report)*. London: HMSO.

Osborne, B. (1999) *The Institutional Distribution of Young People from Low Income Groups*. Address to a joint meeting of the Quantitative Studies and Access Network, Society for Research into Higher Education, 9 February.

Owen, R. (1816) *Address to the Inhabitants of New Lanark*. Available at http://www.robert-owen.com/quotes.htm.

Owen, R. [1835](1965) *A New View of Society and Report to the County of Lanark* (Gatrell, V. A. C. (ed.)). Harmondsworth: Pelican.

Parry, G. and Wake, C. (1990) *Access and Alternative Futures for Higher Education*. London: Hodder & Stoughton.

Robertson, D. (1997) 'Growth without equity? Reflections on the consequences for social cohesion of faltering progress on access to higher education', *Journal of Access Studies*, 12 (1), 9–31.

Schuller, T., Raffe, D., Morgan-Klein, B. and Clark, I. (1999) *Part-time Higher Education: Policy, Practice and Experience*. London: Jessica Kingsley.

Schuller, T. and Bamford, C. (1999) *Initial and Continuing Education in Scotland: Divergence, convergence and learning relationships*. Edinburgh: SCRE. http://www.scre.ac.uk/scot-research/schilinit/index.html.

Scott, P. (1995) *The Meaning of Mass Higher Education*. Buckingham: The Society for Research into Higher Education and Open University Press.

Scottish Executive (2001) *Participation in Higher Education in Scotland*. Available at www.scotland.gov.uk/stats/educ.htm.

SHEFC (1998) *More Opportunities for Part-time Students in Higher Education*. Edinburgh: SHEFC.

Smith, D. and Bocock, J. (1999) 'Participation and progression in mass higher education: policy and FHE interface', *Journal of Education Policy*, 14 (3), 283–99.

Smith, S. J. (2000) 'Retaking the Register: Women's Higher Education in Glasgow and Beyond, c. 1796–1845', *Gender and History*, 12 (2), 310–35.

Spartacus Educational (2002) *George Cadbury*. Available at http://www.spartacus.schoolnet.co.uk/REcadbury.htm.

Squires, G. (1981) 'Mature Entry', in O. Fulton (ed.) *Access to Higher Education*. Guildford: Society for the Research into Higher Education.

Stowell, M. (1992) 'Equal opportunities, access and admissions: tensions and issues for institutional policy', *Journal of Access Studies*, 7 (2), 164–79.

Thomson, A. and Wojtas, O. (2000) 'Scotland booms, England bombs', *Times Higher Education Supplement*, 27 October.

Tight, M. (1996) *Key Concepts in Adults Education and Training*. London: Routledge.

UNESCO (1972) *Learning to Be*. Paris: UNESCO.

University Grants Committee (UGC) (1984a) *Report of the Continuing Education Working Party*. London: HMSO.

University Grants Committee (UGC) (1984b) *A Strategy for Higher Education into the 1990s*. London: HMSO.

Vorhaus, J. (2002) 'Lifelong Learning and New Educational Order? A Review Article', *Journal of Philosophy of Education*, 36 (1), 119–29.

Wagner, L. (1989) 'National policy and institutional development', in O. Fulton (ed.) *Access and Institutional Change*. Milton Keynes: The Society for Research into Higher Education and Open University Press.

Williams, J. (ed.) (1997a) *Negotiating Access to Higher Education: The discourse of Selectivity and Equity*. Buckingham: The Society for Research into Higher Education and Open University Press.

Williams, J. (1997b) 'The discourse of access: the legitimation of selectivity statistics', in J. Williams (ed.) *Negotiating Access to Higher Education: The Discourse of Selectivity and Equity*. Buckingham: Society for Research into Higher Education and Open University Press.

Williamson, B. (1986) 'Who has access?', in J. Finch and M. Rustin (eds) *A Degree of Choice? Higher Education and the Right to Learn*. Harmondsworth: Penguin.

Wojtas, O. (1999) 'Scots class myth debunked', *Times Higher Education Supplement*, 29 January.

Woodley, A. (1991) 'Access to What? A study of mature graduate outcomes', *Higher Education Quarterly*, 45 (1), 91–108.

Woodrow, M. (2001) *Are access policies and current funding arrangements compatible?* Paper presented to the CHERI Conference, *Access and Retention in Higher Education*, City Conference Centre, 18 May.

Wright, P. (1989) 'Access or exclusion: some comments and future prospects of continuing education in England', *Studies in Higher Education*, 14 (1), 23–40.

14

Recent issues and controversies in English education policy

Gareth Evans

Nothing you will learn in the course of your studies will be of the slightest possible use to you in life – save only this – that if you work hard and diligently you should be able to detect when a man is talking rot, and that, in my view, is the main, if not the sole, purpose of education.

(Harold Macmillan 1894–1986)

Introduction

GIVEN THE IMPORTANCE ATTACHED to education by the contemporary discourses of empowerment and utility, it is perhaps not surprising that it should be the subject of wide-ranging and sometimes hostile debate. This chapter examines some of a large number of initiatives which, accompanied by varying degrees of controversy, either relate to or may be held to form elements of recent education policy.

National Strategies, reform and remodelling

The Education Reform Act (1988) introduced the National Curriculum which provided a statutory framework for the teaching of core and foundation subjects in maintained schools in England and Wales. The National Curriculum 2000 (which relates only to maintained schools in England) is its most recent incarnation, encouraging by way of both cross-curricular themes and dedicated provision such individual and societal characteristics as: tolerance and respect for religious and cultural diversity; economic enterprise; parliamentary democracy and the rule of law; and, more recently, education for sustainable development, social inclusion and formal notions of citizenship (Qualifications and Curriculum Authority 1999: 290.)

The framework, variously amended over time, has stipulated the substance of what is to be taught in maintained schools rather than the processes by which this should be achieved. When introduced, the National Curriculum met with widespread professional opposition and perhaps marked the beginning of the contemporary managerialist culture in which league tables, 'performance management' and target-setting for staff, pupils and institutions are common-place and sometimes deemed to be inadequately sensitive to the influence of the complex social, economic and other contexts in which teaching and learning take place. In response to a Government consultation paper on target setting and benchmarking in schools in 1997, the Association of Teachers and Lecturers stated:

> [We] recognise that all school self-improvement is related to the self-esteem, morale and professional commitment of teachers and their sense of professionalism [which] can be affected by resource constraints, social and accidental factors. Perverse and retrogressive effects on matters central to educational opportunities but which are not the focus of specific targets [must be avoided] … to superimpose this definition of what targets must be and to emphasise core subjects will distort the genuine and creative improvement going on in many schools.

> (1997: 1–3)

Among a number of initiatives designed to improve school and pupil perform-ance, the National Strategies for Numeracy and Literacy at Key Stage 2 (Department for Education and Skills 1999a, 1999b) and the national strategies for core and foundation subjects at Key Stage 3 (DfES 2001a, 2001b, 2002a, 2002b, 2003d) may be considered to represent part of a current trend of increasing central Government control of public sector education in England. While the National Strategy for Key Stage 3 at least is a recommendation rather than a statutory requirement, it has been widely adopted in maintained schools in England. The various National Strategies are more prescriptive than National Curriculum Programmes of Study in recommending and providing not only lesson content but also structure and methodology, and a wide range of training and information has been made available by the DfES, the Teacher Training Agency and local education authority consultants.

> A focus on how we teach is key to pupil success. Teaching method reflects and determines the values, skills and attitudes we want children to acquire. Creative teaching promotes pupil creativity … adventure, investigation and reward encourages students to be entrepreneurial … our goal is a teaching force with the flexibility, the

support, the training, the information, the leadership, the funds and the motivation to tailor educational provision to the needs of pupils.

(Miliband 2003)

The Office for Standards in Education (Ofsted) reported on the success and implementation of the National Strategy for Key Stage 3 after its pilot year and again after its first year of national implementation. The second report states that 'there is as yet no evidence of widespread, significant improvement in Key Stage 3 test results in English and mathematics in the schools involved in the pilot since September 2000' (Ofsted 2003a: 3) and refers several times to latency between the introduction of the strategy and the emergence of significant, measurable outcomes. The detail and tone of some observations might be considered indicative of disappointment that while the Strategy has been adopted almost universally, 'many schools need to do more to make coherent use of the Strategy in improving teaching and attainment throughout Key Stage 3' (p. 4). It is interesting to note that in its Government-commissioned study of teachers' workload, PriceWaterhouseCoopers observed that '[teachers] felt that the pace and manner of change was working against achieving high standards, that they were insufficiently supported to meet these changes, and not accorded the professional trust that they merited (PriceWaterhouseCoopers, 2001a: 2) and that 'these pressures are added to by rising expectations about what schools can achieve' (*ibid.*: 3). While expectations have not generally lowered, current initiatives appear to have been significantly influenced by PriceWaterhouseCoopers' report. Their recommendations on 'process redesign' (*ibid.*: 20) include 'remov[ing] tasks from teachers that do not require a teaching qualification', largely achieved as part of the recent National Agreement on Workforce Remodelling (DFES 2003g), at least in theory. From September 2003, teachers can expect: not to routinely undertake administrative and clerical tasks; a reasonable work/life balance; a reduced burden of providing cover for absent colleagues; guaranteed planning, preparation and assessment time within the school day to support their teaching, individually and collaboratively; and a reasonable allocation of time in support of their leadership and management responsibilities (*ibid.*: 2). Recent proposals that specially trained teaching assistants should take on the role of teachers in some circumstances, freeing teachers to engage in other professional duties such as marking, planning and preparation, might be considered to undermine both the professional status of teaching and the work of teaching assistants. As far as the former point is concerned, somewhat undiplomatic and perhaps unnecessary initial concern over 'pig-ignorant peasants' or a 'mum's army' of poorly qualified support staff (Guardian Unlimited 2002) seems to have given way to qualified support from head teachers (Literacy Trust 2003). Foundation degrees are beginning to emerge as a popular training solution (Wilce 2002) and if such training proves adequate and the role of teaching assistants remains limited, accusations of 'deprofessionalisation' may be kept at bay. However, as Todd (2003) observes, teaching assistants work with pupils across a number of subjects, either individually or in small groups, and are able to establish their trust and build strong, purposeful relationships with them as well as observe their performance in relation to varying situations across the curriculum. The nature of and responsibilities involved in whole-class teaching are wholly different – the change in role from an approachable, dedicated source of support to an often busy and sometimes impersonal authoritarian might leave the positive role of the teaching assistant, for some pupils, somewhat diminished.

Reform of the 14–19 curriculum

Changes to provision for 14 to 19-year-olds including greater flexibility for pupils who wish to abandon some or even most academic subjects at school in favour of vocationally oriented courses and/or experience are discussed in some detail in the Department for Education and Skills' 2003 Departmental Report (DfES 2003a). In addition, the Secretary of State for Education and Skills commented:

> Relaxing the sometimes over-rigid demands of the National Curriculum after 14 so that children can follow courses which they enjoy, and on which they thrive, [may be better] than forcing them to study subjects in which they have no interest or aptitude.
>
> (Clarke 2003)

In its recent report entitled *Key Stage Four: Towards a Flexible Curriculum*, Ofsted found a number of 'worrying' features of current school education in England: a large number of pupils become disaffected with school during Key Stage 4, feeling that the curriculum is not relevant to their needs or that they are having virtually no success in it; one in 20 pupils leave school without any GCSE (General Certificate of Secondary Education) qualifications; and only 70 per cent of 16-year-olds go on to full-time further education, a lower level than in most other developed countries (Ofsted 2003b: 1). The report also noted that:

> In four out of five schools the rate at which pupils were excluded was declining. This was due in part to more appropriate and flexible curriculum provision and to the increased use of learning support units, learning mentors and other forms of individualised support.
>
> (p. 3)

As discussed later, such initiatives seem to have heeded the advice of the Social Exclusion Unit, which recently published research indicating a strong correlation between exclusion from or underperformance at school and social exclusion in later life (Social Exclusion Unit 2001).

Following publication of the White Paper *14–19: Opportunity and Excellence* (DfES 2003b), Mike Tomlinson, former Chief Inspector of Schools, was asked to chair the DfES Working Group on 14–19 Reform, charged with developing 'proposals for long-term structural reform of 14–19 learning programmes and qualifications' (DfES 2003e). Its progress report published in July 2003 highlights some interesting issues in relation to various proposals for reform of the qualifications framework currently operating at Key Stage 4 and in post-compulsory ('further') education. The report first suggests that a 'climbing-frame' approach with a number of 'linked but free-standing qualifications' is perhaps most suitable. 'Such a system provides flexible entry and exit points and avoids all-or-nothing choices between different programmes or different levels of study' (DfES 2003e: 8), though the report later states:

> We believe that a framework of diplomas – within which young people would receive a single qualification covering the whole of their programme – offers the best prospect of promoting balanced programmes of general and specialist learning capable of leading to a variety of destinations in further and higher learning, training and employment.
>
> (*ibid*: 43)

These statements are not perhaps contradictory, but might seem to be indicative of a degree of uncertainty as to which style of framework for upper-secondary and further education qualification(s) is likely to be most appropriate. That the working group was asked to look 'particularly carefully at the possibility of baccalaureate-style qualifications' (*ibid.*) might be indicative of a pre-existing Governmental preference. Whatever the shape of things to come, the report suggests that qualifications offered to 14 to 19-year-olds should have:

> Clearer purpose … the traditional academic/vocational distinction does not distinguish effectively between the distinct purposes and destinations of 14–19 learning. For instance, while nominally 'vocational', vocational A levels are increasingly used as a part of the 'academic' route. They appear to offer more practical content and assessment styles than traditional A levels, but with the same outcome – entry to [higher education] rather than direct progression into employment.
>
> (*ibid.*: 13)

Higher nonsense?

A Government Minister recently described some vocational degrees as 'Mickey Mouse' courses, where 'the content is perhaps not as rigorous as one would expect and where the degree itself may not have huge relevance in the labour market' (Hodge in BBC 2003a) and a serialised debate between academics included the remarks:

For the life of me I cannot see the point of some of the new, so-called 'vocational' degrees in car selling, curry making, beauty therapy, rock music and golf, to name but a few ... Everyone loses: students waste three valuable years developing a false consciousness; employers are left with a lot of nonsense to knock out; the raison d'être of universities is compromised; and the country misses out on the practical-technical skills base vital for a competitive economy.

(Smithers in Guardian Unlimited 2000)

The intellectual and practical demands on students (in terms of knowledge of several disciplines; the ability to synthesise this knowledge, to apply it to complex problems and to communicate the results) were certainly comparable to those required in more traditional disciplines.

(Roff in Guardian Unlimited 2000)

'Vocational' A-level qualifications which, as the DfES' working group report remarks, provide entry to higher education, are not offered in subjects of special relevance to prospective medical students, teachers, lawyers, dentists or architects who study 'academic' A levels but enter what is sometimes considered to be 'vocational' training – but in subjects for which there is a market demand, such as business studies and information and communication technology. It seems to be worth noting, as does Knight (in BBC 2003b), that there appear to be a number of ways in which the term 'vocational' in reference to qualifications and careers might be interpreted. If vocational degrees come to replace what would once have been learnt by way of an apprenticeship scheme, for example, then vocational A-level or equivalent qualifications that necessarily lead 'directly to employment' seem inappropriate. In such a situation, vocational qualifications which provide access to higher education seem to be necessary and worthwhile. The different teaching, learning and assessment methods employed in current vocational A-level courses may be considered to leave students less well prepared for the rigours of academia than might academic A-level courses, but without potentially somewhat limiting early specialisation in the vocational arena, some degree of flexibility seems to be required in order to ensure that opportunities for prospective undergraduates are maximised.

Education and social inclusion/exclusion

The Social Exclusion Unit report *Preventing Social Exclusion* (2001) discusses the social, economic and human impact of social exclusion, defined elsewhere as 'a shorthand term for what can happen when people or areas suffer from a combination of linked problems such as unemployment, poor skills, low incomes, poor housing, high crime environments, bad health and family breakdown' (Social Exclusion Unit 2003). Its findings include that such 'linked and mutually reinforcing problems' (2001: 10) are likely to lead individuals and communities experiencing them into 'a complex and fast-moving vicious cycle' (*ibid.*). Similarly concerned research has found that among 14 to 25-year-old offenders and ex-offenders, 'six in ten were educational underachievers' (Prince's Trust 2003: 7) and those who regularly fail to attend school are at particular risk of social exclusion in later life (Centre for Analysis of Social Exclusion 1999). Recent proposals for reform to 14–19 education such as those noted above might be indicative of a certain deference to such findings, particularly in aiming to create a more flexible curriculum for secondary school pupils who are uninterested and/or unsuccessful in meeting the demands of a largely academic programme of study either in the form of the National Curriculum or various qualifications at GCSE level. It seems logical that if pupils take advantage of such opportunities and are indeed motivated by the experience, their risk of social exclusion in later life may be significantly reduced so long as opportunities in life thereafter are sufficient. This view, however, may be oversimplistic and fail to take account of other influences:

> Low educational attainment is a key mechanism translating childhood disadvantage into poor social and economic outcomes in later life. But education is only part of the story, as childhood deprivation is associated with lower adult earnings regardless of educational performance.
>
> (Centre for Analysis of Social Exclusion 1999: 2)

If, as the above would appear to indicate, personal, historical, economic and cultural factors influence and/or serve to restrict lifestyle choices, then it seems clear that the eradication of social exclusion – that is, perhaps, full social inclusion – might only be achievable if the complex, interrelated, catalytic problems associated with it are first eliminated. This dilemma attracts insights and arguments from across the academic and political spectrum and it might be inferred from suggestions such as the following that the very terms employed in the discourse serve to distract the audience from wider issues. Levitas suggests:

> It can be argued that the concepts of exclusion and inclusion obscure the inequalities between the included ... the idea of 'exclusion' permits a basically benign view of 'society' to co-exist with the manifest reality of poverty and deprivation by discursively placing these outside society itself.
>
> (1999: 3)

Given that such problems are complex, 'linked and mutually reinforcing' (Social Exclusion Unit 2001: 10) and the potential importance of lifestyle factors identified above, the role of education in the engineering of a fully 'inclusive' society, whatever that may be, seems unclear. Lifelong learning is one of a number of educational initiatives which might be perceived as either emancipatory or facilitating the kind of conditions in which 'a lifetime entitlement to learning'

(Labour Party 1996: 18) might be considered 'effectively a lifetime obligation to acquire and maintain marketable skills' (Levitas 1999: 12). This might seem especially the case if 'security has been discursively [re]constructed as something individuals achieve through employability, and employability as an individual obligation' (*ibid.*). It seems clear that an education system that includes access to learning opportunities after the student in question has finished his or her compulsory education may provide greater equality of educational opportunity. However, save perhaps for the effects of a potentially better-educated or better-skilled society, it seems to offer little to those who may lack the various means at their disposal required to take advantage of such opportunities.

Performance-related pay

The notorious 'payment by results' system lasted for thirty years, during which time teachers taught to the test, were confined to a narrow, boring curriculum, attempted to arrange the school intake, cheated, ignored bright children and drilled and beat the slower ones until they could satisfy the all-powerful inspectors.

(Chamberlain *et al.* 2001: 1)

According to Hardy (2000), the Victorian system of payment by results which ran from 1862 to 1896 'was nicknamed the "music fine" because it penalised anyone who offered a broad education'. While it seems that the present system of performance-related pay is just that – performance *related* – and the performance-related scale is (a) accessible only to teachers with some years of service and (b) optional, there is still widespread concern that such a system is insensitive, inappropriate and that it may to lead to favouritism and divisive competition. Dolton (2003) states that 'market theories do not necessarily work in the public sector. A bricklayer may lay more bricks if paid a bonus, but this does not apply to teachers, who are highly motivated professionals already working to maximum capacity.'

Guidance for teachers applying to join the performance-related pay scheme, issued by the Department for Education and Skills (2003f), states that applicants' 'knowledge and understanding, teaching and assessment, pupil progress, wider professional effectiveness and professional characteristics' (p. 6) will be taken into consideration alongside 'summarising evidence – in the form of concrete examples from their day-to-day work – to show that they have worked at the standards indicated over the last 2 to 3 years' (p. 7). Former Secretary of State for Education Estelle Morris and others have dismissed claims that the contemporary system of performance-related pay for teachers is a return to the Victorian system of payment by results as 'scaremongering' (Government News Network 1999). From the evidence presented previously, it would seem that such criticism may indeed be somewhat exaggerated since crude statistics, although potentially useless as indicators of teacher performance, are only part of the equation although statistics compiled with greater sensitivity may prove *useful* to some extent if appropriate consideration is afforded to the difference made to pupil outcomes in relation to the context in which teaching and learning occurs – the 'value added' factor.

Alongside Wilby's (2003) consideration that administration alone will have a significant impact: 'the attempt to introduce PRP is a fool's errand … it involves too many forms and a preposterous superstructure of inspection', Kessler and Purcell (1991 in Chamberlain *et al.* 2001: 2) identified that objectives of performance-related pay schemes might include 'weakening the power of unions by making individual rather than collective contracts' – an interesting point to consider alongside certain provisions of the Education Act (2002) discussed later – and 'changing the culture of the organisation' – the latter objective being one that successive Governments have been keen to achieve, and the present Government seems to represent no exception. Ainley (2000: 2) remarks that:

> While education … is presented as the solution to all society's problems and as essential for economic growth … teachers are rarely seen by government as part of the solution but often as the main problem *en route* to the educational progress it desires.

At New Labour's Party Conference in 1999, Tony Blair stated: 'We know how important it is for [teachers] to work as a team. But if we are to get the real step change in your pay you and we both want, we have to link it to performance' (Blair 1999). Shortly afterwards, his speech at a conference for newly qualified head teachers was widely perceived by media outlets and teaching unions as teacher-bashing:

> 'I know that the vast majority of teachers and headteachers do a fantastic job,' he told the heads. 'We are proud of you. But in all reform and change, you meet small "c" conservatives, left and right, who are suspicious of change and who resist change.' Such attitudes could not be tolerated, he emphasised, and nor could 'what I call the "culture of excuses" … that tolerates low ambitions, rejects excellence, and treats poverty as an excuse for failure.'
>
> (Smithers 1999)

Unqualified dislike or suspicion of change may well be considered as one of the many facets of conservatism, but as union leaders have pointed out:

> To question and resist change which [teachers'] professional judgement causes them to believe is not in the interest of the education of pupils is no crime … [They are still] suffering from the untried, untested changes imposed by the Conservative Government.
>
> (McAvoy 1999 in Smithers 1999)

It should be noted that the current promotion of 'performance management' is not exclusively related to performance-related pay and that it seems to have become a term for what may once have been known as 'appraisal', which at the time of writing only seems to feature prominently on the DfES's *TeacherNet* web site in relation to Asset Management. A model policy for performance management states, perhaps confusingly, as part of the suggested rationale:

> We want to improve performance by developing the effectiveness of teachers, both as individuals and as teams [*sic*]. The evidence is that standards rise when schools and individual teachers are clear about what they expect pupils to achieve. That is why performance management is important.

(DfES 2001c)

It seems logical that a situation in which objectives are clearly communicated might facilitate achievement of those objectives better than one in which they are not, but the above does not appear to make a clear case for the importance of performance management of staff, especially when such emphasis is placed upon clear communication of expectations to pupils by the various National Strategy documents. The observation that 'a pupil may have private tuition, help at home, or [be subject to] any number of external influences ... so we may never know objectively whether [performance-related pay] has positive effects on pupil learning outcomes' (Dolton 2003) illustrates flaws in at least one of the criteria upon which performance is judged and might imply a degree of futility in the exercise, at least in relation to some of its specified objectives. While it should be noted that performance-related pay and performance management are separate instruments, it seems that the promotion of any performance management regime to which systemic objectives are very closely related might be a reductive approach to professional development: the 'drip-effect' of continuous bureaucratic accountability seems capable of serving to discourage innovation and/or be considered near-tantamount to the imposition of methodology. As far as the impact of recommended material and methodology is concerned, Ofsted's progress report (2003a) suggests that further research, after a period of maturation, may be indicative of widespread significant improvement. If that is found to be the case, theoretical arguments against such prescriptive recommendations may be marginalised somewhat, although not necessarily weakened, by the success of those recommendations in practice. To some extent, however, as the Association of Teachers and Lecturers remarked above, all improvement of one thing might only be achievable at the expense of another or others' lack of development. The complex nature of the interrelationship between teaching, learning, achievement and its *environs* in the background and day-to-day experience of the learner at least, seems to make subjective any judgement about pupil and teacher performance and particularly the relationship between them.

Public-Private Partnerships

The Private Finance Initiative (PFI) was devised in 1992 by the then-Chancellor of the Exchequer, Norman Lamont, as a way of encouraging private investment in public services. Among a number of others, Ward (2000) discusses the evolution of the Public-Private Partnership (PPP) initiative, whereby private companies become involved in provision of public services including education. It evolved gradually from PFI into the current system whereby corporate bodies from the public and private sectors enter into agreements specifying objectives, costs, completion dates and, if part of the agreement is to provide services following completion of the project in question, service level agreements. The School Standards and Framework Act (1998) empowered school governing bodies to form companies to assist in the running of their school (s.10). The Education Act (2002) provided further 'powers to facilitate innovation' (ch.1) including, with the agreement of the Secretary of State for Education (for schools in England) or the National Assembly for Wales (for those in Wales), that regulations made under the Act may 'designate any curriculum or pay and conditions provision as attracting exemption [seemingly from statutory provision or national agreements, respectively]' (s.7). In what seems a notable departure from previous policy, s.11 imbues governing bodies with the power to form or invest in companies to provide services or facilities for any schools including the exercise of relevant local education authority functions – a rather more significant development than the powers provided by the School Standards and Framework Act (1998) to enable schools acting in consortia to exploit economies of scale in day-to-day purchasing. While this might appear to involve some degree of financial and perhaps moral risk, it should be noted that such powers may not be exercised without the consent of the relevant local education authority and not in any case where the school concerned does not already have a delegated budget. Regulations made under the Act 'may require that the company be prohibited by its constitution from borrowing money, except with the consent of a prescribed person' (s.12(4)). Such provisions appear to be designed as safeguards so that ratification of any such initiative may be achieved by requiring from the outset the involvement of parties from both local and national Government. PriceWaterhouseCoopers' (2001b) review of Public-Private Partnerships seems to have found that some early experiences of the initiative were characterised by a concentration on the letter of contractual agreements rather than the spirit of the initiative: 'the ambiguity of the output specification allowed the private sector to get away with too much' (p. 15) and 'it is currently too easy for the [companies involved] to avoid what were considered by [the public authority] to be contractual obligations' (*ibid.*). Contrastingly, 'The private sector is responsive and improving ... in virtually all cases, there is a consistent view that the private sector is performing better as the [Public-Private

Partnerships] progress' (*ibid.* p. 13). Aside from construction and building main-tenance contracts, Monbiot (2002) discusses how one Public-Private Partnership initiative in education amounts to 'the corporate takeover of childhood'. *Connexions* is perhaps the flagship PPP project in education. Originally designed to replace the DfES Careers Advisory Service, the agency seems to have become, as its name suggests it might be, a kind of portal through which information and advice on a range of subjects affecting young people, and other agencies, can be accessed:

> Once they have registered with this service, schoolchildren are given a swipe card, on which they accumulate points every time they turn up. They trade the points for discounts from the consumer goods listed on the Connexions web site. The choices they make are monitored, and the information is then given to the service's 'commercial partners'. Last year, the education firm Capita, which runs Connexions for the Government, told the *Times Educational Supplement* that companies such as McDonalds and PlayStation Magazine would have 'the opportunity of seeing what these young people take up. They can be a very difficult group to reach '
>
> (Monbiot 2002)

The Public-Private Partnership initiative in particular seems to represent the values often said to be at the core of Third Way politics – the combination of sustainable social provision with economic enterprise. It has been and continues to be the subject of much negative media attention, not least from commentators such as Monbiot, and it would seem that positive reports are either few and far-between or provided by parties somehow interested in its development and continuation. As Monbiot has commented (2001), value-for-money claims cannot easily or readily be subjected to public scrutiny – 'as public services are part-privatised, the business of the state is being shrouded by "commercial confidentiality".' Perhaps only time will tell whether the initiative will make a lasting, positive, cost-effective contribution to society and its institutions.

Conclusion

Most of the issues discussed above are either creations of New Labour or projects from the Conservative era of 1979–97 which New Labour have continued to sup-port and/or develop. Educational change is often controversial. Education, like many public services, is currently undergoing quite radical reform and the process is not yet complete. It seems reasonable to suggest that while bold measures are being enacted, such as those provided by the Education Act (2002), checks and balances are often also imposed and there appears to be little danger that transgressions, be they moral, legal or other, will go unnoticed. Whether, in such circumstances, any effective action to the contrary might be taken, remains to be seen.

Suggested further reading

Docking (2000) provides detailed discussion of New Labour's education policies for schools from 1997 to 2000. Poulson (1998) discusses the relationship between teacher professionalism and accountability in relation to recent initiatives and reforms. Already cited above, Levitas (1999) provides valuable insights into the problematical nature of the concept and presentation of social exclusion and discusses the work of the Social Exclusion Unit and those influential in its establishment in relation to various discourses of inclusion and exclusion. Giddens (2000) offers a comprehensive introduction to the pillars of 'Third Way' politics and discusses opposing perspectives and the interrelation of policy initiatives with social inclusion, education, lifelong learning and the knowledge economy. The Green Paper *The Learning Age* (DfEE 1998) set out the Government's vision for lifelong learning and seems to have significantly influenced future policy and initiatives. Gorard (2000) discusses the quality of contemporary British education and suggests that it serves to promote social justice.

References

Ainley, P. (2000) *Teaching in a Learning Society: the Acquisition of Professional Skills.* Paper presented at the ESRC Teaching and Learning Research Programme First Annual Conference – University of Leicester, Friday 10 November. Available from: http://www.leeds.ac.uk/educol/documents/00003139.doc.

Association of Teachers and Lecturers (1997) *Response to Target Setting and Benchmarking in Schools: Consultation Paper September 1997.* Available from: http://www.leeds.ac.uk/educol/documents/000000408.doc.

BBC (2003a) *'Irresponsible' Hodge under fire.* London: British Broadcasting Corporation. Available from: http://news.bbc.co.uk/1/hi/education/2655127.stm.

BBC (2003b) *In defence of vocational degrees.* London: British Broadcasting Corporation. Available from: http://news.bbc.co.uk/2/hi/uk_news/education/3200524.stm.

Blair, T. (1999) *Tony Blair's Full Speech.* London: Guardian Unlimited. Available from: http://www.guardian.co.uk/lab99/Story/0,2763,202189,00.html.

Centre for Analysis of Social Exclusion (1999) *CASE brief 12: Schools, Education and Social Exclusion.* Available from: http://sticerd.lse.ac.uk/dps/case/cb/CASEbrief12.pdf.

Chamberlain, R. P., Hayes, G., Wragg, C. M. and Wragg, E. C. (2001) *Performance-related pay and the teaching profession: A review of the literature.* Supplementary paper (not presented) at BERA Annual Conference, Leeds, 14 September. Available from: http://www.ex.ac.uk/education/research/bera2001_paper3.pdf.

Clarke, C. (2003) *An Ambitious Programme.* London: Guardian Unlimited. Available from: http://education.guardian.co.uk/specialreports/tuitionfees/story/0,5500,878427,00.html.

Department for Education and Employment (1998) *The Learning Age.* London: HMSO.

Department for Education and Skills (1999a) *The National Numeracy Strategy.* London: HMSO. Available from: http://www.standards.dfes.gov.uk/primary/numeracy.

Department for Education and Skills (1999b) *The National Literacy Strategy*. London: HMSO. Available from: http://www.standards.dfes.gov.uk/primary/literacy.

Department for Education and Skills (2001a) *Framework for Teaching English: Years 7, 8 and 9*. London: HMSO. Available from: http://www.standards.dfes.gov.uk/midbins/keystage3/english_framework.PDF.

Department for Education and Skills (2001b) *Framework for Teaching Mathematics: Years 7, 8 and 9*. London: HMSO. Available from: http://www.standards.dfes.gov.uk/midbins/keystage3/mathematicsframework.EXE.

Department for Education and Skills (2001c) *Skeleton Performance Management Policy for LEAs* London: DfES. Available from: http://www.teachernet.gov.uk/_doc/5177/DfES–0098–20.pdf.

Department for Education and Skills (2002a) *Framework for Teaching ICT Capability: Years 7, 8 and 9*. London: HMSO. Available from: http://www.standards.dfes.gov.uk/midbins/keystage3/ICT_framework.PDF.

Department for Education and Skills (2002b) *Framework for Teaching Science: Years 7, 8 and 9*. London: HMSO. Available from: http://www.standards.dfes.gov.uk/midbins/keystage3/Science_Framework.PDF.

Department for Education and Skills (2003a) *DfES Departmental Report 2003: Transforming Secondary Education*. London: DfES. Available from: http://www.dfes.gov.uk/2003deptreport/uploads/5DfES-Transforming%20Secondary%20Education.pdf.

Department for Education and Skills (2003b) *14–19: Opportunity and Excellence*. London: HMSO. Available from: http://www.dfes.gov.uk/14–19/download.shtml.

Department for Education and Skills (2003c) *TeacherNet*. Available from: http://www.teachernet.gov.uk.

Department for Education and Skills (2003d) *Framework and Training for Teaching MFL: Years 7, 8 and 9*. London: HMSO. Available from: http://www.standards.dfes.gov.uk/midbins/keystage3/framework.ZIP.

Department for Education and Skills (2003e) *Working Group for 14–19 Reform: Background*. London: DfES. Available from: http://www.14–19reform.gov.uk.

Department for Education and Skills (2003f) *Guidance on the Threshold Process in 2003 (Round 4) in England*. London: DfES. Available from: http://www.teachernet.gov.uk/_doc/4794/4953-DfES-Threshold%202003.pdf.

Department for Education and Skills (2003g) *Raising Standards and Tackling Workload: A National Agreement*. London: DfES. Available from: www.teachernet.gov.uk/docbank/index.cfm?id=3479.

Docking, J. (ed.) (2000) *New Labour's Policies for Schools*. London: David Fulton Publishers.

Dolton (2003) *Evidence lacking for (or against) performance bonuses for teachers (Press release)*. London: Institute of Education. Available from: http://ioewebserver.ioe.ac.uk/ioe/cms/get.asp?cid=1397&1397_1=7584.

Education Act (2002). London: HMSO.

Education Reform Act (1988). London: HMSO.

Giddens, A. (2000) *The Third Way and its Critics*. Cambridge: Polity Press.

Gorard, S. (2000) *Education and Social Justice*. Cardiff: University of Wales Press.

Government News Network (1999) *Morris Welcomes ATL Support for Pay Reform Plans*. Available from: http://www.gnn.gov.uk/gnn/national.nsf/0/AABB4625A5BC6B55802567EF005198D6?opendocument.

Guardian Unlimited (2000) *Are new 'vocational' degrees worthless?* London: Guardian Unlimited.

Available from: http://www.guardian.co.uk/debate/article/0,2763,355921,00.html.

Guardian Unlimited (2002) *Morris Prepares for Classroom Changes*. London: Guardian Unlimited. Available from: http://education.guardian.co.uk/schools/story/0,5500,816811,00.html.

Hardy, J. (2000) *Flood Control*. London: Guardian Unlimited. Available from: http://www.guardian.co.uk/Columnists/Column/0,5673,194383,00.html.

Kessler, I. and Purcell, J. (1991) *Performance-related pay: theory and practice*. Cited in. R. P. Chamberlain, G. Hayes, C. M. Wragg and E. C. Wragg (2001) *Performance-related pay and the teaching profession: A review of the literature*. Supplementary paper (not presented) at BERA Annual Conference, Leeds, 14 September. Available from: http://www.ex.ac.uk/education/research/bera2001_paper3.pdf.

Labour Party (1996) *Learn as You Earn: Labour's Plans for a Skills Revolution*. London: The Labour Party

Levitas (1999) *New Labour and Social Exclusion*. Available from: http://www.psa.ac.uk/cps/1999/levitas.pdf.

Literacy Trust (2003) *Heads welcome assistants' role*. Available from: http://www.literacytrust.org.uk/database/teachassist.html#heads.

Miliband, S. (2003) *21st Century Teaching*. London: Guardian Unlimited. Available from: http://education.guardian.co.uk/print/0,3858,4642677–110908,00.html.

Monbiot, G. (2001) *Private Finance – Keep Out!* London: Guardian Unlimited. Available from http://www.monbiot.com/dsp_article.cfm?article_id=449.

Monbiot, G. (2002) *The Corporate Takeover of Childhood*. London: Guardian Unlimited. Available from: http://www.monbiot.com/dsp_article.cfm?article_id=480.

Office for Standards in Education (2003a) *The Key Stage Three Strategy: evaluation of the second year*. London: Ofsted. Available from: http://www.ofsted.gov.uk/publications/docs/3204.pdf.

Office for Standards in Education (2003b) *Key Stage Four: Towards a Flexible Curriculum*. London: Ofsted. Available from: http://www.ofsted.gov.uk/publications/docs/3301.pdf.

Poulson, L. (1998) 'Accountability, Teacher Professionalism and Education Reform in England', *Teacher Development*, 2 (3), 419–32.

PriceWaterhouseCoopers (2001a) *Teacher Workload Study*. London: PriceWaterhouseCoopers. Available from: http://www.teachernet.gov.uk/_doc/3165/Final%20report%205%20December%20CK3dec2.doc.

PriceWaterhouseCoopers (2001b) *Public Private Partnerships: A Clearer View*. London: PriceWaterhouseCoopers. Available from: http://www.pwcglobal.com/uk/eng/about/svcs/pfp/pwc_ppp-study.pdf.

Prince's Trust (2003) *Reaching the Hardest to Reach: Nowhere to Turn*. Available from: http://193.128.182.114/Main%20Site%20v2/downloads/Nowhere%20to%20turn.pdf.

Qualifications and Curriculum Authority (1999) *The National Curriculum for England*. London: QCA/DfES. Available from: http://www.nc.uk.net/download/NC.rtf.

School Standards and Framework Act (1998). London: HMSO.

Smithers, R. (1999) *Unions angered by Blair attack on teachers*. London: Guardian Unlimited. Available from: http://education.guardian.co.uk/news/story/0,5500,94705,00.html.

Social Exclusion Unit (2001) *Preventing Social Exclusion*. London: Social Exclusion Unit. Available from: http://www.socialexclusionunit.gov.uk/publications/reports/html/pse/pse.pdf.

Social Exclusion Unit (2003) *Welcome to the Social Exclusion Unit*. Available from http://www.socialexclusionunit.gov.uk.

Todd (2003) *Not in front of the children*. London: Guardian Unlimited. Available from: http://education.guardian.co.uk/print/0,3858,4656743–48826,00.html.

Ward, S. (2000) *Labour Extends Tory Private Finance Scheme*. London: Guardian Unlimited. Available from: http://society.guardian.co.uk/privatefinance/story/0,8150,395846,00.html.

Wilby, P. (2003) *'Performance pay is the worst of both worlds', Times Education Supplement*. Available from: http://www.tes.co.uk/your_career/pay_pensions/performance_related_pay.asp.

Wilce, II. (2002) *Mum's Army is on the march*. London: The Independent. Available from: http://education.independent.co.uk/higher/story.jsp?story=182832.

15

What is educational research? Changing perspectives

John Nisbet

A repetition of this experiment with 16,000 or 18,000 more cases is needed before final conclusions should be stated.

(Thorndike 1925, spurious)

'Case study' is an umbrella term for a family of research methods having in common the decision to focus inquiry round a single instance.

(Adelman, Jenkins and Kemmis 1977)

'Oh, I can't stand those people,' he said, 'postmodernists or poststructuralists, or whatever they call themselves ... They think there is no such thing as scientific proof and that science is only one interpretation of the world among others equally valid.'
'Well, isn't it?' I said.

(Lodge 2001)

Introduction

THESE THREE QUOTATIONS ILLUSTRATE different ways in which the concept of educational research has been interpreted over the past century. This chapter reviews the history of educational research in Britain, showing how different styles of research have developed, linked with the function that research is expected to perform. A central theme is the growing acceptance of research in education, which paradoxically, it is suggested, may have had the effect of restricting its scope.

In the late nineteenth century German scholars began to think in terms of a subject called 'experimental pedagogy', and this set a pattern which was to dominate research in education in the first half of the twentieth century. Educational research, they suggested, should follow the style of research in the physical sciences, using experiments with representative samples to establish fundamental psychological principles of learning and child development, which could then be applied to guide policy and reform practice. In the USA, this idea was taken up actively, particularly the concept of measurement through tests of mental ability and educational attainment. Educational research in Britain reflected both German and American influences in the early years. But a rather different interpretation of educational research developed in the course of the century. Instead of quantitative studies involving large numbers, mental measurement, standardised tests and statistical analysis, researchers began to use qualitative methods based on intensive case studies of small numbers and sometimes even of a single instance. Quantitative research aimed to produce generalisations: qualitative research gave insights and understanding of the processes in learning and teaching.

The 1960s and 1970s saw massive expansion of educational research. Increased funding led to a pressure for 'relevant' research – which some cynically interpret as limiting research to projects that fit established frames of thought. At the opposite extreme, postmodernist philosophy rejects outright the positivist assumptions in the concept of 'education as a science'. The major change of recent years, however, has been the acceptance of research as a natural and necessary element in educational development, and as an integral part in the professional development of teachers – though that is perhaps more an aspiration than a reality.

Education as a science

The second half of the nineteenth century saw striking advances in science and technology. The scientific model came to be applied with growing success to medicine, engineering and psychology. Could education too be given a scientific base through research?

Traditionally, educational practice was based on tradition and authority, especially the authority of the Bible or of Aristotle or other classical writers: the validity of an idea was judged by the authority of its source. It was this way of thinking that was challenged in the eighteenth-century period known as the Enlightenment, when authority was replaced by rationality: the validity of an idea was to be judged on the basis of evidence. The concept of basing educational practice on empirical research was taken up in the later years of the nineteenth century: in England in 1877, Francis Galton asserted to the British Association for the Advancement of Science: 'It is now possible to inquire by exact measurement into certain fundamental aspects of mind'; and in Scotland in 1879, Alexander Bain published a treatise with the title, *Education as a Science*. But the main thrust of this idea came in Germany. Since philosophers like Kant had dismissed the idea that the mind could be measured, from the 1860s on scholars such as Wundt and

Fechner, and Helmholtz studied aspects of mental activity which *could* be measured – reaction time, sensory discrimination, aspects of sensation and perception, fatigue – studying the senses as an entry to the workings of the mind.

By the first decade of the twentieth century, enough experimental work had been done to enable publication of the first educational research textbooks in Germany and Switzerland. The influence of textbooks is to define the boundaries and content of a discipline. Because the experimental work described in these early texts had their origin in German laboratories, their basis was largely in psychology and physiology: for example, Wilhelm Lay's *Experimental Didactics: its foundations, with some considerations of muscle sense, will and action* (1903); and *Child Psychology and Experimental Pedagogy* (1911) by Edouard Claparède in Geneva. The Introduction to Claparède's text begins:

> That pedagogy ought to be based upon the knowledge of the child, as horticulture is based upon the knowledge of plants, would seem to be an elementary truth. It is, nevertheless, entirely unrecognised by most teachers and nearly all educational authorities.
>
> (p. 1)

In USA, the Child Study movement which was made popular worldwide by Stanley Hall in the 1890s encouraged parents to make systematic observation and recording of their children's development. Cattell's article, 'Mental tests and measurement' (1890) and Thorndike's test scales from 1904 onwards established the measurement approach which dominated educational research in the USA for much of the twentieth century.

Tests and measurements in the USA

American histories of educational research tend to neglect European sources, dating the start of research proper as 1897, when an American researcher, Rice, published the results of his investigations into spelling. He compared class average scores in a spelling test with the amount of time given to spelling in the classroom and found a zero relationship, thus proving 'the futility of the spelling grind', the title of his 1897 paper. Initially, European influence was strong because many American scholars travelled to Germany for their doctoral studies. For example, a major American text in this field, Whipple's *Manual of Mental and Physical Tests*, first published in 1910, reflects in its coverage the influence of Galton (measuring diameter and girth of skull, motor control, strength of grip) and the early German scholars (sensory discrimination, mirror drawing, memory, suggestion), but it also included (at the end) examples from the burgeoning test movement at that time, with tests of reading, arithmetic and spelling.

The leading figure in measurement in these early days was Thorndike, whose doctoral thesis was on learning in animals. Travers (1978) relates how, at Harvard, Thorndike had to keep his animals in the basement of his professor's house (much to the delight of his children); but the story goes that when Thorndike moved to Columbia University there was no room for the animals and so he turned to research on children instead. Whatever the truth of that, he carried over the laboratory scientist role, that of experimentally exploring basic 'laws of learning', such as the law of effect, later called 'reinforcement' (the importance of reward in learning) and transfer of training (learning in one context is generalised to other contexts – such as learning Latin as a training in logical reasoning – only if common elements are stressed). Thorndike's main contribution, however, was in the construction of tests: together with colleagues, he produced the first standardised attainment tests in 1908 and a handwriting scale in 1909, followed by many others. In 1918, an American *Yearbook* listed 109 standardised tests which were in current use in schools: nearly 900,000 copies of one popular test were used in 1917, and several others had sales of over 100,000 each (Monroe 1918).

The idea of improving the efficiency of teaching by setting standards based on tests seems to recur regularly through the century. The 1908 report of the US Commissioner of Education linked efficiency with testing, and his 1910 report proposed setting standards in terms of test performance. Across the USA Boards of Education began to set up 'Bureaus of Educational Research' (sometimes called 'Bureau of Research and Efficiency'). By 1926, there were 105 such bureaus across the country. But gradually they were abandoned, as they tended to be preoccupied with gathering statistics on test scores with which nothing was done (Nifenecker 1918). Travers' verdict on this short-lived movement was that it 'did little for education, neither clarifying the concept of effectiveness nor making schools more efficient … It measured, but did not analyse' (1983: 507).

Research begins to take root

In other countries too, individual scholars were conducting research inquiries and publishing their findings in newly established journals. A fourth edition of Claparède's textbook mentioned above, originally in French and now translated into English, German, Italian, Spanish and Russian, included a new chapter outlining the growth of experimental pedagogy in England, France, Germany, Belgium, Holland and 12 other countries. A feature of the research at this time is that it dealt with issues that are still of interest today; examples from Claparede's text are:

Before learning anything, it is necessary to learn how to learn.

(p. 57)

How far are the various mental functions independent of each other … How far do they reciprocally influence each other (correlation, factor analysis)?

(p. 61)

When we educate a certain function, are we acting upon others at the same time (transfer of training)?

(p. 64)

In England in 1894, an Office of Special Inquiries and Reports had been set up, and its Director, Michael Sadler, pressed the Board of Education (as the equivalent of the Ministry was then called) to establish a national research council, unsuccessfully. Taylor (1972: 4) records an exchange of minutes between Sadler and the Board's Secretary, Morant, which has a surprisingly contemporary ring. Sadler wrote:

In order that the scientific work of educational inquiry may be searching and fruitful, it must be intellectually independent. Those engaged in it must be free to state whatever they believe to be true, apart from preconsiderations as to what may at the time be thought administratively convenient.

Morant replied in terms that were to be echoed in 1970 by Thatcher and in 1971 in the Rothschild Report:

It cannot be too clearly impressed upon you that the work of the Office of Special Inquiries and Reports is done and must continue to be done, for the benefit of the Board, at the instance of the Board, and under the direction of the Board.

Sadler resigned. However, London County Council had its own Inspectors of Schools, and a group of these inspectors carried out numerous experiments and surveys and constructed new tests – especially Winch, who published two books and 38 papers, mostly in American journals, and Ballard, who developed a one-minute reading test standardised on over 22,000 children. (Burt, the most famous of this group, was not appointed until 1915, when he was given explicit responsibility for research.)

In Scotland, Rusk published his *Introduction to Experimental Education* in 1913, acknowledging his debt to Meumann's 1907 text. In 1918 the Educational Institute of Scotland (the teachers' union) set up a Committee on Research, with Boyd as Chair; and Boyd introduced a school-based type of research, with the aim (50 years before the teacher-researcher movement) of getting teachers actively involved in their own research.

In France, Binet and Simon were studying how to identify mentally handicapped children (as distinct from those educationally backward), and from their work they developed an individual test of intelligence in 1905, which was frequently revised and improved.

In the 1930s in the USA, Terman and Merrill revised it extensively to produce a standard version used for the next 30 years. With these tests came a recognition of the wide range of individual differences among children, and the aim of matching instruction to the level of intelligence of the children.

Educational research acquires an identity – and a limited role

By the 1930s, educational research had established a certain degree of respectability and acceptance – 'a certain degree' only, because very few teachers in schools or educational administrators regarded it seriously. Educational research journals grew in number and size, though their readership was almost exclusively members of the academic societies that produced them. Universities set up Departments of Education, but (except in Scotland) these were primarily concerned with teacher training; in England, the Universities of London, Birmingham and Manchester combined this with an active research programme. In 1928 in Scotland, the Educational Institute of Scotland and the Association of Directors of Education had set up the Scottish Council for Research in Education (SCRE), the first such organisation in Europe, but the Scottish Education Department declined to contribute and, as records show (Wake 1984), was wholly sceptical of its value. For the next 30 years, with a staff of only a part-time Director and a secretary, SCRE produced a series of significant research publications based largely on the work of academic staff in colleges and universities, but these remained virtually unknown among teachers.

Similar developments were occurring in other European countries as well as in the USA, New Zealand and Australia. In Sweden, for example, Torsten Husén and Kjell Harnqvist were leading figures in the empirical, psychologically oriented research which influenced Swedish educational policy in the 1950s and 1960s. Institutes for Educational Research were established in many countries (Norway 1935, Denmark 1954, Finland 1954, Netherlands 1965).

However, the common attitude to research at this stage in the century was that it was an academic study out of touch with 'real' problems. In fact, important groundwork was done on reading and other elements of the primary school curriculum, but in Europe the secondary school curriculum remained the province of subject specialists. The unreliability of the examination system was also demonstrated in the research of this period, but that tradition was too well established to be affected by mere research evidence. The 'scientific' approach in the early history of educational research, together with its increasing reliance on the sophisticated statistical methods which were being introduced, resulted in educational research being regarded as a specialist activity, 'done by those *outside* the classroom for the benefit of those *outside* the classroom' (Nixon 1981: 6), requiring extended training (much of it statistical and psychological) and with the function of producing theoretical principles to guide teachers and policy-makers.

> Until about the 1960s, research was essentially a small-back-room activity. Researchers may have dreamed about reforming the world of education, but it was a long-term aspiration, to be achieved by patient scholarship. There was little expectation that policy-makers, administrators or teachers would be much influenced by, or even interested in, research.

> (Nisbet 1984: 3)

This now began to change as the scale of educational research grew and the number of researchers in universities and in specialised units increased dramatically. The role of being the intelligence in the educational system was quite an attractive one for the researchers, even if the system still had only grudging acceptance of the intelligence. By mid-century, researchers had begun to establish this technocratic alliance with the power blocks in education (thus further earning the suspicion of teachers). The 11+ examination, for example, used to select a minority of the year-group for grammar school, relied on standardised tests and statistical analysis which had been validated by research; in this way (though few would have acknowledged it until the mid-1950s) research was used to justify selection as the instrument of a structured society.

Thus for the researchers, the price of acceptance was the demand that research (or at least, funded research) should be 'relevant'. Relegating research to this instrumental role carries risks: trivialising, in pursuing volatile educational fashions; restrictive, in limiting research within the constraints of existing policy frameworks; potentially divisive, creating an elite group of researchers in alliance with authority; and ultimately damaging, in that it can leave the researchers wholly dependent on their powerful partner.

This chapter is concerned primarily with experimental research, and not with philosophical or historical research, or with the extensive individual non-funded scholarship in universities – although some of the points apply equally to these fields. Researchers who choose an unpopular or unfashionable line of inquiry are liable to find that they receive no grants and that their papers are not accepted by journals or, if published, are not widely read or quoted. This restrictive influence of the established orthodoxy is to be found in all science. But the decade of the 1960s in education was to some extent an exception.

The 1960s and 1970s: the 'new look'

The decade of the 1960s was a period of upheaval: it began with major reviews of the educational systems in Britain and major investment in research in the USA to tackle the problem of social disadvantage, and ended with student revolt in

France and across the world. Educational research also experienced challenge to its traditional practice.

Rather unexpectedly (at least for the researchers) national Governments began to set aside substantial funds for research in education. Between 1964 and 1969, expenditure on educational research in Britain multiplied ten-fold; in the USA, expenditure doubled in each year from 1964 through to 1967. An Educational Research Board was appointed within the Social Science Research Council with funds for projects throughout Britain, and in the Scottish Education Department a Research and Intelligence Unit initiated research programmes and funded research in universities and colleges. Major UK reviews of education were commissioned in these years, Plowden on primary education, Newsom on secondary education and Robbins on higher education, and each of these was accompanied by a substantial research and survey programme. It may be argued that, for the most part, the research findings from these programmes were used to strengthen the case for recommendations that the Committee had already reached. This is a limited but wholly valid interpretation of the term 'research-based policy'. In the absence of adequate evidence, Plowden was prepared frankly to proceed in any case:

> The research evidence so far available is both too sparse and too heavily weighted by studies of special groups of children to be decisively in favour of nursery education for all. We rely, therefore, on the overwhelming evidence of experienced educators
>
> (DES 1967: paragraph 303)

It was in these years that educational research began to emerge out of the shadow of the contributory disciplines of psychology and sociology and to develop its own conceptual frameworks, if not actual evidence-based theories. At the same time, a radical change questioned the established experimental style of quantitative statistical research in education. By the 1970s researchers were arguing that qualitative case studies exploring issues in depth with relatively small numbers were more appropriate in education. Quantitative research could show that there were wide ranges of individual differences in every kind of measure but seldom was able to explain the meaning or implications of the findings for everyday contexts: its aim was generalisation for the purposes of prediction and management. Qualitative research in contrast aimed at understanding and insight into the complexities of learning and human behaviour (see Stenhouse 1981).

The practice of measurement was also questioned. In-depth interviews were the basis of what are variously called *ethnographic*, *hermeneutic* or *phenomenological* methods. These approach a topic from the perspective of the interviewee rather than within a framework decided in advance by the researcher. Phenomenography (Entwistle 1981) has its roots in the philosophy of phenomenology, which opposes

285

the positivism or naturalism inherent in contemporary science and technology – the standard scientific approach to knowledge by formulating hypotheses and designing experimental procedures to test these – on the grounds that this finds (or negates) only what the researcher is looking for, whereas the open-ended methods of phenomenography produce data for formulating new interpretive constructs. This approach focuses on awareness or 'encountering', and accepts the role of description in how we perceive situations and how we interpret or 'understand' them. Thus, from the interview transcripts, the researcher derives interpretive categories: for example, the way students speak about their reading and understanding leads to the categorisation of 'deep' and 'surface' learning. Recognising the subjectivity involved, the interpretation must be fully supported by excerpts from what has been said.

Two related innovations about this time introduced new perceptions of educational research: action research and the teacher-researcher movement. Following the Plowden Report in 1967, which had proposed 'positive discrimination' for schools in areas of social deprivation, a large-scale programme of five projects in England and one in Scotland was launched in that year, called the Educational Priority Areas (or EPA) projects, which aimed to combine action to improve conditions with research to identify how best to achieve this. The report, *Educational Priority* (1972), defines this 'novel type of research … [as] small-scale intervention in the functioning of the real world … and the close examination of the effects of such interventions' (p. 165). Action and research have different aims and values:

> Research values concepts such as precision, control, replication and attempts to generalise from the observation of specific events. Administrative action … translates generalisation into specific instances.

> (p. 165)

But in action research those who initiate action also conduct research which directs actions in a developing programme of reform.

Nixon, in *A Teacher's Guide to Action Research* (1981), applies this to the concept of the 'teacher-researcher': 'The case for action research may be stated briefly. By investigating and reflecting upon their own practice teachers may increase their understanding of the classroom' (p. 6).

The teacher-researcher concept was developed in another major project begun in 1967, the Schools Council Humanities Project directed by Stenhouse. The Humanities Project produced materials for the discussion of controversial issues (such as racial prejudice), but an integral part was evaluation by the teachers themselves both to define the research problem and initiate research to guide subsequent action.

> [This] marks a radical departure from the traditionalist view of research as a specialist activity, the results of which teachers apply rather than create … The teacher as a

researcher movement, with its focus on the practical educational problems arising from particular situations, and with the aim of illuminating such situations for those involved, offers an alternative.

(Elliott: 1981: 1)

The teacher-researcher movement has been taken up and given support by both BERA and SERA (the British and the Scottish Educational Research Associations), but 30 years on, it is still a minority group with relatively little published output. But research was now being seen as a professional activity for teachers as well as (or instead of) for specialist researchers, a mode of working to be adopted by all in facing up to problems, whether in policy-making or in school-based projects.

The postmodernist movement goes much further than this in challenging the instrumental view of research, arguing that reality is a social construction.

Postmodernism abandons the enlightenment ambitions of unity, certainty and pre-dictability, because many aspects of life are ephemeral, if not completely unpredictable ... The metaphor of chaos questions progressive betterment, questions the idea that the quality of life has improved. It seeks to understand, but not to reconcile, divisions ... Those who write from a postmodern perspective tend to question the value of rationality, to reject grand theory, to favour local knowledge over systemic understanding, to eschew large-scale studies, and to view the world as an indeterminate place beyond coherent description ... [It is] a requiem for the passing of the modernist quest for certainty, predictability, and the hoped-for advancement of knowledge and society-at-large.

(Constas 1998: 27)

This extreme standpoint takes us back to the nineteenth-century arguments about whether scientific procedures can be fruitfully applied in the field of educational inquiry. At least, it requires us to examine more thoughtfully the positivist assumption that there are 'correct' answers to educational issues which can be discovered by experiment and observation, that there is a reality which may not be immediately obvious but can eventually be discovered (or uncovered) by research if enough effort is put into it.

These were fundamental changes in our perception of what educational research is and what its function should be. Many still hold to the older interpretation, in which the function of research is *instrumental*, that is, it is of value insofar as it can be used to solve problems or guide policy. Empirical research of this kind has been fuelled by the need for predictability. Policy-makers, said Stenhouse (1981), 'seek the reassurance of certainty to ameliorate the agony of responsibility'. The perspective of the 'new look' was quite different. At the conclusion of the 1972 EPA report, Halsey wrote:

The co-operation of research in policy formation has to develop 'organically' rather than 'mechanically'. Action research is unlikely ever to yield neat and definite prescriptions from field-tested plans. What it offers is an aid to intelligent decision-making, not a substitute for it. Research brings relevant information rather than uniquely exclusive conclusions.

(*Educational Priority*, Vol. 1: 178–9)

There is a variety of acceptable forms of research which corresponds to the variety of functions research is seen to perform: to provide answers to problems, to guide policy, to provide insights and understanding, to establish fundamental principles of learning. Can these different styles of research co-exist? They must, for if they are treated as separate, the academic becomes marginal and the practical is superficial.

But there is an inherent danger when we try to integrate the academic with the practical. Practical forms of research, linked to issues arising in current policy and provision, will tend to be given priority over theoretical and long-term studies which often prove eventually more important in that they bring about fundamental changes of attitude and understanding. Today the modern state uses research as an integral instrument of Government. If as researchers we go along with the demands of immediate policy issues, we have access to funds and influence – but at a price. This is a Faustian bargain, for it risks losing autonomy and missing out on basic issues.

Underlying this tension between the applied and the theoretical approaches to research, there is a more fundamental contrast, illustrated by a quotation from the Greek historian, Thucydides. He complained that, among his contemporaries, the ability to understand a question from all sides meant that one was totally unfit for action. There is a sense that worthwhile research must start from a position of uncertainty, and uncertainty is difficult to reconcile with action and decision. Two contemporary European scholars, Husén and Kogan (1984), relate this to the issue of Government funding of research in these terms:

Can national authorities sponsor the generation of uncertainty? Policy makers foreclose on issues … Social science can keep open the space.

(p. 6)

What has been described so far is the trend in the later decades of the twentieth century to move away from the experimental paradigm, whether through qualitative case studies, action research, the teacher-researcher movement or (at the extreme) postmodernism. At the same time, however, a quite different trend can be seen in the increasing recognition of educational research as an integral element in policy and practice. Where research is being funded by Government or public authorities, there is an expectation (or even a demand) that research should be oriented to the requirements of the 'users' or 'consumers' of research. The concept of 'users' is characteristic, in implying that research is done in one place by one group, and then transferred to another group in another place to be put to use. The terms 'users' and 'consumers' implicitly accept an *instrumental* function for research in education. On this view, good research is research which can be used, or which identifies '*What works*', the title of a best-selling American book on current research (Marzano 2003). Evaluation and data gathering studies are more likely to attract funding than theoretical analyses which aim at insights into problems, the *enlightenment* function of research. The emergence of this very different trend is best illustrated by events in Britain from 1970 on.

As Government funding for research increased, the inevitable consequence was a demand by Ministers for a greater say in how the funds were to be spent. Margaret Thatcher, then Secretary of State for Education and Science, declared in a speech to Parliament in 1970:

> There was clearly only one direction that the Department's research policy could sensibly take. It had to move from a basis of patronage – the rather passive support of ideas which were essentially other people's, related to problems which were often of other people's choosing – to a basis of commission. This meant the active initiation of work by the Department on problems of its own choosing, within a timetable and procedure which were relevant to its needs.

This view was quickly taken up in a review of Government research funding in 1971 by Lord Rothschild, who produced the crude 'customer-contractor principle': the customer (Government Department) says what he wants; the contractor (researcher) does it (if he can); and the customer pays. A response from the Social Science Research Council at the time questioned whether following the 'customer's' priorities was best for the advancement of knowledge:

> It is not so much a matter of an ordered hierarchy of priorities, as a process of grasping at opportunities presented by an almost accidental coagulation of interest among a group of able research workers around a chosen problem in order to shift a frontier of knowledge forward.

The words 'an almost accidental coagulation of interest' are a good description of what happens in research, but in the spirit of the times, they were hardly likely to persuade. Later, however, there has been fuller recognition of the importance of theoretical studies which contribute to the underlying disciplines in education – in Britain, especially in the programmes such as the Teaching and Learning Research Programme supported by the Economic and Social Research Council (ESRC). Even the then Minister for Education, David Blunkett, in a speech to the Council of ESRC in February 2000, expressed the point in words that could never have been accepted 20 years earlier:

> There must be a place for the fundamental 'blue skies' research which thinks the unthinkable. We need researchers who can challenge fundamental assumptions and orthodoxies, and this may well have big policy effects much further down the road.

The nature and function of research in education

This review of the historical development of educational research has not dealt with the actual research topics that were favoured at different times: in the early stages, psychological studies of transfer of training and of fatigue in learning; then, the use of tests in selection and the reliability of examinations; in mid-century, sociological aspects such as the influence of home environment; and later a much richer variety of topics, as different styles of research came to be accepted. Instead, the chapter has focused on the concept of research in education – what it is, how it was done and what its function should be – showing how this concept has changed over the past 100 years. At the risk of oversimplification, this can be portrayed as a series of phases, each with different perceptions of research and different implications for the contribution that research may make to education.

1 Initially, research was seen as primarily an academic activity: its contribution to school practice and policy issues was essentially theoretical and long-term.

2 Later, research came to be viewed as the work of experts and specialists, to be used, where appropriate, by teachers and administrators: the profitable business of test construction (involving complex statistical procedures) was a feature of this period.

3 In the 1950s and 1960s, educational research came to be accepted as a discipline in its own right, with its own distinctive procedures and literature: a greatly expanded research activity has extended to cover a wide range of issues.

This third phase has brought research into closer partnership with policy and practice, though in differing ways. Increased funding has given those who commission research a claim to greater say in the design, and sometimes also in the management, of a project and the dissemination of findings. At the same time, the teacher-researcher movement, which initially aimed to support teachers in carrying out research studies themselves, has developed into something more fundamental: a view of research as a key element in a professional approach, a mode of working to be adopted by all in facing up to problems, whether in policy-making or in school-based projects to pilot new curriculum initiatives. In summary, the role of researcher has moved from academic theorist in phase 1, through expert consultant in phase 2, to reflective practitioner in phase 3.

This broadened interpretation of research is the main achievement of the past 20 years: in a word, research has become accessible. Primary school children working on their projects speak of doing research, and we can only hope that they do not subsequently come to regard research as a remote and inaccessible style of working limited to a small elite of specialists. However, it would be wrong to impose a dimension of value on the three phases outlined above: they are essentially a dimension of involvement. All three approaches to researching have their place. There are still some who hold that the underlying contribution of the academic theorist is in the long term the most influential and the most important. Also the need for specialist expertise, and for research that is rigorous and highly skilled, must be acknowledged, for there is a danger of devaluing research if it is too lightly treated as something that anyone can do. A Senior Chief Inspector in England in 1976 complained:

> People say they have done some research when they really mean they have stopped to think for three minutes.

(Nisbet and Broadfoot 1980: 2)

But research has become part of every professional role today, and in education one task of professional development is to weave a research element into the expertise of teachers, leading them to adopt at a personal level the self-questioning approach that leads to reflection and understanding, and from there into action.

Suggested further reading

To get a feeling for the early history of educational research, the best method is to browse in the basement of a university library through the first issues of education journals such as the *Journal of Experimental Pedagogy* (1911), which became the *British Journal of Educational Psychology* in 1931. The American history is told by R. M. W. Travers in Chapter 1 of the fourth edition of *An Introduction to Educational Research* (1978). A short history of educational research in Europe by G. de Landsheere is reprinted in *Educational Research: Current issues*, edited by M. Hammersley (1993, Chapter 1), an Open University textbook which includes 13 other journal reprints on developments throughout the twentieth century. J. Rudduck and D. McIntyre, *Challenges for Educational Research* (1998), covers a range of current issues in educational research, summarised in the *Report of a BERA Colloquium, Educational Policy and Research* (British Educational Research Association 2003). If you wish to explore phenomenology or postmodernism, try a search on the Internet: www.phenomenologycenter.org and www.as.ua.edu/ant/Faculty/murphy/436/pomo.htm.

References

Adelman, C., Jenkins, D. and Kemmis, S. (1977) 'Re-thinking case study: notes from the second Cambridge conference', *Cambridge Journal of Education*, 6, 139–50.

Bain, A. (1879) *Education as a Science*. London: Kegan, Trench & Trubner.

Cattell, J. M. (1890) 'Mental tests and measurement', *Mind*, 15, 373–81.

291

Claparède E. (1911) *Child Psychology and Experimental Pedagogy* (Fourth edition), English translation. London: Edward Arnold.

Constas, M. (1998) 'The changing nature of educational research and a critique of postmodernism', *Educational Researcher*, 27 (2), 26–32.

Department of Education and Science (DES) (1967) *Children and Their Primary Schools (The Plowden Report)*. London: HMSO.

Educational Priority, Vol. 1 (1972). London: HMSO.

Elliott, J. (1981) 'Foreword', in J. Nixon *A Teachers' Guide to Action Research: Evaluation, enquiry and development in the classroom*. London: Grant McIntyre.

Entwistle, N. (1981) *Styles of Learning and Teaching*. Chichester and New York: Wiley.

Hammersley, M. (ed.) (1993) *Educational Research: Current issues*. London: Paul Chapman.

Husén, T. and Kogan, M. (eds) (1984) *Educational Research and Policy: How do they relate?* Oxford: Pergamon Press.

Lay, W. (1903) *Experimental Didactics: Its foundations with some considerations of muscle sense, will and action*. Leipzig: O. Nemnich.

Lodge, D. (2001) *Thinks …* London: Secker & Warburg.

Marzano, R. J. (2003) *What Works in Schools: Translating research into action*. Alexandria, VA: Association for Supervision and Curriculum Development.

Monroe, W. S. (1918) 'Existing tests and standards', in *The 17th Yearbook of the National Society for the Study of Education* (Part 2), pp. 71–113. Bloomington, IL: Public School Publishing Co.

Nifenecker, E. A. (1918) 'Bureaus of research in city school systems', in *The 17th Yearbook of the National Society for the Study of Education* (Part 2), pp. 52–6. Bloomington, IL: Public School Publishing Co.

Nisbet, J. (1984) 'The changing scene', in W. B. Dockrell (ed.) *An Attitude of Mind: 25 years of educational research in Scotand*. Edinburgh: Scottish Council for Research in Education.

Nisbet, J. and Broadfoot, P. (1980) *The Impact of Research on Policy and Practice in Education*. Aberdeen: Aberdeen University Press.

Nixon, J. (1981) *A Teachers' Guide to Action Research: Evaluation, enquiry and development in the classroom*. London: Grant McIntyre.

Rice, E. (1897) 'The futility of the spelling grind', *Forum*, 23.

Rothschild Report (1971) *A Framework for Government Research and Development*. London: HMSO.

Rudduck, J. and McIntyre, D. (1998) *Challenges for Educational Research*. London: Paul Chapman.

Rusk, R. R. (1913) *Introduction to Experimental Education*. London: Longmans Green.

Stenhouse, L. (1981) 'What counts as educational research?' *British Journal of Educational Studies*, 29, 103–14.

Taylor, W. (1972) 'Retrospect and prospect in educational research', *Educational Research*, 15, 3–7.

Thorndike, E. L. (1925) Quotation by H. Wodehouse, in *British Journal of Educational Psychology*, 1 (1), 41.

Travers, R. M. W. (1978) *An Introduction to Educational Research* (Fourth edition). New York and London: Collier Macmillan Publishers.

Travers, R. M. W. (1983) *How Research Has Changed American Schools*. Kalamazoo: Mythos Press.

Wake, R. (1984) *Events antecedent to the founding of the Scottish Council for Research in Education*. MEd thesis, University of Edinburgh.

Whipple, G. M. (1910) *Manual of Mental and Physical Tests*. Baltimore: Warwick & York.

Index